Based in Kathmandu, **Jamie McGuinness** treks and climbs for much of the year and spends the rest planning the next adventure. He manages Project Himalaya who run treks and expeditions. He has trekked the Everest region more than 25 times and has climbed Everest a handful of times. His favourite pastime is exploring remote corners of the Himalaya.

Trekking in the Everest Region
First edition: 1993; this fifth edition: 2009

Publisher
Trailblazer Publications
The Old Manse, Tower Rd, Hindhead, Surrey, GU26 6SU, UK
Fax (+44) 01428-607571, info@trailblazer-guides.com
www.trailblazer-guides.com

British Library Cataloguing in Publication Data
A catalogue record for this book is available from the British Library

ISBN 978-1-873756-99-7

© **Jamie McGuinness 1993, 1996, 1998, 2002, 2009**
Text, maps and photographs

The right of Jamie McGuinness to be identified as the author of this work has been
asserted by him in accordance with the Copyright, Designs and Patents Act 1988

Editors: Henry Stedman, Laura Stone and Anna Jacomb-Hood
Series editor: Patricia Major
Layout and index: Anna Jacomb-Hood
Proofreading: Nicky Slade
Cartography: Nick Hill

Warning: mountain walking can be dangerous
Please read the notes on when to go (pp43-7), health and AMS (pp61-5 and pp285-303).
Every effort has been made by the author and publisher to ensure that the information
contained herein is as accurate and up to date as possible. However, they are unable
to accept responsibility for any inconvenience, loss or injury sustained by anyone
as a result of the advice and information given in this guide.

A note from the author: The world is changing ever more rapidly; thankfully, the joy of
trekking remains much the same. The focus of this book is to help you to plan a trek and
then to show you the region – home to some of the finest trekking on the planet.

There are a couple of philosophies that guided this edition. Firstly, you'll find that I
don't recommend lodges but, instead, I have merely listed the majority of them. Some people judge their accommodation by the cleanliness of the toilet, others by the cosiness of the
kitchen but the bottom line is, I know of so few bad lodges that choosing to recommend one
over another is both unfair and perhaps unhelpful too.

Secondly, my goal was to cover virtually every route and track in the region so that you
have the choice of where to go, because I feel that the availability of information (or lack
of it) should not be a limiting factor. This was partly because I wished to write for everyone, from the first-time visitor to the Nepalophile (I have constantly been surprised at the
number of regulars I meet year after year in the hills). Perhaps, like 90% of trekkers, you'll
still stick to the main routes – but at least that choice is yours. By covering the entire region,
it was also my hope to spread trekkers to equally deserving areas.

For this 5th edition every paragraph and every map has been reviewed and the route
guide refocused to start at Lukla.

We hope you enjoy this edition of the guide and, most importantly, have a wonderful
experience!

Printed on chlorine-free paper by
D2Print (☎ +65-6295 5598), Singapore

TREKKING IN THE
Everest
REGION

**planning, places to stay, places to eat,
includes 83 maps
and Kathmandu city guide**

JAMIE McGUINNESS

TRAILBLAZER PUBLICATIONS

Acknowledgements

I would like to thank the people of the Khumbu for their sincere hospitality, with Natang of Moonlight Lodge and Pasang Thundup of Tengboche-Pangboche deserving of special thanks for sharing their considered opinions on so many matters.

Helena Swinkels reviewed the 'Health Appendix' for the fourth edition and it has stood the test of time by being virtually unchanged here.

Parts 2 and 3 are the combined effort of Anagha Neelakantan, Jamie McGuinness and Caroline Martin building on several other authors' work.

At Trailblazer, thanks to Henry Stedman, Laura Stone, Anna Jacomb-Hood, Nick Hill, Nicky Slade and, of course, Bryn Thomas.

Along the trails in the Khumbu there are so many Nepalis that I'd like to thank by name but, alas, the vast majority are more easily recalled by their smiles and helpfulness – as too are the many foreign trekkers I met.

While I am constantly surprised by the courtesy and warmth of the Nepali people in general, and the majority of government officials I have met, I can only hope that the more faceless side of the government and bureaucracy doesn't destroy the country before they act on the long-known realization that corruption and politicization are the root of all Nepal's current problems.

A request

The author and publisher have tried to ensure that this guide is as accurate and up to date as possible. However, things change quickly in this part of the world. Prices rise, new lodges are built and trails are rerouted.

If you notice any changes or omissions that should be included in the next edition of this book, please email Jamie McGuinness at jamie.mcguinness@trailblazer-guides.com or write to him c/o Trailblazer Publications (address on p2). A free copy of the next edition will be sent to persons making a significant contribution.

Updated information will shortly be available on the Internet at
www.project-himalaya.com/updates-everest.htm
www.trailblazer-guides.com

Front cover photograph: Yaks en route to Lobuche © Jamie McGuinness

CONTENTS

PART 3: KATHMANDU

The city

PART 4: THE EVEREST REGION

Mountaineering history

The people

National parks

Facilities for the trekker

Minimum impact trekking

PART 5: ROUTE GUIDE AND MAPS

Using this guide 156

Trekking from Lukla

Namche and around

To Lobuche and Kala Pattar

To Gokyo and around

INTRODUCTION

The Solu-Khumbu region of Nepal has been a magnet for mountaineers, adventurers and travellers since its opening to foreigners in the 1950s, and with good reason. They may primarily be drawn by a desire to see the world's highest mountain but Everest is only one of many beautiful peaks in the area. Indeed, even if Everest wasn't here, the Khumbu (Everest region) would still be an extremely popular area for it is a superb region for trekking, climbing and exploring.

Passing through populated areas, a trek in Nepal is very different from a wilderness hike in the USA or New Zealand, or a randonnée route in the European Alps. The hills in Nepal are the life and soul of diverse ethnic groups, the most famous of which are the hospitable Sherpa people. What further sets trekking in Nepal apart is the low cost and the ease with which a trek can be arranged. There can be few countries where you can set off for a month-long walk carrying no food or shelter yet be 100% sure that every day you will be able to find these essentials, and on a budget of around US$20 a day. Alternatively, if you want an organized trek with an entourage of guides, cooks and porters to transport you back to the luxurious time of pukka sahibs and memsahibs, this can be quickly arranged with competent staff for a very reasonable cost.

Three areas in Nepal have become popular with trekkers for their scenic attractions and their established network of local lodges for accommodation and food. As well as the Everest region, there's the Annapurna region, north of Pokhara, which may have a greater range of terrain and cultures but receives nearly twice as many trekkers as the Everest region. The third area is Langtang, north of Kathmandu, which is quieter and less developed. What sets the Everest region apart from these two other areas is the fact that once above Namche and Lukla you are right among the mountains, continuously above 3000m/10,000ft with many chances to ascend above 5000m/16,400ft. The greater Khumbu (Everest) region also has immense scope for mountaineering and wild exploration.

Trekking is one of the best holidays there is, a great way to escape the noisy beeping world and rediscover simple pleasures like the enduring glow of a sunset, the magic of flickering flames and the bliss of sleep to soothe naturally exercised muscles. Rural life, little-changed for centuries, surrounds the trekker, thought-provoking and very different from the Western way of life. From the alpine valleys above Namche the scenery is awesome: Ama Dablam, Cholatse and numerous other peaks, while the 8000-metre giants – Makalu, Cho Oyu, Lhotse and Everest – command respect for their sheer height.

The highest mountain on earth has several different names. To the Western world it became Mt Everest in 1865 (and was pronounced 'Eve-rest') but to the Tibetans and the Khumbu Sherpas it has always been Chomolungma. The Chinese have wisely used the local name (transliterated as Qomolangma). Much more recently the government of Nepal has given it the name Sagarmatha. In this guide, it's referred to as Everest only because this is the name most readily recognized by readers. I personally prefer the original name, Chomolungma.

PART 1: PLANNING YOUR TREK

What is trekking?

The prospect of trekking for the first time in the Himalaya can be daunting as well as thrilling. Compared to a week's backpacking in the Rockies or bush-walking in Tasmania, trekking in Nepal is an altogether different experience. Rather than jumping into the wilderness to get away from it all, you walk into a countryside free from roads and discover villages caught in a time warp and terraced fields stacked up huge hillsides. The paths are timeless pilgrimage routes, trails between villages or tracks to high grazing pastures. It is by no means untouched but it is an incredibly beautiful natural world. Higher up in the alpine valleys the villages are replaced by herders' huts and, higher still, the ice castles of the Himalaya.

Trekking is simply adventurous walking: it is not climbing or mountaineering, and the practical aspects are surprisingly straightforward. In the villages and along the way are lodges and teahouses where meals are ordered from menus in English. Alternatively, on an expedition-style trekking tour three-course meals are served by your crew. Either way without the need to carry food and camping equipment, backpacks are light, and if you book with a company you need carry only a daypack. So trekking is really little more than a pleasurable ramble through quaint villages, gazing in wonder at the terraced hillsides and wandering amid incredible mountain scenery.

The satisfaction of trekking is in the process: most trekking days are not particularly long so there is time to spot wildlife, take photographs, chat along the way and relax over lunch or a reviving cup of tea.

But there are challenges. The first and biggest is the physical effort required: as well as the inspiring mountains there are huge hills, some of which must be climbed. Although hopefully lightly laden, hill-climbing still means plenty of heavy breathing and sweat. Pleasure can be had from frequent rests to admire the scenery which, even after a mere ten minutes, alters satisfyingly and often dramatically. Take comfort, too, in the frequent teahouses which are often strategically placed.

The second challenge is the discomfort of sickness. This is Asia and no matter how careful you are, you should count on some bowel problems and possibly a day or two that you would rather forget. Luckily, these seem trivial when compared to the whole wonderful experience.

To enjoy the Himalaya you don't have to be a tough outdoor type. Like backpacks and cameras, trekkers come in all shapes and sizes and with widely differing aspirations. Trekking is physically demanding but certainly not beyond the majority of moderately fit people. The most important thing is knowing that you enjoy the concept. Bring along a traveller's curiosity and a sense of humour and before you know it you will relish the thought of another trek.

Trekking in the Khumbu (Everest) region

Trekking is usually a wonderful experience. However, a reality check is in order. You are heading into an extreme mountain environment. It can snow unexpectedly and emergency facilities are limited. You will also be at extreme altitude and experience its discomfort and problems. Ignorance and foolhardiness on acclimatization can and does still kill, although it is entirely preventable; see pp282-4.

Climbing and exploring

Alpine valleys lure you ever higher, and for some the peaks are the ultimate temptation. With every mountain in the region higher than Mont Blanc, and most higher than Denali, many people want to set a personal altitude record. Do recognize that climbing a 6000m/20,000ft+ peak is real mountaineering, regardless of how the trip is portrayed. The more climbing experience you have, the better, and if you are not experienced, as many people are not, book with a company that understands your level and your needs, or better still, do a climbing course prior. The trek-in to get to the base camp is just trekking and should be enjoyed as such.

Trekking styles and agencies

HISTORY

Nepal, long suspicious of foreign influence and colonial powers, began opening its borders only in 1948. The first tourists (as opposed to mountaineers and researchers) arrived in 1955 but it was not until 1965, when Colonel Jimmy Roberts set up Mountain Travel, that the first commercial treks began. The concept was similar to the expedition approach used by mountaineers, with guide, cook, helpers, porters and separate dining and kitchen tents. These holidays proved to be a great success and essentially the same expedition-style format is still used for remote area trekking and climbing expeditions.

Alongside this self-sufficient approach to trekking is a second, locally based tourism industry catering to the needs of a different type of visitor. Along the main trade routes the hill peoples of Nepal traditionally had a code of hospitality towards travellers. It was only a matter of time before small groups of adventurers started taking advantage of this, staying in basic teahouses and lodges. Now, from Lukla and above, these lodges have developed to the point where they offer distinct advantages over the expedition style.

Trekking is now an industry, but still on a friendly scale. In 1964 just 14 foreigners visited the Khumbu, in 1970 there were 300 trekkers, which grew dramatically to 3000 trekkers by 1973, and in 1974 the first lodge specifically for trekkers was built in Namche. By 1980 there were 5000 visitors, and this doubled to approximately 10,000 in 1990: evenly split between teahouses and expedition style. By 2000 the total number had reached 25,000 with the majority staying in teahouses. Political instability in the following years has meant that only in 2008 will this figure be exceeded.

The latest trekking development is lodge chains, with several companies setting up uniformly high standard lodges in good locations that suit a few days to a week's trekking (see p20).

Now with the variety of facilities and services, it really is up to you how you trek, alone or through a company, staying in teahouses or tents.

EXPEDITION-STYLE TREKKING

The traditional idea of this form of trekking evokes images of an army of heavily laden porters catering for a few pampered sahibs and memsahibs, with sherpas pitching the tents and kitchen staff cooking up three-course meals on tables complete with table linen. In fact this is still essentially the standard format and it's a glorious way to trek, especially off the beaten track where teahouses are rare, or during peak season when the lodges are overflowing. There are big economies of scale so small groups work out at much more expensive per person than a group of four or more.

The crew

The better trekking companies can organize really good camping trips, with everything included. The guide-sirdar will be competent and experienced, with some having even climbed Everest, and the best of them are a real privilege to be around. There will be a sizeable crew, too, even if there are just one or two of you.

The **sirdar** (trekking guide) is an organizer rather than a trained specialist of history and culture. He (virtually never she) will speak English and will carry only his personal equipment. Amongst the sirdar's duties is the hiring and supervision of the porters and sherpas (who are not necessarily from the Sherpa clan, and thus are distinguished from them by the lowercase 's'); they are also usually in charge of the money and wages. It is a powerful position and a good sirdar will ensure that the trek functions in a trouble-free manner. A bad sirdar, on the other hand, can cause endless problems.

The **sherpas** are the sirdar's assistants: general helpers who erect and pack the tents, serve the meals and help in any way they can. They ensure nobody gets lost and carry bags if the members tire. Most speak some English.

The **cook** is another key figure, heading a small army of kitchen helpers, usually called kitchen boys in Nepal.

Porters are load carriers and generally speak little or no English. The standard trekking company load is 30kg/66lbs. For larger groups, yaks and zopkios (a sterile cross between a yak and a lowland cow) are often used, for they can carry double the load of a porter. As a general rule, yaks are normally used only above Namche while zopkios are to be found from Lukla and above.

Tipping your crew

Good crew members are super-heroes. Take the kitchen hands: they prepare all the meals (including for the crew), wash the dishes afterwards until late into the evening and then, early the next morning, you will hear the roar of the stoves well before it is light as they set to work making your breakfast – after which they spend the rest of the day running between the meal stops until it's evening again! And all for around US$5 a day. Similarly, porters are the equivalent of Olympic athletes. Try lifting a load sometime and imagine carrying that every day for the distance you walk.

It has become customary for trekkers to tip their crew – providing they have done a good job. I feel that the trekking companies should pay more realistic wages, and thanks to unionization, this is starting to happen, but tips are still important, and really do make a difference to their quality of life.

Budget something like $50 per trek member per week of trekking: if every member puts this amount in a kitty for you (rather than the sirdar) to divide up at the end, you should have enough to give a minimum of Rs2000 per crew member (though if you tip more, it certainly won't be wasted). It is normal to tip in a graduated scale with porters getting the least and the sirdar the most but there is merit in tipping the porters, sherpas and kitchen hands a similar amount, and the cook and sirdar only slightly more. After all, the cook and the sirdar are in charge of the budgets for the trek and may have already done well out of this.

The majority of crew members take their hard-earned cash back to their family and then try living on this for months – the reality of the developing world can be scary.

Using a Nepali or a foreign company?

Home country or other overseas companies offer tempting and usually well-run trips, and with their fixed departures you will be joining a team of (hopefully) like-minded people. Certainly for ambitious treks and expeditions, they offer good options.

If you are after a custom departure for a couple of people it may make sense to look at Nepali companies, and all foreign operators work through a local company. Do ensure they are experienced at running your itinerary.

TEAHOUSE TREKKING

Dotted along the main trails are privately owned teahouses and lodges. They can provide anything from a cup of tea to a full meal and a bed so, for the entire trek, there's no need to carry food or shelter. Teahouse trekking, as it's usually called, is easy to organize through a company, or independently, just pack and go, and it is also good value.

The level of comfort and facilities in the lodges has improved greatly. Once infamously smoky and rather too authentically mediaeval, many are now modest hotels which generally offer better facilities than the expedition (camping) approach. Because of the way the lodges are managed in the Khumbu, they are regarded as the best in the country, on average significantly better than the lodges in Langtang and better than most lodges in the Annapurna region.

You will be sharing a lodge with other trekkers and a late-night party might keep you (or them) awake: most lodges are not particularly soundproof. On balance, however, teahouse trekking is still more comfortable than camping, and most treks are a fantastic experience.

With a group, your own guide or completely on your own?
Your basic trekking choices are: trekking with a fully organized, pre-arranged group; trekking privately with a guide; or trekking by yourself.

Budget travellers and independent types should trek by themselves (see p15), but if you like the idea of a guide and perhaps porters to assist, the choices are surprisingly broad.

Package treks
Usually booked through a home country operator, these should be well organized with plenty of pre-departure information and offer a knowledgeable guide who can answer almost any question and manage the sometimes diverse range of people on these sorts of treks.

With all arrangements made in advance, from being met at Kathmandu airport, to your departure, everything should flow smoothly. One of the real advantages, apart from a knowledgeable guide to make the trek fun and dates fixed well in advance, is proper backup in case something goes wrong. It is definitely worth checking that the itinerary truly takes altitude into account, and also check on the qualities of the leader, and are they named prior to departure? It is also worth asking what happens if you struggle (due to altitude or sickness). Some simply turn you back without the possibility of a slower ascent or an alternative lower-altitude trek.

Private treks with a guide
Once glossy brochures were the main marketing tool to gather groups, now the internet (and email) is all-powerful, and getting in touch with local trek operators is easy. They are happy to set up a custom trek for one person, two people or a group. This means flexibility and convenience but you might want to do more research (the internet was supposed to save time?) to check/compare the itinerary, the company and perhaps the guide too.

Many foreign trek operators also have either locally guided fixed departure treks where the groups are small, and/or offer custom trips too. The cost will usually be higher but the service should also be more reliable.

The crew for a private trek will normally be a guide and a porter or two, all of whom stay in the lodges as well. The guide generally only carries their own equipment, and porters carry your kitbag, plus their minimal gear, so you are left with your daypack.

Alternatively if you are feeling fit and strong you could arrange for just a porter-guide, someone who can carry 5-10kgs/11-22lbs of your gear (often just your sleeping bag and a few clothes) and also trek with you.

Your guide Once on the trail perhaps the most important factor for a good trek is the guide so it is worth understanding possible strengths and weaknesses. While most local guides speak English, few are truly fluent, and few have been overseas so rarely understand just what a different world you are stepping into, and perhaps how important your holiday is to you. Do realize that the concept of guiding, ie being a cultural interpreter, is only loosely understood and while they should be a knowledgeable trekking companion, standards vary considerably. Some ethnic sherpa guides know their culture well, but explaining it at a philosophical level can be awkward: other guides, usually Hindus, don't always understand Buddhism and the ways of the high country people. Some guides are also often incredibly blasé about altitude sickness: if their advice doesn't sound right read this book carefully and make your own decisions based on the information given here. To be fair though, these issues are more due to Nepal's weak education system. Certainly every guide knows the main trails in a region and can offer at least basic assistance, and answer some of your questions. It should be stressed, also, that many guides are amazingly competent and a real pleasure to trek with.

Once in Kathmandu talk to the guide and maybe even go out for a meal with him; then, go with your instincts: if you have any doubts, ask for someone else.

Porter care Porters are the lowest in the chain and previously often neglected: luckily attitudes are improving. Porters sometimes walk with you but generally set off in the morning and drop the gear where you are staying that evening. They are responsible for their food and lodging. If they are going to high altitudes, and normally you are, insist on knowing the arrangements for the gear they need: will the company provide warm jackets, or are the porters responsible for that themselves? Also understand that trekking personnel look after themselves in most situations but when it comes to bad conditions, with the risk of frostbite and snow-blindness, some are notoriously naive.

Security
Women travelling alone often trek with a guide for security yet occasionally this backfires, and they face hassle from a guide who becomes surly when you won't sleep with him. It is best to be clear from the beginning when dealing with the company: ask for references from women who have used the company/guide and also interview the guide before starting the trek. There are many good, reliable guides.

Service restrictions Normally the trekking company or guide choose the lodges and unless you're willing to pay extra the better lodges and restaurants (eg pizza at Namche bakery) will be off-limits. Some companies use a restrictive 'set meal' arrangement while others allow you to choose from the menu.

Complaints
If trekking with a local company, first try to resolve with the owner. If that doesn't work you should visit the TAAN office (see p84), and it is worth preparing a quick written list of problems. In many cases they will be able to resolve them. The other option is the Ministry of Tourism, where every trekking company has paid a bond to register. Everything has to be done in writing and it pays to present yourself well, be humble most of the time and respect the officials; they have a tough job. They are in Bhrikuti Mandap, the tourist service centre.

Price wars When comparing companies getting caught in a circle of competing on price alone often ends with a lower standard of service, and less loyal staff. It often happens that the guide will be sent out with too little money to run the trek properly and so starts out unhappy. A trick to avoiding this, at least partly, is to book the services of a guide (and porter/s) on a daily basis plus all the flights, but to pay your own lodge bills.

Permits, taxes and staff insurance The trekking company will arrange all the permits you need. Also the company must insure all staff for injury and death, but this does not include helicopter rescue. The bigger companies have block policies, but with smaller companies specifically ask and get in writing that they have insured all your trek staff. The bigger trekking companies also have to pay VAT (Value Added Tax) on some components of a trek, to around 5% of the trek cost, and this is always included, never added on top. Unfairly, as of 2008, small companies don't need to pay but this may change.

Booking in Kathmandu If you have some time in Kathmandu it can make sense to do the research at home but then book your trek when you arrive, once you have met with the company and staff. Almost every street outside the heart of Thamel is lined with trekking companies, though most are on the first or second floors of the buildings, ie above the hundreds of souvenir and clothing shops. Before you walk into an office be clear what services you want – and, just as importantly, what you think you don't need. The majority of trekkers will be looking at hiring a guide or a porter-guide so meet your guide.

Hiring your own guide It is easy enough to turn up in Lukla and hire your own guide or porter-guide. However, this is something the Nepal trekking companies are trying to discourage. Local guides have an 'unfair' advantage of not having an office to run, and don't pay tax either. The companies argue that independent guides are not regulated (trekking companies don't regulate the quality of their guides by compulsory qualifications either) and they are not insured, which is worth bearing in mind; also there is no forum for complaints. Laws covering this are contradictory, as are the ethical questions.

Regardless of the many issues and the fairness or otherwise, now to trek you must have a TIMS (Trekkers Information Management System) permit (see pp83-4); this entitles you to trek either independently (FIT – Free Individual Trekker) or with a company, but not to hire your own staff except in an emergency.

Trekking independently

Many people trek by themselves. The lodges are impossible to miss, route finding presents few problems and basic English is widely understood. Unless trekking during the monsoon or off the standard routes you constantly meet other trekkers in the lodges or on the trail so while you can remain by yourself if you wish, most people end up walking in small groups and staying at the same lodges. This process often begins on the flight (or bus) out to the start, and more friendships evolve during the rest of the walk: this is one of the special joys of Nepal trekking.

> **Want that local experience?**
> On an expedition-style trek and a teahouse trek, although the styles of interac-
> tion with locals are different they are equivalent. Staying in a lodge provides the
> rewarding opportunity to mix with your Nepali hosts, many of whom speak reasonable
> English. How much you interact depends on you: some trekkers seem happy to spend
> all their time just in the company of other trekkers. On an expedition-style trek,
> although being self-sufficient removes the enjoyable need to interact with the villagers,
> this is redeemed by the crew who look after, entertain and add local colour to the trek.

Standard wilderness recommendations are to hike in a group of three or
more, in case of accidents. However, there is less need to apply this reasoning in
the Khumbu because there are several medical posts along the way and lodge
owners and other trekkers can render assistance. While many people would consider it foolish to rely on strangers, in fact very few trekkers have accidents or
ever end up relying on – and inconveniencing – other trekkers so I feel there are
few risks in hiking alone in the Khumbu (ie above Lukla). As a woman the risks
of physical sexual harassment are also negligible above Lukla, for which you can
thank the broad sexual equality accorded by the Sherpa culture. That said, dressing conservatively and behaving modestly is sensible, and when stopping for the
night it's a good idea to check that there is another woman staying in the same
lodge, or head for one of the busier lodges: if heading off the main routes you
should team up with someone else, as much for general safety as anything else.

Trekking below Lukla alone (as a male or female) used to be safe but more
caution is required now. Villagers often ask how many people you are trekking
with and the best reply is always to say that your friend is just behind, or simply
trek with others. Violent crimes against foreigners are still virtually unknown but
the law and order situation in the country has deteriorated significantly.

If you would prefer to begin your trek with a partner, advertise on, or scan,
the noticeboards around Thamel, especially at the Pumpernickel Bakery and the
Kathmandu Guest House boards. There are many internet message boards too
which you can put an advert on or just look at adverts.

As well as being economical, **independent teahouse trekking** gives you
the freedom to alter your schedule and stop where you wish. This is particularly handy if you are sick for a day or two or you feel like a rest: group treks generally have to push on.

Permits To trek anywhere in the Everest region you need a TIMS permit (see
pp83-4) and above Lukla you need a National Park entrance ticket, see p84.

Flights See pp85-6.

Trekking the wild way
Using teahouses where you can and then camping/bivvying up remote valleys
is a fun way to explore: this means you can carry everything you need and a
porter isn't required. At any major village on the main trekking routes you can

pick up enough food, provided you're not a fussy eater, to disappear into the wilderness for a few days or more. The main decisions boil down to selecting exactly what gear to take and deciding if you have enough experience for some of the wilder route options.

Adventure treks and trekking peaks (recreational mountaineering)

For climbers and experienced trekkers the region has an incredible amount to offer. If you are considering a true wilderness trek across some of the wilder passes or fancy climbing a 6000m peak, you are probably better organizing such an expedition through a professional company unless you are supremely confident in your abilities and experience. However, even if you do arrange things through a company, caution is still required. Foreign companies usually assign experienced guides but smaller Nepali companies, despite their claims, are notorious for getting out of their depth. Indeed, few local climbing guides can even *belay* – a standard climbing technique. This is a major failing of the whole trekking industry in Nepal and you should choose the company you sign up with carefully, and also check with them about the guide for the trip. That said, the majority of Nepali-guided expeditions do run successfully.

So how should you arrange this kind of trip? In some places with the lodges being so good, one might assume that staying in lodges until the need to camp might be the best way. Perhaps it is, but sometimes there is little difference in price since the climbing crew still have to trek up to where they meet you, which leads to the question: should they trek with you while you are acclimatizing? Essentially, no. The crew also need to acclimatize, although possibly less so, and in fact might already be acclimatized: check with the trekking company. So you can arrange that you trek around and then meet them at the last village before base camp.

When planning a full camping trip many people wonder if the tables and chairs are necessary, and ask if there is a way to reduce the cost with a simpler service. Certainly trekking companies can lighten loads with less tinned food, lighter dining tents and other details behind the scenes, but when it comes to actually changing the level of service and making major savings, that is much harder. The crew still need their own tents to sleep in, and the kitchen is there to cook both for you and for the crew. So cutting it down to a faster and lighter setup is usually impractical. Instead enjoy the expedition in the classic expedition style.

Permits The list gets longer, although the trekking company will organize this. In addition to the TIMS permit and the National Park entrance fee (p84), you will also need a trekking peak permit from the NMA (Nepal

---

Volunteering
This is now an industry with people paying to join volunteer programmes. Many programmes are genuine, some are not though, so do check with previous volunteers, and carefully consider whether you are helping yourself, or are truly helping a community. The internet is a good place to start.

Cheap trek, but who pays?

Walking the narrow streets of Thamel, Kathmandu's crowded, smog-filled tourist quarter, is to run the gauntlet of hustlers out to convince the gullible Western trekker that the firm they work for is the only one worth bothering with. With every step comes a fresh business card, every second of eye contact a potential booking. And they'll promise the earth to clinch a sale. But just how cheap will they go? I instantly invent a dozen keen trekkers who will join me in a fortnight. Now it's time to do business – and what a deal I can get. For just £12 a day, my imaginary companions and I will be able to walk the mountains of the Annapurna or Everest ranges – sleeping in teahouses by night, three hot meals a day, a rescue service on stand-by. We'll have two nights of three-star accommodation before we start, one porter to every two people. The deal's incredible. But it's not we who are really paying: it's the porters. In the Everest region, a hot shower costs £2, a pot of instant noodles, 65p: it doesn't take a genius to work out that at £12 a day there won't be much flowing through to them. **Stephanie Clark** (excerpt from *The Times*)

Mountaineering Association) or for expedition peaks, an expedition permit from the Ministry of Tourism: this paper chase is definitely a job for a trekking company.

TREKKING AGENCIES IN NEPAL

With over 500 trekking companies, it is hard to know where to start. However, it is worth checking if a company is a TAAN (Trekking Agents Association of Nepal; 🖳 www.taan.org.np) member as you are slightly more protected if there are issues with your trek. However, most companies are members and they are listed on the TAAN website.

It is worth trying to gauge whether the company is big or small, carefully read what the person in charge writes, and if they name or discuss their staff. If they are named, search the internet, and of course search for the company's name as well. For more challenging treks and peaks, ask who the guide/sirdar will be and Google them.

Considering that more than a third of trekkers do book through a local company, the fact that I don't recommend any in particular might seem a bit odd though I do include a list of some (see opposite). For trekking, there is no easy way to distinguish who is good and bad, and this is subjective anyway, how you deal with the company makes a difference, and your luck with the guide and crew. I have seen small companies run good treks, seen the same mess up, and seen bigger companies doing the same.

Expedition-style treks and trek-climbs

Generally, you pay for what you get. If you want a high-standard trek, climbing trip or a trek to a really remote area, it is often better to deal with companies who have offices out of central Thamel – ie the ones who organize mainly internet bookings and expeditions for overseas agents – as they tend to have more experience in arranging these sorts of trip.

Below is a list of Nepal trekking companies, taken from the NMA (Nepal Mountaineering Association) list: each organized five or more trekking peak expeditions in 2007.

I feel the 10 biggest companies have enough business from overseas agents, but list them here all the same: **Summit Nepal Trekking** (⌨ www.summit-nepal.com); **Thamserku Trekking** (⌨ www.thamserkutrekking.com); **Himalaya Expedition** (⌨ www.himexnepal.com); **Asian Trekking** (⌨ www.astrek.com); **International Trekkers (InTrek)** (⌨ www.intrekasia.com); **Sea to Summit Trekking**; **Multi Adventure** (⌨ www.multiadventure.com.np); **Lama Excursions**; **Su-Swagatam Nepal Trek**; **Cosmo Trek** (⌨ www.cosmos trektravel.com).

Any of the following would be worth considering, especially if you are planning an adventurous trek or a trekking-peak expedition:
- **Royal High Mountain Trek** (⌨ www.royalmt.com.np)
- **Arun Treks & Expedition** (⌨ www.arunexpedition.com)
- **IceLand Trekking & Expedition** (⌨ www.ice-landtrekking.com)
- **Nepal Trans Himalayan Explorer** (⌨ www.sherpaadventure.com)
- **Cho-Oyu Trekking** (⌨ www.cho-oyutrekking.com)
- **Nepal Alsace Treks & Expedition** (⌨ www.hikingtrek.com)
- **Explore Himalaya Travel & Adventure** (⌨ www.explorehimalaya.com)
- **Adventure 6000** (⌨ www.adventure6000.com)
- **Wilderness Experience** (⌨ www.wildexp.net)
- **Nomad Nepal Trek & Mountaineering** (⌨ www.nomadnepaltreks.com)
- **Windhorse Trekking** (⌨ www.windhorse-trek.com)
- **Himalayan Glacier Trekking** (⌨ www.himalayanglacier.com.np)
- **Sherpa Shangrila Treks** (⌨ www.trekandclimb.com)
- **Mountain Monarch Adventure** (⌨ www.mountainmonarch.com)
- **Nepal Experienced Adventure** (⌨ www.neatadventure.com)
- **Himalayan Envpro Treks & Expedition** (⌨ www.nepaltibettours.com)
- **Monviso Treks & Expedition** (⌨ www.monvisotreks.com)
- **Exodus Treks & Expedition** (⌨ www.exodustrekking.com)
- **Equator Treks** (⌨ www.equatorexpeditionsnepal.com)
- **Himalayan Guides Nepal** (⌨ www.himalayanguides.com)
- **AngRita Treks & Expedition** (⌨ www.angritatreks.com)
- **Nepal Ecology Treks** (⌨ www.ecologytrek.com)
- **Climb High** (⌨ www.climbhighhimalaya.com)
- **Blue Sky Treks & Exploration** (⌨ www.blueskytreks.com)
- **Himalayan Scenery Treks** (⌨ www.himalayanst.com)
- **Monterosa Treks** (⌨ www.monterosa-nepal.com)
- **Rainbow Treks & Expedition** (⌨ www.rainbowtrek.com.np)
- **Adventure Geo Treks** (⌨ www.adventuregeotreks.com)
- **Annapurna Treks & Expedition** (⌨ www.annapurnatreks.com)
- **Atlante Mountaineering** (⌨ www.trekkingteam.com)
- **Mountain Sherpa Treks** (⌨ www.guidenepal.com)
- **Highlander Trekking & Expedition** (⌨ www.highlandernepal.com)

- **Great Adventure Treks** (🖳 www.greatadventuretreks.com)
- **Regal Excursions** (🖳 www.regaltrekking.com)
- **Community Action Trek** (🖳 www.catreks.com)
- **Mountain Experience** (🖳 www.mountainexperience.com.np)
- **Himalayan Sherpa Adventure** (🖳 www.himal-adventure.com)
- **Kailash Himalaya Trek** (🖳 www.kailashhimalaya.com)
- **Nepal Vision Treks & Expedition** (🖳 www.nepalvisiontreks.com)
- **Peak Paldor Trekking** (🖳 www.peakpaldor.com)
- **Eco Trek International** (🖳 www.ecotour.com.np)
- **Himalayan Journeys** (🖳 www.himalayajourneys.com)
- **Asian Heritage Treks** (🖳 www.asianheritagetreks.com)
- **Nomad Expeditions** (🖳 www.nomadexpedition.com)
- **Unique Adventure** (🖳 www.Internationaluniquetreks.com).

Luxury lodge treks

The lodges are comfortable, all are better than the best independent lodges, and you have a choice of trekking between them, which is better, or taking a helicopter, but be aware altitude issues.

Yeti Mountain Homes (🖳 www.yetimountainhome.com, ☎ +977 1-435 6482) have lodges at Phakding, Kongde, Thame, Namche and Lukla, so a pleasant loop is possible. Their Kongde Lodge is unique, remote and offers a good view of Everest. **Everest Summit Lodges** (🖳 www.nepalluxurytreks.com, ☎ +977 1-437 1537) have lodges in Monjo, Mende (between Namche and Thame), Tashinga (between Namche and Tengboche), Pangboche and Lukla, making them convenient for cultural day trips while avoiding the trekking masses.

OVERSEAS TREKKING AGENCIES

Some companies offer a general range of treks while others specialize in climbing and adventure treks. Brochures and websites usually stress the level of experience required for treks and climbs advertised. Don't, however, lose sight of the fact that although trekking is made easier by the need to carry only a daypack, it is still your legs that do all the walking. Don't be afraid to quiz the company on who is leading the trek, their group numbers policy, and on the detailed itinerary. All profess to follow comfortable acclimatization rates but the hard reality is that some don't.

Compared to Nepali companies the prices quoted by foreign agencies are higher, often much higher, but you'll also get a much higher standard of preparation and trek too. Furthermore, you have the consumer rights of your country on your side, so you should be well protected. In contrast, if booking through a Nepali company you'll have to deal with the slow-moving Ministry of Tourism should anything go wrong.

Tours and trekking agencies in the UK

- **Bufo Ventures** (☎ 01539-445445, 🖳 www.bufoventures.co.uk) organizes tailor-made treks for groups or individuals.

- **Community Action Treks** (☎ 01228 564488, 🖳 www.catreks.com) is a trekking company founded by Doug Scott, the first Briton to climb Everest, largely to support his charity, Community Action Nepal (🖳 www .canepal.org.uk). Offers several treks including the standard Everest Base Camp trek.
- **Classic Journeys** (☎ 01773-873497, 🖳 www.classicjourneys.co.uk) offers three treks in the Everest region.
- **Exodus Travel** (☎ 0845-863 9600, 🖳 www.exodus.co.uk) has a wide range of guided treks with accommodation in tents or teahouses.
- **Explore Worldwide** (☎ 0844-499 0901, 🖳 www.explore.co.uk) offers a number of treks in the Everest region.
- **Footprint Adventures** (☎ 01522-804929, 🖳 www.footprint-adventures. co.uk) operates a 17-day Everest Kala Pattar trek and a 24-day Ultimate Everest trek, both guided and both taking in the Base Camp.
- **Great Walks of the World** (☎ 01935-810820, 🖳 www.greatwalks.net) runs three treks in the region.
- **High Places** (☎ 0845-257 7500, 🖳 www.highplaces.co.uk) operate a trek to Everest Base Camp as well as a 15-day Mountains & monasteries trek and Gokyo and Island Peak.
- **Himalayan Frontiers** (☎ 01737-224294, 🖳 www.himalayanfrontiers.co.uk) specialize in Nepal and have an office in Pokhara. They offer a number of treks including treks up Mera, Tent, Island and Chulu peaks.
- **Himalayan Kingdoms** (☎ 01453-844400, 🖳 www.himalayankingdoms.com) operate several treks including a 17-day Base Camp and Gokyo trek, a less-strenuous 11-day Sherpa Villages family trek, and a 29-day Sir Edmund Hillary Trust (UK) Everest trek which visits schools and medical centres built by the trust.
- **Intrepid Travel** (☎ 01373-826611, 🖳 www.intrepidtravel.com) have the standard treks and have added Mera and Island Peak as well as a trek on the southern approach to Everest.
- **Jagged Globe** (☎ 0845-345 8848, ☎ 0114-276 3322, 🖳 www.jagged-globe.co.uk) offers more ambitious trekking and mountaineering holidays.
- **KE Adventure Travel** (☎ 017687-73966, 🖳 www.keadventure.com) has a long history of treks and trekking peak climbs in the Everest region.
- **The Mountain Company** (☎ 020-7498 0953, 🖳 www.themountaincompany. co.uk) offer adventure, classic and luxury treks from 14 to 26 days.
- **Naturetrek** (☎ 01962-733051, 🖳 www.naturetrek.co.uk) offers bird-watching and botanical tours in several regions of Nepal including a 22-day (15 days trekking) Mount Everest and Gokyo Lakes trip.
- **Palanquin Travels** (☎ 020-7436 9343, 🖳 www.palanquintravels.com) Specialists on the Indian subcontinent, with treks including a 34-day 'Looking Behind Mount Everest' expedition on the high route from Maluku base camp to Lukla via the East Col (6150m), culminating in an ascent of Mera.
- **Ramblers Worldwide Holidays** (☎ 01707-331133, 🖳 www.ramblersholi days.co.uk) offer a teahouse trek in the Everest Region.

- **Peregrine Tours** (☎ 0844 736 0170, 🖳 www.peregrineadventures.co.uk) British branch of popular Australian chain (see opposite).
- **Sherpa Expeditions** (☎ 020-8577 2717, 🖳 www.sherpaexpeditions.com) has a wide range of guided treks including a standard 18-day trek to Everest Base Camp and an 8-day Everest Panorama trek.
- **Terra Firma** (☎ 01691-870321, 🖳 www.terra firmatravel.com) offers several treks in the region and a high adventure holiday including trekking, rafting and trailbiking.
- **Tribes Travel** (☎ 01728-685971, 🖳 www.tribes.co.uk) offers small-group and tailor-made treks including Everest Base Camp and Gokyo Lakes.
- **Walks Worldwide** (☎ 01524-242000, 🖳 www.walksworldwide.com) offer an Everest in Style trek and Everest Base Camp.
- **World Expeditions** (☎ 020-8545 9030, 🖳 www.worldexpeditions.com/uk) operate a wide variety of treks in the Everest region.

Trekking agencies in Continental Europe
- **Austria** Reiseburo El Mundo (☎ 316-81 06 98, 🖳 www.elmundo.at) is an agent for Exodus (see p21).

- **Belgium** Divantoura (☎ 09-223 00 69, 🖳 www.divantoura.be), an Explore agent (see p21). **Joker** (☎ 02-648 78 78, 🖳 www.joker.be) is an agent for Exodus (see p21), Intrepid (see p21) and GAP (see opposite).

- **Denmark** Hannibal & Marco Polo (☎ 33-76 67 00, 🖳 www.hannibalog marcopolo.dk); **Kipling Travel** (☎ 47-16 12 20, 🖳 www.kiplingtravel.dk); **Topas** (☎ 86 89 36 22, 🖳 www.topas.dk).

- **France** Club Aventure (☎ 08 26 88 20 80, 🖳 www.clubaventure.fr).

- **Germany** DAV Summit Club (☎ 089-64 24 00, 🖳 www.dav-summit-club.de).

- **Ireland** Abbey Travel (☎ 01-804 7153, 🖳 exodus@abbeytravel.ie). Agents for Exodus UK (see p21).

- **Netherlands** HT Wandelreizen (☎ 0522-241 1146, 🖳 www.htwandelrei zen.nl). **Nederlandse Klim en Bergsport Vereniging** (☎ 0348-409521, 🖳 www .nkbv.nl). **Snow Leopard Adventure Reizen** (☎ 070-388 28 67, 🖳 www.snow leopard.nl); **Flach Travel** (☎ 0343 592659; 🖳 www.flachtravel.nl), an agent for Exodus (see p21).

- **Spain** Banoa (☎ 94-435 51 19, 🖳 www.banoa.com).

- **Switzerland** Acapa Tours (☎ 056 443 32 21, 🖳 www.acapAdventures .com) is an agent for Exodus (see p21) and Peregrine (see p21).

Agencies in the USA
- **Adventure Center** (toll free ☎ 800-227-8747, ☎ 510-228-8747, 🖳 www .adventurecenter.com) offer a large number of treks in the Everest region.
- **GAP (USA)** (toll free ☎ 800-676-4941, 🖳 www.gapadventures.com); see GAP (Canada) for a description.

- **Geographic Expeditions** (☎ 415-922-0448, toll free ☎ 800-777-8183, 🖥 www.geoex.com) run several tours around Nepal including a Himalayan Leadership trek and a Sherpa Villages and Everest trek.
- **Journeys International** (☎ 734-665-4407, ☎ 800-255-8735, 🖥 www.jour neys-intl.com) includes some treks specially for families.
- **Mountain Travel Sobek** (☎ 510-527-8100, ☎ 888-687-6235, 🖥 www .mtsobek.com) offer an Everest Base Camp trek and an Everest Escapade as a group trek or a tailor-made holiday.
- **Wilderness Travel** (☎ 510-558-2488, toll-free ☎ 800-368-2794, 🖥 www .wildernesstravel.com) offers a 25-day 'Ultimate Everest' tour including a 20-day trek to Everest Base Camp via the top of Kala Pattar, as well as a gentler 9-day 'Private Journey' trek from Lukla.
- **World Expeditions** (☎ 415-989-2212, toll-free ☎ 1-888-464-8735, 🖥 www .worldexpeditions.com) is a volume operator with a wide variety of trips.

Agencies in Canada
- **Canadian Himalayan Expeditions** (☎ 416-360-4300, toll free ☎ 800-563-8735, 🖥 www.HimalayanExpeditions.com) is one of the few Canadian companies that runs their own treks, rather than acting as agents for other companies, and offers a wide variety of walks in the Everest region.
- **GAP (Canada)** (☎ 416-260-0999, toll-free ☎ 1-800-708-7761, 🖥 www .gapadventures.com) is a very large, well-run organization offering an Everest Adventure, Everest and Annapurna and Everest and Kailash treks.
- **Trek Escapes** (☎ 1-888-456-3522, 🖥 www.trekholidays.com) has branches all over Canada and acts as an agent for Exodus (see p21) and Peregrine (see below).
- **Worldwide Adventures** (☎ 613-241-2700, toll free ☎ 1-800-567-2216, 🖥 www.worldexpeditions.com.ca) act as agent for World Expeditions; see below.

Agencies in Australia
- **Peregrine Travel Centre** (Melbourne ☎ 1300-655433 or Sydney ☎ 1300-854 444, 🖥 www.peregrineadventures.com) offer a large number of treks in the Everest region as well as tailor-made holidays.
- **World Expeditions** (☎ 1300-720000, 🖥 www.worldexpeditions.com.au), have a number of branches in Australia and are the main competition for Peregrine. As well as a range of standard treks, some climbing expeditions are offered and one trek includes a chance to help on the Junbesi School Project.

Agencies in New Zealand
- **Project Himalaya** (🖥 www.project-himalaya.com). Run by the author of this guidebook.
- **World Expeditions** (☎ 09-368 4161, toll-free ☎ 0800-350354, 🖥 www .worldexpeditions.co.nz); see above.

Agencies in South Africa
- **Shiralee Travel** (☎ 028-313 0526, 🖥 kim.kirsten@harveyworld.co.za). Agent for Explore (UK); see p21.

> **Acute mountain sickness (AMS) – a primer**
> The key to planning a trekking itinerary is awareness of altitude sickness: going up too fast causes a medical condition serious enough to kill you. The higher the altitude, the less oxygen there is in the air. On the lower summit of Kala Pattar (5554m/18,222ft), for example, there is 50% less oxygen than at sea level. Your body needs many days to adapt to this phenomenon so for a safe trek it is absolutely essential that you **allow sufficient time for acclimatization**.
>
> The doctors at Khunde Hospital and the HRA Pheriche clinic all stress that in virtually every case they treat, the patient has ascended faster than the guidelines. In a surprising number of cases trekkers were forced to ascend too quickly by their group's itinerary. Sometimes this has been because a delayed flight has meant they have had to cut out a vital acclimatization day. The Japanese are perhaps the most notorious for rushing and also seem to be highly susceptible to AMS. See box p25 and box pp28-9 for more information as well as the appendix (pp290-9).

How long to go for

If time is the ultimate luxury a trekking holiday should be a decadent one. The more time you have in the mountains the better, especially if the concept of trekking appeals. It takes a day or two to adjust to the trekking lifestyle and exercise, and it's usually only in the last couple of days that you'll start to feel it is time to clean up and fatten up. If you want to sample trekking rather than eat the whole pie, a week to ten days is a good length: anything less is just a stroll.

Time planning
Arriving in Nepal from Australia or Europe it's best to allow a whole day in Kathmandu (ie two nights), while from North America allow two whole days (three nights) to start to recover and adjust to the different time zone and climate. If arranging a trek on arrival, two or three full days are better. Try to have at least one day in Kathmandu at the end of a trek in order to clean up and shop. More time can easily be filled by exploring the Kathmandu Valley, relaxing in cafés and bargaining with tea-serving Kashmiri carpet salesmen and Thangka-hawking Tibetans. Slowly Nepal is becoming an adventure destination, so plan extra time if rafting, bungee jumping, canyoning, mountain-biking, paragliding or visiting Tibet appeals.

Avoid the trap of planning a whole itinerary down to the last minute and allow plenty of time for the inevitable delays and interruptions to your schedule. Domestic flights can be delayed, so allow an extra day or two to accommodate for this. Once on the trail, especially on a longer trek, allow a couple of days for inclement weather, sickness or a gloriously lazy day for eating and reading. Although many people have never been hiking for more than four or five days at home (or indeed never been hiking at all), two or three weeks in the mountains of Nepal usually flies by all too quickly.

PLANNING YOUR TREK

Route options

Since ancient times caravans have followed trade routes across many parts of Asia. The advent of motorized transport brought great changes but these developments passed Nepal by until the 1950s. The first road link, the Rajpath between Kathmandu and India, was opened only in 1956 but road construction is now a government priority (rail is impractical). With much of the countryside being not far off vertical, only the low-lying Tarai (Terai) and the Himalayan foothills have been penetrated and even then the roads are rough.

The rest of the country still relies on the footpaths and mountain trails that form an age-old network across the country. Looking at a map it's easy to plan some weird and wonderful routes in wild and isolated areas. However, only a few major routes are suited to trekkers wanting to stay in lodges – but what routes some of them are.

PLANNING

Most people start planning with the intention of seeing Everest. Basically this entails going to the Khumbu region and up a hill to view the mountain. So the majority of trekkers fly to Lukla, trek to the top of Kala Pattar, then fly out of Lukla. This standard route is popular, and with good reason, but the options are much broader.

All routes to Everest pass through Namche (except a few tough options mentioned later) so the first decision to make is how you're going to get there. If you plan to fly one way only, flying out is best since the walk-in aids

---

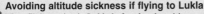

Avoiding altitude sickness if flying to Lukla

Most flights arrive in Lukla before lunch so it's usual to hit the trail and stay at Phakding or Monjo for the first night. Nevertheless, some sensible planning is required to lessen the risk of altitude sickness occurring later. Already at Lukla there is only 70% of the oxygen compared to sea level. Altitude-specialist doctors recommend taking a minimum of 2-3 nights to reach 3000m/9843ft. Lukla is at 2850m/9350ft so you are already close to that altitude limit and Namche, at 3450m/11,319ft, is well above it: yet most trekkers who fly in then trek to Namche in just over 24 hours. These people are twice as likely to experience troublesome AMS (Acute Mountain Sickness) and form the majority of serious cases. Caution at this point will undoubtedly lessen the impact of problems experienced later. Diamox may also help; see p295.

There are many people in the trekking industry who would consider the above advice over-cautious. However, two American studies found that 9-12% of people who ascend directly to 2800m (ie Lukla's altitude) suffered noticeable AMS, admittedly usually non-life-threatening, but definitely uncomfortable. The AMS tended to resolve itself within 2-3 days of staying at the same altitude. Arriving directly at 3860m (ie Syangboche) caused AMS in 84% of people.

❏ TREK TIMEFRAMES – KATHMANDU TO KATHMANDU

The following are overall times needed for a trek, assuming normal pace with acclimatization days and including travel days. Remember to allow an extra day or two for flight delays, sickness etc. See box pp28-9 and pp282-4 for suggested itineraries.

Flying in and out of Lukla
● **Quickest Everest view** (to Namche with a day trip there) 5-6 days
● **To Tengboche Gompa** 7-9 days
● **Khumbu culture** (with time around Thame, Namche, Tengboche) 8-12 days
● **Everest Base Camp** (actually Kala Pattar) 13-16 days
● **Gokyo Lakes** 12-14 days
● **Explore the Khumbu** (Gokyo, Kala Pattar, Chukhung) 18-21 or more days
● **Attempt Island Peak** (or similar) 18-21 days
● **Mera Peak** 19-23 days
    For flying in to Phaplu instead of Lukla, add 4-6 days

Walking into the region
● **Expedition route** (Jiri start, trek to Kala Pattar then fly from Lukla) 20-22 days
● **Explore the Khumbu** (Jiri start, look up the main valleys then fly from Lukla) 23-28 days
● **Expedition route in, Salpa end** (Jiri start plus walking out via Salpa-Arun to Tumlingtar) 27-30 days
● **Salpa-Arun route** (fly to Tumlingtar, trek to Kala Pattar then fly from Lukla) 22-25 days
● **Tilman-Shipton route** (bus to Leguwa Ghat, Salpa-Arun to Kala Pattar, fly from Lukla) 23-26 days

acclimatization (the process of getting used to altitude, see box pp28-9) and fitness. If flying in and out, although the vast majority of people begin and end in Lukla, flying in to Phaplu is a sensible alternative (see p30). For sample itineraries see pp282-3.

FLYING IN

To Lukla (2850m/9350ft)
This is the most popular way to begin the trek because it's the quickest: Lukla is only one-and-a-half day's walk from Namche. However, the risk of altitude sickness is double that of alternative routes unless at least one extra acclimatization day is scheduled (see box p25). Trekkers in organized groups should particularly note this; see p282. Consider, too, the use of Diamox, a drug that aids acclimatization: see p295.

Lukla flights are surprisingly reliable given that they are fair-weather only, although at the end of the trek it is still a good idea to plan an extra-just-in-case-day in Kathmandu before you fly out of Nepal. While the international airlines in Kathmandu tend to be forgiving if you get stuck in the hills, they cannot always arrange to put you on the next available flight, and home country domestic airlines tend to take a much harsher approach.

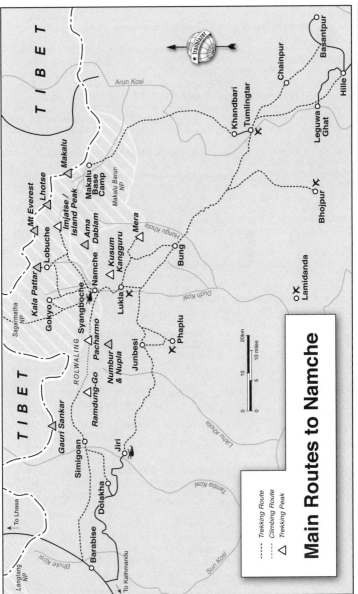

Main Routes to Namche

Legend:
- - - - Trekking Route
.... Climbing Route
△ Trekking Peak

❖ Itinerary planning and altitude awareness

Kala Pattar is 5600m/18,373ft and Gokyo Ri is 5340m/17,519ft – they are high! You might sleep at the same altitude as the top of Mont Blanc. Even on a shorter trek you could top out at 4000m/13,120ft. It is essential to understand that your body needs time to acclimatize to these altitudes and process takes days. So, it is essential to plan a trek with this in mind.

After a high percentage of the early trekkers died of a mysterious pneumonia, it was realized there was such a thing as altitude sickness. After several studies, it was recommended that trekkers spend 2-3 nights at around 2000-3000m/6560-9840ft before going higher, then ascend an average of approximately 300m/984ft a day in sleeping altitude, and have a rest day every three days. This is the safe and relatively comfortable ascent rate for most people, although it is still possible for the occasional person to get seriously sick, even with this caution. If you go faster to altitude you run bigger risks, and a greater percentage of people get hit with altitude sickness. Despite these facts, many trekking companies offer treks with much faster ascent rates – beware, or at least be aware that you run a greater risk of getting into trouble or having to turn back.

In the following tables, you end up with a long itinerary if you stick exactly to the guidelines, so the compromise itinerary is one that is a day shorter but still altitude-aware, and is one that many people have completed. Although many people do trek the 'unwise' options, usually at least one person, sometimes several in a group, will have to turn back, and there have been plenty of rescues on this sort of itinerary.

Diamox is a drug that helps acclimatization, read more on p295.

Do also allow a day or two or some flexibility for possible intestinal sickness, especially if this your first visit to Nepal, or in case your domestic flights in or out of the region are delayed. Note that once you have acclimatized, and slept up high, you don't need to acclimatize again on a trek. See pp290-9 for a more detailed discussion.

Standard Kala Pattar trek itinerary

Day/ altitude	Good	Advised sleeping altitude good	compromise	unwise	unwise	Advised sleeping altitude rounded up
Day 1/	Phakding/ Monjo	Phakding/ Monjo	Phakding/ Monjo	Phakding/ Monjo	Phakding/ Monjo	
2-3000m	2650m	2650m	2650m	2650m	2650m	**2-3000m**
Day 2/	Monjo/ Namche	Namche	Namche	Namche	Namche	
2-3000m	2650m/ 3450m	3450m	3450m	3450m	3450m	**3000m**
Day 3/	Namche	Namche	Namche	Namche	Namche	
3000m	3450m	3450m	3450m	3450m	3450m	**3333m**
Day 4/	Namche	Namche/ Thame	Namche	Tengboche	Tengboche	
3300m	3450m	3450m/ 3780m	3450m	3860m	3860m	**3666m**
Day 5/	Tengboche	Khumjung	Pangboche	Pheriche	Pangboche	
3600m	3860m	3790m	4000m	4280m	4000m	**4000m**
Day 6/	Pangboche	Pangboche	Dingboche/ Pheriche	Pheriche	Pheriche	
3900m	4000m	4000m	4350m/4280m	4280m	4280m	**4000m**

(cont'd) Day/ altitude	Good	Advised sleeping altitude good	compromise	unwise	unwise	Advised sleeping altitude rounded up
Day 7/	Dingboche/ Pheriche	Dingboche/ Pheriche	Dingboche/ Pheriche	Lobuche	Pheriche	
3900m	4350m/ 4280m	4350m/ 4280m	4350m/ 4280m	4940m	4280m	**4333m**
Day 8/	Dingboche/ Pheriche	Dingboche/ Pheriche	Thuklha/	Gorak Shep Chukhung	Lobuche	
4200m	4350m/ 4280m	4350m/ 4280m	4600m/ 4750m	5150m	4940m	**4666m**
Day 9/	Thuklha/ Chukhung	Thuklha/ Chukhung	Lobuche	Gorak Shep	Lobuche	
4500m	4600m/ 4750m	4600m/ 4750m	4940m	5150m	4940m	**5000m**
Day 10/	Lobuche	Lobuche	Gorak Shep	Pheriche	Pheriche	
4800m	4940m	4940m	5150m			**5000m**
Day 11/	Gorak Shep	Gorak Shep	Gorak Shep	Namche	Namche	
5100m	5150m	5150m	5150m			
Day 12/	Gorak Shep	Gorak Shep	Pheriche/ Pangboche	Lukla	Lukla	
5100m	5150m	5150m				
Day 13	Pheriche/ Pangboche	Pheriche/ Pangboche	Namche	fly to Kathmandu	fly to Kathmandu	
Day 14	Namche	Namche	Lukla			
Day 15	Lukla	Lukla	fly to Kathmandu			
Day 16	fly to Kathmandu	fly to Kathmandu				

Gokyo trek itinerary

Day/ altitude	Advised sleeping altitude Unwise	Compromise	Day/ altitude	Advised sleeping altitude Unwise	Compromise
Day 1/	Phakding/ Monjo	Phakding/ Monjo	Day 7/	Gokyo	Machermo
2-3000m	2650m		3900m	4750m	4410m
Day 2/	Namche	Namche	Day 8/	Gokyo	Gokyo
2-3000m	3450m	3450m	4200m	4750m	4750m
Day 3/	Namche	Namche	Day 9/	Dole/Mong	Gokyo
3000m	3450m	3450m	4500m		4750m
Day 4/	Khumjung	Namche/ Thame	Day 10/	Namche	Dole/Mong
3300m	3790m	3450m/3780m	4800m		
Day 5/	Dole	Khumjung	Day 11/	Lukla	Namche
3600m	4040m	3790m	5100m		
Day 6/	Machermo	Dole	Day 12/	fly Kathmandu	Lukla
3900m	4410m	4040m	5100m		
			Day 13		fly Kathmandu

To Phaplu (2350m/7710ft)

If you wish to fly, flying to Phaplu is an under-used route and yet a sensible choice. It saves what some consider an arduous day on a bus to Jiri and a few days' walking. Compared with flying to Lukla, it allows a safer and more gentle introduction to altitude and reveals a richer cultural variety with the added bonus of being able to visit Junbesi and Chiwang Gompa.

To Syangboche (3700m/12,139ft)

There are no scheduled flights to Syangboche, the airstrip just above Namche, only helicopter charter flights. Without previous acclimatization, flying to Syangboche and descending to Namche, at 3450m/11,319ft, is uncomfortable and potentially dangerous: Lukla is a much-better option.

ROUTE OPTIONS ABOVE NAMCHE

Above Namche there are four main valleys (see map opposite), each spectacular and worthwhile exploring. The westernmost valley in the Khumbu is the **lower Bhote** featuring Thame with its old gompa – a good day or overnight trip from Namche.

The **upper Bhote valley** leads to the 5700m Nangpa La trading pass which was opened to trekkers in 2002, although you can only go to the top of the pass and cannot actually cross into Tibet. Above Arye there are no lodges so any walk here is serious wilderness trekking, and spectacular – perfect for some wild exploration; see pp224-6.

Moving eastwards, the **valley featuring Gokyo** has a stunning set of turquoise lakes, multiple Everest viewpoints and offers incredible potential for exploration. Its lower reaches are good places for wildlife spotting.

The next valley east features **Kala Pattar**, the most popular point for viewing Everest and Everest Base Camp. These are accessible from Lobuche and Gorak Shep, the highest places you are likely to stay. One detail that should be clearly understood is that although most people are initially drawn to Everest and want to visit Everest Base Camp, there are actually no views of the upper part of the mountain from base camp. For this reason almost everyone climbs Kala Pattar, for its glorious panorama, including Everest. If you wish to visit both, plan an extra day in your itinerary.

The final valley above Namche is home to **Chukhung** and offers good exploring and climbing, although no Everest views. Chukhung is the starting point for the climb of the ever-popular Imjatse/Island Peak, 6173m.

In addition to trekking through each valley, there are also several high passes that run between them and provide a greater challenge. All are possible to cross relying on teahouses.

Other considerations are the gompas – **Buddhist temples** – that dot the region. **Tengboche**, en route to Lobuche and Chukhung, is popular and well set up to accept visitors. It is also modern, having been rebuilt on a grand scale after a fire in 1989: as such, a comparison with centuries-old gompas such as Pangboche, Thame or Khumjung can be enlightening. Although many visitors

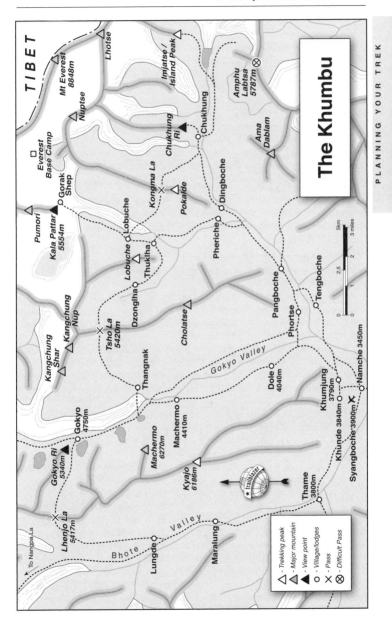

The Khumbu

TIBET

Mt Everest 8848m
Lhotse
Nuptse
Everest Base Camp
Pumori
Kala Pattar 5554m
Gorak Shep
Lobuche
Lobuche 4930m
Thukla
Dzonglha
Kangchung Shar
Kangchung Nup
Tsho La 5420m
Thangnak
Gokyo 4750m
Gokyo Ri 5340m
Machermo 6270m
Machermo 4410m
Kyajo 6186m
Lhenjo La 5417m
To Nangpa La
Lungde
Bhote Valley
Maralung
Thame 3800m
Syangboche 3900m
Khunde 3840m
Khumjung 3790m
Dole 4040m
Namche 3450m
Gokyo Valley
Phortse
Pangboche
Tengboche
Cholatse
Pheriche
Dingboche
Pokalde
Kongma La
Chukhung
Chukhung Ri
Ama Dablam
Amphu Labtsa 5787m
Imjatse / Island Peak

Key
△ - Trekking peak
◺ - Major mountain
▲ - View point
○ - Village/lodges
✕ - Pass
⊗ - Difficult Pass

Scale: 0   1   2   3 miles
0   2.5   5km

PLANNING YOUR TREK

are keen to experience the **Sherpa culture**, to do so in depth is more difficult than you would expect; see pp34-5.

The amount of time spent above Namche varies with your ambitions. To see Everest from the top of Kala Pattar, or Gokyo Ri in the Gokyo Valley, a minimum of thirteen days must be allowed (including a day for flying out). This includes several consecutive nights spent at the same point while ascending: this is essential for adequate acclimatization. Lovers of grand mountain scenery and explorers, however, could spend weeks wandering up the high valleys above Namche, only returning to hunt down a hot shower and good pizza. In addition to incredible scenery, staying in quieter lodges and spending time with the Sherpas is all part of a rewarding experience. It is this that separates trekking in Nepal from trekking in wilderness areas in Western countries.

Lobuche or Gokyo?

Years ago, heavy marketing for treks to Everest Base Camp excluded other less goal-orientated options. This is still reflected in the brochures of many trekking companies which barely mention a trek up Gokyo Valley. It is, however, well worth considering.

The pros and cons With the Lobuche option, the views from **Kala Pattar** (near Lobuche and Everest Base Camp) are fantastic. Although only the upper part of Everest can be seen, spectacular sheer mountains and glaciers entirely surround you. Most people don't end up visiting Everest Base Camp, partly because many don't have enough time and also because the trail there is rough and the only view is of the fearsome icefall. However, during the main expedition season, April-May, visiting the tent city is fascinating.

From **Gokyo Ri** the mountains are just as spectacular but not so close, affording views that extend into the distance. The sunset from Gokyo Ri far surpasses that from Kala Pattar. But perhaps the major advantage is Gokyo's exploration potential: multiple day trips are possible, with all offering a view of Everest.

Trekking to Gokyo also has the advantage of taking one day less and the highest sleeping altitude is lower too, at 4750m as opposed to Lobuche's 4930m or Gorak Shep's 5170m. On the other hand, if you plan to spend only a single day at one or the other, Lobuche is possibly the better option because the views are great from nearby Kala Pattar and the walk is perhaps more spectacular, although tougher.

If you have more time the options increase. Having been to one of either Gokyo, Lobuche or Chukhung, you should now be acclimatized sufficiently so that you no longer have to plan with altitude in mind. The distances in the Khumbu are not, in fact, very great, with each valley being only a day or two apart. Deciding between visiting Chukhung en route to Lobuche or going to Lobuche first and then Gokyo is such a difficult choice that it's tempting to add a couple more days and visit all of them!

Some examples of itineraries are given on pp28-9 and pp282-4: they can be joined together to create more interesting combinations.

Gokyo *and* Lobuche

Keen to visit both? If you plan to visit both but not Chukhung, it may be slightly more sensible to visit Gokyo first since the maximum sleeping altitude there is slightly lower. Crossing the Tsho La (Cho La) between the valleys takes most people two days while walking around the bottom route via Phortse takes two to three days.

If you plan to visit Chukhung as well beginning with Gokyo or Chukhung makes equal sense. Gokyo and Chukhung offer many days' worth of side trips while Lobuche/Gorak Shep is more limiting.

The Tsho La / Cho La / Chugyima La (see p217) is a tempting option when contemplating visiting both Gokyo and Lobuche valleys but the conditions must be good. This trip normally takes two days. The alternative walk via Phortse offers a less alpine landscape but is just as rewarding, though it involves two or, more normally, three longer days trekking.

The Lhenjo La / Renjo La (see p221) is now possible to cross exclusively using teahouses, which will increase both the number of trekkers who use this route and the possibilities nearby. For acclimatization purposes, it is significantly better to cross in the Gokyo to Thame direction.

Flying out

The majority of trekkers fly out of Lukla. Although the walk from Namche to Lobuche or Gokyo takes a week going up, the return trip takes most trekkers just two days, then one more to Lukla. It isn't possible to fly out of Syangboche, except by helicopter charter.

WALKING IN

From Jiri – the expedition route

Jiri–Shivalaya, a day's journey by bus from Kathmandu, is the usual starting point for trekkers who prefer to walk-in. This route features lodges and teahouses catering for trekkers and while during the peak season the regions above Lukla are congested, the Jiri walk-in never suffers this feeling. Virtually all trekkers are without guides, giving the lodges a carefree air. It is a surprisingly strenuous walk with the route crossing three large ridges, but it's also a rewarding one that prepares you for the higher altitudes ahead. See p231 for more details.

The Salpa-Arun route from Tumlingtar

On this route, compared with the Jiri to Namche walk, the number and height of the hills are similar but the overall distance is slightly greater. Route-finding is more challenging and many lodges are a half or full day's walk apart so it's better attempted by trekkers with some experience. Most lodges don't have menus (or flush toilets) so it is still a surprisingly rustic experience: there have been hardly any changes in the last 20 years.

Flying to Tumlingtar is good value, relatively reliable and generally the better option. Air fares have risen much less than bus fares, narrowing the difference to the point where the only reason for taking a bus is for the experience or if you are travelling with your trekking crew.

The road from Hille has now been extended to Tumlingtar and Khandbari, although a couple of vital bridges are still missing (and will probably be built by 2010). At the time of writing buses went as far as Leguwa Ghat, around 10-12 hours from Kathmandu and small buses/jeeps ply the rest of the route, except over the river without a road bridge.

Once another large bridge across the Arun is constructed at Leguwa Ghat, the road will also go to Bhojpur, a possible starting point for trekking. The route is not touristy and the facilities are less than basic.

Beginning with a wet-and-wild rafting trip, the Sun Kosi is a great way to combine a rafting expedition with a Salpa-Arun trek. The rafting finishes at Chautara and it is easy enough to get transport up to Hille-Leguwa Ghat. The Salpa route was used for the first few expeditions into the Khumbu but didn't catch on, perhaps because they trekked it during the monsoon. The trail notes start on p246.

Walking in and out
Starting from Jiri is more sensible, and then finishing with the tougher trek out to Tumlingtar. However, retracing your steps to Jiri is not a boring alternative: returning, the views are different and the seasons change the colours of the countryside. You'll get a warm welcome from lodges you return to and, being wiser to the ways of the land, you'll probably find this part of the walk more rewarding than before.

OTHER OPTIONS

Cultural treks
The Salpa-Arun and Solu-Khumbu regions are perfect areas for a culture-oriented trek. In many ways time is the most important factor. Taking a Sherpa guide and staying in lodges gives you an immediate introduction to a local house (ie their lodge). If the lodge isn't busy you can sit at the kitchen fire and chat with the owner. This is more easily accomplished off-season from Namche and above. Thame and the small settlements en route, Upper Pangboche and Phortse are less frequently visited villages.

Below Lukla the main trails aren't heavily trekked and there are few trekkers in the shoulder season, eg late September, December to March and mid-May to mid-June. You can get off the tourist-frequented routes by either taking an expedition crew or, if you have the right guide, simply by staying in people's houses. But be warned the food will be simple and there may be little privacy. Perhaps the best way to experience the culture is to briefly live it, eg help with the harvest.

There are some loops that take you off the main trekking routes. For a sample of **Rai culture** consider staying in Bung or Gudel for at least several days and visit a few of the villages nearby, eg Cheskam. There is a route south of the main trekking route, via Somtang, to or from Phaplu.

Phaplu and the surrounding region is barely visited by trekkers. There are several interesting old and new gompas and Salleri is the district headquarters, the real Nepal, although half modern. Chialsa is a **Tibetan enclave**, as is Thubten Choeling, north of Junbesi. Trekking up from Okaldunga to Phaplu would be an experience. Around Bhojpur, Dingla, Tumlingtar, Khadbari and Chainpur is a mainly Hindu region. Trekking to the Rolwaling Valley is rewarding and it is possible to exit via a different route. You will have to camp a few nights but the hardy could mostly stay in local lodges and people's houses.

For all the ideals involved in taking a cultural trek, it is difficult to really experience or get deeply into the culture, especially without speaking the language. It helps to read as much background information as possible, particularly anthropological papers, and have a particularly communicative and patient guide.

Other non-technical trekking routes into the Khumbu

The standard routes (Jiri and the Salpa-Arun) are the most logical and direct ways into the Khumbu, reinforced by convenient lodges. However, walking from Barabise to Jiri is feasible, as is flying into Lamidanda, Okhaldhunga, Bhojpur, or trekking up from the Okhaldhunga road to the south. These alternatives are not on difficult or dangerous trails but they traverse hot low country and lack lodges, so they are better attempted with a guide and after acquiring some Nepalese trekking experience.

Alternative treks

The psychological omnipotence of Everest is so great that few people contemplate trekking in this region without the aim of seeing it from close quarters. Star attraction aside, there are other areas that offer fantastic trekking amid stunning mountains. However, these all require a degree of self-sufficiency and camping. Many would be particularly suited to the classic style of Nepal trekking – a crew to carry the excess and a few Sherpa companions to round off the experience.

Alternatives to the Everest region

The Everest region trails are particularly crowded during October and November, and this is the perfect time to explore alternative regions. All are expedition-style camping treks. The **Kanchenjunga region** (home to the third-highest mountain on the planet) has long alpine valleys and plenty of side valleys to explore; the **Manaslu circuit**, a trek around the eighth-highest peak, is in a far less-developed region where teahouses are not an option and features both picturesque middle-hills villages and classic Tibetan villages in the higher reaches; around **Dhaulagiri** (#7) is extreme trekking and a relatively untouched culture in the lower region; while the **Makalu** (#5) region has wilderness trekking in the upper reaches; and across the border in Tibet, the **Kharte Valley** trek to the Kangshung face of Everest is remote, stunningly beautiful and surprisingly under-trekked.

If you are worried the trek may be too strenuous for you, another alternative for seeing Everest close up is a jeep tour from Lhasa to Kathmandu, driving via Everest Base Camp on Everest's north side, which offers the added bonus of allowing you to experience Tibet.

> **A second trek**
> Trekking can be addictive! Around 20% of trekkers do it again in the same hol-
> iday. Trekkers also have one of the highest tourism return rates in the world: an
> amazing number of people just keep coming back year after year. After a first trek
> you'll know how the teahouse system works and be comfortable with the way Nepal
> is in general. Teahouse trekking is still only easy in the three main areas of Annapurna
> (Trailblazer publishes *Trekking in the Annapurna Region*), Everest and Langtang, but
> using the teahouses some wild routes with plenty of exploring are possible.
>
> On a more generous budget (US$35-100 a day, plus flights), heading away from
> the main areas and camping makes sense. During the October-December season, or
> late spring, the more ambitious may want to throw in a 6000m/c20,000ft trekking
> peak too. A map of Nepal is useful for planning.

Going without local support is for the tough and experienced and even then a
porter for some sections would be invaluable. The best suggestions are:

● **Exploring above Junbesi** to Dudh Kund (Milk Lake) below the holy mountain of Numbur and in the Lumding Kharka area, south of Kongde (a 'trekking
peak') and Nupla. This could be combined with the trek to Namche.

● **South of the Rolwaling Valley** is a region that hides untold exciting possibilities – high *kharkas* (grazing areas) and ridges littered with mountains a
touch under 6000m/19,685ft. Several circuits are possible over unused passes.

● **The Hinku and Hongu valleys** offer challenging and remote treks amongst
mind-blowing mountains. A circuit including Mera would be attractive.

● **The Barun and Makalu region** This is an isolated area with only a fraction
of it used for grazing and expedition access to Makalu. Otherwise it's impenetrable forest topped by savage mountains. A trek to Makalu Base Camp is the
only feasible option.

PEAKS AND PASSES

Mountaineering adventures take careful planning but the possible rewards are
satisfying too. Broadly, there are several ways of planning these expeditions.

The first is to arrange everything through a company, as a complete trip.
This feels like a real expedition. The second is to acclimatize on a teahouse trek,
and then meet the crew for the climb or ambitious pass crossing.

At the planning stage do also consider what the alternatives would be if you
fail in your first objective, whether this is a pass or a peak: every few years it
does snow heavily at an inconvenient time – will that shorten your trip or are

> **Mountain-biking**
> A picture of a Japanese man astride a mountain bike atop Kala Pattar set off a
> raft of would-be imitators. Each found the hard way that bikes have to be car-
> ried at least 95% of the time, effectively the whole way. Now, sensibly, Sagarmatha
> National Park has put a ban on mountain-biking in the park.

there worthy alternatives? Whichever mountain you tackle, do plan a sensible acclimatization program, and trek first, then climb. So for Island Peak do a trek to Kala Pattar/Everest Base Camp then go climbing.

Note that on even a basic expedition the costs quickly mount up so especially for less-focused, novice or budget mountaineers it is generally better to simply go exploring around the Khumbu. There is a glorious freedom in the host of 5800m scrambles and 5400m pass crossings, unencumbered by harness, rope or guide.

Trekking peaks

Fancy climbing a 6000m Himalayan peak? In the jagged world of the Everest region there are a few peaks that can be relatively straightforward to climb and some of these so-called 'trekking peaks' have become increasingly popular objectives. Despite the term 'trekking peaks', all involve real mountaineering, and climbing at 6000m is more challenging than most people expect.

For many climbers and would-be climbers, the combination of a trek to Everest Base Camp and the climb of a 6000m/20,000ft peak has unbeatable appeal – it's one of the reasons **Island Peak**/Imjatse (6173m/20,252ft) is the most popular of the 'trekking peaks'. That means it is busy during the main October-November season, sometimes chaotically so. With ropes fixed along all the tricky sections it is simply a case of clipping on a jumar (a one-way device) and heading off, hopefully to the summit. The second busiest peak is **Mera** (6476m/21,246ft), offering a sensational summit panorama including a bunch of 8000m mountains. It is little more than an intimidating snow plod up, so it suits people with little skill. It is in a remote area with no villages (although there are some lodges), which contrasts with Island Peak.

On both mountains there is a mixture of clients, from those whose mountaineering experience is close to zero and are on guided ascents to more skilled climbers using basically the same techniques.

Other relatively straightforward peaks in the region include **Pokalde** (5794m/19,009ft), which is a rock scramble but below the magic 6000m/20,000ft mark. **Parcharmo** (6273m/20,580ft) is basically equivalent to Island Peak, but is off the main trails so requires more time and commitment. It begs to be combined with crossing the Tashi Labtsa; see p263.

(cont'd on p40)

Trekking peak statistics

Island Peak is by far the most popular peak with around 2000 people a year, or on average 15 people or more a day (during the season), and during peak season there could potentially be as many as 30 or more climbers, seriously consider if you want to climb with that number of people around; do consider other trekking peaks within your ability.

Mera Peak is the next most popular with around 800 people in a year, and this will grow. Parcharmo and Lobuche come in at around 250 a year, Pokalde around 150, and all the other Khumbu trekking peaks have less than 50 climbers a year.

PLANNING YOUR TREK

❖ OTHER ACTIVITIES

Nepal offers a lot more than just trekking. Some of these activities require advance planning, others can be booked in Kathmandu on arrival: just remember to allow some extra time to make the necessary arrangements. For mountain biking, rafting, canyoning and bungee jumping there are a collection of companies with small offices in the centre of Thamel. Check the courtyards in Kathmandu Guest House, the one beside that with The Last Resort Office and others including the one leading to Northfield Café. See also box p40 regarding trips to Bhutan or Tibet.

Rafting (2-12 days; $35-65 a day) While Nepal is famous for its mountains it should also be renowned for rafting. Huge mountains mean big, steep rivers, which are perfect for rafting and **kayaking**. For thrill-seekers no trip to Nepal would be complete without a wild-water expedition. The nervousness, no, the plain fear of being committed to a rapid, then the sheer exhilaration of running and surviving the huge white-water make rafting one of life's most thrilling experiences. Between the roller-coasters are peaceful stretches, chances to splash around and relax, letting the adrenaline highs give way to that priceless inner glow. Also special is the warmth and fun of being an integral part of the team.

For a mild, cheap intro try the **Trisuli**: almost every rafting company runs this river with two- to four-day trips possible, virtually year-round. If you know you will enjoy the thrills and spills don't muck around, hit a river with a higher scare factor. The **Bhote Kosi** (two days) and the **Marsyangdi** (five days) are steep, technical and fun. For the ultimate try the massive waters of the **Karnali** (six to seven days plus three travelling) and the **Sun Kosi** (eight to nine days plus two travelling), which have rapids that will make even the coolest cucumber gulp in disbelief. Another world-class river is the exhilarating **Tamur** (Kanchenjunga region), with its magic trek-in and approximately 130 rapids in 120km. For a shade off full throttle consider the cultural **Kali Gandaki** (three days, out of Pokhara) or the **Sun Kosi** in low water. The high-water season, for those with no fear, is late September to early October and May. Trips run into November then begin again in March and taper off by late May.

Wherever you go, safety should be paramount. The more difficult the river is, the more you should check the company's ability, and make sure you ask if the rafting guides and safety kayakers are swift-water-rescue trained. Take a look at Peter Knowles's *Rafting: a consumers' guide*, available in Kathmandu; for more info on all the rivers of Nepal read his delightfully written *White Water Nepal*.

Want to learn how to kayak? Kayak Clinics come highly recommended, though first ensure the instructors are qualified.

Mountain biking (1-4 days; $20-65 a day) The Kathmandu Valley and the surrounding hills offer some of the best mountain biking there is: endless interesting trails, many technical and, much more than that, a cultural experience and insight into the real Nepal. Although you can go alone, the guides know the best loops and the companies have good bikes.

Trips can be organized through **Pathfinders**, **Himalayan Mountain Bikes**, **Dawn till Dusk** (🖳 www.nepalbiking.com), **Nepal Mountain Bike Tours** (🖳 www.bikehimalayas.com) and others in Thamel.

Canyoning ($80-120 including transport)

More fun. Up near the Tibetan border both **The Last Resort** (🖳 www.thelast resort.com.np) and **Borderlands** (🖳 www.borderlandresorts.com) offer canyoning in the stunningly steep hillsides around there.

Bungee jump ($80 including transport) This is the ultimate for adrenaline junkies, a leap off a bridge 160m/520ft (!) above the Bhote Kosi, or try the world's highest canyon swing. **Bungy Nepal** (🖥 www.bungynepal.com) is based at the Last Resort (see opposite) and offers bungee jumps; these can also be combined with canyoning and rafting.

Paragliding Frontiers Paragliding (🖥 www.nepal-paragliding.com) runs courses (€500) and tours from Pokhara: check out parahawking which is flying with eagles, kites and vultures.

Motor-biking around the city ($12-25 a day) With the dust, pollution and lack of road rules few people ride in Kathmandu for pleasure but once outside the city limits it's a different story, and exploring by motorbike can be fun.

Mountain flight ($166, allow 3-4 hours) Almost every morning during the high seasons, Buddha Air, Yeti Airlines and others operate a 'mountain flight' for close-up views of the Himalaya including Everest. It departs only if the sky is relatively clear. Tickets are refundable and bookings may be moved to the following day if the flight is cancelled. Taking any other domestic flight is, if the weather's perfect, also spectacular.

Visiting Pokhara ($15 bus/$100 flight) Beside a lake gazing up at the huge Annapurna range, the delight of Pokhara is that there's nothing to do besides enjoying the cafés. It is also a good base to begin or end Annapurna treks and ties in well with trips to Chitwan National Park and rafting the Trisuli, Seti and Kali Gandaki.

Chitwan National Park wildlife safari (3-4 days) Staying in the park costs $175-450 for two nights (plus $80 by tourist coach, $250 by car with a driver, $200 by air) and outside the park (Sauraha) from $75.

Fancy shaking trunks with an elephant or sipping exotic cocktails under a crimson sunset? How about wildlife spotting by dugout canoe and elephant-back or watching rhinos forage in the savannah from the breakfast table? Royal Chitwan National Park is one of Asia's premier game parks, a mix of jungle, grasslands and river plains teeming with wildlife, including the endangered **royal bengal tiger**, the rare **gangetic dolphin** and the usually seen **one-horned rhino**.

Safari, Asian style, is quite different from the African approach. The game, although abundant, is often more elusive and shy. It is also better hidden in the long elephant grass or jungle undergrowth, hence the advantage of spotting by elephant-back, from canoes and from *machans* (hides or blinds). However, you will see lots of game and there's a special thrill finding it in its natural environment.

There are two distinct ways of enjoying Chitwan: staying inside the park, or staying outside. Sauraha, the travellers' haunt outside the park, is the cheaper but less satisfactory alternative: the Government-run elephant ride is short so most of the game spotting is done on foot (and by climbing trees if a rhino charges) or by jeep. And in the cosmopolitan village you miss the absolute serenity of the morning and evening jungle. So, while the experience is good, there is a better way.

Scattered through the park jungle, the wildlife resorts are secluded and more than comfortable. The well-planned activities flow and the service is superb. Each resort has its own fleet of elephants, dugout canoes and jeeps, handled by guides who know the animals' habits, usually spotting game long before you do. The resorts are peaceful and deliciously relaxing, making the Chitwan experience a brilliant way to begin or end a holiday in Nepal.

(cont'd from p37) For people who consider themselves confident or experienced mountaineers and want an uncluttered peak-season climb there are other mountains worthy of your attention, see pp280-1.

Technical passes into the Khumbu

There are four challenging 5700m-plus (18,700ft) passes that drop into/out of the Khumbu and require mountaineering competence. There are two broad approaches to these expeditions; either plan the pass crossing/s as the focus of the trip and start with them, or tack them on at the end.

Beginning in the Rolwaling or Mera areas means camping expedition-style with a full crew and spending time acclimatizing and possibly climbing a peak as well. This sort of trip is centred around the passes and peaks. Once you are in the main Khumbu region you could keep the crew with you, but more usually you would switch to teahouses and the crew could head down.

If instead you want to travel light and fast that means you must already be acclimatized and strong, so teahouse trekking around the Khumbu then heading over the passes makes sense. Carrying all your own equipment is possible but tough. A hybrid method is to take an experienced climbing sherpa to assist, and then hire porters as needed/available, on the easier sections.

The tough and dangerous **Tashi Labtsa** is at the head of the Rolwaling Valley and can be reached from Barabise or Dolakha. If you're trekking with a group, a climb of the trekking peak Ramdung-Go is usually included for acclimatization and to ensure you are capable of the crossing: you pass temptingly beneath Parcharmo too.

 VISITING TIBET AND BHUTAN

Visiting Tibet

If you already have a Chinese visa, you can sometimes cross the border as an individual, though often it is prohibited. Since there are (officially) no buses, you often have to hire a Landcruiser (minimum US$100 per person) to Shigatse. This also gets around random permit problems.

An easier and quicker way is to book one of the 8- to 11-day fixed departure tours in Kathmandu, though you should book well in advance as the operators need time to book the flight and process the paperwork. These drive to (or from) Lhasa, stopping at most points of interest along the way. The budget versions cost US$600-1000, including the US$273 flight between Kathmandu and Lhasa; an 11-day Tibet-side Everest Base Camp tour costs $1200-1500 including flight. Tours generally run from March to mid-November. There are four or five operators in Thamel, with little to distinguish between them and most trekking and travel companies organize through them too.

Visiting Bhutan

The Land of the Thunder Dragon is an exclusive, particularly rewarding destination. The friendliness of the people and the smooth organization come at a price of around US$200 a day whether trekking or travelling. It also takes time to arrange – a minimum of two weeks – and allowing more time is better.

The **Mingbo La** and **Amphu Labtsa** are technically difficult, isolated and are generally only crossed in conjunction with climbing the trekking peak Mera (6476m/21,246ft) or crossing a couple of 6100m/20,013ft passes from Makalu Base Camp. Read the route descriptions on pp223-4 for scare factors. The **Nangpa La** (5716m/18,753ft) is the highest and one of the more arduous trading passes in the world. It was recently opened to visit but not to cross; see pp224-6.

The high passes of the Khumbu and the trekking peaks are better attempted during the October to Christmas season, or from mid-March onwards.

Budgeting

The price of material progress is too often to replace a smile with a worried frown, the god being money instead of inner peace   **Tom Weir,** *East of Kathmandu*, **1955**

Nepal is undoubtedly one of the cheaper countries to travel around. It's possible to survive on US$12 a day and for around US$30 a day you can live quite comfortably. There's also a tempting array of services and souvenirs to mop up any excess funds.

COSTS IN KATHMANDU

Your choice of hotel will largely determine the amount spent on basics. A spartan double room with communal bathroom facilities goes for US$3-6/£1.70-3.36/€2.07-4.14 a night, and with attached bathroom US$5-12/£2.80-6.70/€3.45-8.30; a pleasant 2- or 3-star room is US$20-50/£11.20-28/€13.80-34.50. Five-star hotels begin from $140/£78.40/€96.60 a night but vary considerably depending on the political situation.

Eating out in the better Thamel restaurants will cost around $12-20 a day. What you spend on drinks depends on your poison: a large bottle of beer or a glass of wine is around $3-4, a nip of local spirit slightly cheaper.

For a budget traveller, around US$150/£84/€103.50 a week is adequate for cheap hotels, good food and sightseeing. It is the avoidable one-off expenses, such as flights, rafting trips and quality souvenirs that will have a large impact on your budget plans. With less than US$100/£56/€69 per week careful budgeting is required.

THE TREKKING BUDGET

Package treks
With all the money paid upfront it's simply a case of following company guidelines and allowing for the few extras. While trekking there are no expenses bar the odd bottle of beer so just allow for souvenirs, bars of chocolate and the tips for your crew (see box p12).

Private treks (with a local company)

Clarify with the company exactly what you are paying for and, more importantly, what is extra. All the wages for the crew must obviously be included. But how about crew flights, taxes, and the National Park entrance fees – are they included in the price too? Decide also how much should be paid for extra days, which could happen if, for example, you decide to trek for longer, or if the flight is delayed.

There are big economies of scale so small groups work out much more expensive per person than a group of four or more.

Independent trekkers

Budget trekkers with more time than money will want to start from Jiri or Tumlingtar, where there are still dormitories (and twin-bedded rooms) and meals are cheap. Spending less than $12 a day is quite possible, until Namche, where the prices climb as steeply as the hills, and $15-20 is more realistic.

Trekking comfortably above Lukla without a budget to stick to costs around $25 a day: allow an extra $15 a day ($20 if you are on your own) if you want to treat yourself to a room with attached bathroom, now available at most main places.

It is most important to have a considerable amount of extra money on you to allow for emergency situations. Many trekkers end up taking a doctor's consultation at Khunde or the HRA post, and a few end up being rescued or hiring a porter. Doctors in Nepal report that many budget trekkers don't have enough cash on them. It's best to take at least $150-200/£84-112/€103.50-138 in rupees more than your budget. You will most likely spend this in Kathmandu upon your return or, if heading to India, this can easily be converted to Indian rupees.

Namche also offers souvenirs and trekking and mountaineering gear: if you are likely to be tempted take extra cash.

CURRENCY

The Euro, British pounds, as well as US, Canadian, Australian, Hong Kong and Singapore dollars are accepted in Nepal, both in cash form and as travellers' cheques. Major credit cards are accepted by: star-class hotels, some shops and trekking companies; and for cash advances at a few banks. Kathmandu and Pokhara have cash machines (ATMs). Be aware that normally there is a daily limit on your transactions (set by your bank).

As in the rest of Asia some US$ cash is handy.

For rates of exchange see p87.

Money for the trek

It is best to take all of what you think you will need for your trek in Nepalese rupees. When you change money, ask for some smaller denominations. Tips are best paid in rupees, although hard currencies do work as well, at a pinch.

Independent trekkers trekking below Lukla should take particular care to have plenty of change. If you are planning to buy a ticket at a rural airport, note that payment is in hard currency only.

When to go

Trekking the standard routes in the Khumbu is possible and can be pleasant at almost any time of the year: just tailor your route and your expectations to the prevailing seasonal conditions.

The **post-monsoon season** (October and November edging into December) traditionally offers the clearest weather and stunning views but is also the busiest time and many lodges are full. **Winter** in the Himalaya is more manageable than you would first think since the weather is mainly fine, so for the well-prepared trekking is still rewarding, with delightfully few trekkers too. Winter thaws to the **spring** reawakening: the flowers bloom, leaves sprout and the rhododendrons blossom for the March to May trekking season. Conditions tend to be more variable than Nov-Dec, with some longer fine periods, but often more hazy skies and afternoon cloud, but it is still a good time to trek.

By the end of May and into June it's hot and the approaching **monsoon** occasionally shakes its clouds. When this does arrive, in the middle of June, everything flourishes under the life-giving rain: in the middle hills leeches abound and coupled with the humidity, trekking is tough. It is often cloudy and does rain in the high country, but is still pleasant, delayed flights are the issue.

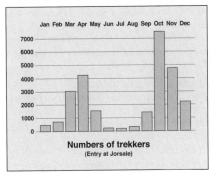

Jan Feb Mar Apr May Jun Jul Aug Sep Oct Nov Dec

7000
6000
5000
4000
3000
2000
1000
0

Numbers of trekkers
(Entry at Jorsale)

For climbing and crossing high passes the classic trekking time (October–December) is best, with April to early June second, with often more variable weather.

SEASONAL CONDITIONS

Early autumn (mid-September to late-October)

The monsoon has dwindled but some tail-end clouds and showers (or short-lived snow at altitude) must be expected. Locals and trekkers simply take cover in the nearest teahouse and wait the afternoon shower out. There's also a chance that the monsoon may not quite have ended (see box p45). It's most important to note is that Lukla flights are often disrupted at this time, so allow an extra day or two to cope with this. The Jiri to Namche section is either hot and sweaty under the fierce sun or perpetually grey and cloudy, while higher up it's pleasant with cool but mostly frost-free nights. If you skip the lower country, this is a particularly pleasant and under-trekked season. At this time the whole country changes from a lush, verdant green into the harvest colours.

The approach of winter (mid-October to December)

This is classic trekking time, famed for clear skies and fantastic weather. Early October through to late November is also the busiest period with most lodges and campsites brimming with trekkers.

The long fine periods are occasionally broken for a day or two by a front sweeping overhead causing high cloud or cloud banks that roll up the valleys, then usually clear at altitude with the sunset. The odd stronger front brings a spot of wet weather as well but it is impossible to tell (even the locals can't) whether a front contains rain. Barring unusual conditions during this trekking season, perhaps two or three periods of showers and drizzle, or short-lived snow at altitude, can be expected. In an unusual year there is perpetual high cloud and less than crystal-clear skies.

Tengboche begins receiving frosts in October and by November at altitude evenings are chilly. During a cold clear snap in the up-valley lodges (Lobuche, Gokyo and Chukhung) a water bottle beside your bed will partially freeze overnight and the lakes above 5000m/16,404ft begin to ice over. Shorts can still be worn above Namche on windless days by the determined but light trousers/pants feel more comfortable. December is one of the most pleasant months for trekking because statistically it is the driest month of the year and the vast majority of trekkers have already headed down. The shorter winter days are cooler but on the walk-in you'll still sweat on the hills. Above Namche it is cold but a thick down jacket, good sleeping bag and lots of hot drinks can ward the cold off effectively.

Winter (January to March)

New Year or sometime into January/February usually brings a week or so of disturbed weather. Frequently this is the snowfall that puts a stop to the easy pass-hopping and climbing, or at least brings more challenging conditions. This

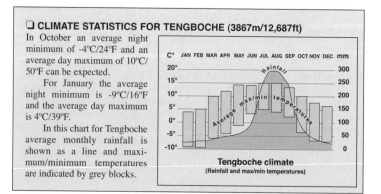

❏ **CLIMATE STATISTICS FOR TENGBOCHE (3867m/12,687ft)**

In October an average night minimum of -4°C/24°F and an average day maximum of 10°C/50°F can be expected.

For January the average night minimum is -9°C/16°F and the average day maximum is 4°C/39°F.

In this chart for Tengboche average monthly rainfall is shown as a line and maximum/minimum temperatures are indicated by grey blocks.

Tengboche climate
(Rainfall and max/min temperatures)

Global warming

Global warming is now a fact, though how it affects us is still being debated. The recent changing of weather patterns is not temporary, so the weather of the last five years or so is a guide to future changes, with greater fluctuations likely. For the trekker expect a large dump of snow (rain in the low country) in October or November as a cyclone degenerates on the Himalaya but otherwise it should be mostly fine at this time of year.

Another effect of global warming is that monsoon-like conditions sometimes seem to prevail earlier, occasionally as early as May, although the official monsoon still seems to begin around mid-June. However, these days it tends to begin more lightly than in the past, with heavier rain usually falling later, resulting in flooding and landslides. What's more, towards the end of the season the monsoon often appears to retreat, only to then return and stage a dramatic finale.

semi-regular fall is sometimes followed by more winter storms breaking the fine periods. Two closely spaced storms can lead to snow drifts above Namche. A bad year will see the high lodges snowed in for a few days and a sudden rush on plastic boot rentals in Namche. The shaded snow has no chance of melting while the rest of the snow patchily clears over a week or two. In other years, and this is increasingly the trend, there'll be only light falls that burn off quickly in the sunny spots. Air temperatures stay around 0°C/32°F during the warmer days, and nights are all below this and can even hit -30°C/-22°F at 5000m/16,404ft. All the high-altitude lakes sport ice thick enough to skate on and many (for example Gokyo lake) will not thaw until May.

March has a reputation among the Sherpas as being colder than December, and with snow lying around, trekking is more challenging. This is no time to take an expedition-style trek: stick to teahouse trekking. Below Namche, down to an altitude of about 2600m/8530ft, periodic snow falls and ice can occasionally be expected. Flights to Lukla are sometimes disrupted by snow during January and February but only for a day or two.

Spring (April to early June)

The second trekking season commences at the end of March and continues into May. The fine periods will be broken by lots of cloud rolling up the valleys during the afternoon, often bringing drizzle that clears during the evening. On the trekking peaks and above there is a pattern of daily light powder snow that shortens the usable part of the day. A torrential pre-monsoon downpour is also possible, though rare.

The temperatures warm up considerably and by the end of April are hot at low altitudes and sometimes on the warm side higher up too. The rain, sun and warmth spark a flourish of growth with rhododendrons painting the hillsides, beginning in late February at lower altitudes and blooming ever higher during March and April.

In May the middle hills are sweltering: beginning early, having a long lunch and sometimes walking in the late afternoon minimizes the discomfort. The low-altitude haze and occasional cloud reduce the strength of the sun. In the high country, early May is an under-utilized time. While the weather may be less stable than November-December, the warmth, lushness and the comparative lack of trekkers mean it is still great trekking. This is also the Everest expedition season.

Summer and the monsoon season (mid-June to early October)

The Indian monsoon rains usually hit the eastern Himalaya around mid-June, although it can, rarely, be as much as a month early or late. Below 3000m/ 10,000ft it's oppressive, muddy and leeches abound but flights still operate (on an irregular schedule: planes may not be able to get to Lukla for many days in a row) so it's possible to avoid the worst areas. There are frequent showers, mainly in the afternoon and at night, and occasional heavy deluges, especially in July and August. Everybody dives under the nearest shelter to drink tea and wait it out. Infrequently these cloudbursts create dangerous flash-floods and mudslides; find safe shelter.

Above Namche the days are warm and the nights are frost-free though short-lived snow can fall on Kala Pattar and even down as far as Chukhung and Gokyo. Rainfall is uneven with the southernmost mountains bearing the brunt: this is the reason the glaciers on Numbur and in the Hongu/Hinku are so big. Above Namche is a partial rain-shadow area and consequently in the higher reaches of the main valleys the rain is reduced to occasional showers and drizzle. The rain pattern is not regular: it might be misty and rain every afternoon for a week, then clear for a couple of days. Slippery trails can be a problem, particularly for porters. The monsoon always eventually manages to find its way into tents and dining tents are restrictive for an afternoon's rain: it's better to stick to teahouse trekking. Overall, the almost perpetual cloud cover is more of an annoyance than the drizzle. The views are stunning when they clear but you often wait days for this to happen, though Kala Pattar does clear more frequently. The rewards of this season are lush green valleys carpeted by petite flowers, though this is also true of late May and early June. For a person who likes wandering, rather than trekking to a schedule, it's a wonderful time to observe the other way of life of the Sherpas: the monsoon cycle of agriculture and festivals.

By September the monsoon is in retreat. Officially the monsoon rains usually stop around mid-September but sometimes they cease as early as the beginning of the month or as late as mid-October.

Although the monsoon conditions in the Bay of Bengal may have finished, the unsettled pattern of cloud and periodic drizzle usually continues into early October. Increasingly frequently, during October or November the remains of a Bay of Bengal cyclone unload in a torrential downpour lasting a day or two. This falls as troublesome deep snow at altitude that generally clears rapidly in the sunny regions.

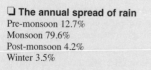

❏ **The annual spread of rain**
Pre-monsoon 12.7%
Monsoon 79.6%
Post-monsoon 4.2%
Winter 3.5%

THE KATHMANDU CLIMATE

At the moderate altitude of 1350m/4450ft, the capital's climate is quite mild. The monsoon showers keep the temperature down mostly to the high 20s°C/80s°F during summer, although it's humid and uncomfortable if it does not rain. By the end of September the tropical temperatures cool and by late October the evenings are a little cold for just a shirt. The early winter days are sunny and agreeable, the evenings require a jacket and there's the occasional frost.

From Christmas onwards a morning fog pattern sometimes settles on the valley making rising early a challenge. This also disrupts some flights but by 10 or 11am schedules are back to normal. Visiting Kathmandu is pleasant during any of the seasons although spring and autumn are the most popular, and crowded, times.

What to take

FOR TEAHOUSE TREKKING

Lukla and above

Flying in, you skip the hot middle hills country. It can be sunny and fine, almost shorts weather, up to and around Namche; a drizzly afternoon can also be surprisingly cold. Don't be alarmed though, this region often feels as cold as anywhere else on the trek.

Above Namche the days are cooler and a set of interchangeable warm and/or windproof layers is best. These layers will also do for sitting around in the high lodges from late April to October but at other times a toasty insulated (down) jacket for cold mountain tops and evenings in the lodges is essential. An important key to staying healthy is sleeping well and warmly so that your body doesn't waste energy trying to keep you warm. Don't skimp on your sleeping bag.

During the main trekking season (October to December) it is nearly always dry so you need one set of clothes, ie only what you can wear at once (plus an extra shirt and a change of underwear). During late winter into May clothing may get wet so an extra thermal or light fleece might be appreciated.

All this can add up to a lot of equipment and since you (or a porter) must carry it all consider carefully how to keep it to a minimum. On domestic flights in Nepal the usual luggage limit is 15kg (34lb) before excess charges apply.

Middle hills trekking (below Lukla)

With altitudes ranging from 350m to 3500m (1200-12,000ft) you need a variety of gear to cope. For the most part, no matter what time of year, when the weather is fine it is hot and sweaty while trekking so you'll want mainly cool, loose clothes and sun protection. Pass crossings are often windy and cold though so have some warmer layers and a windproof/waterproof jacket: note it can snow on the middle hills passes in late autumn and winter. Being toasty in the evenings is so much more comfortable than skimping, so do bring a light down

The bare necessities

What to take is simply a question of what is essential. I met some Tibetans travelling without yaks over the 5716m/18,735ft Nangpa La, on a camping trip. We looked at each others' lunches (my biscuits and their *tsampa*) and then compared rucksacks: my fancy expedition-sized pack versus their grubby day-packs. One Tibetan unpacked the rest of his bag to show me what the essentials were: gloves, an extra pair of socks and shoes (Chinese shoes are not known for durability), a jersey and grass (for starting yak dung fires). After lunch into the bag went a 2kg sack of tsampa, a stomach of butter, a brick of tea, spoon, cup and the ancient teapot, and on top went the all-too-thin bedding roll. A hat was already on his head and his jacket pockets held a knife and lighter. They laughed as I shouldered my 20kg backpack and followed them.

Teahouse trekking Assuming you will be staying entirely in lodges, confident trekkers can get away with very little equipment:
- **For Sept-Oct and May-June**: a 40-litre backpack, T-shirt, thermal top for evening wear, light down jacket (or a thick thermal plus fleece top), rain jacket, mid-weight longjohns/softshell pants, light trekking trousers/pants and some sort of light sleeping bag (supplement with lodge blankets)
- **For Nov to May**: a 50- to 60-litre backpack, two thermal tops (one for walking, one for the evening), down jacket (thicker is better), good breathable rain jacket (Gore-Tex or similar), softshell pants, insulated trousers/pants or longjohns, light trekking trousers/pants (optional), snow gaiters (optional), good 4- to 5-season sleeping bag.

jacket and some warm fleece pants. Only having a good fleece jacket just doesn't seem quite enough.

The layering principle

If you wear a number of thinner layers of clothing you can simply shed a layer if you get hot or add a layer if the temperature drops. In spite of the fact that this keeps your clothing dry (more comfortable and much warmer than if wet) you still see many people wearing an insulated jacket and dripping with sweat during the day. Of course the layer next to your skin will probably get wet with sweat so you should carry an extra T-shirt or thermal top. When you stop, change the wet top for a dry one and then put an extra layer or two on to keep warm.

Don't under-estimate the high country cold

Above 4000m it is cool year-round. Even after a warm, sunny day the evening temperature is dramatically lower. From November to April the nights are *very cold*. And whereas lodge dining rooms have a fire, the rooms are not heated at all. While many Canadians, Americans and Scandinavians understand the cold, Brits, Kiwis and Aussies don't have exposure to these low temperatures. High-altitude winter night temperatures are similar to your freezer at home (which is

❏ Is it cold?

'My friend lent me a nice light sleeping bag...'

'It might be good for Swedish summers,' said Tim, from Sweden, in disgust, deciding that his sleeping bag isn't good enough for Gokyo in September.

> **The top half**
> Working out a good combination of tops can be tricky, especially if you want to travel light. I go without a fleece jacket, instead taking a mid-weight thermal top and expedition-weight top, both zip T-style, ie zip neck rather than crew (or an airy t-shirt and expedition-weight thermal for a warm season trek), a light but good down jacket and a soft shell or Gore-Tex jacket.
>
> A friend uses a completely different combination: wicking T-shirts and the occasional thin thermal top with a Windstopper/softshell jacket and a down or fleece vest. If it is likely to be wet he includes a Gore-Tex jacket: if it is winter, a thick down jacket.

normally set at -18ºC) and even in the trekking areas night temperatures can drop to as low as -30ºC.

In real winter a windless sunny day doesn't feel cold, even though the air temperature might be around 0ºC, but a blustery, cloudy day requires being well protected.

There is another factor that conspires to cool you – the lack of oxygen. It is largely oxygen in the blood that keeps fingers and toes warm. When bottled oxygen was first tested on Everest in the 1920s the first effect noticed was that everyone felt warmer. The trick at altitude is to carefully manage and regulate your body temperature. If possible avoid getting sweaty and damp and the moment you start cooling down add some layers. The most critical time is at the end of the day, when you might be low on energy. Having a snack at this time or, a hot drink helps. It is far easier to stay warm than try to warm up after getting cold.

What to sleep in when it's cold

Surprisingly, if you put on all your clothes to go to bed you feel constricted and not a lot warmer. Using a sleeping sheet and one layer of comfy thermal underwear is better and if that's not enough put your down jacket over your sleeping bag. Alternatively, wear the down jacket but with only a T-shirt or thermal top on underneath. What keeps you warm is trapped air, not the materials themselves. Pull the draw-cords tight and ensure your head and shoulders are well insulated. A hot water bottle is the ultimate luxury: make one using your aluminum or tough plastic water bottle in a sock.

> **The bottom half**
> A good, comfortable pair of trekking trousers/pants is almost indispensible: thinner for the warmer seasons and thicker for the cold season. You could pair them with leggings/longjohns, though having a separate pair of fleece pants is cozy and more comfortable. In late autumn or winter in the high country some lighter (ie more versatile) soft shell pants work really well. Tight leggings generally look out of place on the Nepal trails.
>
> Many people pack expensive, waterproof, breathable trousers /pants. Most of the time they remain unused, so don't bother with them. They come into their own, especially bibs, when climbing in winter though.

Foot care
Your feet will be doing far more work than they're used to so take great care of them. The rest of your body has the luxury of changes of clothes but your feet are confined to a single pair of boots that must cope with the extremes of heat and cold: so air them, and your socks and boots, frequently – lunch in the sun is an ideal time. Consider changing your socks more than once during the day and wash your feet and socks, if nothing else, at least every few days. If you feel a hot spot or a blister developing, you should stop immediately and treat it (see p301) before it's too late to prevent damage.

EQUIPMENT LIST

Major items
● **Sleeping bag** Essential: a down bag is lighter and more compact than a synthetic one of the same warmth. From late April to the end of October a three-season bag is adequate, ie 700 grams of good down. For the cold months, November to March, take particular care to choose a warm four-season bag, ie 900+ grams of high quality down. When buying a down bag look for good and even thickness: the down should be fluffy and light. An inside muff around your neck makes a big difference to overall warmth.

In Kathmandu you can easily rent ordinary sleeping bags and there are also a few good down bags. Trekking companies often provide bags but if you already have a good one it's worth taking it instead. There are also fleece liners for approximately US$12 that can boost a tired bag's warmth.

Above Lukla, most lodges have relatively clean blankets or quilts to supplement a less than adequate sleeping bag.

● **Sleeping-bag liner** (cotton or silk) This saves washing your sleeping bag and adds warmth. Lightweight silk is deliciously luxurious, imitation silk is not as good. Hygiene fanatics may also want to bring their own pillowcase.

● **Rucksack/backpack** It's important to have a comfortable one. The feature that will help most in this respect is a good waistband – it should fit snugly without riding up your stomach (which interferes with breathing). At the same time it must not sit too low and touch your walking muscles. Small backpacks are neat and look trendy but often are not big enough. For winter a larger pack is preferable since gear does not have to be tightly compressed and this makes packing easier. Group trekkers will need only a daypack but once you put in a down jacket, wind trousers/pants, camera and water bottle, plus more odds and ends, you will doubtless find that you need a bigger one, 30-45 litres or so: again, a proper waistband will make it far more comfortable. A good range of daypacks and small- to medium-sized backpacks are available in Kathmandu.

● **Boots** One of the most important things for ensuring a happy trek is having comfortable feet. Carrying a backpack places a greater load on your feet than normal so stiffer supportive yet light boots will feel more comfortable in the long run. It's possible to trek in trail running shoes but the new generation lightweight trekking boots are superior. Trekkers seem to get away with these boots even in winter but this can be dangerous during a snowfall. Sturdy but fairly light all-leather boots are better for cold weather (although should be water-proofed after a snowfall or if the trails are muddy).

When choosing boots look for good ankle support, plenty of toe room essential for the long descents (but don't overdo this) and a stiff sole (helps prevent tired feet by lessening twisting). Check the inner lining – leather is OK but Cambrelle (which can destroy the bacteria that causes foot odour) is even better. The trend is towards Gore-Tex or a similar waterproof but breathable inner lining. These render boots even warmer, very often too warm for normal trekking. For the drier seasons less technical boots are more comfortable.

Lightweight trekking boots generally have good shock-absorbing qualities but some foams can actually be crushed if too heavily loaded. Boots must be worn in before trekking and this should include some steep hills.

For independent trekkers, weight and space are of prime importance so a single pair of comfortable boots is generally enough. If trekking with a group, another pair of shoes for relaxing around camp can be useful. In cold weather, down booties are an option worth considering.

Clothing

● **Down jacket** This is essential during the cold months and useful at all other times. Light down jackets are easily packed and feel comfortable over a wide range of temperatures. For winter if you are not carrying it, find one of bum-warming and hand-warming length, big and thick with a hood: these can be rented in Kathmandu for a dollar or two a day.

● **Down pants/trousers** These are a good idea if you are on a high-altitude camping trip between December and March. Teahouses are much warmer and down pants are completely unnecessary: go with some fleece pants instead, cheaply available in Kathmandu.

Dress standards

These vary considerably around the country. Kathmandu is the most liberal and culturally diverse place though Western women will find dressing modestly attracts far less attention. The well-off (locals and foreigners) are expected to dress casual but clean. Along the regular trekking routes the Nepalese are used to (though have never understood) the comparatively odd and occasionally indecent ways in which Westerners dress, but in less-frequented areas locals may still be quite shocked. Even with the Khumbu Sherpas' familiarity with foreigners, you will rarely see more than their head and forearms. Being dressed in a culturally acceptable way gains you much greater respect among the local people, a fact that many trekkers have commented upon.

For men longer shorts are acceptable. T-shirts are OK, but singlets, running shorts or cycle shorts/pants, despite the fact that some porter-guides wear them, are going too far. Bare chests are rude.

For women double standards exist. Long baggy shorts are worn but $3/4$-length pants or light baggy trousers are definitely more appropriate. A T-shirt is the minimum for modesty; Lycra shorts/pants invite unwarranted attention.

PLANNING YOUR TREK

● **Wind/rain jacket** Essential. High up, if the sun is shining, it can be wonderfully warm. When a breeze picks up the true air temperature becomes apparent and wind protection is a necessity. Since it rarely rains all day – or even at all in peak season – having an expensive, totally waterproof jacket (if there is such a thing) is not necessary. When it starts raining everybody simply takes cover in the nearest shelter. During the finer months the daring have got away with Windstopper or soft-shell fleece and no waterproof jacket. Plastic ponchos are only of use during the monsoon: an umbrella is better.

● **Jersey/fleece top** Opinions vary: when it's cold people with down jackets consider down essential, but those with only fleece say it's adequate. Fleece is no substitute, however, for a down jacket in real winter. From May to October, the wet times, fleece may be a better choice.

● **Shirt/blouse** T-shirts are popular but thin long-sleeved cotton shirts/blouses or travel shorts are versatile: the collar protects the back of your neck and the sleeves can be rolled up or down. Take two so that you have a dry one to change into after trekking. For winter trekking ditch the shirt and take high-neck thermals instead.

● **Underwear** Along the trails into Namche washing every day or two is never a problem. Higher up, when it is cold, the inclination to change your underwear and wash may occur less frequently. Four to five pairs of pants/briefs is plenty. (When Ranulph Fiennes and Mike Stroud crossed Antarctica they took only one pair each for over 100 days, though this just about ended the expedition.) If you frequently wear a sports bra bring two: otherwise, what you normally wear is fine.

● **Thermal underwear** Longjohns/leggings and some sort of warm top are essential unless substituted by fleece for the warmer times. In winter a midweight zip T is good at lower altitudes, and higher up layer this.

● **Pants/trousers** Light material, loose and dirt-coloured is best. Synthetic travel pants/pack pants are perfect. Throwaway cotton pants are easily bought in Kathmandu. Jeans are not practical: they are restricting and cold when damp.
For colder weather and in the high country softshell pants plus travel pants are a good combination.

● **Fleece pants** Good to have though during the warmer seasons they are not strictly necessary: thermals and walking pants will do. In winter they are almost essential.

● **Windproof/waterproof pants/trousers/bibs** If your trekking pants are partly windproof an additional waterproof pair isn't needed.

Old clothes needed by Kathmandu charity
Child Workers in Nepal (CWIN; ☎ 428 2255, ☎ 427 8064, 🖳 www.cwin.org .np) is a charity working for the rights of children and the abolition of child-bonded labour (16% of children in the country are bonded labourers). They also run a 'Common Room' to support the thousand children who live on the streets of Kathmandu. Clothes are always needed: children's clothes are best but they can alter adults' clothes. They can also make use of any medicines you may have left after your trek. CWIN is near Soaltee Holiday Inn in Kalamati.

● **Socks** Most of the time your feet will be warm or even hot while walking so quality cotton-mix sports socks or light, technical wool mix socks are better than thick trekking socks, at least until it gets really cold. Few people seem to believe this so I suggest you test this out at home. Three to four pairs are enough. It's during some evenings and a few cold days that you will need really thick, warm socks. Lightweight trekking boots generally fit snugly so wearing two pairs of socks at the same time (originally used in stiff boots to prevent blisters) is not practical. Instead a single pair of quality socks is quite adequate, with an extra pair in reserve.

Other items
● **Warm hat** Essential.
● **Sun-hat** Essential. A light hat with a wide brim is good, as is a cotton scarf with a visor.
● **Neck gaiter** The lighter multifunctional buff-style works well to moisten your breath if you get a throat tickle.
● **Mittens/gloves** Essential except during the monsoon. Fleece or Windstopper fleece gloves (cheaply available in Kathmandu) are fine for anything except winter climbing; thinner liner gloves will even do. Ski gloves tend to be too warm and heavy.
● **Snow gaiters** Leggings that protect from the ankle to the knee are useful in Nepal only when it has snowed heavily. On the main trails, after a large fall of snow a path is cleared quickly so if you can wait you can survive without gaiters. Off the main trails or when climbing they are essential and often, in combination with a longer waterproof jacket, are a good substitute for waterproof pants.
● **Towel** Doesn't need to be big. Quick-drying sarongs seem to be better than most high-tech travel towels.
● **Bathing suit** Only useful while walking along the Arun, where the water is less than glacial in temperature.
● **Insulating pad** Not needed for teahouse trekking unless you plan to spend a night or two outside. For expedition-style treks you will be provided with a pad of sorts but a self-inflating (Thermarest) pad is an improvement.
● **Water bottle** A one-litre water bottle is essential and should be leakproof, tough and able to withstand boiling water. Two are useful, but unless you will be in the hot country, not essential as lodges and teahouses are frequent. Some people swear by the convenience of drinking systems but they often fail. In winter they are not worth the trouble, even insulated tubes often freeze in a trekking setting.
● **'Green tea' (pee) bottle/jar** The effects of altitude test even the largest of bladders. Some people would consider this a luxury; once you have used it though, you realize it is an essential. One litre is the minimum.
● **Sunscreen** Essential. The ultra-violet (UV) concentration increases around 4% for every 300m gain in altitude and snow reflects 75% of UV. Having said that, the sun is not nearly as strong as in the ozone-hole Oceania regions. Generally the thick white high-factor creams are unnecessary, less messy ones are effective enough. Do apply frequently, even on cloudy days and in snow or bright days offer some to your crew too.

● **Sunglasses** These are essential and must protect against UV – virtually all sunglasses, even the cheapest, now do. For prolonged high-altitude sojourns side pieces are useful but ski goggles are not. If you wear prescription glasses it's best to get a pair of prescription sunglasses made. Alternatively, detachable dark lens have proved adequate.

● **Contact lenses** Wearers report problems with grit and pollution in Kathmandu but few problems in the hills except cleaning them in cold conditions. To prevent the cleaning solution from freezing it's best kept in your sleeping bag on cold nights. Also bring your glasses. Many people become blasé about cleaning/changing their lenses but complacency often leads to problems later.

● **Torch/flashlight** Essential. LED-based torches are perfect for trekking, and a set of new batteries will often last a trek. Head torches are particularly handy for group trekkers in tents. Budget trekkers may get by with a cheap Chinese LED torch from Kathmandu.

● **Trekking poles** Particularly useful for stiff descents on rough terrain. If you are already in the habit of using them, bring them. If you are exploring with a heavier pack they are invaluable. If you have never used them, consider buying one if you are older or feel twinges in your knees. They really can make a difference.

● **Umbrella** Most useful during late spring and the monsoon through to the end of September, an umbrella also offers great protection against the sun and, coupled with a good rain jacket, is essential for surviving the monsoon. Available in Kathmandu: look for a big and sturdy one.

● **Pack cover** Potentially useful from March to the end of September. A large, carefully cut plastic bag can be a reasonable substitute. Both are available in Kathmandu: you can also buy plastic bags in main villages on the trail.

● **First-aid kit** See p302.

● **Water purification kit** It is possible to get away with using lodge-boiled water or environmentally unsound bottled water but you have more flexibility with another solution, see pp289-90.

● **Reading matter** Owing to the social nature of trekking, there's often not much time for reading. One or two paperbacks are usually enough for a deliciously lazy day and can be exchanged in Namche or with another trekker.

● **Diary** Many people like to write a diary while they trek.

● **Money pouch/belt** Most people find wearing one while trekking a hassle and keep it buried in their pack until they stop for the evening. More money belts are left behind under pillows than stolen: think of a better way of hiding it at night and develop a habit.

If you plan to stay only in lodges camping equipment (tent, foam pad, stove, food, cutlery, plate and mug) is not needed. On an expedition-style trek everything is provided but you may want to bring your own self-inflating mattress (eg Thermarest) as an improvement over what will be supplied.

Toiletries

This is where you can really save some weight. There is no need for a half-litre bottle of shampoo: chances are you will only wash your hair a few times and one-use packets are available in Kathmandu. Finding hot water for a shave is not always easy and there are no plugs for electric razors except in Namche. The smallest size of toothpaste sold is perfect for a month. Most critically don't forget your deodorant ('the trekker's shower').

● **Toilet paper** Available on main routes so start with only one roll.

● **Lighter** Handy for lighting candles in lodges, buy in the region to avoid flying with it.

● **Moisturiser** A small tube for sensitive or well cared for skin is useful as the air is dry and the sun harsh.

● **Lip balm with sunscreen** Essential to prevent chapped and blistered lips. From Namche and above use all the time, even on cloudy days. Banana Boat seems to be the best brand.

● **Tampons/sanitary towels** Tampons are available in Kathmandu but in the hills only pads are available.

● **Pre-moistened towelettes ('Wet ones')** Handy for group trekkers but bulky for individuals.

● **Earplugs** Earplugs can be useful to block out a persistent snorer; if you haven't already got any, most airlines have them available on long-distance flights.

Camera choice

Compact digital cameras can give great results when trekking but carefully test how photos with snowy mountains come out: often a little compensation to make the picture slightly darker is needed (don't overdo this though).

Your basic choices are either a truly pocketable (cigarette-pack sized) camera, which is less versatile but extremely convenient; or a slightly larger, better 'superzoom' compact. Either way find a good case for your pack waist band or shoulder strap so that you can keep it really handy. Most compacts have a zoom that begins from 35/38mm equivalent but for trekking a wider-angle zoom from 28mm is far more useful.

As a rule, it is better to buy more memory and shoot at full resolution on the best quality setting.

Digital SLRs produce fantastic results, give better results in low light, and are worth the extra weight but once again you need to work out how you will carry it. A neoprene cover works well, so you can carry it with a shoulder strap which means that it will always be handy.

Lens strategies can be sticking with one general 'Street' lens, to having several that cover very wide angle to real telephoto, for more creativity and to really capture the varied scenes. Bring all your lenses if you are unsure.

If you enjoy playing with/editing pictures do shoot in RAW format: the results are far better and those blown-out white mountain shots in jpeg often have good detail in RAW, and you can convert to preserve this.

Especially if shooting jpegs, a polarizing filter is useful and learning its tricks can be fun. It can significantly cut down reflection, giving skin, landscapes (tree leaves in particular) and the sky a deeper, richer colour. It does this best when used in bright sunlight at approx 90° to the sun. It should not be used for every shot and it's possible to overdo the effect.

Services in Nepal Recharging camera batteries is possible at all major settlements above Lukla, though often at a price. It is still a good idea to have one spare battery or even two if you like looking at your photos frequently.

If you are running low on memory you can reliably burn your photos onto a CD/DVD in Namche and sometimes at other places too.

A reasonable selection of memory cards, cameras – both compacts and SLRs – plus good lenses, batteries and cases are readily available in Kathmandu. The most comprehensive camera review site is 🖥 www.dpreview .com: read their conclusions particularly carefully.

EQUIPMENT AVAILABLE IN NEPAL

In Kathmandu

Everything for a trek can be bought in Kathmandu, mostly for less than in the West. A lot of equipment is locally made, some well designed and strong, most of it adequate or barely so, but you pay for what you get so gear doesn't cost much. In contrast to the uniformly high standard of gear in the West, you will have to look carefully at every aspect of design and manufacture in Kathmandu: in particular carefully feel the quality of down. Some store owners are happy to point out the differences in quality along with the commensurate differences in price, though the less honest will still sometimes insist that a fake label is genuine.

You can rely on finding an odd variety of lightweight trekking boots, daypacks and smaller backpacks, large 'porter'/duffel/kit bags, down jackets, down sleeping bags, fleece jackets, trousers/pants and accessories, and also a variety of semi-waterproof breathable jackets and pants. Now that Gore-Tex is out of patent similar material is available, usually from Korea. It is basically waterproof but generally the seams are not sealed.

A limited range of thermals is available but in general you are better bringing them from home. Large-volume backpacks are hard to find.

The vast majority of accessories are genuine: branded knives and pliers sets, trekking poles, torches, sunglasses, harnesses, karabiners, gas stoves, crampons, ice axes and altimeter watches. A few things are conspicuous in their absence, such as: drinking systems, GPSs and walkie talkies. Increasingly original gear is available, there's a Mountain Hardwear shop and several other major brands will probably open up too. Be aware that stylish items often sell out.

Renting

There's a great variety of rental equipment here which saves buying expensive specialized gear. Easy-to-rent items include down jackets, sleeping bags, insulating pads, plastic boots, ice axes and crampons.

If you are flying in and out of the Khumbu it's better to rent most of the equipment you require in Kathmandu. You can rent passable sleeping bags, down jackets and down booties. Comparing daily rates, renting gear in Namche tends to be marginally more expensive than in Kathmandu though you don't have to carry it up or pay for the time it's not in use.

If you have forgotten anything, a full range of budget gear and often some good-quality original gear is available. For the latter, the prices are often similar to those of the US, but sometimes there are real bargains around too.

ADVENTURE TREKKING EQUIPMENT

Group trekkers are provided with extensive lists. Climbers and experienced adventure trekkers planning to camp out frequently really need to plan carefully: too much is horribly heavy unless you recruit a porter, and too little is limiting.

If trekking alone, or in a small group without a full trekking crew, it's really worth employing a porter who has trekked the route before. Not only will all your packs be lighter (often making the difference between an endurance test and an enjoyable trek) but experienced porters know the bivvy caves, the local herders, the track details and the latest on where you can find supplies in unusual places.

In Namche it's possible to rent everything necessary to climb a trekking peak: harnesses, snow stakes, ropes, crampons, tent etc, but the quality leaves a lot to be desired. If you have your own favourite gear, bring it.

Local snow bars are untested and locally made, but generally do. Most ice screws are Russian titanium. Serviceable down suits are made for 8000m expeditions and the warm Millet Everest boots are available both new and used.

High altitude
In October Day temperatures rarely drop below zero, except above 6000m, so a good fleece and thick thermals are enough although down jackets are still handy and a better choice. Although the weather is mostly fine you should be prepared for a fall of snow. Good leather boots are adequate for 6000m peaks and the high passes in perfect conditions: however, most people attempting trekking peaks do wear plastics.

In November & December Be prepared for real cold. Day temperatures range from 10°C/50°F to -10°C/ 14°F and at night expect -10°C/14°F to -25°C/-13°F .

Day wear for climbing should include soft shell pants or thin/mid-weight longjohns plus semi-windproof trousers, technical T-shirt or mid-weight top with a second, expedition-weight top (or fleece) and a Gore-Tex shell for more demanding conditions. Windstopper gloves are essential, backed up by something more substantial. The higher you go the better your mittens must be. Conditions vary considerably and often you can get away without waterproof pants/bibs but they are invaluable if windy while climbing.

Choosing boots is the most difficult bit: starting early in the morning for a 6000m peak is extremely cold and must be planned for. Modern leather or synthetic-leather technical boots are a good balance for climbing and hiking at high altitude but you will feel better in lighter boots around Namche altitudes. This generally means taking two pairs of boots, so there is little difference in having a good pair of lighter trekking boots and climbing in plastics. An alternative is to go with slightly less technical but still heavy-duty trekking boots that can take crampons, and then use full over-gaiters for the climb. Foot care is incredibly important and should never be neglected: if there is only one part of you that you wash in weeks at high altitude, it should be your feet.

In the evening you'll need a substantial down jacket, thin balaclava, and perhaps thick longjohns or fleece pants. Down pants are a luxury.

At night, for several people a tent might be comfortable but during a fine spell sleeping out in a five-season sleeping bag works (provided you have an emergency space/survival blanket for an unexpected snowfall). A self-inflating mattress (Thermarest) with a very thin back-up pad is a comfortable and safe combination: otherwise, a thick foam pad will suffice for a few nights.

From January to early April   Be prepared for extreme cold. Light down jackets or, better, thermals with fleece, and stretch fleece leggings are comfortable to walk in. Well insulated leather boots/plastic boots above 4000m/ 13,123ft are good for trekking if it has snowed, with some trekking crews and most lodge owners wearing them; they are essential for climbing. If trekking in leather boots use gaiter protection and take care to keep them dry.

A tough tent is essential. You must be prepared for savage cold and infrequent snowstorms. Above 5000m/16,404ft a cold clear night can put thermometers off the scale.

Frostbite is something to be aware of. For hands, windstopper gloves are invaluable and good mittens are essential too. Take great care of your feet too: lacing boots tightly compresses both the lining and the socks that are meant to keep your feet warm and restricts vital circulation. Inner boots may need lacing only around the ankle. The soles suck heat out and insulating inner soles are invaluable. A single extra layer of material around the whole boot (like a stuff sack) can make a big difference on the coldest mornings when climbing in crampons.

In mid-April & May   The warmer conditions are tough with soft, wet and often deep snow. Bring an alarm clock for early starts and a few novels for long snowy afternoons. Tents and clothing should be waterproof and plastic boots are still best for climbing. Gore-Tex pants/bibs and fleece are in their element: carry spare dry clothing and perhaps some shoes for walking around camp at day's end.

General gear
● **Stoves** Epigas-Primus and most other canisters, with matching stoves, are available in Kathmandu and Namche. Ask the supplier if they have been refilled with Kathmandu gas, which smells more, or are original. Dirty, low-quality kerosene is available in small quantities at virtually every lodge above Namche.
● **Water bottles/bags** A total capacity of three litres per person is useful for camping.

Climbing gear
For a first trip in the Himalaya, I strongly advise beginning with a trek and a light climb or exploration rather than focusing on the vertical. With this approach you can get away with just bringing enough for walking on glaciers and one or two pitches. There's lots of new and second-hand climbing gear for

sale in Namche and Kathmandu. Always available are cheap titanium ice screws, snow stakes, jumars, karabiners, slings, ice axes, crampons (step-in and strap-on) and new and used ropes (fixed and climbing, but exercise caution).

Don't neglect your crew's equipment

While you may have the latest and best equipment your crew certainly will not. Sirdars usually have reasonable gear although it is worth checking their climbing gear and sleeping bag. The sherpas and kitchen hands are less well-equipped and generally appreciate cast-offs, perhaps a Kathmandu fleece or a good piece of clothing as part of the tips. Porters have nothing and appreciate clean serviceable clothes of any sort and especially old running shoes or boots. See box p12 for notes on employing and looking after crew.

RECOMMENDED READING

Kathmandu has the world's best selection of books on Nepal and the surrounding mountain areas and prices are often below normal cover prices so it's also an attractive place to buy them. The Thamel area boasts many secondhand bookshops with hundreds of cheap paperback novels. See also pp308-9.

Guidebooks

Most guidebook titles have fallen off the trail, leaving just a few that are current. The standard *Lonely Planet Nepal* is comprehensive and good on practical information, with some four- to ten-day treks covered.

The *Rough Guide to Nepal* offers stiff competition, with its comprehensiveness and enthusiastic chatty style and introductions to the treks.

When it comes to trekking details the choices seem less satisfactory. Lonely Planet's *Trekking in the Nepal Himalaya* (8th edition) is thorough in many ways, covering all the main treks, but lacks detailed trail information. What's more, it expects everyone to stick to their daily itinerary. The new edition, rewritten from scratch is due at the end of 2009. Finally, Stephen Bezruchka's seventh edition of *Trekking in Nepal* (2007) has no lodge info but it does cover obscure treks.

Trailblazer publishes detailed regional guides to trekking in other parts of the Himalaya – *Trekking in the Annapurna Region* and *Trekking in Ladakh* (see p319).

Mountaineering books

Everest has become mainstream news with morality and the philosophy questioned, but there are still few books that stand the test of time. Most expedition books are still more for the avid climber. The books I particularly enjoyed are listed below.

Bill Tilman and Eric Shipton are names closely linked with much of the early exploration of the Himalaya and Karakoram. Even judged by modern standards the ground they covered and the peaks that they conquered is incredible. Their legacy is a series of books written in elegant prose with vivid and interesting descriptions that twinkle with penetrating insights, often curiously and hilariously funny. Their individual books have been reprinted in several volumes.

Eric Shipton's *The Six Mountain-Travel Books* (The Mountaineers, Seattle, 1985) includes two books about Everest: *Upon That Mountain* and *The Mount Everest Reconnaissance Expedition 1951*. HW Tilman's *The Seven Mountain-Travel Books* (The Mountaineers, Seattle, 1983) includes *Mount Everest 1938* and *Nepal Himalaya*, which has been reprinted and is widely available in Kathmandu.

Everest by Walt Unsworth (Oxford Illustrated Press, 1989) is a climbing history capturing the hopes and fears of the attempts on Everest.

Everest: The Best Writing and Pictures from 70 years of Human Endeavour, edited by Peter Gillman (Little, Brown & Co, London 1993) features interesting historical snapshots of the climbing of Everest.

Cho Oyu by Favour of the Gods by Herbert Tichy covers the first ascent of Cho Oyu. With only three members this was not the usual grand expedition, and neither is the book written in the traditional heroic style.

Nothing Venture Nothing Win by Sir Edmund Hillary is an interesting autobiographical account of his adventures including the scaling of Everest. His *Schoolhouse in the Clouds* offers an insight into the development of the Khumbu and other Sherpa areas.

Sherpas: Reflections on Change in Himalayan Nepal by James F Fisher is an interesting and readable investigation into the changes in the Khumbu that tourism and schooling have brought, with perceptive feedback from local people.

Into Thin Air by Jon Krakauer is the compelling story of how so many climbers died (and some miraculously lived against the odds) on two commercial expeditions in 1996, but to get a sense of the other side of the story, read *The Climb* by Bourkreev.

MAP RECOMMENDATIONS

This guide specifically includes many maps, enough to cover a normal trek to the Khumbu from Jiri or Lukla. However, for identifying the many surrounding peaks and features, detailed topographic maps are invaluable – and essential for exploration off the beaten track.

Google Earth is also well worth exploring, for getting a better sense of the valley and ridge systems and especially for access to less frequented places.

In Kathmandu there is an almost bewildering range of maps, some pocket-sized, with some designed to cover just the specific area in which you are trekking, whether it is above Lukla or starting from Tumlingtar or Jiri. There are even maps that are specifically designed for climbing a particular peak, such as Mera Peak etc.

❏ **Further information and useful websites**

For more information and links to websites see the updates section for this book at 🖥 www.trailblazer-guides.com.

Out of Nepal, however, finding maps can still be a mission with very few available to buy, even via the internet.

● **The Schneider 1:50,000 series** is published by Freytag-Berndt und Artaria of Vienna and covers the entire area without overlap in beautiful but now dated four-colour topographic maps. The *Khumbu Himal* is the most useful for all trekking, exploring and climbing from Namche to the north. Check the other titles if you are exploring other areas.

● **The National Geographic series** has maps of the Everest, Annapurna and Langtang regions. Despite their heritage they still have minor mistakes but nevertheless are great both for planning and once on the trail.

The yellow-bordered magazine published a beautiful map of the area surrounding Everest but, unfortunately, it does not cover the Gokyo Valley, or even below Pangboche. Inserted in the 1988 centennial issue, it was the most accurate and detailed 1:50,000 map ever made. Use it for the Amphu Labtsa, Mingbo La, Sherpani Col and climbing around Chukhung. Colour photocopies are stocked by most bookshops in Kathmandu.

● **The Himalaya Kartographisches Institut series and the Nepa map series** These are maps produced in Nepal and readily available in Kathmandu and, increasingly, overseas. Confusingly they come under several more names, including Himalayan Map House and Map Point, and in a bewildering variety of titles, though all are similar. Search carefully for the most detailed scale for the region you need. The pocket size is handy and few details are compromised.

Generally, the other series of maps available in Kathmandu are simply rip-off copies of the above. There is little to choose between them and even 'Latest updated editions' are loaded with minor inconsistencies, though you should find them adequate for trekking.

The names and spellings used in this book are more accurate than any map.

Pre-trip health precautions and inoculations

INTRODUCTION

The majority of Nepal's population has limited access to basic infrastructure, so the health situation is extremely poor. Disease and malnourishment are rife and even the kind of sickness that's easily cured by simple measures can often lead to death without basic health education. Visitors arriving with immunizations, healthy bodies and access to clean water are at much less risk. A bout of diarrhoea, however, is almost inevitable, no matter how careful you are.

The physical aspects of trekking

Trekking means walking almost every day for four to seven hours, often for three weeks or more. Many people begin only moderately fit but generally cope well and end the trek feeling amazingly healthy. A few find the reality of continuous walking difficult. If you lead a sedentary life plan an exercise pro-gramme well before you go. Brisk walks are a good start, building up to include walking up and down hills while wearing the boots you plan to wear trekking, to introduce your body to the rigours of hill walking. Jogging and aerobics are reasonable substitutes. Muscles strengthen fairly quickly, although painfully if you overdo exercise.

It is important to realize that while trekking you can be a long way from help and sometimes you will have to be your own doctor. However, the Khumbu region is better endowed with medical facilities than anywhere else in rural Nepal. There is an excellent small hospital at Khunde (an hour above Namche). The Himalayan Rescue Association post at Pheriche is staffed by short-term volunteer doctors and open for 7-8 weeks during the peak of the two main trekking seasons.

SPECIFIC AGE GROUPS

Many recently **retired people** have made it to the top of Kala Pattar (5600m/18,373ft) so age alone need not be a barrier. The older you are, the more important prior fitness preparation is. Older trekkers are also more likely to have chronic medical conditions that should be assessed by a doctor before committing to a trek.

Caution should be exercised when taking (**young) children** trekking. Although younger people seem to acclimatize as well as adults, they generally trek much slower. Very young children have difficulty in communicating exact-ly how they feel, which can lead to confusion regarding illness. Remember with small children, if in doubt: descend.

Cautious doctors recommend a safe maximum altitude for pre-teenage chil-dren of 3000m/9843ft, though there is little evidence to support this recom-mendation. After all, a number of young children have made it to the top of Kala Pattar, and even 18-month-old babies have visited Everest Base Camp and stayed several days there.

Trekking with children can be very rewarding and bring you closer to the locals. You share a common bond for there are few people without children in Nepal. Little legs are easily carried by a porter when tired, and Sherpanis are good babysitters. Remember, however, that's it's not only the altitude that's a potential problem but also the fact that you'll be visiting a remote area.

There is no evidence to suggest that **teenagers** adapt more slowly to alti-tude than adults. However, they do appear to be more at risk. This is likely to be because of competitiveness and a will not to give in. School groups should allow an extra day or two over and above even the most conservative itineraries and be particularly watchful. An extended conservative itinerary allows for greater flexibility necessary to cope effectively with illness and other problems that typically arise.

MEDICAL CONDITIONS

Anyone with heart, lung and blood abnormalities or a continuing medical condition should have a check-up and get a medical opinion before setting off. A summary letter from your doctor describing your medical condition, treatment including any medications and contact information should be carried with your personal documents. It is important that you remember to pack a second set of any required medications, and that they are stored separately while flying and trekking so a back-up is available should a bag be delayed, misplaced or stolen.

● **Asthma** Having asthma is no reason to avoid trekking. Except in polluted Kathmandu there are fewer irritants in the air at high altitude so most asthmatics actually feel better while trekking. Look after your medication by keeping it with you at all times – wear your inhaler on a chain around your neck or keep it in a pocket. There is still the normal risk of a serious attack so brief your companions on what to do.

● **Diabetes** If it is well-controlled, diabetes is no reason to avoid trekking. You cannot afford to lose the medication so keep it with you at all times. Advise your friends on the procedures in case there's an emergency. Your increased energy expenditure will change carbohydrate and insulin levels so it's **very important to monitor your glucose levels** frequently and carefully and to keep blood sugar levels well controlled. Insulin that has been frozen loses potency, so care must be taken to adjust your dosage in relation to blood sugar levels measured by your monitor.

● **High blood pressure (hypertension)** Blood pressure will fluctuate more and be higher than usual while on a trek, particularly as you ascend to high altitude. Therefore it is important that your blood pressure be well-controlled prior to your departure. You should seek the advice of a doctor who is aware of the history of your condition.

● **Previous heart attacks** The level of exertion required on a trek is more significant than the altitude factor for normal trekking elevations. If your condition at home is well controlled during brisk exercise levels comparable to trekking, going on a trek may be a reasonable decision for you. However, do consider that you are just as likely to suffer a recurrence abroad as at home, and you will be entering a remote region of the world with very limited health facilities. Seek the advice of your doctor.

● **Epilepsy** There may be a small increased risk of a seizure at altitude but this is not necessarily a reason to stop trekking if your condition is under good control at home. Your companions must be briefed on all the relevant procedures.

● **Pregnancy** To embark on a trek to moderate altitude while pregnant is a personal decision. Prior to the 35th week of the pregnancy, and assuming there have been no complications, there is no convincing evidence against trekking. After 35 weeks, however, airlines do not allow air travel on normal passenger flights. Furthermore, one must consider that you are entering a remote area, so should any problems or concerns develop, medical care may be a long way away.

INOCULATIONS

'For residents and travellers, one proper jab now can save dozens later....'
Dr Jim Litch, ex-Khunde Hospital

There are no official immunization requirements to enter Nepal but the following should be considered. It is worth checking if there is a specialist travel clinic near you, though some regular clinics now have the ability to advise you on travel vaccinations too. On the internet check ⌨ www.ciwec-clinic.com, which offers great advice and is also the most professional medical clinic in Kathmandu. Also check the World Health Organization site (⌨ www.who.int) and the American Centers for Disease Control and Prevention (⌨ www.cdc.gov).

● **Hepatitis A** Usually passed on in contaminated water: immunization is considered a must by most doctors unless you have had hepatitis A before. The older and less effective alternative is a gamma globulin injection which should be given just before departure and be repeated every 4-6 months while travelling. There is also a combined hepatitis A and B vaccination that should be considered.

● **Hepatitis B** Like HIV, it's passed by unprotected sex or contaminated blood products – think out-of-the-way hospitals. There is a vaccine.

● **Meningitis** Occasional cases of meningococcal meningitis occur in Nepal. The disease is often fatal but the vaccine is safe and should be considered.

● **Cholera** The World Health Organization no longer recommends this vaccination. It is only partially effective, whereas early treatment with antibiotics is extremely effective. The risk of travellers acquiring cholera in Nepal is extremely low.

● **Typhoid** This is common in Nepal. There are various vaccines and one should be obtained: the injectable vaccine has been found to be more effective than the oral one.

● **Tetanus-Diptheria** This vaccine is recommended if you have not had a booster in the last 10 years.

● **Polio** If you did not receive this immunization as a child a series of vaccinations is recommended. If you have not had a booster as an adult, one may be required. Check with your doctor.

● **Measles, mumps and rubella** If you did not have these diseases (or the vaccinations) as a child you may need a vaccination.

● **Japanese Encephalitis B** This disease is transmitted by mosquitoes who have fed on domestic pig, is endemic in rural areas in the Tarai and has spread to rural areas near Kathmandu. As a trekking visitor the risk is extremely low, and the vaccination is not in the recommended category. Consider the vaccination if you will be in Kathmandu for a month or more between August and the end of October, the higher-risk months.

(Opposite) Faces of the Khumbu region.

LORD BUDDHA PHARMACY
D.D.A. 15197
Namchebazar, Solukhumbu, Nepal.

SAVE TIBET

· · · · · Got sore legs?
· · · · · Tired of walking?
And, Still want to Complete the Tre

What Shall One DO

HIRE A HORS

Please contact here.

घोडा भाडामा छ। 馬に乗って楽にトレッキングしません

● **Rabies** This deadly virus is transmitted by the bite of an infected animal, usually a monkey or dog. The risk of being bitten is small but should the animal be infected with rabies you will die unless you get treatment, though thoroughly washing the site immediately following the bite, with disinfectant or even soap and water, has been found in one study to be effective in preventing rabies. That said, travellers have died of rabies in Nepal. A vaccination is available but even if you've had it you'll then need a follow-up course of two further injections for full protection after a bite. If you've not been vaccinated and are unlucky enough to be bitten, a single injection of a very expensive rabies immune globulin and a series of five injections of vaccine over a four-week period is required. These should be started as soon as possible: preferably within a week of the bite. The rabies immune globulin and vaccine are available only from the CIWEC clinic in Kathmandu.

● **Malaria** Carried only by the anopheles mosquito, a less dangerous form of malaria exists in the Tarai (Terai) and middle hills in Nepal, ie below 2000m/6562ft. A more dangerous form exists but is rare. There's no risk in Kathmandu, Pokhara and while trekking. For Chitwan and rafting in the low country between October and May the risk is so low that prophylaxis is not recommended. Staying in the Tarai during the monsoon is more complex. If you are starting or finishing a course for other countries it's vital to take your medication at the recommended time.

The first line of protection, however, is to avoid being bitten. The anopheles mosquito is active only between early evening and dawn so you should cover up well between these times and use mosquito repellent on any exposed skin.

If you are behind on any of the immunizations listed above, they can be safely obtained at clinics in Kathmandu.

MEDICAL INSURANCE

A combined travel/medical insurance policy is a sensible choice for any traveller and a requirement for most tours booked in your home country. Specifically, check whether helicopter rescue is included and, if not, look for another policy that does.

Independent trekkers can register with their embassy, often now online: alternatively, forms are available at each embassy and the Himalayan Rescue Association in Kathmandu. Note that a rescue mission does not take place unless there is a guarantee of payment by a third party such as a trekking company, embassy or your insurance provider (see p303).

For health clinics in Kathmandu see pp118-19, and see p285 for a detailed discussion of staying healthy on the trek.

(Opposite) If you're in Namche and you've 'got sore legs' you could take the advice of the sign (bottom) or visit the Lord Buddha Pharmacy (top right). For retail therapy there are numerous tourist shops (top left).

PART 2: NEPAL

Facts about the country

GEOGRAPHICAL BACKGROUND

Sandwiched between India and China, Nepal is roughly rectangular in shape, 800km long by 200km wide (500 miles by 125 miles). With a total area of 147,181 sq km it's about the same size as England and Wales combined, or Florida, USA. Although Nepal's geographical claim to fame is indeed the Himalaya (eight out of ten of the world's highest peaks are here) there is a tremendous range in elevation across the country. Everest, the top of the world, stands at 8848m/29,028ft while the lowest place in Nepal is a mere 70m/230ft above sea-level.

Nepal's population is estimated at approximately 28 million, and growing rapidly.

Mountains, valleys and plains

Nepal conveniently divides into three distinct regions, running as east–west bands across the country:

The true **Himalayan range** stretches around 2400km (1500 miles) from Nanga Parbat (8126m/26,660ft) in Pakistan to Namcha Barwa (7782m/ 25,531ft) in Eastern Tibet in three parallel ranges. The highest is the northernmost and in the Nepalese section includes eight of the world's fourteen 'eight-thousanders' (as mountaineers refer to peaks over 8000m/26,247ft). Some definitions also include the Karakoram, Hindu Kush and Pamirs as part of the Himalayan region. The range is so high it stops the monsoon system from entering Tibet.

Lying between the Himalaya and the southern lowland, the **middle hills region** comprises mountains and hills, river valleys and basins, including the Kathmandu and Pokhara valleys. It covers about half the country. Running parallel to the Himalaya are the Mahabharat, rising to 4877m/16,000ft and the Siwaliks (or Churia) ranging from about 600m to 1500m (2000ft to 5000ft).

❏ **Mother Earth**
When geologists first came to Nepal, Sherpas were horrified to see them breaking rocks and digging holes without first apologizing to the land. Sherpas perceive the earth as Mother Earth: the soil is her flesh, the rocks her bones, the water her blood. They depend on her for their lives and when they die their flesh becomes one with the earth.

Along the southern border with India is the lowland plain known as **the Tarai** (Terai), covering a little under a quarter of the country. Once a dense sub-tropical forest, much has now been cut down to make way for settlers and provide firewood and building materials for both India and Nepal. Some of the remaining forest areas, such as Chitwan, have been set aside as national parks. Almost 60% of the country's cultivated land is in this area, its fertility enriched by the alluvial soil washed down annually from the mountains to the Tarai.

Rising peaks, deepening valleys

The Himalaya were formed by the collision of the Asian and Indian continental plates, the Indian plate forcing up the edge of Tibet on the Asian plate. This collision is still continuing today, at the rate of a few millimetres each year, resulting in landslides, erosion and mountains that are still rising. Quite how fast the Himalaya are growing is difficult to say since not all peaks are pushed up at the same rate. The annual growth rate is estimated at between 1mm and 3mm (up to one eighth of an inch).

These are also the youngest mountains in the world and geographers are especially interested in the fact that they don't form the watershed. This is further north on the Tibetan plateau which is why the major rivers that flow through Nepal into India's Ganges have their sources north of the Himalaya, cutting south through deep valleys. On the Jomsom trek you follow the world's deepest valley, the Kali Gandaki, and at one point you stand almost three miles (4.8km) below Dhaulagiri and Annapurna I. Several of these valleys form ancient trade routes with Tibet.

CLIMATE

Nepal is at the same latitude as Florida, USA, and Cairo, Egypt, so the climate in the lowland areas is hot with temperate winters. The trekking areas are, however, well above sea level and consequently temperatures vary considerably.

The climate comprises distinct seasons but with an important additional feature: the monsoon. This moisture-laden wind amasses in the Bay of Bengal and sweeps up across India to spend its forces on the Himalayan mountain chain between late June and mid-September. It does not rain continuously or even every day. Rather there may be a heavy downpour during the day that usually last less than an hour, keeping the summer heat down to bearable levels. Sometimes it rains only at night. The middle hills areas are mostly cloudy and humid during the monsoon. After the monsoon retreats, the climate is mainly dry and sunny for the remainder of the year.

Autumn is renowned for clear skies and pleasant temperatures. By winter the high hills take on dry brown shades and the mountains are occasionally dusted with fresh snow. The colourful spring, March to May, is punctuated by the odd shower of life-giving rain but the heat builds until the monsoon relief arrives. The trekking seasons are detailed on pp43-6.

HISTORICAL OUTLINE

Facts and fables

Nepal's early history is clouded in folklore and legend. One story relates how the Kathmandu Valley, then a huge sacred lake, was emptied through a channel cut by the stroke of a god's sword. The Chobar Gorge, which drains the Valley, indeed fits the description and geologists maintain that the soil in the Valley gained its renowned fertility as a lake bed.

At the time of the Buddha, in the second half of the 6th century BC, the Kirati ruled the Kathmandu Valley. They were a Mongol race whose descendants include the Rai and Limbu now settled in the east of Nepal. Buddhism spread slowly and the arts and architecture developed under the 28 successive kings. Around AD300 the Indian Licchavi dynasty invaded Nepal, introducing the caste system and Hinduism, which intermingled with Buddhism, a process continuing to this day. Around AD900, power struggles enveloped the Valley and it was not until AD1200 that the Malla dynasty became established. The caste system was rigidly defined and (although there was occasional in-fighting that laid the towns of the Valley to waste) trade, cottage industries and the enduring Newar culture blossomed. The 1400s left the wealth of architecture, carving and sculpture that surrounds the Durbar squares in Kathmandu, Patan and Bhaktapur. Known then as Kantipur, Lalitpur and Bhadgoan respectively, these three cities divided into separate flourishing but quarrelsome kingdoms in 1482 on the death of Yaksha Malla.

Unity, treachery and extravagance

In 1768 Prithvi Narayan Shah of Gorkha (a princely kingdom between Kathmandu and Pokhara) conquered the Kathmandu Valley and began the Shah dynasty that continued by direct bloodline to the last king, Gyanendra. He started by consolidating the many individual kingdoms that now form the basis of Nepal. His successors, although 'honourably defeated' in the 1814 war with British India, were able to resist colonial domination, a fact that the Nepalese are proud of to this day.

Overall control by the Shah dynasty was undermined by the rich nobles whose constant struggle for power often led to violence. However, in 1846 unequivocal control was seized by Jung Bahadur Rana who killed all the ministers and high officials in what became known as the Kot Massacre. He declared himself Maharajah, and the founder of a second line of Nepalese kings. To ensure continuity of the line his family married into the Shah dynasty and other high-caste families. Jung Bahadur Rana alone fathered over a hundred children. He and his heirs effectively ruled the country, although the king, kept in seclusion, was the highest authority.

The Rana family amassed incredible wealth, visible in the numerous European-style palaces (inspired by Jung Bahadur's visit to Europe) which now house various government departments in Kathmandu. This feudal dynasty held Nepal in its grip for over a century until 1950, when the puppet king Tribhuvan outwitted them.

The Gurkhas

Forming what is probably the world's most famous fighting force, the tough Nepali hill men who fill the Gurkha battalions within the British and Indian armies are renowned for their bravery and resilience. Stories of their fearlessness have been sending shivers down the spines of every enemy they've faced since recruitment began in 1815.

During the Falklands Conflict, it is said that rumours were circulating through Argentinian ranks that the Gurkhas were not only tough fighters but that the extent of their ruthlessness included decapitation of their victims (with the famous khukri) followed by ritual cannibalism! In June 1983 when it was leaked that Gurkhas would be used in an assault on an outpost near Port Stanley, the Gurkhas arrived to find that the enemy had fled.

Since Britain began recruiting the soldiers of the disbanded Gorkhali Army nearly two centuries ago these 'Gurkhas', as they came to be known, have served in every conflict that has involved Britain or India. In World War I, 200,000 Gurkhas served; 250,000 in World War II. When India became independent in 1947 six of the ten Gurkha regiments remained with the Indian Army; the others becoming part of the British Army.

Gurkha wages, pensions and payments for associated services (eg frequent charter flights for families of Gurkhas going on leave or returning from Nepal) were, until recently, the country's largest source of foreign currency. They are still a vital source of earnings, accounting for about 20% of Nepal's GNP.

There are now about 100,000 Gurkhas in the Indian Army and 4000 in the British Army. When the Hong Kong base was closed in 1997 as the colony reverted to China, Gurkha numbers fell by 2500. There are two infantry battalions, one based in Britain and the other in Brunei, where one battalion is already on loan to the Sultan.

In Britain the army is having difficulty in finding enough British recruits – despite a £17.5 million advertising campaign. In Nepal they are swamped with applicants. Since the fitness test used for British recruits is too easy for Nepalis tougher tests have been devised. They must complete the $1\frac{1}{2}$-mile run in $9\frac{1}{2}$ minutes, $1\frac{1}{2}$ minutes less than the test used for British soldiers. In Nepal, the 2001 recruitment tests attracted 25,000 young hopefuls – for just 270 places with the British Gurkhas.

The post-war period

Following the end of the Second World War much of Asia was in turmoil. Newly independent India, and China, both seemed to have their hungry eyes on the tiny neighbour that divided them. Political discontent and fear were growing in Nepal.

Now known as the father of democracy in Nepal, BP Koirala managed to undermine the Ranas' control and India assisted in engineering the return to power of King Tribhuvan in 1951. In a checkmate move, ostensibly on a tiger-hunting trip, the king drove into the Indian Embassy, giving the Ranas the choice of giving up power or giving up the country to India. Nepal quickly invited foreign countries to open consulates in Kathmandu, keen to maintain its independence. Thus ended more than a century of isolation.

Arranged to heal or to share?

In 1971 in a grand ceremony Birendra, then the crown prince, and his two brothers married the daughters – all sisters – of the most powerful Rana family. This shrewd move meant there was never an outside family who could kill the king to gain more power through the queen's family, and meant the unplanned transition from Birendra to Gyanendra was surprisingly smooth.

More troubling to believers is an old astrological prediction that the Shah dynasty would last 10 generations only; Birendra and Gyanendra are the 10th generation, and so it has apparently been proved.

The panchayat system

In 1955 King Tribhuvan died and was succeeded by his son, Mahendra. The constitution was reformed and in 1957 the people of Nepal voted in the Nepal Congress Party with a decisive majority. However, bribery and corruption played a large part in the country's first elections and continued in the new government. This gave King Mahendra the excuse to step into power and at the end of 1959 he arrested the entire cabinet. He took direct control himself, later instituting the *panchayat* system. Under this system the locally elected leaders of village councils nominated the candidates for higher posts, all ultimately under the king. In theory, this was quite a reasonable system and was endorsed by the new Eton-educated King Birendra when his father died in 1972.

Democracy established

Corruption and self-interest prevailed and popular discontent spread again, erupting in 1979 with violence in Kathmandu. The panchayat system was put to the test by public referendum and survived, but only just. Its days were numbered and the government's inability to solve a serious trade dispute with India in 1990 and its continued persecution of the opposition caused public protest. Meetings dispersed with bullets became riots and the palace was surrounded by machine-gun-toting soldiers.

Under mounting public and private pressure King Birendra lifted the ban on political parties in April 1990. He readily agreed to become a constitutional monarch and a temporary government was formed.

In 1991 the promised elections were held in a first-past-the-post system. The Nepal Congress Party (symbol: the tree) won, putting the Communist Party (the sun) in the role of opposition party.

The Nepali Congress have a supposedly pro-business stance and in this respect can be compared with the Conservative party in the UK and the US Republican parties; like those parties, many perceive the Nepali Congress to be arrogant and out-of touch with the man on the street, particularly as the party is made up largely of high-caste people. The communists are the opposite, mainly from the low castes and, despite a red name, are more socialists – the equivalent of the (Old) Labour party in the UK, or the US Democrats. The third main party, the RPP, are the remaining members of the reformed Pancha (Panchayat) leaders who, despite being well connected and articulate, have never become a force to be reckoned with.

Demo-crazy

Fifteen years of democracy and an equal number of governments later, there was little to show except frustration. The political parties and the stagnant bureaucracy perpetuated the old feudal caste attitudes, and corruption and apathy consumed the political will to improve life for ordinary Nepalis. Elections were dirty, and winners spent all their time siphoning away development money and further politicizing the bureaucracy to ensure another victory. Parties in opposition used every tactic, moral and immoral, to remove the incumbents, and forced or show-of-power closedowns (*bandh* or *bandha*) became ruinously common. Even with a clear majority parties broke into factions in an attempt to split the pie. Predictably, large parts of rural Nepal were utterly neglected, to the Maoists' advantage.

To be fair, the UML (United Marxist Leninist) party, in its brief mid-1990s reign, introduced a far-reaching decentralization policy. This programme allotted a yearly allowance to the smallest administrative unit, the Village Development Committee (VDC) so they could help themselves. Then a faction of the party split off, confusingly calling itself the Communist Party Marxist-Leninist (CP-ML or ML) and though both parties came together again in 2002, they never trumped the Nepali Congress. This should have been an ideal opportunity for development since Congress were in power for more than six years, but institutionalized corruption, set in place by the NC's geriatric leader, destroyed the faith of the general population in the party and possibly even in democracy.

Divisions

At the height of the Maoist crisis in 2002, the Nepali Congress split into two factions, Koirala's NC, and the NC (Democratic), run by Deuba, who was prime minister at the time. The 'democratic' tag was to show that the party practised

The royal massacre

In June 2001 the country was in political crisis but the massacre of King Birendra and much of the family overshadowed everything. On the night of June 1, Crown Prince Dipendra, slightly intoxicated by alcohol and dope, returned to a family dinner, heavily armed and in combat fatigues. He coldbloodedly shot his father with an M16 rifle and then injured or killed 11 other family members. The queen and Nirajan, Dipendra's brother, initially escaped but he shot them outside. The rules of accession were clear: he knew he was now king. But then, distraught, he turned a pistol on himself. Though he lived in a coma long enough to be declared king, he died a couple of days later.

As in a Shakespearean tale, Dipendra had everything he could want except the woman of his dreams. He was in his 30s and frustrated: his choice of wife was the bright and beautiful Devyani Rana, a woman of most royal blood but from a family that the queen's side of the family had been feuding with. The queen insisted he marry one of two other women.

In the period of disbelief and disillusionment after the massacre, the king's brother Gyanendra was crowned king.

The Maoists

In 1992 Baburam Bhattarai was an elected member of parliament from the Maoist party. He was a different sort of politician from what Nepal was used to, an architect with a PhD in urban planning: he had also designed the Rastriya Banijya Bank building (a Government-owned bank) opposite Singha Durbar, which is still considered the best-designed office building in Nepal. As an MP, though, he grew increasingly disillusioned with what he saw: the slow pace of development in rural Nepal, the encouragement of the private sector without adequate social safeguards, and the feudal attitudes at all levels of bureaucracy and politics.

In 1994, after the Maoist party split in two, Bhattarai lost power and decided to go underground. His faction released a 40-point list of demands, all reasonable measures aimed at educating and empowering Nepalis. However, the methods Bhattarai and his party chose are objectionable. On 13 February 1996 the underground Communist Party of Nepal (Maoist) declared a 'People's War' that aimed to overthrow the state. The Maoists' core tactic was to attack isolated police posts and remote district headquarters in overwhelming numbers, and kill or maim people in government or the administration seen to be influential or corrupt. It wasn't surprising they amassed a reasonable amount of grassroots support in poor regions of the country: corruption and government mismanagement had reached monumental levels, and much of the blame could be laid at the doors of the opulent houses and shiny four-wheel drives of the ruling Nepali Congress.

In mid 2001 the Maoists agreed to a ceasefire at a time when they were winning nearly every battle with the under-equipped police. However, the Maoists fooled the new Deuba government, merely using the time to regroup and strengthen their forces, to take on the newly constituted Armed Police Force (APF; since the King would not sanction using the army against the Maoists). Boldly they attacked military bases for the first time in November 2001, taking on all the forces of the Nepal state. Until that point the army had been confined to their barracks, not allowed to help the police. It was an audacious move and many commentators predicted this would be their downfall but the Maoists had judged accurately.

By changing tactics and only fighting on their terms, the Maoists continued their campaign in the middle hills of west Nepal, and slowly pushed into the less impoverished eastern hills. By 2005 the Maoists had full or partial control over more than 20 of the country's 75 districts, sadly ruling entirely by fear. However, while there were large swathes of the countryside under Maoist control, it was equally the case that many villages 'belonged' to whichever side was patrolling them at any given time of the day, the military or the Armed Police, or the Maoists. Who was stuck in the middle? The general population, and they suffered horribly. By this stage, there was only one realistic solution to stop the killings and horribleness of it all, and that was to bring the Maoists into government, either that or a descent into eventual civil war. So the Maoists joined the government on the conditions that a Constituent Assembly election be held, with the constitution being rewritten, and that the monarchy end.

During the fighting the Maoists received absolutely no support from China and only diplomatic meddling from India, and, most tellingly, during their fighting phase suffered a lack of weapons and ammunition in a continent awash with guns.

The issues were seemingly easy enough to solve in the beginning, instead with the narrow-minded, short-sighted, selfish and incompetent political leaders, Nepal has lost more than a decade of development: 15,000 people were killed directly, and many, many more died unnecessarily, indirectly. Many of these leaders who took the country on this path to ruin are in the new government: it does not bode well.

internal democracy as, almost incredibly, the NC barely do. However, NC 'undemocratic' was still the most powerful force with Girija Prasad Koirala as leader. A skilled power broker, he led a loyal coterie of family members and friends, and ruled by cunning and sheer force, displaying a feudal-lord-like obsession with consolidating power rather than promoting development and progress.

With such arrogant selfishness, and the Maoists steadily gaining ground in the hills, it was only a matter of time before the system fell apart. The King appointed governments but none was strong and real elections were repeatedly postponed because of the security situation, the government only existing in the district headquarters, yet nothing was done to improve any aspect of governance or to push development out where it mattered so that control would return naturally. Almost inevitably King Gyanendra took over by emergency rule on 1 Feb 2005 and some of the citizens breathed a sigh of relief.

Royal solution

The King came in as ruler of last resort with the wary support of most people, despite the controversial death of his brother. Clearly the need was to remake the country and fix the political system. Obviously the way to bring the country together was by acknowledging that the Maoist demands were legitimate and reasonable (apart, debatably, from getting rid of the monarchy), and tackle the problems the political parties wouldn't touch, such as opening the hugely corrupt fuel distribution system to private companies, and depoliticizing the bureaucracy. Clearly if the King did this nobody could complain but instead he brought in autocratic leaders from the Panchayat times, pushed aside the political parties and commanded the army to destroy the Maoists, grossly increasing the already-shocking army human rights' abuses. Many people wonder if his brother would have been as misguided.

After a few months it became obvious that the King was only making a bad situation worse, giving the political parties and the Maoists ammunition to erode all support for the monarchy. Eventually he gave in to 'Jana Andolan II', the second people's movement.

The non-Royal solution

NC lobbied hard and in April 2006 the last elected government (of 1999) was reinstalled, GP Koirala was Prime Minister again, heading the SPA (Seven Party Alliance), and immediately cut the powers of the king. Soon after the government declared a truce with the Maoists, eventually bring them into the 'Loktantra' or Democracy government by agreeing to hold a Constituent Assembly (CA) election.

Can a tiger change its stripes? Koirala is a forceful old man and a consummate politician but neither a statesman nor visionary and certainly not a democrat. Similarly the Maoists publicly led by 'Prachandra' had internal divisions, and what they say and what they do are entirely different. For both, talk was easy, action not, and even with some simple '8-' and '12-point agreements' still nothing happened. Months after the deadlines still neither side had disclosed what had happened to the 'disappeared people', undoubtedly all gruesomely murdered, the Maoists had not stopped extortion or given back land they had confiscated and nor had the politicians (or the Maoists) stopped repeating mistakes made in the past.

Delays

In 2007 the Constituent Assembly elections (a body to rewrite the constitution) were postponed twice, and whatever else was said, the real reason was neither side felt they could win. In fact, the Maoists were so worried they might not even make the 5% threshold, they thundered that full proportional representation was the only fair way to vote, a shrewd move that conned a lot of people who didn't realize the previously agreed MMP (Mixed Member Proportional voting where each voter is given two votes, one for a person from their region and one for the party of their choice) is actually more fair. Delaying tactics only, and the price was a loss of mandate and respect from the international community.

With political paralysis the Tarai flared up, the historically neglected 'madhesis' or people of plains origin, demanding an end to the historical discrimination. The power vacuum was been filled with multiple violent groups, more anarchic than previous bad times, and further complicating the power balance.

The trick election

It is sometimes said that 'you can't fool all of the people all the time', but it seems that in desperation for something – anything – positive to happen the political parties did. Compromises on the split of proportional representation and the opaqueness of who would run the country while the Constituent Assembly was rewriting the constitution meant that with all the elected people having to belong to a political party, and the other 26 out of over 600 members being chosen by the Prime Minster (strictly the Council of Ministers), there is no room for lawyers or the intelligentsia, or anyone wanting to curb the politicians' lust for power through constitutional means.

Eventually on 10 April 2008 elections were held with the Maoists pushing past the boundaries of fairness, but still the results reflected the frustration with the previous lack of direction, many people willing to give the Maoists the benefit of the doubt ('none of the above' was not an option on the ballot sheet: it could have been popular). They won just under half the seats, comprehensively beating the other three main parties: voters were showing the main parties the door.

Trick solution

While the election meaning was clear, the result ended up being a very complicated balance of power, and the Maoists had already alienated almost everyone, especially the CP-UML, ideologically close to them, with killings and denunciations. That made a consensus government a tricky solution, especially as the Maoists were making a blunt power grab and had not renounced their dictum of taking over by any means, or acted on any agreements such as returning confiscated land etc. However, the option of all the fragmented parties (many smaller ones founded along ethnic or regional lines) joining against the Maoists, ie a grand coalition, throwing the Maoists out and potentially leading to civil war, wasn't really a long-term workable solution.

The king out, a president in

As part of the political solution, the newly elected Constitutional Assembly rubber-stamped the political agreement to remove the monarchy (the only political agreement of the multiple 8-, 12- and 21-point agreements that was implemented on time). With surprising dignity the king left the palace in June 2008, moving to Nagarjun, a forest park on the outskirts of Kathmandu that historically had been the family property. The politicians displayed no such dignity and squabbled for a full four months before even deciding how to elect a president, with the opposing sides trying to ensure that neither Koirala or Pushpa Kamal Dahal (Prachandra) became the first president, and also arguing over the role of the president: unbelievably this had not been previously decided.

Miscalculating, the Maoists failed to get their candidate elected – Ram Raja Prasad Singh, a lawyer but also convicted bomber (eight dead in a political campaign) – so almost by accident Nepal ended up with a stalwart Nepali Congress ex-minister, Ram Baran Yadav as a largely ceremonial president, but still political arbitrator of last resort. He is a Madhesi, ie from the Tarai, as is the vice president, Parmananda Jha, previously a corrupt judge, and so already shows a less-discriminatory face of the government. The president tries to be scrupulously fair in public so it seems that Nepal could have ended up with far worse.

Default Prime Minister

The Maoists' brute force and contempt of everyone else had to be tolerated, and in the end worked for them, even though the NC suddenly put the interest of the country first, but far too late. Finally Pushpa Kamal Dahal, previously called 'Prachandra', one of the Maoists' central committee leaders, was elected Prime Minister in August 2008, four months after the election, with the CP-UML having to swallow their pride and the NC left sulking.

While the details are messy, the fact that the Maoists have joined the government by facing the electorate is impressive, and so perhaps the wiggle room, closed-door dealings and tolerance of broken agreements has resulted in the chance of avoiding civil war. Unfortunately it is these traits that got the country into this situation in the first place.

What now?

At the time of writing the Maoists had been in power for a few days: not enough time for any judgements. Dahal and the Maoists undoubtedly want to and need to transform the country. However, will the policies make hard economic sense?

Second, and perhaps most importantly for the citizens' quality of life, while improving governance, will the Maoists turn a blind eye to their comrades extorting and murdering? If real law and order isn't brought back, their still publicly undefined 'Prachanda Path' will prove to be a gruelling trail of more human suffering.

ECONOMY

Nepal's rural backwardness may be attractive to tourists but the mediaeval way of life is not easy for most Nepalese. In the past tenant farmers, the majority of the population, paid crippling taxes to landlords in a vicious semi-feudal system. The 1964 reforms sought to redress this by land redistribution and reducing rental to a (still unbearable) 50% of the crop but they were only partly successful.

In 2000 the bonded-labour system was abolished but despite assistance being readily available the freed *Kamaiya* have struggled against Government indifference (high caste bias) to get their government-promised land. Even now, 90% of Nepal's population lives off the land with the majority existing at subsistence level. It's a simple, hard life with virtually no money.

This legacy means the prospects for the farmers' children are bleak. Nepal's astronomical birth rate and a lack of new arable land are the main problems. The ever-expanding population has been partly absorbed by the Inner Tarai but the amount of arable land available per person continues to drop. Crop yields have increased but up until 2007 low prices and the lack of roads inevitably turned Nepal into a net food importer. There are dire predictions about the decline of land fertility and the destruction of the forests; already there are food and firewood shortages. Without development miracles this situation can only get worse.

Nepal is barely industrialized. Demand for jobs far outstrips supply resulting in exploitative wages and appalling working conditions. Nepal's biggest export and biggest earner is labour, with more than a million people working overseas and repatriating more than a billion dollars a year, an 8th or 12.5% of the GDP: this is the only reason the country isn't bankrupt. That doesn't include the more than two million Nepalis surviving in India, and yes, that means more than an eighth of the population work (are exploited, mostly) overseas because of economic hardship at home.

Tourism is a big, reliable earner: perhaps the country will finally break the half-a-million-visitors-a-year barrier soon. Other industries such as carpet, pashmina and ready-made garments have gone through boom–bust cycles but there is hope that ayurvedic medicinal ingredients, cardamom, tea (and perhaps coffee) might be more durable. Undoubtedly more cash cropping in the hills is needed.

For comparison, the per person GDP is equivalent to around a dollar a day, although if using purchasing power parity, the equivalent is more like $1600 per year in developed country terms (imagine trying to live on $30 a week). There is money in Kathmandu but little anywhere else.

For the most part the functioning economy is Kathmandu, with some industry in the eastern and central Tarai, and lots of agriculture. In the eastern and central hill regions some farmers also cash crop, so somehow mostly the east seems more comfortable than West Nepal's appalling, persistent poverty.

DEVELOPMENT

Classified as one of the least-developed countries (LDCs) in the world, in virtually all comparative measures Nepal is ranked in the lowest 25%, anywhere from 125 to 150 out of approximately 177 countries that can be measured. Literacy is around the 50% mark, and just under 50% of the population speak Nepali as a first language. Nepal has received plenty of foreign aid and there are many, many successful small and medium projects that have made a real difference to people's quality of life. However, more broadly Nepal's government is failing its people, on one side with government apathy and on the other by failing to direct aid projects effectively; many smaller organizations focus on doing what they want to rather than what is best overall for the country because of government apathy and corruption. It is easy to criticize everything, and everyone does, but so far the Nepal government has not been able to show enough leadership and commitment to make everything work better.

No money, no problem

Although it seems strange, there is more than enough money available for development, it is Nepal's absorption capacity that is the problem, actually spending the money. The hold up is often anti-corruption measures: correspondingly bureaucrats are less likely to allow a project to function smoothly, and with constant revolving doors – power struggles – at the highest levels, there is no continuity. The hard reality that few people will voice is that developed countries are comparatively wealthier because they are more organized, have a drive to constantly self-improve and most public officials truly care; this is good governance. The less-developed countries are simply just not as organized, whether it is corruption, additional paperwork, cultural issues or lack of visionary leadership. Surprisingly natural resources have no bearing – think Singapore and Taiwan – and while Nepal is landlocked, so are Austria and Switzerland. Yes, there are some injustices in international trade and other inequalities that people harp on about, but using these issues is just a cover up for bad governance.

This is easy to say but what, really, needs to be done? Take these two seemingly simple examples. The roads in Kathmandu (and the rest of the country) need improving: perhaps a city strategy to discourage cars would be useful, perhaps bigger roads would be better – many different approaches are possible. Regardless, in the short term better roads mean less dust pollution, traffic moving more smoothly, more room for bicycles and alternative transport. So the Kathmandu Municipality planned many useful road projects and has plenty of money for them (without a drop of aid needed) – so far, so good. To keep costs down and by government rule, these contracts are advertised and the cheapest contractor that can satisfy the conditions wins. The road works started then soon stopped and only half of the budget for the year was spent. Why? The price of tar had risen substantially (like crude oil), yet there was no mechanism to allow for that, nobody worked out an easy way to solve this relatively minor issue.

Second, let's consider education. This is a no-brainer: better education is the key to unlock the potential of the country, and the sky is the limit with aid money and assistance, if used effectively. While there are many complex choices, fundamentally quality education is needed and everybody agrees with this. Again Nepal has failed miserably due to the politicians and the Maoists. Sadly more than a few people in power have sabotaged education because an educated population would be less compliant (fewer winning votes with free alcohol on voting day) and more critical of feudal ways. And who staffs most voting booths? Teachers, but many are not teachers at all: they just pick up the salary as their reward for rigging elections, and accordingly Nepal has more than five times as many temporary (often unqualified) teachers as qualified, permanent teachers yet the court cases about this have dragged on for more than five years because of political interference.

During the long insurgency the Maoists were just as bad. Currently school education is free at government schools but the standards are so abysmal that private education, even with barely trained but more enthusiastic teachers, is far superior. The Maoists want to nationalize private schools and have already put an unofficial cap on fees, intent on destroying the system before any plans of rebuilding, and only because private schools are less willing to spread their doctrine.

What about colleges and universities? Don't ask. The student unions are strong and are the rent-a-mob proxies for political parties, and of course they are a huge vote bank. The facilities are abysmal and lecturers barely attend, instead running more lucrative parallel private tuition for their classes after hours. So the chance of just letting in overseas private universities that are already operating in other countries and have everything worked out, is zero.

During the insurgency neither side cared, and every year weeks of education were lost to strikes, despite the general population being behind having schools as a 'zone of peace'. So, education has been hijacked for many selfish, unrelated reasons, and it is the country that suffers in the long run.

The development that is needed to get Nepal on track is in governance. The whole government needs modernizing and an attitude change. However, there is huge resistance to change – cutting off the easy money, or even just the unknown. At the moment promotion is on seniority rather than performance and it is virtually impossible to fire someone: retraining is needed for the dedicated, and non-performers and the corrupt need to be got rid of. The justice system is weak: almost anyone with money can get away literally with murder. The government routinely ignores court judgements against it, and a business case can drag on so long that the result is meaningless, so of course business investment is a nightmare too. It is the poor who suffer under this as the laws only apply to them.

What is needed is comprehensive and fair laws that apply to everyone without wiggle room, and an end to discrimination. For example, until recently women were not allowed to inherit property and rape in marriage was not thought possible; still police are loath to enforce equality when caste issues erupt surrounding drinking from the same taps or entrance into temples. There have been hundreds of challenges to the archaic and caste-biased laws through PILs (Public Interest Litigation), but justice for the people is still a long, long way off. With a solid rule of law and strong consumer advocacy and protection, business and the economy can flourish: if only the Government would take the role of encouraging business by clear-headed regulation rather than trying to meddle or run competing enterprises.

Freeing the economy is a proven way of lifting lower middle-class people into the solid middle class, and of course the wealthy benefit hugely but what about the real dollar-a-day poor?

Initially people joined the Maoists because their situation was helpless and the Maoists were at least trying to do something to overthrow the old, corrupt system, but their tactics of coercion, fear and extortion without any real benefit in the villages and towns always worked against them, and during the insurgency they never changed their stripes either. Essentially they were as incompetent as the government. The one necessary and lasting change they have made is the introduction of unionism to the ordinary workers. Wages and working conditions are slowly improving (8-hour shifts for restaurant staff, instead of 10-12 hours), but now Maoist-supported unions fight against UML-supported unions, trying to control the union fees rolling in: a sad loss of direction.

The poor will benefit the most from careful and directed government attention, better education means real opportunity and for farmers, a better price for produce and roads to access markets can make a real difference. Fire up the economy and particularly help the poor.

Nepal has lost a very real decade to the troubles, and at the current rate will take another to sort itself out: it's no wonder it is one of the poorest countries in the world. Very sad.

RELIGION

Nepal is now officially secular but until recently was a Hindu Constitutional Monarchy. Official statistics (2002) state that 80.6% of the population is Hindu, 10.7% Buddhist, 4.2% Muslim, 3.6% Shamanist and Animist, 0.4% Christian

The peoples of eastern Nepal

A cultural bridge between Tibet and India, Nepal is a colourful patchwork of ethnic groups, castes and clans. Although officially the only Hindu kingdom in the world (until 2006), tides of history have also deposited Buddhists and even a few Muslims and Christians here. Unlike in India the caste system is not institutionalized and is generally only observed by the beneficiaries, the higher castes.

Newars, with their rich urban-based culture and separate language, are the traditional inhabitants of the Kathmandu Valley, responsible for much of the famous architecture and art. Outside Kathmandu they are mainly merchants, particularly shop owners. **Brahmins** are the high Hindu priestly caste rather than an ethnic group. Traditionally they earn money from performing religious rituals and must avoid being polluted by people of a lower caste. Many now work in the government and in business.

Sherpas (see pp137-42) and **Kirat** (Rai and Limbu, see pp142-3) are the ethnic groups most commonly encountered on the Everest trek. **Rais** are found south of Solu and Pharak, particularly in the area between the Khumbu and the Arun. The villages of Bung and Gudel are exclusively Rai and you'll also meet them at Namche's Saturday market. Usually stocky and short, the Rai have Mongoloid features, a round face and a tanned but fairly light skin and they wear light-coloured clothing. The diet staples are rice, maize, wheat and millet, mixed with a variety of vegetables. The Rais are well represented in Gurkha battalions of the Indian and British armies. **Tamangs** are people of the middle hills who very often act as porters. The women are distinctive with nose jewellery that hangs over their lips while the men wear a rough sleeveless woollen tunic when it is cold. They are Buddhists and, like the Sherpas, have their roots in Tibet.

and 0.02% Jain. Since being both Hindu and Nepali-speaking can confer greater employment opportunities and higher social standing, it's likely that there are more Buddhists and fewer Hindus than these figures suggest.

The long tradition of religious toleration has led to a blurring of distinctions, especially between Hinduism and Buddhism. You'll see Buddhist prayer-flags fluttering over a Hindu temple and statues of Hindu gods in Buddhist gompas (monasteries). In fact, many Hindu deities have their Buddhist counterparts.

Hinduism

The most complex of all religions is also the most tolerant – in Nepal, at least, if not in India. In theory, Hinduism accepts all other beliefs as true and allows for forms of worship which range from simple animism to deepest philosophy. Its many paths even include *tantra* which maintains that enlightenment can come through absolutely anything in life; and that includes drink, drugs and sex.

Central to Hindu belief is **reincarnation**, the belief that all living things go through a series of rebirths which lead eventually to *moksha*, salvation in the form of escape from the cycle and unity with the Creator. What determines whether you're reborn in the next life as a flea or a wealthy landowner is *karma*. Good and bad karma are the direct result of good or bad actions during your lifetime.

The Hindu **caste system** still has a profound influence on the lives of most people in Nepal. It was actually extended by the Malla king, Jayasthiti, to bring Buddhists into this rigid form of social control. The main Hindu castes are the **Brahmins**, the priestly caste (some Brahmins are still priests but many are now employed in the civil service), **Chhetris** (warriors and rulers), **Vaisyas** (traders and farmers) and **Shudras** (artisans). Below them are the **untouchables** (butchers, tailors, sweepers and those who carry out other menial tasks).

The Hindu pantheon has three main gods: Brahma the creator, Vishnu the preserver and Shiva the destroyer and god of reproduction. Most Hindus are Vaishnavites (followers of Vishnu) or Shaivites (followers of Shiva). On the Jomsom–Muktinath trek you may meet a *sadhu*, a Shaivite pilgrim (carrying a trident as the symbol of Shiva) on a pilgrimage to Muktinath.

Other popular deities include Saraswati (Brahma's consort and the goddess of science and wisdom), Kali or Durga (Shiva's blood-drinking consort, the goddess of death), Rama and Krishna (the seventh and eighth incarnations of Vishnu) and Hanuman (the monkey god).

Buddhism

In its purest form Buddhism isn't actually a religion since it's concerned not with gods or the saving of the soul but with personal enlightenment dependent solely upon the works of the individual. Buddhism grew out of Hinduism in the 5th century BC and shares with Hinduism the belief in reincarnation. For Buddhists, however, escape from the cycle of rebirth brings *nirvana*, the extinguishing of self and desire.

The Buddha was born **Prince Siddhartha Gautam** in 560BC in Lumbini, southern Nepal. Overcome by all the suffering and pain in the world, he tried to

Puja
A *puja* (act of worship) can be anything from a quick prayer to a festival of several days but offerings of some sort are usually involved. Hindus offer flowers, food and coloured powders and light incense and butter lamps. They receive a *tika* (a red mark on their forehead) as a blessing from the deity. Hindu pujas to mark the year's most important festivals require animal sacrifices (formerly human sacrifices) and at Dasain thousands of buffalo and goats are beheaded.

Buddhist pujas are rather more humane. Juniper is burnt as incense, mantras (see box p140) are chanted and prayer wheels are spun. Lamas are sponsored to say prayers and invoke the blessing of the gods on certain people.

find the reasons first in philosophy, then as an ascetic submitting himself to a round of tough penances. These included sitting on thorns, sleeping by rotting corpses and eating a diet so low in calories that he is reputed to have been able to feel his backbone when he grasped his stomach. He became so weak that one day, walking along a river near **Bodhgaya** in India, he fainted and fell into the water. Coming to he decided that enlightenment was not to be found in extreme deprivation. He restored himself with a good meal and sat down under a tree (the famous bodhi tree) to meditate.

The Middle Way In his meditation, it was revealed to the Buddha that human desires cause people to be locked into the eternal circle of rebirth. Only when people cease to desire can they escape this cycle of suffering and achieve final peace. He realized that he couldn't have achieved enlightenment before because it was what he desired.

He realized that extremes of self-mortification and self-indulgence were not the answer; the 'Middle Way' is the path to enlightenment. This involves mastering the **four noble truths** (that all life is suffering, that desire is the cause of all suffering, that it is possible to escape from this state and achieve nirvana, and that this can be done by following the Eight-Fold Path of right views, right thought, right speech, right action, right livelihood, right endeavour, right mindfulness and right concentration).

Buddhist sects Soon after the Buddha's death in 480BC, a schism occurred amongst his disciples that eventually divided Buddhism into two main camps, Theravada and Mahayana; but there are now many sects within these.
● **Theravada Buddhism** ('the tradition of the elders') is closer to the Buddha's original teachings that enlightenment comes through your own endeavours, not through divine interference. Also known as Hinayana (the 'Lesser vehicle'), it's followed in Sri Lanka and the countries of South-East Asia.
● **Mahayana Buddhism** is entirely different. It's much more like a religion with a colourful pantheon of enlightened beings known as *bodhisattvas*. The Buddha himself is seen as a divine being, just one of a number of Buddhas who've come down to earth (and some who have yet to come) to help everyone achieve nirvana. Buddhism was given a much wider appeal because converts

NEPAL

did not have to give up their old gods; they could continue to worship them as bodhisattvas.

● **Tibetan Buddhism** or Lamaism is the main form of Buddhism practised in Nepal. When Mahayana Buddhism reached Tibet in the 7th century, it absorbed the deities of the native religion, Bon. Lamaism emphasizes the importance of magic and the reciting of magical phrases from *tantras* (manuals) to achieve certain ends; it's often referred to as Tantric Buddhism. Tantrism was formerly popular also in Hinduism, and it taught that there are two parts to each deity, male and female. It was thought that a mystical union with one or other part of the deity was possible by mortals through sexual excess. In the 11th century, Tibetan Buddhism was purged of these extreme tantric elements by the monk, Marpa.

In Tibetan Buddhism, spiritual teachers are known as *lamas* and live in the gompa (monastery) that is usually attached to the temple. In the course of Tibetan history these lamas achieved greater power than the kings.

There are four main orders of monks. The **Nying-ma-pa** (the Ancient Order or Red Hat school) was founded in the 8th century by the monk Padmasambhava (also known as Guru Rinpoche), who spent some time in Nepal. Most of the Buddhists in the mountain regions here are followers of this order (see p140). The **Sakya-pa** and **Kagyu-pa** (founded by the reforming monk Marpa) have few adherents in Nepal, although there are monasteries of the Sakya-pa sect in the north Annapurna region. The **Geluk-pa** (Yellow Hat school) is led by the Dalai Lama, the exiled Tibetan leader who now lives in India. Many of his followers came to Nepal after the invasion of Tibet by China in 1959.

● **Newari Buddhism**, as practised in the Kathmandu Valley, is not derived from Tibetan Buddhism but from earlier influences from the south. The religion of the Newars is an interesting mixture of Hinduism and Mahayana Buddhism. Their Buddhist priests do not live in monasteries but marry and belong to a hereditary caste.

● **Bon-po** is a sect which mixes pre-Buddhist beliefs with religious practices close to Buddhism.

Animism

Even older than the established religions in Nepal is a belief in the forces of nature which are able to affect human beings. The sun, the moon and the stars, mountains, rocks and rivers are all thought to have an *anima* (spirit) which needs to be placated or a delicate balance will be upset that will lead to some human misfortune. Particularly amongst the mountain people there are still **shaman**, or faith-healers (*jhankri*) who intervene between the deities and mortals, especially when the latter are ill.

Practical information for the visitor

VISA AND TREKKING REGULATIONS

Visas

All visitors except Indians require a visa for Nepal. This is easily obtained on arrival at the airport or border, or at Nepali embassies abroad, though this is often the more expensive option. Wherever you get it, your visa application must include a passport-size photo.

At the time of writing (October 2008) a 2-day transit visa costs US$5, 15 days $25/£15, 30 days $40/£25, and 90 days $100/£60. However, these rates and the kinds of visa available may have changed by the time you read this. The fees are payable in any major convertible currency and visas can be turned into multiple entry for an additional $20. Visas are valid from the date of entry into Nepal, whether you are in Nepal all that time or not.

Visas are free for **children** under 10 years old.

The 48-hour **transit visa** is actually good for three days with the standard official one day's grace (see p84) but that still won't get you far in the hills.

For information on **other visa categories** (diplomatic, official, study, pilgrim, non-tourist and business visas) talk to Immigration or see their website (🖳 www.immi.gov.np).

Visa extensions and conversion

Visa extensions cost US$30 per 15 days (paid in equivalent Nepali rupees; they don't take dollars), for a maximum of 150 days in one calendar year (1 Jan-31 Dec). If your visa expires within this timeframe you must pay the extension fee plus a fine equivalent to $1-3 per day, depending on how many days you are over. If you are late because the Department of Immigration is closed – for public holidays but not strikes – there is no fine.

In Kathmandu, applications for extension are accepted at the Department of Immigration, Maitighar. The Department is open every day except for public holidays, from 9am to 3pm in summer and 9am to 2pm in winter. If you apply in the morning your passport will be ready by 5pm in summer, 4pm in winter, and earlier if they are not busy. The Maitighar office is a taxi ride (approximately US$2) from Thamel. Taxis drop you at the entrance of an alley, walk up the small street at this complicated and large intersection. Touts sometimes promise a special service but you won't need their services unless you want something special.

TIMS permit

Nepal used to have an odd trekking-permit system but this was scrapped for the main trekking regions, including the Everest and Rolwaling regions, in 1999, and the short-lived and hated TRC – Trekkers Registration Certificate – is also dead.

In 2008 a new system was introduced: the TIMS – Trekkers Information Management System – permit which is a way of tracking roughly where you are in case of trouble, collecting statistics, and also a way of regulating the trekking industry. If **trekking with a company** they will provide one for you. They need a passport copy and two passport-sized photos (readily available in Thamel).

Independent trekkers get a differently coloured FIT (Free Individual Trekker) permit, available free from TAAN's office at Maligaun, Ganeshthan (☎ 442 7473, 444 0920, 444 0921; $2 by taxi from Thamel) and from Bhrikuti Mandap, the tourist service centre. You can also buy from trekking agencies in Thamel, just look for the distinctive green TAAN signs. There's service charge of between Rs200 and Rs500, but that saves you taxi rides across the city, and of course some of these offices are open much later than the counters.

While TIMS is still in its infancy, TAAN (the Trekking Agents Association of Nepal) has ambitious plans: for example at the numerous police posts where you have to write your full name, passport details (all of them), visa details and what you had for breakfast, instead, they will just take your name and TIMS permit number.

You need to carry your TIMS permit at all times when trekking, and also have a copy of your passport details page and Nepal visa, or your passport, and a backup passport copy.

National Park entrance

For trekking above Lukla you have to pay the Sagarmatha National Park entrance fee of Rs1000. If trekking from Tumlingtar or climbing in the Mera area you pass through a corner of the Makalu-Barun National Park, also Rs1000. If trekking with a company, these permits are normally included.

The National Park fees collection counter has moved from Thamel to Bhrikuti Mandap, which all taxi drivers know: it's $2-3 from Thamel. You can also pay the fee at the entrance to the national park, which saves a taxi ride: don't forget to budget for it though. However, for conservation areas such as ACAP (Annapurna Conservation Area Project), you have to pay the Rs 2000 fee in Kathmandu or Pokhara, or pay double at the actual entrance.

Leaving the country

You are given one day's grace, ie allowed to leave the day after your visa expires. For those heading to India, excess Nepali rupees are easily converted into Indian rupees but do this in Kathmandu or at the land border. In India, even in Delhi and other major centres, it is almost impossible to change Nepali rupees.

GETTING TO NEPAL

By air

Now that Nepal has introduced third-country landing rights the variety of air-lines flying into Kathmandu has dramatically increased and changes frequently. Coming **from Australasia** and the **west coast of America**, Star Alliance's Thai still has a big hold on the market, while **from Europe** and **America's east coast**, Qatar (twice a day), Gulf and Etihad are popular choices.

Check your routing and stopovers carefully: flying via Delhi usually involves an inconvenient and late overnight stop, and requires getting a visa before leaving. As a general rule avoid Nepal Airline Corporation (NAC; formerly RNAC), for they are particularly unreliable.

Flying from India is a bit of a lottery as the Delhi route, particularly, is at full capacity. Jet Airways is the best but there are plenty to choose from.

You can also fly direct between Kathmandu and Varanasi, Mumbai, Kolkata and sometimes Bangalore, and between Biratnagar and Kolkata and Patna.

The land route **from Tibet** is the more interesting but you can fly between Kathmandu and Lhasa with Air China's monopolistically priced flight.

See pp97-9 for information on arrival at Kathmandu airport.

Overland from India
From Delhi there are direct buses to Kathmandu but it is a tough journey taking 36-60 hours. Enquire at Tibet colony: the final stopping point in Kathmandu is Bauddha. An alternative is to take a train to Gorakhpur and then catch a local bus (don't believe touts who say there is a tourist bus) to the border crossing of Sunauli/Belahiya. From Varanasi you can take a train or bus to Gorakhpur, from where it is approximately three hours to Sunauli.

Immigration is staffed from dawn to dusk although the border does not physically close at night. If you arrive late simply walk across and stay at the better hotels on the Nepalese side, then visit immigration the next morning. Without a visa and exit and entry stamps you'll encounter a big problem in Kathmandu or when leaving. Buses to Kathmandu (11 to 14 hours) leave from 5am to 9am for the day service and from 4pm to about 8pm for the night buses. For much of the way the route follows the Trisuli River and the scenery is an impressive introduction to the middle hills of Nepal.

From Kolkata (Calcutta) there are two routes: one is via Patna to the border at Raxaul/Birganj, followed by a 15-hour bus ride to Kathmandu; the other is by train to Siliguri, near Darjeeling, and then an hour-and-a-half to the border by bus or taxi. Cross the border into Kakarbhitta (spelt various ways), from where it is 10 hours or so to Kathmandu.

LOCAL TRANSPORT

Nepal has an extensive network of **domestic flights** to make up for the lack of roads. With many competing airlines, services, although basic, are surprisingly convenient. Since there are no radars at hill strips cloudy weather can occasionally postpone flights, sometimes for several days. Tickets can be bought direct from the airlines but travel agents and trekking companies get them for the same price too. Avoid the grossly mismanaged national airline, Nepal Airlines (NAC), if possible – though for the more unusual sectors they are often the only choice. Fares must be paid in hard currency, cash or travellers' cheques, not rupees. For more details see p122. Domestic tickets are not readily available over the internet.

Once the domestic fleet was almost exclusively sturdy Twin Otters but with the proliferation of airlines, demand and improved airstrips a variety of turbo-prop planes are now flown. There are still no regional runways long enough to take 737 jets.

Increasingly, small helicopters are used for sightseeing, charter and rescue. Charter charges run from US$1500 to $2000 an hour.

Long-distance bus services are run using sturdy Indian buses that cope well with the rough roads. Night coaches are for masochists but the only choice for longer routes. The day buses are often filled to bursting point and feature a variety of seating, mostly unsuitable for long legs. The spectacular scenery can, however, make up for the lack of comfort.

For journeys to Pokhara and Chitwan, tourist coaches, with seated passengers only and safe luggage storage on the roof, are the best, especially as they depart from near Thamel, saving a taxi journey. See a travel agent or hotel reception for tickets.

Taxis are plentiful and relatively cheap. In Kathmandu they have meters, in other places mostly not. **Cycle-rickshaws** are environmentally sound and found in all major towns. Make sure to fix a price before you set off. Auto-rickshaws are banned from Kathmandu but can be found in various states of repair in other cities close to the Indian border.

Hiring a vehicle is best organized direct with a driver for a tourist car, or through a travel agent for minibuses and four-wheel drives. In theory you should have an international licence to **hire a motorbike** but mostly you can get away without this and just leave a security deposit with the owners. Costs start from US$10 a day.

Cycling around on a 'Flying Pigeon' or a (copy) **mountain bike** (see p38) with clanking gears can be pleasant anywhere except Kathmandu.

LANGUAGE

Nepali, a Sanskrit-based language similar to India's Hindi, is the country's official language. For approximately half the population Nepali is not the mother tongue; ethnic languages such as Sherpa and Newari are widely used in local areas, and in some places adjacent valleys can be home to completely different languages. The 2001 census counted 93 languages.

Nepali is the medium for government-run schools but most private schools teach in English, often odd Nepali English that students are not always comfortable using.

In the tourism industry English is the main language, though it is by no means fluently spoken. In the main trekking areas it is quite possible to get by speaking only English.

Learning Nepali is rewarding and will provide many amusing reactions. Simple spoken Nepali is not difficult and most Kathmandu bookshops sell small phrasebooks, *Basic Spoken Nepali* is the best for really learning the language.

ELECTRICITY

The electricity grid covers only the major towns and cities and load-shedding power cuts are frequent literally several hours a day in the winter and spring. In theory the supply is 220V and 50Hz with round two-pin and three-pin sockets in two sizes; unfortunately, it will always be the other size from your plug.

In general, rural Nepal has little electricity, although some houses now have a cheap solar panel and battery that can power a couple of small fluorescent bulbs.

In the Khumbu, though, there is reliable electricity in Lukla, Namche, Khumjung-Khunde, Thame, Tengboche and Pangboche. At most other places at least a couple of lodges have solar panels and converters for recharging camera batteries for a price.

TIME

Nepal is 5 hours and 45 minutes ahead of UTC (Coordinated Universal Time)/ Greenwich Mean Time (GMT), and 15 minutes ahead of India (as a show of independence). There is no daylight saving scheme.

MONEY

The Nepalese rupee (Rs or NC) comes in banknote denominations of 1, 2, 5, 10, 20, 25 (rare), 50, 100, 250 (rare), 500 and 1000 rupees, each featuring an animal. There's a surprising variety of coins worth from 1 to 10 rupees, and plans for bigger denomination coins; so far, all of these coins are confusing to foreigners because the value is written only in Nepali.

Note that Indian Rs500 and Rs1000 notes are illegal in Nepal and will be confiscated if found. This is because at one time Pakistan forged them and distributed them through Nepal.

Changing money

The days of changing money at black-market rates in carpet shops are almost gone; instead every Thamel street has a dozen moneychangers. You can buy Nepali rupees at your star-class hotel, at a bank or a moneychanger.

Rates of exchange vary a little depending on whether the exchange is an official government transaction or one being made by a tourist in a commercial bank or moneychanger but the spread of rates is not great, so unless you have a large amount to convert, there's not much point shopping around.

❏ **Rates of exchange**

The Nepali Rupee is tied to the Indian rupee and tracks it at exactly 1.6 times the value.

UK£1	Rs127
€1	Rs102
A$1	Rs50
C$1	Rs63
NZ$1	Rs46
US$1	Rs80
Indian Rs1	Rs1.60

Current exchange rates are available on: ⌨ www.nepalnews.com and ⌨ www.xe.com/ucc

When changing money for trekking, try to get some smaller denominations, Rs100 notes especially. Out of season or on minor routes it can be hard to change a Rs1000 note.

Tipping

Once virtually unknown in Nepal, this custom has spread: at many tourist hotels and restaurants a compulsory tipping charge is now levied. If no TSC – Tourism Service Charge – is listed a 5% tip or the small change will be appreciated. Tipping trekking crews is now normal; for guidelines see box p12.

POST AND TELECOMMUNICATIONS

Nepal's **postal system** is slow and unreliable. Letters and postcards take anywhere from two to six weeks, surface mail three to six months, and often neither arrives. The numerous cargo offices are the best alternative for sending home excess gear and souvenirs.

The **international telephone code** for Nepal is ☎ 977, followed by 1 for Kathmandu, or simply 977 for mobiles: all mobile numbers begin with a 9. The phone system in the capital is overloaded and international tariffs are high compared to global trends. Most home-country **mobile phone services** work but SMS messages are sometimes received 20 times. **Internet cafés** are everywhere. Many of the ones in tourist areas have card readers and will burn your photos onto a CD or DVD. Many internet cafés also offer cheap international calls. There are some wi-fi connections in Kathmandu, see p118.

MEDIA

All but budget hotels have cable **television** with a range of popular channels.

Radio Nepal's short-wave transmissions reach the whole country. News in English is broadcast at 7.30am, 2pm and 8pm, followed by the general weather forecast, usually 'mainly fair throughout the kingdom'. The Met Office has a hopeless record in predicting huge snowstorms. Increasingly, private FM stations in Kathmandu are broadcasting over the rest of the country in shortwave, some in trendy English, others in a Nepali mishmash. You could also try the BBC. Note, however, that none provides long-range weather forecasts; the internet is a better alternative.

There is a crop of local English-language daily **newspapers** – the state-run *Rising Nepal*, *The Kathmandu Post*, which has good news but can be terribly cheesy, and the more stylish *Himalayan Times*. They all cost less than Rs5 and are often available at your favourite breakfast spot. The *Nepali Times*, a colour weekly that comes out on Friday, is absolutely the best paper overall. All publications are available online.

HOLIDAYS AND FESTIVALS

Government office hours are 10am to 5pm (to 4pm in winter) Sunday to Friday, with only Saturday as a holiday. Embassies take the whole weekend off.

Increasingly, banks are open for at least a few hours on Saturdays, Sundays and public holidays but don't rely on this. Of course, the cash machines don't close, although they have a habit of running out of money during festival periods. Souvenir shopping and sightseeing are possible every day though all museums are closed on Tuesday.

With the rich patchwork of cultures and religions in Nepal it is a land of colourful festivals and these are celebrated with fervour, especially by the less well-off masses. In fact, there's a festival going on somewhere at least every other day. The main season for festivals, however, comes in August and September as the monsoon withdraws.

The main festivals which are celebrated in Kathmandu or the Annapurna region are listed below. Since almost all are determined by the lunar calendar they occur on a different day each year. The Ministry of Home Affairs issues a list of the 25 official holidays at the beginning of each year.

Festivals
● **Dasain** (Durga Puja) is the biggest of Nepal's festivals, lasting at least 10 days and beginning at the end of September or early October. The whole country grinds to a halt as people return to their villages for family reunions and feasts. It's a Hindu festival, which celebrates the triumph of good over evil, symbolized by the victory of the Hindu Rama over Ravana and the goddess Durga over Mahisasur, the devil who took the shape of a buffalo. Consequently numerous buffalo (and goats, sheep and cockerels) lose their heads during the eighth and ninth days of the festival and the roads literally flow with blood. Every form of transport, from the cycle-rickshaws of Thamel to Nepal Airlines' Boeing 757, has its wheels doused with sacrificial blood to bring good luck for the year ahead.

● **Tihar** (Deepavali) lasts five days and usually falls in November, two weeks after Dasain. It's known as the 'Festival of Lights' after the thousands of oil lamps that are lit in windows to welcome Lakshmi, the goddess of prosperity. Children go singing door-to-door for donations, houses are cleaned, sisters perform pujas for their brothers and everyone decorates the local cow.

● **Losar**, the Tibetan New Year, falls in February. If you're in Kathmandu at this time, Baudha is the place to be. On the fourth day thousands of Tibetans converge on the stupa for prayers.

● **Shivaratri** is celebrated in February at Pashupatinath in Kathmandu. It's a day of ritual bathing and puja that attracts Hindus to this Shiva temple from as far away as India.

● **Holi** If you're in any Hindu area in March you can't escape this boisterous spring festival. It involves tossing buckets of water over everyone and 'playing colours' (throwing handfuls of coloured powder). Westerners (particularly women) are a favourite target so put on your old clothes, stock up with bags of powder and water squirters and keep your camera covered.

● **Bisket Jatra** is Nepalese New Year's Day, which falls in April. The main celebrations are in Bhaktapur and then in Thimi the following day.

● **Raato Machhendranath** The god Raato ('Red') Machhendranath is the protector of the Kathmandu Valley, worshipped by both Hindus and Buddhists.

Held in April or May to ensure that the monsoon will reach the Valley, this festival lasts at least a month. An image of the god is pulled on a huge chariot through the streets of Patan in a smaller version of the Jagannath procession that takes place in Puri in India.

● **Buddha Jayanti** is the birthday of the Buddha, celebrated in May. Conveniently, it's also the anniversary of his enlightenment and death. In Kathmandu the main celebrations take place at Swayambhunath but there will be pujas at most Buddhist temples.

● **The Dalai Lama's birthday**, on 6 July, is celebrated particularly by Tibetans.

● **Janai Purnima** falls in August on the full moon of Shraaun and is centred on the Kumbeshwar temple in Patan. High caste Brahmins and Chhetri change the sacred red thread (*janai*) that they wear over their left shoulder and under their clothes. The festival also attracts shamans.

The **Gai Jatra** ('Cow Festival') follows the next day, to honour those who have died within the last year.

● **Teej**, celebrated in August/September, is a women's festival that begins with a feast and is followed by a day of fasting. Husbands are honoured and women take ritual baths at Pashupatinath in Kathmandu to cleanse themselves from the 'sin' of touching a man during menstruation.

● **Indra Jatra** This important festival marks the end of the monsoon in September. It lasts eight days and in Kathmandu there are mediaeval pageants and masked dances. Prithvi Narayan Shah conquered Kathmandu to unify Nepal during Indra Jatra in 1768 and this historic event is remembered during the festival.

An important part of the festival is the appearance of the Kumari, the 'living goddess' (see p120), in Durbar Square. She rides in a chariot to greet the image of the god Bhairab in Hanuman Dhoka, whereupon beer flows from a pipe between his teeth. To get a sip of this brings good luck.

Sherpa festivals

● **Mani Rimdu** is the popular three-day Sherpa festival held at Tengboche in November and at Thame in May. Monks perform ceremonies and dances, both serious and fun. It is a major social occasion.

● **Losar** (Tibetan New Year) is celebrated during mid-February. It is a time to receive new clothes (making them is a winter job) and put up new prayer flags.

● **Orsho** is a rite to protect the crops and takes place at the beginning of April.

● **Ch-rim**, to rid the land of evil spirits, occurs twice a year. The rite is enacted first after potato planting, then again after the harvest when the livestock returns from the summer pastures.

● **Dumji** is an important five-day festival that takes place during the monsoon, over the anniversary of the Khumbu's patron saint, Lama Sange Dorje. The gods are requested to subdue the evil spirits of the village. A group of eight families (different each year) lays on the feast. There are separate festivals in Namche, Thame and Khumjung.

FOOD

Dal bhaat is most commonly cited as the archetypal Nepali food, and it is almost universal around the country. Each ethnic group and geographic region has its own take on this basic meal of rice, lentils, greens, and vegetables, but standard flavouring is onion, garlic, ginger, and chilli, though in some places you're down to just chilli.

That said, dal bhaat isn't as universal as it's made out to be. In the Khumbu, potatoes form a major part of the diet of the Sherpas, and in many middle-hill areas carbohydrate comes in the form of wheat, buckwheat or millet *dhido*, a very filling polenta-like dish favoured after a hard day in the fields or on the trail. If you see someone plunging their fingers into a neon green puddle – it's *sisnu*, made from stinging nettles. Nepalis love meat but it's a real indulgence for most hill people.

The only really distinctive regional or ethnic cuisine is that of the Kathmandu Newars. It's full of rich, strong flavours and lots of herbs and spices, and includes many kinds of regular meat and organs, fermented bamboo shoots, and pancakes.

In Kathmandu

Eating habits are slowly changing. Tibetan momos (meat or vegetables encased in dough and steamed or fried) and a noodle soup known as *thukpa* are popular lunches. There is also plenty of decent tandoori and North Indian vegetarian food around. Unfortunately, the latest national dish is MSG-laden instant noodles, promoted by catchy jingles on radio.

Many cheaper travellers' restaurants offer an amazing variety of dishes, from Indian to Chinese, Mexican and Italian. Sometimes they are edible but the better restaurants tend to specialize in one type of cuisine only.

'Buff' (buffalo) steaks feature on many menus, the slaughter of cows still being outlawed in this newly, supposedly secular kingdom. Beef is available at some restaurants, imported from, of all places, India. The home-style cakes and pies available here are a real post-trek delight. For details see pp107-14.

DRINK

Be paranoid: all **water** should be treated (see p289) before it is safe to drink, especially in Kathmandu where you should not even use the tap water to brush your teeth. Mineral-water bottles are an environmental nightmare but there are few alternatives, as only the five-litre and 20-litre bottles are recycled.

Several **beers** are brewed in Nepal, some under licence from foreign companies; all taste similar and give hangovers. Cheap locally produced **spirits** are widely available; Khukri rum and the various whiskies are favourites. There's a widespread culture of home-brewing with a variety of grains but be careful with *chang* (fermented, 'beer') and *raksi* (distilled, spirit). The hangovers can be terrible and sometimes the dubious brewing conditions leave hangers-on in your gut too.

THINGS TO BUY

The souvenir shops in Kathmandu and Pokhara are stuffed full of carpets, crafts and knitwear, some of it well made but there's also some real tourist tat. It's best to do your shopping near the end of your trip, once you've had a chance to see what's available. Compare goods and prices in a number of shops and always bargain. The tourist shops in expensive hotels are not a good place for a bargain but they may have some high-quality goods.

Read Jeff Greenwald's *Shopping for Buddhas* for an amusing portrait of Western consumers in Nepal. If it's real antiques you're after note that you need an export permit for anything that looks as if it could be more than a hundred years old. For other 'antiques' a receipt from the shop will suffice as long as it contains a detailed description of the item. You should be aware that your own country will probably have some restrictions on the value of goods you import duty-free.

Clothes and sweaters Clothes shops sell the latest pseudo-hippy fashions (including loose-fitting cotton trousers, which are recommended) and they also do a good line in embroidery. T-shirts are emblazoned with everything from 'Tintin in Tibet' to 'I love Kathmandu'. Pashmina is a best buy, similarly woollen sweaters. They're hand knitted in attractive colours but need careful washing as they lose their shape easily. Garments and pashmina are a large export earner for the country.

Carpets The Tibetan carpet industry, started as a refugee relief programme in the early 1960s, expanded to become Nepal's largest export, but has now been overtaken by garment export. The industry has never really recovered from being banned by Germany due to child labour concerns that neither the government nor some of the companies were interested in addressing. Children are probably involved in the making of many other kinds of souvenirs sold in Nepal. Prices vary according to the number of knots per square inch – from about 50 up to 100 for the best quality. They're usually made from wool and colours are mainly pastel hues but there also are striped tiger rugs: these were once a trendy alternative to real tiger skins. Kashmiri traders have also opened shops in Nepal selling rugs in Kashmiri, Indian and Central Asian styles in silk or wool.

Thangkas Many shops specialize in these Tibetan religious paintings. They're bright, highly detailed and done on cloth but may not be quite as old as you're led to believe. Some thangka painters are also producing humorous modern paintings in this style. There are some good shops off Patan's Durbar Square as well as in Thamel and Pokhara.

Jewellery A wide range of jewellery is available but you have to know your gems or you could be fobbed off with glass. Silver filigree bangles, earrings and coral and turquoise necklaces are all popular. Strings of colourful beads are sold at the bead market in Kathmandu. Alternatively, you could have some earrings made up by a goldsmith in Kathmandu.

Trinkets and other souvenirs There's a wide range of interesting little souvenirs including attractive papier-mâché boxes and vases in Kashmiri shops, puppets, masks, Nepalese caps and incense sticks. Nepalese tea also makes a good present. Handmade paper is a traditional craft and you can buy block-print calendars, writing-paper and cards. There are also cloth-covered notebooks and photograph albums with traditional-style black paper leaves.

The streets of Thamel are thronged with boys hawking Tiger Balm, flutes and khukris. Some sell 'Nepali padlocks'. Made from brass in the shape of animals, these make unusual little presents. Thimi, near Kathmandu, is famous for its pottery and makes an interesting bicycle excursion but most pieces are too large and heavy to be convenient souvenirs.

Bargaining
Throughout Asia, bargaining is a part of life, although trekking exposes you to few situations that require bargaining. Most lodges have a menu with fixed prices that really are fixed – where you eat or stay is your choice. Buying at markets or from a farmer or hiring a porter may require some negotiation. As a foreigner (incredibly wealthy in comparison to most rural Nepalese) you start at a disadvantage and this will be utilized. Bargaining need not be aggressive – it's better to treat it as a game with smiles and jokes. Basically you are trying to agree a price that leaves you both happy. After a price has been agreed it must be honoured. Once the transaction is complete that is the end of the matter, all is forgiven and forgotten. Harbouring resentment comes across as a small-minded Western attitude.

SECURITY
Before you go
It is well-worth checking out the current travel and security situation and getting advice on the risks, even if the level of detail is sometimes off-putting. Most countries enable you to register online so your details are readily available, should you get into trouble when in Nepal.

British citizens should contact the Foreign and Commonwealth Office (🖳 www.fco.gov.uk), Americans the US Department of State (🖳 www.travel.state.gov/travel), Australians the Government Department of Foreign Affairs (🖳 www.smartraveller.gov.au), New Zealanders the Ministry of Foreign Affairs and Trade (🖳 www.safetravel.govt.nz/) and Canadians Foreign Affairs and International Trade (🖳 www.voyage.gc.ca/consular_home-en.asp).

In Nepal
Kathmandu is safer than most Western cities. Violent crime is virtually unknown and it is safe to take taxis, cycle and walk the streets and alleys at night, although women may be safer in a group.

Despite the relaxed atmosphere in hotels, staff are honest, rooms have barred windows and managers are security-conscious, keeping an eye on who goes in or out. In the cheaper hotels other travellers are a greater risk, if anything. The better hotels have security boxes for valuables and all will store luggage safely while you trek.

At bus stations be aware of the adept pickpockets. The usual ploy is to distract you with conversation or by pretending to be interested in your watch, or simply to rush and jostle as you board a long-distance bus. Pickpockets have a field day at busy festivals. Keep your money in safety deposit at your hotel or in a pouch or moneybelt and never let your camera and other valuables out of your sight.

In **Thamel** the nightlife has blossomed and so has the late-night trouble. After 11pm or so single women walking home have (rarely) been hassled, usually by Nepali guys that have followed them out of a club. Inside occasional fights erupt, often over young foreign girls who are acting naïvely, and pickpockets sometimes work the clubs so either leave valuables at the hotel or be extremely careful. The Thamel bars which close around 11pm or so and the chill out lounges are generally trouble-free; it is the nightclubs where things can happen.

The **trekking regions** were once crime-free but as the population is exposed to the wider ways of the world, occasional cases of theft now occur. Violent attacks are almost unheard of in the Solu-Khumbu. Trekking crews are trustworthy, although if you lend gear you might have to ask to get it back. In the crowded lodges during high season occasionally the odd thing goes missing, generally a camera or valuable trekking equipment, but in a quiet lodge things are absolutely safe.

You are incredibly wealthy by most rural standards so don't flaunt your gear or openly display large quantities of money and camera equipment. You should show that you value and care for all your belongings.

LUGGAGE STORAGE

Most hotels will store whatever you want to leave behind when you set off on your trek. Normally there's no charge if you'll be staying on your return. Do lock everything. The better hotels also have a safety deposit box.

PART 3: KATHMANDU

The city

Nepal's capital city (population around 800,000 million) is a fascinating mélange of mediaeval and modern that combines astounding beauty with appalling squalor and poverty. Time has stood still in parts of Kathmandu Valley. In the narrow alleys, around the numerous temples and shrines and along the banks of the (now filthy) Bagmati River people go about their daily lives in much the same way as their ancestors did hundreds of years ago. Yet, it is a city on the edge of disaster, the traffic is close to gridlock during rush hours and the air and water pollution are major public health hazards.

For first-time visitors to Asia, Kathmandu is a chaotic visual feast, but for long-term travellers who've journeyed up from India it's also a feast of a more basic nature. The city's restaurants, some of the best on the subcontinent, dish up pepper steaks and enchiladas, pad Thai and tiramisu. Budget accommodation, too, is good and can be better value than in the big Indian cities.

It's well worth setting aside at least a few days to see something of the city, and it can be a fun place to hang out for longer, as attested by the number of expatriate workers here.

HISTORY

Origins

The name Kathmandu is believed to be a corruption of Kasthamandap ('Square house of wood'), the 1000-year-old dharamsala (rest-house) that still stands in Durbar Square.

The first identifiable civilization in the Kathmandu Valley was that of the Kirats, who occupied a number of sites in the region in the second half of the first millennium BC. They were succeeded by the Lichhavi in the 9th century AD and the Malla in the 13th century. The settlements were centred around religious sites known as *piths* or power places, usually on the tops of hills.

Early urban planning

Kathmandu was a town of almost 2000 houses by the beginning of the Malla period (13th century), centred on Pashupatinath. Like the other two large towns in the Valley, Patan and Bhaktapur, it was an independent kingdom. Religion controlled not only the lives of the people but also the layout of these towns. Wandering through the chaotic maze of streets and temples in modern Kathmandu, it's difficult to believe that there has ever been any town planning here; but, in fact, centuries ago Hindu philosophy determined the design of whole towns based on the Vastupurusa Mandala, a complex layout in the shape of a square. This was composed of many smaller squares assigned to different deities and their temples. The main temple and palace, the centres of spiritual and temporal power, were symbolically placed at the very centre. Agricultural land surrounded each town.

Newar architectural heritage

The dominant culture in the Kathmandu Valley, until the unification of Nepal by the king of Gorkha in 1768, was that of the Newars. They are best known for their spectacular architectural legacy – the temples and palaces that surround the Durbar squares in Kathmandu, Patan and Bhaktapur. They built with brick, wood and tiles and are said to have invented the pagoda. Until the introduction of reinforced concrete in Nepal in the 1970s, Kathmandu was truly the Florence of the East. Visiting in 1959, Michel Peissel described the city as 'simply one vast work of art, from the humblest of the peasant's rectangular brick homes to the most impressive of the two-thousand-odd pagodas whose gilt roofs rise above the neat rows of houses. Each house, each temple, each shrine is deco- rated with delicately carved beams representing gods and goddesses, or animals drawn from reality and from fantasy, carved in dark wood that stands out against the background of pale pink bricks' (*Tiger for Breakfast*).

Rigid town planning did not allow for the enormous growth that has taken place in the area. Satellite towns were developed to house the growing popula- tion and these often became associated with a particular industry: Thimi, for example, is still a pottery centre. Most of the towns in the Kathmandu Valley did, however, manage to conform to their original plans at least until the time of the Ranas. Jung Bahadur, the first of this line of prime ministers, visited Europe in 1850 and introduced the bizarre neo-classical style of architecture exemplified in the vast whitewashed edifices that can be seen in various stages of dilapidation in the city. Large areas of agricultural land were taken over for their construction.

Modern Kathmandu

The real attack on the strongly inter-related cultural, social and religious frame- work of the Valley's urban centres did not, however, really begin until the 1950s after the restoration of the monarchy and the opening up of the country. Since the late 1980s the effects have been dramatic, though, and many parts of Kathmandu have degenerated into an urban sprawl of unsightly concrete and brick buildings. The district of Thamel, that today looks no different from tourist ghettos in other Asian capitals on the backpackers' route, was largely fields in the 1970s. Kathmandu Guest House (see p103), opened in 1968 to house Peace Corps volunteers, was the first hotel here.

Kathmandu today is plagued with the problems that beset all rapidly expanding, developing-world cities: overcrowding, severe pollution and traffic

(**Opposite**) **Top**: The stupa at Bodhnath (Baudha, see p121) is one of the biggest in the world and the centre of a large community of Tibetan Buddhists. **Bottom**: The interiors of Buddhist temples are decorated with murals often including fearsome temple protectors.

Living and travelling with shutdowns
Like most of South Asia (and Bangladesh in particular), *bandhs*, or enforced shutdowns, are a show-of-power political tool, and are annoyingly disruptive and of dubious effectiveness. A bandh can be called by any of the opposition parties (or student union proxies) and on occasion even by the party in power. With varying degrees of success they manage to close down shops and stop public transport and taxis from running for anywhere from one to three days. Some bandhs only affect transport, although all destroy the economy.

In Thamel you can find small grocery stores, restaurants and the odd cybercafé or even bar open on a bandh day, often in the evening. If you plan to go sightseeing and the bandh is especially successful you may have to walk all over town, though it is sometimes possible to get one of a handful of taxis that run with blacked-out licence plates, and tour companies also organize vans draped in huge banners proclaiming 'Tourist Only'.

There is an upside to all this: during bandhs, particularly during multi-day ones, the air clears up considerably and it is a real pleasure to roam the streets on foot or bicycle. Flights run on schedule and airline offices remain open, as do medical facilities and some government offices. For many Nepalis who don't have to live on a daily wage, a bandh is a welcome day off to catch up on chores, chit chat and soak up the sun.

congestion to name but a few. The population of the Kathmandu Valley now stands at 1.5 million, with a high growth rate of around five per cent.

ARRIVAL AND DEPARTURE

By air
Arrival Tribhuvan International Airport is a 20-minute drive from the centre of Kathmandu. Once off the plane you are led to the Arrival Hall and **immigration**. If you already have a visa look for the appropriate queue. If you need to get one, fill out a visa form (available in the hall or in advance from the internet) and line up at the queue for paying visa fees (see p83). You can pay in most hard currencies, cash only. You also need a passport photo: it's usually possible to get one here but it is better to bring one from home.

In the Arrival Hall there's a basic but cheap duty-free shop and a foreign-exchange counter or two. Once through Immigration head downstairs to the **luggage carousel** staffed by predatory porters for whom the money you give is never enough (although a dollar or equivalent should be plenty) and luggage carts designed to travel in every direction but straight ahead.

Customs don't generally offer problems for tourists, although you may be required to put all your luggage through an X-ray machine (they are looking for gold being smuggled in).

KATHMANDU

(**Opposite**) **Top**: Making momos (veg- or meat-filled dumplings, steamed or fried) in the kitchen of a lodge in Jorsale. **Bottom**: A typical double room in a trekking lodge: simple, clean and all you need for a good night's sleep after a day on the trail.

Through customs is the quiet main hall where the **tourist information booth** gives out free copies of *Travellers' Nepal* (in which the star-class hotels advertise heavily) and a free map of Kathmandu, both worth picking up. There's a **bank** open during the day. The **hotel-reservation counter** deals with reservations for star-class hotels and organizes a free taxi service. The **pre-paid taxi counter** organizes transport into town for around the rupee equivalent of US$6. Sometimes bargaining with the taxi drivers outside is slightly cheaper but often more hassle. There is no bus service.

Outside the building is a chaotic scene similar to any developing-world airport forecourt. Most of the people there work directly for a hotel so commissions are rarely involved. If you have a good recommendation for a hotel it is worth emailing them and their staff will meet you at the airport. Otherwise, taxi drivers will pull you every which way offering discount hotel rooms while boys eagerly try whisking away your luggage to another taxi. It is extremely rare for anything to be stolen but expect to have to tip: a dollar is plenty, or possibly coins from your home country (they collect them and then ask other tourists going home to buy them). There are also plenty of hotel representatives, with

Welcome to Thamel!

Arriving in Thamel leaves many travellers feeling as though they've been plunged into a three-ring circus plus freak show. Limbless beggars, mothers with crying babies, filthy urchins, and Tiger Balm vendors all beseech tourists. Drug dealers trail you whispering 'sssssmoke hassheeesssh??'; touts ('rafting? trekking?') pester you, and rickshaw or taxi drivers almost literally run you down. In amongst them all, to the tune of incessant horn-honking and see-sawing *sarangis* (see box p116), are the stick-wielding *chowkidars* (security guards) trying to maintain some order and keep the riff-raff out of the guesthouses and and restaurants.

Few things distress the first-time visitor more than the sight of the young street kids: all filthy faces, ragged clothes and outstretched hands. Like many things in Nepal, it's not quite what it seems. See the plastic bag many of them clutch to their face, repeatedly huffing and puffing? It holds model airplane glue. Most of the kids are glue-sniffers, a habit that burns out their brain cells. The glue is sold at every corner shop: any money you give will be used for their next buzz. Still, the endless pleading tugs at many a visitor's heartstrings. The tactic 'Buy them off with five rupees or a packet of biscuits – just so they'll leave me alone' creates instant monsters. Finding you an easy mark, the kids then hound you mercilessly for more. So what should you do?

If you spot a greying blond, blue-eyed Irishman darting about scolding the begging kids in Nepali, it's **Declan Murphy**, an activist who has been working with Thamel's street kids for six years now. His sincere, weary advice is: *'Don't give them anything at all.'*

'I can't expect a tourist visiting for two or three weeks to understand everything I've learned over the years,' Declan sighs. *'But every bit of food, money, or even attention you give to these kids just encourages them to stay on the street. The truth is, there are very few genuine orphans or hungry kids here in Thamel. Most of them are 'created' beggars – they dropped out of school and started hanging out in the tourist*

many offering a free taxi if you check out their hotel first. Travellers usually head for Thamel for budget to mid-range accommodation. Taxi-drivers recommend the marginally more expensive Thamel hotels (where they can sometimes get commission) but it's easy enough to find your own hotel once you have got rid of the taxi driver.

The several routes to Thamel pass through narrow streets lined with crumbling red-brick houses and shop after tiny shop. You know you've arrived in Thamel when, after driving by a few roundabouts, you see Westerners everywhere and the road ahead narrows to a jumbled mass of vehicles. This is as good a place as any to get out. Alternatively, ask for Kathmandu Guest House, to land yourself in the centre of it all.

Departure If you leave Nepal by air there is a departure tax of Rs1695 (Rs1356 for India and SAARC countries) which is payable in local currency only at the labelled bank counter. In the bank here you can reconvert rupees into hard currency. Alternatively you can dispose of surplus rupees at the shop in the corner of the departure hall that sells gift packs of tea and Coronation Khukri rum in exotic khukri-knife-shaped bottles.

---

district for fast money and handouts. Some have even been dressed 'dirty' by their parents and sent out to glean a bit of fast cash.' Your offering may make you feel momentarily generous, but it's hurting them in the long-run.

Look twice at those sari-clad mothers with hands outstretched, carrying infants – they also are not what they seem. Many have borrowed a baby from someone, for the specific purpose of begging. Residents have seen the same women for years, often with several different babies. Their favoured scam is to plead for the tourist to buy them 'milk – baby.' Then they cash back the unopened packets, and at several dollars a packet, this is far easier than collecting coins.

Lest all this sounds heartless, the elderly and extremely disabled are exceptions; in Nepali society they have few other options. Rather than government pensions as in the West, local culture includes a tradition of giving to the old and disabled. The able-bodied beggars, however, are professionals, many of whom weren't here just weeks ago: they have 'commuted' from peak tourist spots in India. The easiest way to deal with all this is just to ignore, and never make eye contact, perhaps give a polite 'no' and just keep walking.

If you want to do some good, reward the many hard-working people of Nepal with tips. Your hotel security guard stands some 12 hours a day for minimal wages, and watches tourists give handouts to the glue-sniffing wastrels. The cigarette seller on the corner, trying to support her kids with honest work, sees foreigners hand more than her day's salary to the begging 'rent-a-baby' mothers. Don't contribute to the perpetuation of the begging sub-culture. Donate instead to one of many worthy organizations including **Maiti Nepal** (🖳 www.maitinepal.com), which rescues young Nepali women from human trafficking rackets, or Declan's own **Just One** (🖳 www.just-one.org), which assists the kids long term to get their lives back on track in whatever way seems to suit their situation.

Help keep Nepal's children in school and off the streets. When tourists stop giving handouts, the 'street kids' will begin to disappear.   **Caroline Martin**

> **The phenomenon of a new tourist**
> Whether it is the smell, your ultra-clean clothes or simply your visible won-
> der at the density and chaos of it all, many shopkeepers, tiger-balm sellers and
> trekking touts know you are new to the city, and this is the time to beware. There are
> many sincere, good people struggling to make a living but there are also many who
> will take you for a ride, price-wise. Use your instincts. See also box pp98-9.

By land

Most **buses** terminate at the main bus station, north of the city. If you're coming
into Kathmandu by bus it's worth asking the driver to drop you off as near to
Thamel as possible. From the main bus station, however, there are frequent packed
Toyota Hiace mini buses (Rs12-15 plus the same for your large backpack) which
pass by the northern end of Thamel on their way to Ratna Park or the original bus
station near the clocktower. A **taxi** to Thamel costs the equivalent of US$4-5.

ORIENTATION

Greater Kathmandu, which includes Patan as well as Kathmandu itself, lies at
about 1350m/4428ft above sea level. The Bagmati River runs between these
two cities. The airport is 6km to the east, near the Hindu temple complex of
Pashupatinath, with the Buddhist stupa at Baudha 2km north of Pashupati. The
other major Buddhist shrine, Swayambhunath, is visible on a hill in west
Kathmandu. The third city in the Valley, Bhaktapur, is 14km to the east.

Within Kathmandu, most tourist hotels, guesthouses, and restaurants are to
be found in Thamel, north of the historic centre of the city, Durbar Square.
Freak St, the hippie centre in the '60s and '70s, is just off Durbar Square and
still offers some cheap accommodation. Some of the top hotels and the international airline offices are along Durbar Marg, which runs south from the modern
royal palace museum, scene of the grisly murders (see box p71) in June 2001.

WHERE TO STAY

Hotel areas

Most travellers find **Thamel** the most convenient area to stay in. This traveller's
haven has rooms to suit every budget, with over 100 guesthouses and hotels, good
restaurants, souvenir shops, bookshops, ATMs, communication centres and travel agencies. Away from this tourist scene are other areas: in the halcyon days of
the '60s and '70s when Kathmandu was a major stopover on the hippie trail,
Freak St, just off Durbar Square, was the place to hang out. Although the hash

> ❏ Some hotels and guesthouses 'specialize' by catering to particular nationalities,
> often with staff conversant in the appropriate language. Look for websites, signboards
> and business cards in Korean, Chinese, Japanese or Hebrew characters.

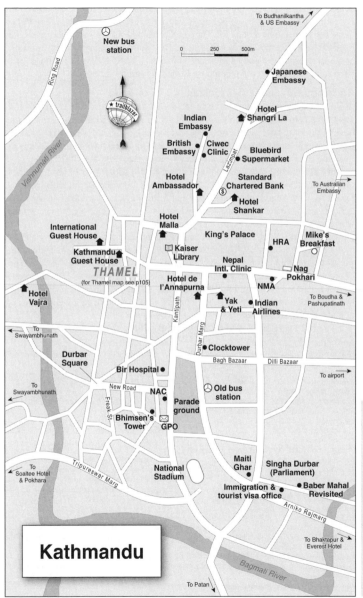

Kathmandu

To Budhanilkantha
& US Embassy

New bus
station

0   250   500m

Japanese
Embassy

Hotel
Shangri La

Indian
Embassy

British   Ciwec
Embassy   Clinic

Bluebird
Supermarket

Hotel
Ambassador

Standard
Chartered Bank

To Australian
Embassy

Hotel
Shankar

International
Guest House

Hotel
Malla

King's Palace

HRA

Mike's
Breakfast

Kathmandu
Guest House

Kaiser
Library

Nepal
Intl. Clinic

Nag
Pokhari

THAMEL
(for Thamel map see p105)

NMA

Hotel de
l'Annapurna

Hotel
Vajra

To Boudha &
Pashupatinath

Yak
& Yeti

Indian
Airlines

To
Swayambhunath

Durbar
Square

Bir Hospital

Clocktower

Bagh Bazaar

Dilli Bazaar

To airport

To
Swayambhunath

New Road

NAC

Old bus
station

Parade
ground

Bhimsen's
Tower

GPO

To
Soaltee Hotel
& Pokhara

Tripureswar Marg

National
Stadium

Maiti
Ghar

Singha Durbar
(Parliament)

Immigration &
tourist visa office

Baber Mahal
Revisited

Arniko Rajmarg

To Bhaktapur &
Everest Hotel

Bagmati River

To Patan

Ring Road

Vishnumati River

Lazimpat

Kantipath

Durbar Marg

Freak St.

trailblazer

KATHMANDU

dens are now closed the area retains a timeless charm. Its five or so hotels and restaurants are all in the rock-bottom to cheap bracket. Across the bridge in **Patan** there are two budget hotels off Durbar Square and also a few good upmarket hotels. The less central areas of **Boudanath ('Boudha')** and **Swayambhunath**, home to two of the Valley's most recognizable UNESCO World Heritage sites, have some simple hotels favoured by Buddhists and travellers.

Rock-bottom places (US$5/£2.80/€3.45 or less)

In Thamel there are around 40 places to choose from in this bracket, and though most have common baths, in some you'll get an attached bathroom. A few hotels have triple- or quad-bed rooms. Check that the toilets and hot water work (though hot water will rarely be available 24 hours), and try to get a room that faces away from the roads – Kathmandu is plagued by noisy dogs and honking taxis.

In this category, you will find bare-bones accommodation with few amenities: often places do not provide towels, toilet paper, or room service. In recent years, a few of the lower-end budget places have unfortunately downgraded into 'massage parlour' arrangements. Clean and bright lobbies, family-staffed operations, women working behind the front desk, an active notice-board, and a shelf-full of travel guides are some indicators of places catering to genuine travellers. A few of the old rock-bottom stalwarts off Thamel Chowk have been nearly subsumed by store fronts offering hippie clothes and hand-made paper goods, but they're still there. There are clusters of cheap guesthouses: on Z Street (pronounced 'Zee') – now a sort of Freak Street North; on a small hillside adjoining Z Street called Paknajol; in Narsingh Chowk (the alleys behind Pumpernickel Bakery); on lower Jyatha; and in Chhetrapati, an area adjoining Thamel to the south.

The following are **keyed to the map on p105**:

Acme GH (470 0236; acmeguesthouse.com)
Cherry GH (425 0675)
Classic Down Town GH (217 4349; b2magar@hotmail.com)
Cosmic Hotel (470 0415; hotelcosmic.com)
Deutsch Home (470 0989; allnepaltour@gmail.com)
Eco 2000 (470 0213; eco_hotel@hotmail.com)
Family Peace GH (438 1138; peace_family@hotmail.com)
Global Hotel (425 8320)
Green Lotus Inn (425 8996)
Happy Home GH (691 0479; happyhomeguesthouse.com)
Himalayan KTM Peace GH (426 2597; dhrubakmshrestha@yahoo.com)
Holyland GH (443 3161; lodgenepal.com)
Iceland GH (470 0686; icelandgh@yahoo.com)
Kathmandu City GH (426 0624)
Ktm Garden House (438 1239; hotel-in-nepal.com)
Ktm Holiday Inn (423 3892)
Ktm Peace GH (438 0369; peaceguesthouse.com)
Khangsar GH (426 0788; khangsar@wlink.com.np)
Laughing Buddha Home (442 5056)
Legend Highlander (425 9086)
Lhasa GH (422 8019)
Lily Hotel (470 1264; kajbabu26@hotmail.com)

Lucky GH (9841-831607)
Mt Annapurna GH (422 5462; raj_kumarb@hotmail.com)
Mt Holiday (425 3555; emholiday@gmail.com)
Mustang GH (470 0053; mothersland.com)
My Home (425 7111; salilbasu@wlink.com.np)
Namche Nepal (441 7067; hotelnamchenepal.com)
New Dhaulagiri GH (470 0761; nwdhaulagiri@yahoo.com)
Nirvana Peace Home (438 3053; nirvanapeacehome.com)
Om Tara GH (425 9634; bhim15@hotmail.com)
Over There GH (470 0129; surendra21st@gmail.com)
Planet Hotel (422 0258; hotelplanet.com.np)
Poon Hill Hotel (425 7666; visitnepal.com/poonhill)
Potala Hotel (470 0680; potalahotel.com)
Puskar Hotel (426 2956)
RP GH (441 3881; htlredplanet@wlink.com.np)
Red Planet (470 0879; redplanet_thamel@hotmail.com)
Royal Gorkha GH (426 6602)
Seven Corner Hotel (470 0405; hotel7corner.com)
Shangri La GH (425 0188; shangrilathamel.com)
Shiva's Damaru GH (425 9928)
Souvenir GH (441 0277; souvenirguesthouse.com)
Student GH (425 1448; studentgh@htp.com.np)
Tibet Peace GH (438 1026; tibetpeace.com)

Trekker's GH (219 1318)
Visit Nepal Hotel (435 8362)
Yak Lodge (425 9318; yakreslodge@yahoo.com)

Yellow House (438 1186; theyellowhouse2007@g
mail.com)
Yeti Guest Home (470 1789; yetiguesthome.com)
ZZang (aka Jjang) (4701536; nepal-jjang.com)

Hotels in Thamel

Most Thamel hotels offer a range of room prices and features – from bare-bones simplicity to a few luxury rooms with all the extras. In all rooms, clean sheets and blankets should be evident; the better ones will also supply towels, 24-hour hot water, room service, phones, toilet paper and perhaps carpeting. Little features to check: is there a vent or window in the bathroom, a clothes line and a rooftop or terrace garden? Features aside, when choosing a hotel, go by the reception staff – are they friendly and helpful or lackadaisical? Do the lobby and rooms look and smell clean, or are they stuffy and musty?

There are plenty of hotels in every direction. However, the centrepiece is the long-running *Kathmandu Guest House* [65] (see p106), a Thamel landmark with a wide range of room prices, which is bursting in the high season. A good alternative is the cluster of clean, quiet and budget-to-moderate hotels down an alley towards Chhetrapati, including *Tibet Guest House* [98].

Budget hotels (US$6-20/£3.40-11.20/€4.20-13.80)

The following are **keyed to the map on p105**:

Ambassador Garden Home (under construction in 2008)
Annapurna GH (441 7461; annapurnaguesthouse.com)
Blue Diamond (422 6907; hotelbluediamond.com.np)
Buddha Hotel (441 3366)
Diplomat Hotel (426 7798; hoteldiplomat.com.np)
Discovery Inn (422 9889; hotel_discoveryinn@ya
hoo.com)
Dolphin Guest House (442 5422; dolphinguesthouse.com)
Down Town Hotel (470 0471; hotel-downtown-
nepal.com)
Easy Hotel (470 1462; hoteleasy@yahoo.com)
Elite Hotel (422 7916; hotelelite@hotmail.com)
Encounter Nepal (444 0534; encounternepal.com)
Excelsior Hotel (425 7748; excelsiornepal.com)
Florid Nepal (470 1055)
Garuda Hotel (470 0766; garuda@mos.com.np)
Great Wall (425 3543; hotelgreatwallnepal.com)
Greeting Palace (441 7212)
Hana Hotel (442 4683; hotelhana.com.np)
Heera Hotel (425 9671; annapurna_t@yahoo.com)
Holy Lodge (470 0263; holylodge1983@live.com)
Horizon Hotel (424 8738; hotelhorizon.com)
Impala Hotel (470 1549; hotelimpala.com.np)
Imperial GH (424 9339; imperial_guesthouse@ya
hoo.com)
Jagat Hotel (425 0732; jagathotel.com.np)
Karma Hotel (442 5476; hotelkarma.com)
Lucky Star Hotel (443 7569; hotelluckystar.com)
Marco Polo GH (425 1914; marcopolo@wlink.com.np)
Millennium Inn (426 2013; millennium@mail.com.np)
NamTso Hotel (425 1238; namtso4h@wlink.com.np)
Nana Hotel (470 1960; nana@info.com.np)
New Gajur (422 6623; taishan88zst@yahoo.com.np)

Newa GH (441 5781; newagh.com)
Norling GH (424 0734; hotelnorling.com)
Pilgrim's GH (444 0565; pilgrimsguesthouse.com)
Pisang Hotel (425 2540; hsitaula@wlink.com.np)
Pokhara Prince (424 9579; omshantiok@yahoo.com)
Potala GH (422 0467; potalaguesthouse.com)
Potala Tourist Home (441 0303; potalatourist
home.com)
Prime Hotel (426 0855; hotelprime.com.np)
Prince GH (470 0456; princeguesthouse@hotmail.com)
Pyramid Hotel (424 6949; trip-nepal.com)
Shakti Hotel (441 0121)
Shree Tibet Hotel (470 0902; sritibet@wlink.com.np)
Si Hai Hotel (423 8109)
Siesta House (9851022200; siestaguesthouse.com)
Silver Home (426 2986; hotelsilverhome.com)
Sun Rise Cottage (425 6850; src@mos.com.np)
Sweet Dream Hotel (470 1880; sweetdreamthamel
@yahoo.com)
Tashi Dhele Hotel (425 1720; tashidhele1@hotmail.com)
Tashi Dhargey Inn (470 0030; hoteltashi
dhargey.com)
Thorong Peak GH (425 3458; thorongpeak.com)
Tibet GH (426 0383; tibetguesthouse.com)
Tibet Himalayan GH (422 5319; tibethimalayan.com)
Utse Hotel (425 7614)
Villa Everest (441 1593)
White Lotus (424 9842; hotel_whitelotus@hot
mail.com)
Wonderland Inn (441 8197; wonderland@eco
mail.com.np)
Yanki Hotel (425 6851; hotelyanki.com)

KATHMANDU

> ❏ **Hotel receptions are not trekking companies**
> Many of the budget hotels pressure new arrivals into booking a trek at reception. Naturally this involves a hefty commission usually to the detriment of the services, and some hoteliers will tell outright lies ('it is impossible to find the way, there are so many trails') in their attempts to get you to sign up. Move hotels if they don't desist.

ACCOMMODATION IN THAMEL

61 Acme GH
76 Ambassador Garden Home
29 Annapurna GH
122 Blue Diamond
70 Blue Horizon
23 Buddha Hotel
67 Centre Point
92 Cherry GH
59 Classic Down Town
14 Cosmic Hotel
16 Courtyard Hotel
64 Deutsch Home
132 Diplomat Hotel
115 Discovery Inn
28 Dolphin GH
53 Down Town Hotel
19 Easy Hotel
46 Eco 2000
129 Elite Hotel
27 Encounter Nepal
79 Excelsior Hotel
2 Family Peace House
15 Florid Nepal
121 Fuji Hotel
51 Garuda Hotel
80 Global Hotel
111 Great Wall Hotel
108 Green Lotus Inn
24 Greeting Palace
39 Hana Hotel
93 Happy Home GH
110 Heera Hotel
87 Himalayan KTM Peace GH
120 Holy Himalaya Hotel
52 Holy Lodge GH
40 Holyland GH
95 Horizon Hotel
20 Iceland GH
8 Impala Hotel
116 Imperial GH
55 International GH
133 Jagat Hotel
41 Karma Hotel
101 Kathmandu City GH

65 Kathmandu GH
3 Kathmandu Garden GH
106 Kathmandu Holiday Inn
4 Kathmandu Peace GH
103 Khangsar GH
26 Laughing Buddha Home
78 Legend Highlander
125 Lhasa GH
18 Lily Hotel
134 Lucky GH
11 Lucky Star Hotel
34 Malla Hotel
7 Manang Hotel
47 Mandap Hotel
74 Marco Polo GH
10 Marshyangdi Hotel
56 Millennium Inn
127 Mt Annapurna GH
102 Mt Holiday Hotel
50 Mustang GH
119 Mustang Holiday Inn
89 My Home
88 Nam Tso GH
22 Namche Nepal
63 Nana Hotel
13 Nature Hotel
48 New Dhaulagiri GH
128 New Gajur Hotel
75 Newa GH
96 Nirvana Garden Hotel
1 Nirvana Peace Home
31 Norbu Linka Hotel
130 Norling GH
60 Northfield Hotel
107 Om Tara GH
66 Over There GH
25 Pilgrim's GH
90 Pisang Hotel
123 Planet Hotel
100 Poon Hill Hotel
113 Pokhara Prince
77 Potala Hotel
105 Potala GH
69 Potala Tourist Home

82 Prime Hotel
58 Prince GH
83 Puskar Hotel
94 Pyramid Hotel
71 RP GH
62 Red Planet Hotel
91 Royal Gorkha GH
38 Samsara Resort
57 Seven (7) Corner
32 Shakti Hotel
117 Shangri-La GH
84 Shiva's Damaru
45 Shree Tibet Hotel
126 Si Hai Hotel
112 Siesta House
114 Silver Home
35 Souvenir GH
73 Student GH
97 Sun Rise Cottage
12 Sweet Dream Hotel
85 Tashi Dhele Hotel
42 Tashi Dhargey Inn
104 Tayoma Hotel
9 Tenki Hotel
37 Thamel Hotel
86 Thorong Peak GH
98 Tibet GH
124 Tibet Himalayan GH
72 Tibet Holiday Inn
6 Tibet Peace GH
54 Tradition Hotel
81 Trekker's Guest Home
131 Utse Hotel
44 Vaishali Hotel
33 Villa Everest
17 Visit Nepal Hotel
118 White Lotus
68 Wonderland Inn
109 Yak Lodge
99 Yanki Hotel
5 Yellow House
49 Yeti GH
21 ZZang Hotel ('Jjang')

> ❏ The Kathmandu **area code** is 01. If phoning from outside Nepal dial +977-1 for landline phones. Mobile phone numbers all start with 98; from overseas dial +977 98.

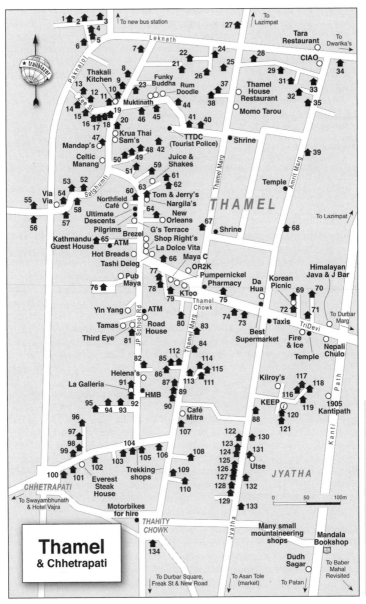

To new bus station

To Lazimpat

To Dwarika's

Leknath

Tara Restaurant

CIAO

Paknajol

Thakali Kitchen

Teen St

Funky Buddha

Rum Doodle

Thamel House Restaurant

Momo Tarou

Muktinath

Krua Thai

Sam's

TTDC (Tourist Police)

Shrine

Mandap's

Celtic Manang

Juice & Shakes

Saghumti

Temple

Via Via

Northfield Café

Tom & Jerry's

Nargila's

New Orleans

THAMEL

To Lazimpat

Ultimate Descents

Pilgrims

G's Terrace

Shop Right's

Shrine

Brezel

La Dolce Vita

Kathmandu Guest House

ATM

Hot Breads

Maya C

Himalayan Java & J Bar

Tashi Deleg

OR2K

Pub Maya

Pumpernickel Pharmacy

Korean Picnic

Da Hua

KToo

Yin Yang

ATM

Thamel Chowk

Tamas

Road House

Taxis

To Durbar Marg

Third Eye

Best Supermarket

Fire & Ice

Nepali Chulo

Temple

Helena's

La Galleria

Kilroy's

HMB

KEEP

1905

Kantipath

Café Mitra

Everest Steak House

Trekking shops

Utse

JYATHA

Kanti

CHHETRAPATI

To Swayambhunath & Hotel Vajra

Motorbikes for hire

THAHITY CHOWK

Many small mountaineering shops

Mandala Bookshop

Dudh Sagar

To Baber Mahal Revisited

Thamel
& Chhetrapati

To Durbar Square, Freak St & New Road

To Asan Tole (market)

To Patan

KATHMANDU

0   50   100m

Moderately priced hotels (US$20-40/£11.20-22.40/€13.80-27.60)

There are numerous hotels in this price range, most of them with an in-house restaurant. All rooms have attached bathrooms with hot water; the better rooms feature satellite TV and perhaps an air-conditioner and heater. Some hotels in this price range have a few de luxe rooms. Their online rates might be higher; try contacting them direct for better tariffs. Once again, a little bargaining can go a long way if they're not full and it's out of season.

The following are **keyed to the map on p105**:

Blue Horizon (442 1971; hotelbluehorizon.com)
Centre Point (444 4399; hotelchangcheng.com)
Courtyard Hotel (470 0476; hotelcourtyard.com)
Fuji Hotel (425 0435; fujiguesthouse.com)
Holy Himalaya Hotel (426 3172; holyhimalaya.com)
International GH (425 2299; intguesthouse.com)
Kathmandu GH (470 0800; ktmgh.com)
Mandap (470 0321; hotelmandap.com)
Mustang Holiday Inn (424 9041; mustangholiday.com)

Nature Hotel (470 0822; hotelnature.com)
Nirvana Garden (425 6200; nirvanagarden.com)
Northfield (470 0078; hotelnorthfield.com)
Tayoma Hotel (424 4149; tayomahotel.com)
Tenki Hotel (470 1483)
Thamel Hotel (442 3968; hotelthamel.com)
Tradition Hotel (470 0217; hoteltradition.com)
Tibet Holiday Inn Hotel (441 1453; hotelgnr@col.com.np)

Three-star standard/four-star hotels (US$30-160/£16.80-90/€21-110)

(See also box opposite) Around the three-star standard are two well-managed hotels built in traditional Nepali style. *Hotel Vajra* [see map p101] (☎ 427 1545, 🖳 www.hotelvajra.com) was conceived and paid for by a Texas billionaire, and built by Newar craftsmen, with wall-paintings by Tibetan and Tamang artists. Rooms range from luxurious with private terrace to budget rooms with washbasins and shared bathrooms. It is located near the culturally Buddhist area of Swayambhunath. The traditionally decorated *Summit Hotel* (☎ 552 1810, 🖳 www.summit-nepal.com) in the Kupondole Heights area of Patan is popular with expeditions seeking a peaceful location. Both Summit and Vajra have a tranquil atmosphere, attractive gardens, restaurants and amenities such as massage – and in Summit's case, even a swimming pool.

Close to each other in north Thamel are *Hotel Marshyangdi* [10] (☎ 470 0105, 🖳 www.hotelmarshyangdi.com) and *Hotel Manang* [7] (☎ 470 0121, 🖳 www.hotelmanang.com): both are popular with trekking groups. A few blocks away in a more secluded area is the Tibetan-themed *Hotel Norbu Linka* [31] (☎ 441 0630, 🖳 www.hotelnorbulinka.com). *Hotel Vaishali* [44] (☎ 441 3968, 🖳 www.vaishalihotel.com), tucked away in a relatively quiet corner, is Thamel's first four-star hotel. Travel agents can offer substantial discounts. *Samsara Resort* [38] (☎ 441 7711; 🖳 www.samsararesort.com), Kathmandu's only designated 'Smoke-Free Hotel,' is located down its own lane round the corner from the Vaishali. Travel agents can offer substantial discounts.

Five-star hotels   [also see map p101]

The closest five-star hotel to Thamel is the newly renovated *Hotel Malla* [34] (☎ 441 8385, 🖳 www.hotelmalla.com), right on Thamel's edge at Lainchaur and very convenient. *Hotel Yak and Yeti* (☎ 424 8999, 🖳 www.yakandyeti.com) has a world-famous name and good Durbar Marg location, but is other-

wise nothing special. The nearby *Hotel de l'Annapurna* (☎ 422 1711, 🖳 www
.annapurna-hotel.com), just down the block from the erstwhile Royal Palace, is
similar. In **Lazimpat**, a short taxi ride or a 20-minute walk from Thamel, are
Shangri-La (☎ 441 2999, 🖳 www.hotelshangrila.com) with its idyllic
Shambhala Garden, and the *Radisson* (☎ 441 1818, 🖳 www.radisson.com/kath
mandune), with its rooftop pool and Splash Bar. If proximity to central
Kathmandu is not a priority, the *Hyatt Regency* (☎ 449 1234, 🖳 www.kathman
du.regency.hyatt.com), a 20-minute taxi ride away in the Tibetan area of
Boudha, is an excellent choice. Set amongst acres of garden, it's walking dis-
tance from the famous Boudhanath Stupa.

Away from Durbar Marg, in an area called Gaushala, is probably the best hotel
in Kathmandu: *Hotel Dwarika's* (see box p110; ☎ 447 9488, 🖳 www.dwa
rikas.com), a true heritage hotel. If Kathmandu is a living museum, this is the ultimate place to experience it. Every room (US$175/180) is an individual work of art.
Even the swimming pool is created in the fashion of a traditional Newar fountain.

WHERE TO EAT AND DRINK

Kathmandu's days as a remote mountain outpost are long over. One can easily
fill days and nights in sophisticated coffee shops (most with Wi-fi), restaurants
and go club-hopping – without even leaving Thamel.

With liberal licensing, all restaurants serve alcohol, and smoking is allowed
(only a few places have smoke-free areas). Many places also have garden terraces, which suits the temperate climate. This is real Asia too: there are few
truly quiet, peaceful places.

Prices are reasonable, certainly by Western standards, although added taxes
(see box below) mean it is not the value it once was. In the better Thamel restaurants main courses are mostly $3-6, a litre of water less than $1, a large (650ml)
bottle of beer $3 and a glass of wine $3.50, all excluding tax.

For those on a strict budget, eating for $2 a meal is becoming a challenge;
some places in that range are dangerously dire.

Taxes and tipping

Tax and service charges increase hotel and restaurant bills by around 25% in
the better places, as the otherwise negligent government drags business into
the modern world. There is a 13% VAT (value-added tax) charge which is added to
hotel bills and is sometimes included in restaurant menu prices, but sometimes not.

A more recent addition is a 10% service tax, an automatic tip, which is shared
among all employees including kitchen staff. It also covers incidental costs (such as
broken dishes), with a portion of the tax going directly to the union office itself. This
was part of a Maoist-inspired union package that also limits working hours, but is
mostly only enforced in the better (tourist) restaurants.

Do check your bill: if there is a 10% service charge (SC), I suggest that is
enough, unless the service was truly exceptional. For places without a service charge,
understand that basic wages are dismal and not enough to support a family. Tips really make a real difference to their quality of life. Small change amounting to approximately 5-10% of the bill is appropriate.

> **Hygiene alert**
> Be especially careful about what you eat before you set out on your trek; you're much more likely to pick up a stomach bug from dirty Kathmandu water than in the hills. A test on the quality of the tap water in Thamel showed it to contain more than ten times the WHO recommended safe maximum level of faecal matter. **Don't even brush your teeth in tap water (yes, it is that bad)**. The better restaurants are serious about hygiene with all kitchen water filtered, but don't believe all restaurants that tell you their salads have been soaked in iodine.
>
> If you have only a few days in Thamel before your trek and are concerned about hygiene, I suggest sticking to these central time-tested restaurants: *New Orleans Café*; *Northfield Café*; *La Dolce Vita*, *Roadhouse*; *La Galleria*; *K-too!*; *Kilroy's*; *Yin Yang* and *Pumpernickel Bakery*.
>
> The jury is still out on eating **salads**. I think they are safe in the above-listed places; some insist you should play it safe and avoid them everywhere.

Unless otherwise indicated, the restaurants described are in Thamel (see map p105), but there are good restaurants in nearby neighbourhoods: **Durbar Marg** is walking or cycle-rickshaw distance from Thamel and services the business and five-star hotels there (each with a 24-hour casino). **Lazimpat**, the diplomatic area, is a walk to the north, and a bit decentralized; it's home to expats and several embassies.

A taxi ride south across the Bagmati will take you to **Patan** (Jawalakhel, Pulchowk, Sanepa) which is littered with NGO and INGO compounds, expats and up-market neighbourhoods, and restaurants to serve them. Patan has a surprising variety, particularly on Pulchowk's growing 'Restaurant Row.'

Breakfast, brunches, lunches

Most hotels and guest houses offer a mediocre breakfast or snacks, either as room service or in their own dining room. Outside, you'll get a better selection. Try *Pumpernickel Bakery, Brezel Bakery* and *Hot Breads*, with their selection of cinnamon rolls, apple strudel, cakes and also muesli. All have a terrace and are cheap, and usually quick, and good for a quick lunch snack too.

For a bigger choice and all cooked options, *Mandap's* has a bakery and imported Illy coffee. *Helena's* has breakfast specials and an extensive view from its high (seventh floor) roof terrace.

For a leisurely meal in the open air a few places merit special mention: *New Orleans* has perhaps the best yogurt and their *Mexican Morning* and *Eggs Hollandaise* are matchless. *La Galleria* has the best coffee (see opposite), good fruit and their *Ultimate Omelette* is just that, even if they only have a small balcony terrace. *Northfield Café*, in a large garden, also has good fruit and free coffee refills, and the pancakes come with endless syrup.

Coffee

Caffeine corporates such as Starbucks have yet to arrive in Nepal but superb European-style café coffee is available, in the form of Illy and Lavazza. Some baristas are trained; all serve a selection of teas as well.

Himalayan Java brought coffee culture to the area, using fresh Nepali-grown beans, with cakes, cookies, sandwiches and salads in a comfy lounge indoors or out on the noisy terrace. It's a popular Nepali Saturday and after-work hangout.

La Galleria with fantastic Illy coffee is smaller, with an upbeat, modern feel and superb food. Both serve decadent cold coffee creations (such as Iced Mocha).

Chikusa has a friendly coffee counter, which boasts of its 'real' brewed and ground coffees, as well as sandwiches and meals. On a hot day, the iced coffee made with frozen coffee ice cubes delivers an outstanding buzz. No doubt by the time you read this more spots will have sprung up.

Quick eats

If Thamel is lean on anything, it is places to fill up in a hurry. McDonald's, KFC, Pizza Hut and the other fast-food chains that have infested neighbouring Asian countries are thankfully still absent.

La Galleria features grilled panini sandwiches or wraps served with a smile and a side of fries. You can grab a falafel plate and various sandwiches at *OR2K. Hot Breads'* spinach-mushroom quiche can be microwaved and eaten on the run, or upstairs. Their strawberry tart (in season) will bring you back. Opposite is *Shop Right's bakery*, but it doesn't have a terrace. *Pumpernickel's* sandwiches are good too.

Western & Continental meals

K-too! is a cheerful beer and steak house with a sports-bar vibe. A great no-brainer is the toasted minute steak 'Bookmaker'; they also have full-flavoured onion, anchovy & spinach quiche and to go with the large screen TV is a decent range of bar snacks.

For a refreshingly different menu and great atmosphere don't walk past *New Orleans*; it's down an alley opposite Pilgrim's Books. Try their *Jambalaya* (chicken or veg) or for a lighter meal spinach rice & steamed vegetables. A true 'resto-bar', a White Russian made with blended ice cream will even do as a dessert. *Helena's*, in its own seven-storey building, is an everything good, nothing outstanding place; main dishes cost Rs155-355.

Many places have **steaks** on the menu, which in traditionally Hindu Nepal is usually buffalo steak, of an ordinary cut. It's often served as a 'sizzler' and arrives in front of you on a heated cast-iron plate with sound effects to match. You can ask whether the featured steak is 'beef, or buff'.

Wine
Wine has arrived in the Valley, with most of the better restaurants serving both by the glass and by the bottle. Avoid the cheaper French and Italian wines – the Australian, Chilean and South African wines tend to be pleasantly drinkable, and readily available in some Thamel corner shops. *Kilroy's* has the best variety but no restaurant has a sommelier.

The enduring *Everest Steak House's* speciality is a wide range of real beef fillet steaks from, of all places, India. If you have the appetite of a yeti, try the Rs1650 Chateaubriand (it's better split between 3-4 people), or the half-order for Rs950. In this Chhetrapati restaurant, there are virtually no vegetarian dishes.

G's Terrace is a Western-Nepali joint venture with a diverse range of cuisine, including authentic Bavarian. Try the *Schwabischer Zwiebelrostbraten* (special roast beef) at this pleasant roof-top restaurant which features live bands some evenings. Another Kathmandu institution is *Rum Doodle*, famed more for its displays of historic Everest summiteer signatures than the food, but it is one of the very few places that offers mashed potatoes. Try lemon grilled chicken or the Rum Doodle BBQ. During winter enjoy a real fire without guilt: the logs are made from crushed rice husks.

Kilroy's has an original, rich menu and competes to be the finest restaurant in Thamel. For a starter try chargrilled market vegetables. Their *Royal Dal Bhaat* is truly regal, as the former King and Queen of Nepal ate here. Irish stew and even a Beef and Guinness hotpot give away the Chef's heritage. Lunchtime sandwiches (including smoked salmon) are good value. For a more intimate atmosphere, *Café Mitra* offers nouvelle cuisine with its petite portions and a romantic setting.

Venturing outside Thamel, the five-star hotels have some excellent Western-style restaurants. One of the best is at the *Hyatt* in Boudhanath, and similarly modern is the Radisson. *Yak & Yeti* (a great name) is better for specialty functions than food.

Nepali & Newari

There are many cheap Nepali places in Thamel that serve the local standards – dal bhaat or momos – usually for less than Rs150. *Thakali Kitchen* upstairs on the corner of Z St stands out for cleanliness and value (refillable 'dal bhaat thali' meals Rs85 veg, Rs135 non-veg). Next door to Funky Buddha is the very similar *Muktinath Thakali Kitchen*. Tour groups often go for a Nepali banquet experience, which is actually mostly Newari food. These restaurants seek to recreate a complete traditional Newari dining experience – an historical re-enactment complete with period utensils, seating and staff in national dress, many include traditional folk song and dance in the package.

Thamel House has perhaps the largest traditional Nepali menu in the neighbourhood. Set in a renovated 100-year-old Newar building, it's the only one of

Dwarika's

Worth the taxi ride for a special occasion is the heritage hotel Dwarika's (in Gaushala, a little off the road to the airport). It's a bit like dining in an open-air museum. The late Dwarika Shrestha devoted his life to collecting the rapidly vanishing woodcarved masterworks that traditionally adorned local houses, then built this hotel to house them. The result is almost a world unto itself.

Krishnarpan (just one of their restaurants) offers a lavish, traditional Nepali-Newari meal ranging from 6 to 22 courses; you must book in advance (☎ 447 0770).

its kind in Thamel. Nepali khasi (boneless mutton) is Rs165: order separately or go for a set menu. A great accompaniment is tomato achaar, a traditional boiled tomato sauce, which is rarely found on menus. They also have a popular range of fish dishes: the grilled trout is superb and good value too at Rs195. Main dishes start from Rs180; the nine-course set meal costs Rs695.

Heading out of Thamel, at Baber Mahal's *Baithak* in their grand long gallery, portraits of royals past stare down as you feast on recreated 'delicacies from the Rana court.' Main dishes are Rs500 and the set dinner, the Maharaja's Feast (Rs945), is recommended. Advance booking is required (☎ 426 7346).

An elegant, ceremonial dining Nepali experience is offered by *Krishnarpan*, inside the heritage hotel **Dwarika's** (see box opposite).

Bhanchha Ghar in Bagh Bazaar (near Durbar Marg) offers wild pork or dried deer meat to accompany drinks and the dinner menu is similarly exotic. *Nepali Chulo* (Tridevi Marg at Kantipath), in an old Rana mansion, is an easy walk from Thamel, immediately past the long wall of Phora Durbar, the American Club. Both offer cultural shows with folk music and dancing.

Tibetan

While Tibet is not generally known for its cuisine, *momos* (meat or veg dumplings) are now the quintessential Nepali fast food. To venture beyond momos, the best-known Tibetan place is *Hotel Utse*. A plate of momos is under Rs100, or try *thenthuk* or *thukpa* (home-made noodle soups). Their Tibetan banquet, suitable for 5-6 people, requires a few hours' advance notice. For a real authentic Tibetan experience, ask for salted butter tea (*sol cha*) with some sawdust-like *tsampa* (roasted barley flour).

The informal *Tashi Deleg* is a great place to go for all of the above, or to get toasted on *Tungba* (millet-based Tibetan beer, served in a distinctive metal container resembling an oil can). See also Yangling p113.

Indian

Decent North Indian food, as well as its relaxing tatami room in back, has made *Third Eye* popular but *Mandap's* is more consistently delicious, even if the menu is limited and pricier. Try the spicy (but not chilli hot) Yogurt Chicken or Palak Paneer (spinach with homemade cottage cheese): go with friends to try more dishes. Those craving quality **South Indian** dosas will have to venture outside Thamel – the brightly lit *Angan*, next to Bluebird Supermarket in Thapathali has the self-serve ticket system, and serves superb 'pure veg' *dosas*, *idlis* and *uttapam*. Closer to Thamel is the cheap and cheerful South Indian snack spot *Dudh Sagar* (Kantipath); it is a pity that *Pilgrims*, through the bookshop, is rather ordinary.

Italian

Many restaurants serve pizza and pasta, but one stands way above the rest. *Fire & Ice Pizzeria & Ice Cream Parlour*. Run by an Italian woman who imported her own computer-controlled Moretti Forni pizza oven, some of the best pizzas on the subcontinent are turned out here. Prices range from Rs210 to Rs350. *Ciao* (formerly Marco Polo's) on the edge of Thamel near Malla Hotel also has

KATHMANDU

a dedicated following for its wood-fired pizzas and home-style pasta dishes, and offers parking. Back in central Thamel *La Dolce Vita* and *Roadhouse* deliver wood-fired pizzas at two-thirds of the price, with good pasta and variety.

Cha Cha is a quirky Japanese-owned pasta joint, hidden away down an alley near Kilroy's with only seven seats along the counter. The meals in this tiny spot are prepared in front of you – literally. Neopolitan Carbonara is Rs170 for normal size, Rs 245 for large.

Chinese

Most cheaper 'do-everything' restaurants have spring rolls and chowmein on their menus, usually unmemorable. Better to try the Chinese-run places, which seem to be multiplying. The *New China Town Restaurant* is good, sometimes excellent but inconsistent.

Probably the best Chinese restaurant is the *Imperial Pavilion* at Malla Hotel, just north of Thamel. *Da Hua* (upstairs on Amrit Marg, Thamel) is an informal, clean, cheap 'n' cheerful Chinese.

Thai

Yin Yang, next door to Third Eye, is one of Thamel's best restaurants, with its authentic Thai chef and fragrant outdoor garden. Their Phad Thai for Rs210 is the most consistent and best, and with the curries you have a choice of heat. They also have a range of Western cuisine and their pastas in particular are good value. Most dishes are available in their vegetarian varieties. *Krua Thai,* near Mandap's is an old Thamel favourite, with excellent curries too.

Japanese

Tucked away upstairs in corners of Thamel are a surprising number of small Japanese places, all radiating quality and cleanliness. Tea and warm towelettes greet you; the dishes are works of art. If you're unfamiliar with the cuisine, photo-menus help you decide. Servings tend to be smaller, so are good for a lighter meal. The informal *Momo Tarou* (Bhagawati Bahal) is great value and serves sushi and imported Asahi beer.

Round the corner, off Thamel Chowk, *Itta* and *Okufuro No Aji* have more extensive menus. *Lotus Coffee Gallery* on Jyatha is a neighbourhood counter restaurant which doubles as a Thangkha gallery without the hard sell.

Korean

The helpful photo-menus simplify ordering; everything is accompanied by a side dish of the obligatory *kim chee* (spicy pickled cabbage). *Korean Picnic* (off Tridevi Marg, near Himalayan Java) is astounding value, a clean, informal place run by Nepali women. The nearby *Villa Everest*, attached to the Korean-orient-ed hotel of the same name, has an outdoor garden. *Hankook Sarang* (near the Third Eye) is cheap and popular for Korean-style sushi set (called Kimbebap).

Mexican

Northfield Café is the only place for a tostada. The Californian owner has brought some excellent Tex-Mex into Thamel; try the enchiladas (chicken or veg). *Mike's Breakfast* in Naxal (a taxi ride) also serves a Mexican selection.

Vegetarian/Middle Eastern

With its Day-glo murals, floor-cushion seating and trance music, *OR2K* is a trippy scene of its own. It's also one of the few dedicated vegetarian restaurants. Catering to Israelis, there is falafel (Rs135) and a hoummus plate (Rs110), but also pasta, pizza, salads, Thai curries and their own creations such as cauliflower pie (Rs190) – all good value. They also serve breakfast.

Celtic Manang is another chill spot; mostly vegetarian, with salads, sandwiches and brown rice available. See also Nargila's below.

Juices/smoothies

The tiny, innocuous *Just Juice and Shakes* down the alley heading to Hotel Red Planet is a favourite with Thamel insiders. Their secret? Using frozen fruit and yogurt, rather than ice, to make incredibly thick, cold shakes. A sublime coffee-banana-chocolate shake is Rs65, and they were innovators with one of the first cappuccino machines in town.

Ultra cheap

Over on Freak St, a handful of restaurants offer main courses that start for about US$1 and top out at around US$2. *Chameleon Diner, Ganesh Restaurant* and *Cosmopolitan* are all that remains of the street's heyday. *Snowman* remains but now serves only sweets (see Desserts, below). *Organic World & Fair Future* is a new community-based venture featuring all organic coffees and teas, baked goods and pizza.

Back in Thamel, restaurant prices are higher, but there are still places a budget traveller can get a clean, filling meal. At the long-running *Tashi Deleg,* many items are Rs100-150, and steaks are around Rs200. *Nargila's* is good value, and popular with Israelis for its middle Eastern food: a plate of falafel with pita, tahina and salad is Rs105. *OR2K* (see above) is also good value.

There are many local momo and dal bhaat spots often with added parasites as an invisible bonus. The hygienic places are *Yangling* (near Satgumthi) for budget Tibetan, and *Thakali Kitchen* (see p110) where the menu includes an unusual selection of local liquors.

Desserts

After a long trek there's often space in your stomach for a substantial dinner *and* dessert. Harking back to Kathmandu's hippy heritage, *New Orleans'* sweet updates are delicious, from the Dutch-inspired apple pie to the solid carrot cake. *La*

Baber Mahal Revisited

The crumbling stables of a Rana palace near the Singha Durbar parliament building have been transformed, with help from the Kathmandu Valley Preservation Trust, into a chic shopping and dining enclave that wouldn't look out of place in Beverly Hills. There are some exclusive boutiques, art galleries and a handful of classy restaurants, including the expat favourite, *Chez Caroline*. Caroline's has an elegant, eclectic continental menu with extensive desserts, including creme caramel, flourless chocolate cake, homemade ice-creams and sorbets.

Galleria serves the best New York-style cheesecake. *La Dolce Vita's* tiramisu, served in a cocktail glass, is the best in Thamel, but perhaps the finest sweet in the area is *Kilroy's* lemon tart. The skill Thomas Kilroy gained making over 20,000 lemon tarts in Bermuda shows in these delightful desserts; one may not be enough. On Freak St, where people really know their munchies, *the* place is the long-running *Snowman*. The wall murals and lanterns haven't changed since its colourful hippy past, and the desserts are still astounding value at Rs40 for a slice of chocolate banana cake, apple crumble, Black Forest cake or lemon meringue pie. If you're craving **ice-cream** there is no Ben & Jerry's or Haagen-Dazs, but a banana split or the brownie sundae from *Northfield* might hit the spot. *Fire and Ice's* soft serves have a classic choice of toppings. By the scoop, there is *Pumpernickel's* homemade style and a Baskin-Robbins ice-cream bar in *Roadhouse*.

NIGHTLIFE

Thamel has become the nightlife centre for all Kathmandu, with the fashionable young Nepali middle class partying alongside travellers. Hot spots can roughly be sorted as loud rock 'n' roll bars, traditional pubs, chill-out lounges, and discos.

Rum Doodle Restaurant & 40,000^{1}/2ft Bar is a Kathmandu institution, where yeti footprints inscribed by the members of many a mountaineering expedition (the 40,000^{1}/2 'feet') adorn the walls. It's a good place to catch stories at the end of the expedition season over a hot rum punch.

Live music
In Thamel this generally means deafening rock bands doing 1960s-70s classics, plus a bit of Pearl Jam. It's hard to ignore the thump between 7pm and 11pm within the 'Miracle Mile.' *G's Terrace, Reggae Club, Funky Buddha, Lhasa* and even the tiny *Full Moon* all regularly feature live rock 'n' roll, with Nepali musicians playing credible covers of everything from AC/DC to U2.

Trance and techno have made their forays, with internationally known DJs from places like Ibiza, London and Mumbai making appearances at places such as *Funky Buddha* or *Electric Pagoda*. Look for event flyers in the telltale 'trippy' script. For acoustic sounds, there are jazzy fusion/jam sessions with sitar, guitar, vocals or tabla at open-air places like *New Orleans* and *Jatra*. In particular, Sunday nights at New Orleans have set the standard for fusion jams.

Jazz Upstairs, with live jazz and cheap drinks, is a bohemian hangout straight out of vintage Greenwich Village. Wednesdays and Saturdays are the most 'happening' nights; entrance Rs200. It's hidden opposite the French Embassy in Lazimpat. *Via Via,* part of a small international network of backpacker way-stations, has a long-standing Open Mike Night every Friday. With its laid-back aura and library of travel guides (very clearly marked 'Stolen From Via Via' to prevent theft) it's otherwise a great place to lounge and read up on your next destination.

The **Alliance Française** and **Russian Cultural Centre** occasionally sponsor a play, jazz night or film festival; details are listed in the City section of local dailies. The 5-star hotels put on big theme parties well advertised in the papers.

Pubs

Tom & Jerry's (aka 'Thamel Base Camp') is an institution – noisy and popular, with pool tables and satellite TV. *Full Moon, Buddha Bar, Pub Maya, Tongues 'n' Tales* and *Maya Cocktail Bar* are all neighbourhood stalwarts.

Sam's Bar is a friendly local old-style pub with small outdoor terrace and ingenious retractable roof for monsoons and winters, it is opposite Mandap's, upstairs. Round the corner, *Funky Buddha* is larger, an all-rounder with bar, dancefloor, outdoor garden and juice bar, featuring trance DJs Fridays, hip-hop and live music other nights.

Chill-out lounges

These are the millennium version of the '70s Kathmandu hash dens, featuring capacious couches and a mellow, conversational, trendy ambience where locals mix with the international crowd. You're equally welcome to party, or to pass out.

Comfort Zone is a spacious rooftop lounge run by a Korean couple. There's a good BBQ, the best, most generous cocktails in Thamel, jazz-oriented music with large screen video, and Monday night movies. *Tamas*, set in a renovated Rana mansion, the luxurious Tamas (Sanskrit for 'relaxation'), verges on decadence. Room after room of couches unfold with a variety of intimate or 'open' spaces. Himalayan Java is a coffee house by day, but evenings find it transformed into *J-Bar,* a small but de luxe lounge upstairs inside the Java complex on Tridevi Marg. Open Tuesday-Sunday 6-11pm.

Electric Pagoda's cozy bar opens onto a garden setting. A newcomer to the neighbourhood, it's set in another traditional Rana-era house round the curvy street known as Satghumti (Seven Corners). The music is mostly trance and there is a 'pass-out room.' *Full Moon*, with its intimate floor cushion seating was an early trendsetter and remains popular with lounge lizards. There's no dance-floor in this tiny bar but food is available.

Funky Buddha's garden, lounge and psychedelic murals qualify it for the Chill-out category, with an underground feel. They also serve food, and are open quite late on weekends (see Nightclubs below).

If you're jet-lagged and want to hit the town from 11pm to 4am, look for the #1905 'bowling alley' sign on Kantipath: *Saturdays at 1905 Kantipath* features relaxed drinks and dining (lunch and dinner daily).

Nightclubs

Most of the disco dance floor action is outside Thamel, Nepali crowds. Typically there is a cover charge (entrance fee).

One of the most happening places is *Club Platinum* (inside Yak & Yeti Hotel, Durbar Marg). Like its name, it's sleek and shiny; it's open nightly.

Funky Buddha's upstairs disco comes alive at the weekend – thumping trance music and hip-hop goes on well into the wee hours. The garden terrace and downstairs lounge offer crash-friendly spaces.

Fire Club, in the heart of Thamel by Kathmandu Guest House, has an edgier scene with a large hip-hop oriented dance floor. It's one of the few truly late-night spots (to around 5am at weekends). The sleek *J-Bar* (inside Himalayan

KATHMANDU

Java) is open Tue-Sun 6-11pm, with dancing on Fridays in this small but trendy spot: it's very popular with stylish young Nepalis.

In the sunken garden of a vintage bungalow *Saturdays at 1905 Kantipath* becomes an all-night outdoor party on Saturdays in the trekking season (Mar-Apr and Sept-Nov). There is a modest cover charge: you can party till dawn.

With lurid signboards and names like Pussy Cat, Krazy Girl, and Striptease, 'shower bars' have mushroomed in recent years; there are dozens around Thamel. 'Shower bar' is a euphemism for what's basically a strip joint, and they add to Kathmandu's dubious reputation as a growing centre for sex tourism. At the time of writing there were no controls in place to prevent exploitation of either dancers or patrons. However, it is likely a stronger government will crack down on them.

Casinos

The five-star hotels all operate 24/7 casinos. If you flew into Nepal recently you're entitled to Rs100-worth of free coupons if you show your air ticket.

ENTERTAINMENT

Dohori

A folk music tradition, Dohori is a lyrical challenge match, a sort of call-and-response courtship ritual in which men and women alternately tease one another in lighthearted song. Mixing flirtation with social commentary, it's very popular with working Nepalis. Though most performers in Thamel are professionals, there's some spontaneity and even audience participation. Try **Gambesi Dohori Nachghar**, or **Pokhara Dohori Nachghar**, next door to one another on Tridevi Marg near Himalayan Java. Singing starts around 7.30pm and continues till past midnight; no entrance fee.

Cinema

Current shows for **Jai Nepal** and **Kumari Cinemas** are listed in the local English-language papers. Along with Bollywood hits, they show select Hollywood blockbusters ('English movies'). Note that some shows sell out, shows are typically at 6.30pm, with late shows (9pm) only on weekends. Kumari is a taxi ride away while Jai Nepal, past the old Royal Palace and Durbar Marg, is a 15-minute walk from Thamel.

Starting at a more convenient 8pm, **Kathmandu Guesthouse's** cozy (about 25 seats) in-house cinema is a modest Rs100. The reception noticeboard displays the evening's feature. In season in the early evening, the Guesthouse

> ### Thamel's Sarangi sellers
> Part of the regular cast of Thamel Street Theatre are the *sarangi* vendors. Many are members of the Gandarbha (musician) caste, who were formerly guaranteed employment at traditional functions, or serenaded on long-distance buses prior to loud stereos. With the modern break-down of the caste system, they have turned to making, playing and selling the *sarangi* (folk violin sounding a great deal like a country fiddle) for tourists. Some have CDs of their own music for sale too.

also hosts **Chris Beall's slide shows** which cover the main trekking regions of the country. He's a professional photographer and lecturer and the slide shows offer good unbiased advice for trekkers about to head into the hills and are well worth the ticket price.

SERVICES

Banks
Larger hotels can change money at reception, and around every corner in Thamel are authorized moneychangers.

There are **automatic cash dispensers (ATMs)** all around central Kathmandu. In Thamel the most convenient machines are in the Kathmandu Guest House courtyard, in front of the reception of the Garuda Hotel and adjacent to the Roadhouse Café. There have been no reports of theft or muggings around ATMs but use your judgment at night. There is a withdrawal limit of Rs40,000 (a little under $600) per transaction set by the machines, but the limit for your card might be set lower by your bank.

Depending on your bank system at home, you can also withdraw in person from banks, either in rupees or travellers' cheques, but not in foreign currency. Sometimes the amount is unlimited, sometimes it's limited by your bank. The most convenient **foreign-exchange counter** in a bank is the branch of Himalayan Bank, in the same building as Fire & Ice, but the place is often chaotic. The Standard Chartered branches on Lazimpat and Nabil on Kantipath are convenient too, and the branch of Nepal Investment Bank on Durbar Marg is open 365 days a year, though only from 9am to noon at the weekend and on public holidays.

Bookshops Kathmandu has some of the best bookshops on the subcontinent, including second-hand shops where you can trade in your novel for another.

International papers and magazines The *International Herald Tribune*, *USA Today*, and the *Asian Wall Street Journal* are sold everywhere as are magazines including *Time*, *Newsweek*, *Fortune*, *The Economist*, *Stern* and *Der Spiegel*. Once it was all news, but now you don't have to miss much at all with fashion magazines such as *Cosmopolitan* and *GQ*, and car and computer magazines also on the stands. There's a plethora of Nepali magazines, many advertising tourist-orientated services and interests.

Tourist police?
Set up to help tourists, this one-roomed office is where you report incidents of theft so you can get a police report for insurance purposes. The trouble is they often doubt you and will not provide complete reports. That may sound ridiculous but there is little you can do other than insist on seeing a superior or gently insist they do their job properly. They have zero interest in actually solving crime. They are located in Bhrikuti Mandap, the same building as the Tourism Board and Department of Tourism, but right around the back.

> ❏ **Embassies**
> For a handy list of the foreign embassies in Kathmandu see 🖳 www.embassiesabroad
> .com/embassies-in/Nepal
> ● **Australia** (☎ 437 1678, 🖳 www.nepal.embassy.gov.au), Bansbari
> ● **China** (☎ 441 1740, 🖳 www.chinaembassy.org.np), Baluwatar
> ● **France** (☎ 441 8034, 🖳 www.ambafrance-np.org), Lazimpat
> ● **Germany** (☎ 441 6832, 🖳 www.kathmandu.diplo.de), Gyaneshor
> ● **India** (Consul, ☎ 441 0232, 🖳 www.south-asia.com/Embassy-India), Lainchaur
> ● **Israel** (☎ 441 1811, 🖳 www.kathmandu.mfa.gov.il), Bishramalaya House, Lazimpat
> ● **New Zealand** (Honorary Consul ☎ 441 2436, 🖳 www.nzembassy.com), Dilli Bazaar
> ● **Russia** (☎ 441 2155, 🖳 www.nepal.mid.ru), Baluwatar
> ● **Sweden** (☎ 422 0939, 🖳 www.swedenabroad.com), Khicha-pokhari
> ● **Thailand** (☎ 437 1410, 🖳 www.thaiembassy.org/kathmandu), Bansbari
> ● **UK** (☎ 441 0583, 🖳 www.britishembassy.gov.uk/nepal), Lainchaur
> ● **USA** (☎ 441 1179, 🖳 www.nepal.usembassy.gov), Pani Pokhari

Communications

There are **internet cafés** everywhere; before you start just check how grimy the keyboard is. The rates are around Rs30-40 an hour. Many internet cafés also offer **internet phone services** but the quality is random, although so are calls through the monopolistically expensive **Nepal Telecom** service.

There are an increasing number of **wi-fi** connections around Thamel, a few still free but most are better-quality paid services.

Most **home-country mobile phone services** work but SMS messages are sometimes received 20 times. A **local SIM card** is available at any corner shop with their sign. Prepaid cards start from Rs500, with GPRS and EDGE services and even internet, if your phone is capable. You can call overseas and receive calls but most **SMS messages** don't seem to get through.

For parcels, in addition to the post office (GPO), a 25-minute walk south of Thamel, you have the choice of **cargo agents** scattered in Thamel who will reliably send your stuff through international couriers – at a price – as well as air freight bigger consignments.

Medical clinics

CIWEC (☎ 442 4111, 🖳 www.ciwec-clinic.com; Mon-Fri 9am-4.30pm) is an exceptionally competent clinic located between the British and the Indian embassies, a ten-minute walk or a five-minute taxi ride from Thamel. Consultations cost US$49 or equivalent in any currency and they also have a new dental clinic there too.

The long-running **Nepal International Clinic** (NIC; ☎ 443 4642, 🖳 www .nepalinternationalclinic.com; Sun-Fri 9am-1pm and 2-5pm) is also good. A first consultation costs US$45 or equivalent; a follow up is US$25. Consultations on Saturday are between 3pm and 5pm: callout ($75) is also possible. It's 200m east (ie continuing away from Thamel) from the main Durbar Marg Palace gate. CIWEC and NIC are the best places to ask if hospital or specialist attention is required, and are two of the few places that take Visa and MasterCard.

There are a couple more convenient and slightly cheaper clinics in Thamel. Try **Himalayan Traveller's Clinic** (☎ 426 3170, after hours ☎ 437 2857), on the edge of Chhetrapati, or **Himalaya International Clinic** (☎ 422 5455, daily 9am-5pm) virtually next to Hotel Norling in Jyatha. Some **pharmacies** also have a doctor in attendance, especially in the evening. There is one slightly down from Hotel Manang, and more along in Chhetrapati.

The closest 24-hour hospital with emergency facilities is in fact right on the northern edge of Thamel, **Manmohan Memorial hospital** (☎ 442 0822, ☎ 441 1605), down Lekhnath Marg. All the doctors speak English but the facilities are fairly basic. For **dental problems** try **Healthy Smile** (☎ 442 0800) on Lazimpat, opposite Ambassador Hotel, or the new CIWEC Dental Clinic, opposite their medical clinic. In both the dentists are competent and experienced and have been trained overseas.

With all clinics there are additional charges for medicines and lab services.

TRANSPORT

The Kathmandu traffic is always a nightmare and is reaching the point of grid-lock during the 9-10.30am and 4.30-6.30pm rush hour. Avoid travelling at these times if you can.

Catching metered **taxis** for sightseeing, visiting exotic restaurants and office hopping is the easiest option but it really helps to know the area name (rather than street name); ask your hotel reception staff to write it down. Just hop in, tell them where you want to go (for example, 'Bhrikuti Mandap jaan-hos') and check they turn the meter on once moving. Even if the meter is some-times rigged, this is often better than bargaining first. There is a special night rate, also on the meter, between 9pm and 6am.

Ruthlessly driven Toyota Hiaces compete with electric three-wheeled **tempos**, which are a mix of electric SAFA tempos (*safa* means 'clean' in Nepali), and petrol-engine versions. There are no route maps or any easily visible way of working out where the vehicles are going. As a tourist, taxis are usually easier.

Cycle rickshaws seem to be favoured by the really drunk who in turn are loved by the rickshaw wallahs – perhaps because Rs500 notes look similar to Rs10 notes! Make sure you arrange a price before you go. They are useful for getting to Durbar Square but are not suitable for finding Swayabunath or other places that are up hills or far away.

KATHMANDU

Kathmandu Environmental Education Project (KEEP)
Raising environmental awareness among trekkers and the trekking industry, KEEP is a real treasure trove. The **information centre** (☎ 421 6775, 🖥 www .keepnepal.org; 9am-5pm; see map p105) near Kilroy's features log books filled with comments from previous trekkers, which are perhaps the best source of up-to-date information. The documentary *Carrying the Burden* made by the BBC is shown at 2pm each day and is well-worth watching. Also consider buying *Pocket First Aid and Wilderness Medicine*, an amazingly concise tome and a must for the serious trekker.

Bicycles can be pleasant during strikes, on Saturdays (when the traffic is lighter) and for exploring outside the city. There are Indian clunkers, copy mountain bikes and good mountain bikes for rent in Thamel; see p38.

Be sure you are comfortable riding in Asian traffic before even contemplating riding a **motorbike** here. There are no real road rules that are followed so intersections are a dangerously confusing mess. Give way and forgive. Helmets are compulsory.

WHAT TO SEE AND DO

A virtual living museum, the Kathmandu Valley is crammed with sights and scenes and it's well-worth setting aside several days to take some of them in. The most popular attractions are mentioned below. Aimless wandering through the narrow streets also has its rewards. Amongst the colourful confusion you'll come upon numerous temples, stupas and other holy places. Most hotels and travel agents can arrange custom **sightseeing tours**. To get the most from these ensure you will be accompanied by a qualified guide. For a small group half-day guided tours cost around US$20-50 each, depending on entrance fees.

Durbar Square First stop on the Kathmandu sightseeing trail is Durbar Square, also known as Hanuman Dhoka. This complex of ornately carved temples and monuments includes: the old royal palace (closed Tuesday; entry Rs250); the Kumari Bahal (the home of the Kumari, the 'living goddess', a young girl chosen as the incarnation of the Hindu goddess, Durga); the Kasthamandap (the wooden pavilion from which the city's name is said to have been derived); and the tall Taleju temple, built in the 16th century. The best time to be here is early in the morning when people are going about their daily pujas.

There is an entrance fee of Rs200 to get into the square. Whilst this has raised complaints from travellers, nobody should begrudge paying – the entire square has, after all, been declared a World Heritage Site by UNESCO and vast funds are required to restore and maintain the many buildings.

Having paid the fee, visit the offices at the southern end of Durbar Square (to the west of the entrance to Freak St, behind the souvenir market) to pick up a free **Visitor Pass**. Bring one passport photo and your passport. You can then visit Durbar Square as often as you like for free for the rest of your stay.

Swayambhunath From this huge stupa on a hill in the west of the city, the all-seeing eyes of the Buddha overlook the entire Kathmandu Valley. It's also known as the Monkey Temple and dotted around it are several other shrines and temples. There's a pilgrims' rest house, a Buddhist library and gompa (Buddhist temple) as well as a Hindu temple dedicated to the goddess of smallpox.

Behind on a smaller hill is a favourite temple for children, dedicated to Saraswati, the goddess of learning. Walking (half an hour from Thamel) through the colourful streets is the most pleasant way of reaching the hill.

Pashupatinath Beside the sacred Bagmati River, this is one of the most revered Hindu temples on the Indian subcontinent. Entry to the main temple is barred to non-Hindus but there are numerous other shrines in this large religious complex. Dedicated to Shiva – the destroyer and creator – stone linga fertility symbols are everywhere. Cremations take place on the banks of the river, providing a morbid tourist attraction.

You'll see lots of sadhus, saffron-robed holy men, who perform various feats here (including rock-lifting – with their penises no less!). Pashupatinath, on the eastern outskirts of Kathmandu, is easily reached by bike or taxi.

Bodhnath (Baudha) One of the largest stupas in the world, Bodhnath is surrounded by a thriving Tibetan community. Prayer wheels line the mandala-shaped base. These must be turned clockwise, the direction in which you should always walk around the stupa.

There are lots of souvenir shops as well as Tibetan restaurants and a few guesthouses. Around sunset it's particularly atmospheric. Close by are a variety of Tibetan gompas. Leave a small donation when visiting.

Patan Once a separate city-state, this ancient historical centre is now a southern suburb of Kathmandu. It's an architectural feast, at the centre of which is Durbar Square. Temples abound and it is best to explore on foot or by bicycle.

The outskirts of the town are beautiful and semi-rural, the most desirable residential area for wealthy Nepalese and expatriate staff.

Bhaktapur Compared with Kathmandu and Patan, the other cities in this mediaeval trio, time has stood still in Bhaktapur. Wandering round the narrow streets and temple-filled squares is fascinating and schoolboys act as surprisingly knowledgeable guides, though they'll want some baksheesh (Rs100 or so, though they'll try for more). Staying here overnight, especially during a festival, is well worthwhile. It's 14km from Kathmandu and you can get here by taxi, minibus or trolley-bus. You can also cycle here although the pollution is horrific. Hiring a mountain bike to combine with a steep ride to Nagarkot makes for an adventurous expedition.

Nagarkot Perched on the eastern rim of the encircling hills, the Himalaya from the Annapurnas to Everest are visible from Nagarkot on a clear morning. It's a popular overnight excursion though the exploring possibilities on foot or by mountain bike warrant more time. There are plenty of cheap lodges, and buses from Bhaktapur leave every hour or so. Overnight and early morning sunrise tours are easily arranged by travel agents or with a taxi driver. Close by is **Dhulikhel**, another favourite viewing spot. Just off the Arniko Highway, this is also easily reached.

Dakshinkali Sacrificial blood flows freely on Tuesdays and Saturdays for the goddess Kali at this temple. Like hungry hyenas, tourists jostle to take red-splashed photos and a few turn vegetarian. It is 20km from Kathmandu, an uphill cycle ride. Alternatively, buses leave from Martyrs' Gate, just east of the post office in Kathmandu.

Budhanilkantha Reclining on a bed of huge coiled snakes, this image of Vishnu, the creator, was carved from a single block of stone and is most impressive. It is often called the Sleeping Vishnu.

Budhanilkantha is north-west of Kathmandu and it is definitely worth visiting on a mountain-bike trip: alternatively, ask locals where to catch a bus. There is no entrance charge yet.

GETTING TO THE KHUMBU

By air

The popular Lukla tourist sector is flown by a handful of airlines, with Yeti Airlines (🖳 www.yetiairlines.com) offering the most flights a day; it is also generally the most reliable. Other airlines also work although you are better to avoid the inefficient and corrupt (but safe) state-run Nepal Airlines Corporation (NAC; formerly Royal Nepal Airlines. There is no e-ticketing system yet for domestic airlines in Nepal but you can book online and then pay on arrival in Kathmandu. This system may improve by the time you read this.

If you are already in Kathmandu it is a question of finding who has space, a job best left to a travel agent or trekking company. It is better to book well in advance but even if you book a day before it is usually possible to find seats.

Schedules and fares   Airline tickets are priced in US$ and cannot be paid for with Nepalese rupees. The flight timetables are approximate only (take a magazine), but as a rule flights start from early morning: the first flights are from 5.30am to 6.30am, depending on sunrise times, to get the clearest weather. Flights continue in the morning and there is the occasional afternoon flight, but these tend to be less reliable. In December and January ground fog often delays flights to mid-morning. The fares for different airlines for the same sector are all similar. There are no early booking discounts and return fares are double one-way fares, although discounting on this is starting. Only double-sector flights are cheaper than adding the two single sector fares together. There is a (possibly temporary) insurance and/or fuel surcharge on most tickets. A departure tax of Rs165 is payable at the airport for all domestic flights.

Sample fares excluding surcharges are: **Lukla** US$109 (return $198); **Tumlingtar** US$89; **Biratnagar** US$108; **Phaplu** US$103; **Syangboche** charter helicopters only; **Mountain flight** US$140; **Pokhara** US$86.

Nepalis (such as your trekking crew) get significantly cheaper fares (eg Lukla Rs2355, Phaplu Rs2090 and Tumlingtar Rs2810, plus surcharges) so getting tickets for them is sometimes more difficult when the flights are nearly full as airlines refuse to take them.

By bus

Most bus rides are long and uncomfortable but stops are made for meals. Roadside stalls sell biscuits, fruit, sweets and soft drinks. Restaurants serve little more than dal bhaat and instant noodles and are not always clean. It's wise to be cautious, especially at the start of your holiday. Buses for Jiri, Dolakha and Barabise still use the central bus station near the clocktower, not the bus station north of Thamel. See the route guide sections for bus information on getting to Jiri pp228-30: Dolakha-Singhati p262 and Leguwa on p247.

For the Salpa-Arun and Leguwa Ghat–Tumlingtar see pp247-8.

PART 4: THE EVEREST REGION

Mountaineering history

EVEREST

Meantime let us count our blessings – I mean those thousands of peaks, climbed and unclimbed, of every size, shape and order of difficulty, where each of us may find our own Mt Everest. **IIW Tilman** *Mount Everest 1938*

The search for the world's highest mountain
In 1808 the Survey of India began the daunting task of mapping the whole of the subcontinent. One of the goals was to discover if the Himalaya was indeed the highest mountain range in the world, as had previously been suspected. Already challenging, the project was made even more difficult by the fact that Nepal and Tibet, wary of foreign intervention, were closed to outsiders.

By 1830 the survey had reached the border between India and Nepal. Unable to cross into Nepal, surveyors resolved to continue the project from the plains. A baseline the length of the range was marked and in 1847 surveying of the northern peaks began, using trigonometrical calculations based on the heights and distances of known points. Conditions were terrible: malaria was rife and monsoon rain eroded the observation towers each year.

Until the mid-19th century it was thought that Kanchenjunga, in Sikkim, at about 28,000ft (8534m), was the highest peak in the range. In 1856 calculations published by the Survey of India revealed that a mountain on the border between Nepal and Tibet was higher. This mountain was designated 'Peak XV' and its height stated to be 29,002ft (8839m); Kanchenjunga was 28,156ft (8582m).

The accuracy of this first survey is astounding considering the fact that the mountains were measured from survey points between 108 and 150 miles away from the peaks. In their calculations surveyors had to take account of the earth's curvature and the changing air density, which bends light. They also waited 18 months for perfect conditions and good visibility, with the pollution from all the wood fires used in cooking often obscuring the views.

The generally used height of Everest is just 26ft (less than 9m) higher than their estimates, at 8848m/29,028ft, a figure produced by an Indian survey taken in Nepal in the 1950s. It's interesting to note that when National Geographic made their much lauded 1:50,000 map of Everest, instead of re-measuring the mountain they used its accepted height as a base for all the other altitudes on the map. However, there is controversy over whether this height is that of the mountain including the hard ice on its very top or just the rock base. In 2006 the Chinese measured again and, excluding an allowance for the summit ice, came up with a figure of 8844m (29,015ft). A GPS reads as high as 8866m (29,087ft) on the snow summit.

The naming of Everest

It was not until 1865 that Peak XV was named. The accepted method of naming peaks at the time was to use the local name if one could be found. The first map of the area, made in the 1700s, marked this peak as **Tschoumoulancma** but the Surveyor General, Andrew Waugh, chose to name Peak XV **Mount Everest** after his predecessor, Sir George Everest, who oversaw the great survey of India.

This appropriately grand appellation stuck in the West but Tibetans and Sherpas have always used a variation of the name used on the 18th-century map. The Dalai Lama, giving permission for the 1921 Reconnaissance Expedition, called it **Chha-mo-lung-ma**, the name adopted by the Chinese (but transliterated as Qomolangma or Chomolungma). This is also the name that the Sherpas use. Difficult to translate directly, it is usually said to mean: 'Mother Goddess of the World'. Sherpas sometimes translate it as 'Home of the Goddess of the Wind' or 'Home of the God or Goddess that Looks After Mothers'. (Makalu is said to be the home of the deity who protects daughters.)

The Nepali government's name is an even more recent creation than the English designation. They call it **Sagarmatha**, which has been variously translated as: 'Forehead Touching the Sky', 'Head in the Sky', 'Head above All Others' or 'Churning Stick of the Ocean of Existence'.

The Dalai Lama permits the first Everest expedition

Once Everest had been identified as the world's highest mountain, nearly three-quarters of a century were to go by before an expedition could be set up to reach the area. The main interest was originally from the British but Nepal and Tibet were suspicious of this colonial power's intentions. Nepal already had a British Resident living in Kathmandu, installed as a permanent observer after they had lost the 1814 war to the British, and one resident foreigner was more than enough. Tibet's capital Lhasa had been a closed city for more than a century but in 1904 Francis Younghusband led a British expedition which fought its way through Tibet, killing many Tibetans, ostensibly to negotiate trade links between the two countries. For more than a decade the Dalai Lama withheld his permission for a British party to make an attempt on Everest. However, eventually he yielded to British demands and the first expedition was mounted in 1921. It was organized by the Royal Geographical Society with climbers from the Alpine Club and was followed by further attempts in 1922 and 1924.

1921 Reconnaissance expedition

The first expeditions were remarkable for a number of reasons. Many of the most promising young mountaineers had been lost in the battles of the First World War so the average age of members of the reconnaissance expedition was an almost geriatric 44. Although composed of experienced mountaineers, their experience was of European mountains half the height of Everest. Very little was known about the effects of altitude and their equipment and clothing, although the best available at the time, would seem totally inappropriate by modern standards. It was not a strong team and only six of the nine members reached the base of the mountain after the long walk from Sikkim.

A major figure in the first expeditions was George Mallory. With his mountaineering partner, GH Bullock, he first spent a tough month exploring the area to find the easiest access to the mountain, the hidden East Rongbuk Glacier. It was immediately obvious that summer, the monsoon period, was not the most favourable time for climbing. But despite this and their appalling equipment, three Sherpas and three climbers reached the North Col, 7000m/23,000ft. By the end of the expedition a thorough exploration of the Tibetan side of the Everest Massif had been made, and Mallory had even peered into the Western Cwm, as he named it, from the Lho La.

Frozen spaghetti on the 1922 expedition

The 1922 expedition, led by Brigadier-General Charles Granville Bruce, arrived before the monsoon and boasted a 13-member team (including a film crew) and rather superior food supplies. As well as champagne and caviar there were tins of Heinz spaghetti which, like most of the other foodstuffs, froze solid at the higher camps.

They may have been better fed but the team members were still woefully under-clothed. A famous picture of Mallory and Edward Norton, high on the mountain, shows them dressed in wool trousers and jackets with little room for more than a jersey or two and longjohns under this. They sported medium brimmed hats and, aside from the goggles, ice axes and rope, would not have looked out of place strolling in an English park on a winter's morning.

A series of camps was established. Camp IV was set up on the North Col and the primitive Camp V at a height of over 7600m/25,000ft. Although experience showed that this was too low for a serious attempt on the summit, the first attempt was launched from here. Nevertheless, Mallory, Norton and Howard Somervell reached a height of 8150m/26,738ft without oxygen, before descending, all slightly frostbitten.

The second attempt was by George Finch, accompanied by Bruce's son, Geoffrey. Spurred on by hot tea and the discovery that using oxygen at night aided warmth and sleep, they climbed to 8320m/27,300ft. For Bruce's son this must have been especially satisfying since this was his first climbing trip. It was also the first time that oxygen had been used on Everest and some members of the group were very much against it, maintaining that its use was most unsporting.

The third attempt ended prematurely, 200m below the North Col with a fatal avalanche. Nine Sherpas were caught and seven of them killed. The Everest toll had begun.

'Because it's there' – the 1924 expedition

It is immaterial whether or not Mallory coined the immortal phrase 'Because it's there', when asked in 1923 why anyone would want to climb Everest; it's

THE EVEREST REGION

for his pioneering contribution towards its conquest that he should be remembered; the fateful 1924 expedition was to be his last.

Team members were still inadequately clothed; they had no down clothing. Each climber was given an allowance of £50 to kit himself out. Norton boasted windproof overalls and a leather, fur-lined motorcycle helmet plus the usual all-too-thin layers, hardly sufficient against temperatures as low as -40°C (-40°F).

Early storms battered the group forcing them to retreat to Rongbuk Monastery. Here they received the Lama's blessing which they'd imprudently not bothered to seek out when they'd first arrived in the area. The freak weather patterns held up stocks of oxygen sets, leading to a shortage at Camp IV on the col; despite this, Camp V was established. Camp VI was set at an altitude of 8170m/26,804ft, with Norton and Somervell staying there overnight. They set off early the next morning but Somervell was overcome by a serious coughing attack. He had developed frostbite in his throat and almost choked on a lump of his own frostbitten flesh which he later coughed up, giving him much relief. Norton was forced to struggle on alone and, labouring up steep ground covered with powder snow, reached a record altitude of 8570m/28,126ft, a phenomenal achievement. One has to wonder how much further Norton would have been able to climb if he had had an oxygen set.

That evening, with Norton suffering from snow-blindness and Somervell also out of action, Mallory chose Sandy Irvine to accompany him the next day, probably because of his familiarity with the oxygen sets. Sherpas climbed with Mallory and Irvine up to Camp VI then returned. The next morning, with the weather less than perfect, it was assumed that Mallory and Irvine had left after sunrise since they left their torch and magnesium flares behind. Later, Noel Odell climbed from Camp V to Camp VI to study the geology of the rocks along the way, and through a brief hole in the clouds saw the two climbers ascend a step. Initially he was inclined to think it was the second step before the summit but later suffered doubts. This was at around 1pm so the climbers were far behind their schedule: Mallory had intended to be at the second step by 8am. A snow storm blew up and then cleared two hours later, leaving the ridge and the summit cone fully visible, but there was no sign of either Mallory or Irvine. The night was also clear and a watch was kept on the ridge to the summit but there was still no sign of either man.

Their disappearance began endless conjecture as to whether or not they reached the summit before they died. Subsequent climbers have remarked that Odell's description of where he saw them fits the third and final step better than the second; climbers are still easily visible at that point. However, in 1999 Conrad Anker tried climbing the second step without the recently installed ladders and reported that it was most unlikely they had managed to make it up. To the day he died Odell wasn't sure which step he saw them on but thought likely that they had attained the summit. Largely as a result of his uncertainty, there is now an armful of books discussing in depth exactly how far Mallory and Irvine got up the world's highest mountain.

> **The finding of Mallory's body**
> In May 1999, a season of exceptionally little snow, an expedition dedicated to researching the Mallory-Irvine mystery found Mallory's body, intact and in an amazingly preserved condition, high up on Chomolungma on the Tibetan side. Intriguingly, one of Mallory's or Irvine's oxygen bottles was found at a point higher than the fall, indicating that Mallory, at least, was returning from a higher point. It is also significant that the clip for his oxygen mask was found in his pocket, indicating that he had taken it off, either because of a malfunction or, more likely, because he had used up all his oxygen, a supply of 8-11 hours.
>
> Also intriguingly, one of the climbers of the 1975 Chinese expedition reported finding a body with a hole in the cheek, which could only have been Mallory or Irvine. Mallory's body was discovered further away from this reported location than would have been expected and his cheeks were not damaged. No more is known because the Chinese climber who told this to one member of the Japanese Women's Everest Expedition died the next day.
>
> The search for Irvine's body continues and there is still not enough information to definitively confirm whether or not they did actually summit.

Telephones on Everest – the 1933 expedition

It was not until 1933 that another attempt was made. This boasted technical innovations: radio and, from Camp III to Camp IV, a telephone line. It was a strong team but bad weather interrupted the process of setting up intermediate camps, putting the expedition behind schedule. Nevertheless, they equalled Norton's altitude record, climbing without supplementary oxygen on bad snow.

British institutions such as the Royal Geographical Society and the Alpine Club considered Everest their own preserve, jealously guarding it from attempts by outsiders. They were not amused, therefore, by the announcement, in 1933, by the wealthy adventurer, Maurice Wilson, that he would climb Everest alone. He bought a light aircraft and flew himself from Britain to India. Despite having no previous climbing experience he managed to get as far as the North Col before succumbing to the cold. His body was found by the next expedition.

The 1935 Reconnaissance expedition

Led by Eric Shipton, this was the first of several expeditions to be headed by this famous explorer-mountaineer. He preferred to travel light, living off the land, which was a major departure from the normal expedition approach. Since eggs were the most accessible source of protein they regularly appeared on the expedition menu, and Shipton notes that 'though many of them were rather stale we consumed enormous quantities. Our record was 140 in a single day between four of us, and many times our combined party of seven put away more than a hundred.' (*Upon that Mountain*).

One of the Sherpas Shipton took with him was an enthusiastic nineteen-year-old named Tenzing Bhotia (later Norgay), who proved to be ambitious and strong. Amongst the other team members was Dan Bryant, a cheerful Kiwi. The expedition had instructions not to climb Everest but the monsoon broke late so there would, in fact, have been time for a serious attempt that season. It was, however, a surprisingly successful climbing expedition in other respects, with an impressive total of 26 peaks over 6095m/20,000ft climbed by the seven-man group, and all for a total cost of £1500, around the price of a Rolls Royce at the time.

Monsoon stops play

The following year the 1936 Everest attempt, for which the 1935 expedition had been preparing the way, was unfortunately washed out by the early arrival of the monsoon. Then came a low-budget expedition in 1938 led by HW Tilman (recounted in his *Mount Everest 1938,* see p60). Having learnt lessons about the monsoon from previous expeditions, they arrived early but to no avail. The monsoon broke three weeks earlier than it ever had previously. Still, they continued, even trying a different route, until worsening snow conditions for the last 1000m forced them to retreat.

Nepal at last

In 1948 the Kingdom of Nepal for the first time opened its doors a crack, though only to parties interested in scientific research. Tilman was not a scientist (he claimed that he 'had hitherto refused to mingle art with science') but he compromised his principles and was allowed in the following year. He was allocated the Langtang area, which to his delight was marked 'unsurveyed' on his map. Later he was lucky enough to be invited to visit Namche, walking in from Dharan via the Arun River. As part of this trip he made the first ascent by a foreigner of the now famous Kala Pattar.

The 1951 Reconnaissance Expedition

After the Chinese invasion of Tibet the northern route to Everest was sealed off with the closure of the border. An expedition, led by Shipton, was dispatched to reconnoitre an alternative, southern route through newly opened Nepal. Although Shipton had turned down many suitable applicants for the team in Britain, recalling instead New Zealander Dan Bryant from the 1935 Expedition, in a moment of weakness he accepted a request from the NZ Alpine Club for two unnamed climbers to join the team. They were George Lowe and Edmund Hillary. It was to be the first time that a party had climbed after the monsoon, the traditional season being in the 'lull before the storm'. They arrived in Namche at the end of September and climbed to the Western Cwm. In spite of the danger from the Khumbu Icefall it was clear that the south side route up Everest was indeed feasible.

1952 – the competition closes in

Time was running out for the British and what they arrogantly considered their exclusive 'right' to the area. In 1950 the first 'eight-thousander' (8000m peak), Annapurna, had been conquered by the French. After the British 1951 Reconnaissance Expedition to the Khumbu, there came an unwelcome piece of news: the Swiss had been given permission to make an attempt on Everest in

1952 and the British would have to wait until the following year. A French attempt was scheduled for 1954. Surprisingly, the Swiss almost agreed to a joint Anglo-Swiss expedition (obviously wanting to make use of Shipton's wide experience of the mountain) but the details could not be worked out to everyone's satisfaction. The Swiss chose Tenzing Norgay (see box below) as their sirdar. He held them in high esteem because it was with two of the Swiss expedition members that he had successfully stood on top of a peak in 1947, his first despite 12 years climbing with expeditions.

The trek to Base Camp took 23 days from the newly opened airfield in Kathmandu. They established five camps between Gorak Shep and the head of the Western Cwm and conclusively proved that it was a feasible route. Tenzing and Raymond Lambert climbed to just below the south summit but could go no further. It was realized that an additional camp and further logistical support were needed for an attempt to succeed. Their second attempt after the monsoon was dogged by bad luck, bad planning and the ferocious high-altitude winter winds.

Preparations for the 1953 British Everest Expedition

The Swiss attempts gave the British a chance to prepare properly. Training included an expedition to Cho Oyu in 1952, led by Shipton. Although they failed to reach the summit (see pp135-6), the expedition was of great value: as a result important refinements were made to oxygen sets and clothing.

In planning the 1953 expedition internal politics played a large part. Though Shipton had led many previous expeditions and had immense popularity with the public, some members of the Alpine Club committee felt that he might not be the right man to lead an expedition of such size and under such pressure. This would surely be the final chance for them to reach the summit first. Diplomatic to the last, Shipton agreed that he was indeed happiest climbing with the minimum of encumbering resources and it was decided that John Hunt, an army officer, should lead the expedition which would be run on military lines. Strangely, most of the committee had never met Hunt, and he had been turned down for the 1935 Everest expedition for reasons of health.

'We knocked the bastard off!' – success in 1953

The 1953 expedition was an all-out assault. It was decided that oxygen was to be used to the limit of its advantages, for aiding sleep and climbing – anything

---

Tenzing Norgay was Tibetan
Throughout his life Sherpa Tenzing was coy about where he was brought up. It turns out he was Tibetan, only briefly spending time in Thame, Nepal. The reason for the cover-up was that he had no passport and with the backing of Prime Minister Nehru, it was the Indians who gave him one, much to the annoyance of the Nepali authorities who would have loved to claim him as their own. Either way, neither country wanted to hand a propaganda coup to the Chinese, who had recently invaded Tibet.

to conquer. With all this equipment the walk-in was on a grand scale: the first of two groups of porters numbered some 350 people. Since the only currency accepted in the hills at the time was silver coins it took several porters just to carry the wages. There were 13 climbers, with Tenzing Norgay added to the climbing ranks, plus a reporter and cameraman.

The team spent two weeks climbing in the Khumbu area to aid acclimatization before tackling the Icefall. It was while forging a route through this monstrous obstacle that Hillary and Tenzing first got to know each other and Tenzing demonstrated that he could match the very competitive Hillary. Once the camps in the Western Cwm were established sickness took its toll, setting back the schedules. However, after a 13-day struggle, Camp VIII on the South Col was established.

Charles Evans and Tom Bourdillon made the first summit attempt from this camp although it was clearly too far away to allow a safe return if they did succeed. In the event snow conditions deteriorated and one of the oxygen sets caused problems, so the climbers settled for the south summit. This was less than 100m/328ft below the real summit, but at that altitude, even with oxygen, the climbers estimated it to be three hours away.

The second assault was better planned. A higher camp, Camp IX, was established and Hillary and Tenzing rested here for the night, drinking quantities of hot lemon and even eating a little. At 6.30am on 29 May, they began the climb. They reached the south summit by 9am, and the snow conditions past this first critical point were good. What is now known as the 'Hillary Step', a 13m/43ft barrier, was overcome by chimneying up a gap between a cornice and the rock wall, a dangerous but necessary move. The summit, only a short distance away, was reached at 11.30am. In the words of Hillary:

I looked at Tenzing and in spite of the balaclava, goggles and oxygen mask all encrusted with long icicles that concealed his face, there was no disguising his infectious grin of pure delight as he looked all around him. We shook hands and then Tenzing threw his arm around my shoulders and we thumped each other on the back until we were almost breathless.   John Hunt *The Ascent of Everest*

By evening they had struggled down to the South Col where Hillary told his team mate: 'Well, George, we knocked the bastard off' – though this was not exactly what was printed in the press at the time!

Chinese attempts on Everest

The pressure bubble burst with the success of the British expedition. It was some time before further attempts were considered as now the other unclimbed 'eight-thousanders' commanded attention. The Swiss climbed Everest after their conquest of Lhotse in 1956. In 1960 the Indians came close to success and at the same time the Chinese attempted the pre-war route via Tibet.

It was a mammoth affair, mounted on a grander scale than any previous attempt. Success was announced but no photos could be produced and the expedition account, after being suitably embellished by the propaganda department, made entertaining reading but was inconsistent with the mountaineering thinking of the time. We join them on the second step on a four-metre wall:

Each one made several attempts but fell back each time. They looked at each other for inspiration. Time was marching on mercilessly, and according to the weather-station forecast, it was the last day of the fine weather period ... Then Liu Lien-man had an idea that the 'courte echell' (short ladder) technique might help, so crouching down he offered his companion a leg-up. Ignoring the biting cold and the danger of freezing, Chu Ying-hua took off his high-altitude boots and his eider-down stockings to make the climb easier ... It had taken them five full hours to overcome this obstacle ... dusk came and an icy wind howled dolefully. The three members of the Communist Party of China, Wang Fu-chou, Chu Ying-hua and Liu Lien-man, discussed the situation and it was decided to leave Liu Lien-man behind and press on.

Mountaineering in China (People's Physical Culture Publishing House)

They claimed to have left a plaster bust of Chairman Mao Tse-tung near the summit. Although at the time the attempt was ridiculed by the Western media (this was during the Cold War) it's now considered that the expedition did succeed in reaching the summit.

Sydney Wignall, in his book *Spy on the Roof of the World*, suggests another reason for the attempt. In 1955 he gained permission to climb Nalkanbar, on Nepal's far western border with Tibet. In fact they planned to make a clandestine attempt on Gurla Mandhata, 7694m/25,243ft and the 34th highest mountain on the planet. They made the mistake of confiding in Tibetan traders, whom they later found out could only cross the border with a Chinese spy among them, who ensured they said only good, entirely fictitious things about the invaders. They were soon caught and taken to Taklakot, where they were interrogated for two months.

In desperation to please his captors, Wignall told them that Hillary and Tenzing had placed a sort of nuclear-powered radar capable of seeing all the way across Tibet to Lop Nor (where, unbeknown to him, the Chinese were developing their first nuclear weapon). Among his interrogators was the General in charge of Tibet. He appeared technologically naïve. Later, after a diplomatic hiatus they were released but were allowed to return only over a route known to be impossible in winter. Much to the dismay of the Chinese the mountaineers succeeded in returning; as a result it was proved the Chinese had been lying since they had announced that they had released them a month earlier in a different region. Wignall brought valuable information out, which unfortunately was ignored by India: the Chinese invasion of Indian Aksai Chin (Ladakh) should not have been a surprise at all.

There were rumours of another Chinese attempt in 1966 in which 24 climbers died but Chinese officials refused to discuss the incident. In 1969 it was claimed that three surveyors reached the summit without oxygen or additional support; and in 1975 another Chinese team was said to have reached the summit. Proof of their success was found by Doug Scott and Dougal Haston of the 1975 British South-West Face Expedition; on the summit they came upon a red Chinese tripod.

❏ Conquering the world's top 20 peaks

The world's 20 highest mountains were almost all climbed in a relatively short span of frenetic mountaineering activity between 1950 and 1960.

1	Everest/Sagarmatha/Chomolungma	8848m	29,028ft	1953
2	K2 (Pakistan/China)	8611m	28,251ft	1954
3	Kanchenjunga (Nepal/India)	8586m	28,169ft	1955
4	Lhotse (Nepal/Tibet)	8501m	27,890ft	1956
5	Makalu (Nepal/Tibet)	8463m	27,765ft	1955
6	Cho Oyu (Nepal/Tibet)	8201m	26,906ft	1954
7	Dhaulagiri (Nepal)	8167m	26,794ft	1960
8	Manaslu (Nepal)	8156m	26,758ft	1956
9	Nanga Parbat (Pakistan)	8126m	26,660ft	1953
10	Annapurna (Nepal)	8091m	26,545ft	1950
11	Gasherbrum I (Pakistan/China)	8068m	26,470ft	1958
12	Broad Peak (Pakistan/China)	8047m	26,401ft	1957
13	Gasherbrum II (Pakistan/China)	8035m	26,261ft	1956
14	Shishapangma (Tibet)	8027m	26,335ft	1964
15=	Gasherbrum III (Pakistan/China)	7952m	26,089ft	1975
15=	Gyachung Kang I (Nepal/Tibet)	7952m	26,089ft	1964
17	Annapurna II (Nepal)	7937m	26,040ft	1960
18	Gasherbrum IV (Pakistan/China)	7925m	26,001ft	1958
19	Himalchuli I (Nepal)	7893m	25,896ft	1960
20	Distaghil Sar I (Pakistan)	7885m	25,869ft	1960

1996: the best guides or not, Everest is still the limit

In 1996 some high profile deaths and some surprising survival stories put Everest in the world headlines again. Rob Hall, a Kiwi guide who had summitted Everest three times previously, and Scott Fisher, who had summitted previously without oxygen, were the respective leaders of two commercial groups of climbers. Due to some bickering between the climbing sirdars, ropes up the Hillary step were fixed late, creating a bottleneck. Then, unheralded, a light storm caught the late climbers unaware. A group made it down to the 8000m South Col, only to lose their way, forcing them to spend the night huddling together for their lives.

In a brief early morning clearing a few struggled into camp. Rescuers dragged a couple more climbers back but left Beck Weathers and Yakuso Namba, who were badly frost-bitten and barely alive, to die.

Amazingly, in the morning Weathers suddenly awoke and staggered into camp. After a heroic rescue effort including a 6000m helicopter landing, he survived losing a hand, fingers and his nose to frostbite. Namba died on the col.

Meanwhile, higher up the mountain a similar struggle was happening. Rob Hall and Andy Harris, New Zealand guides, valiantly struggled with Doug Hansen on his second attempt at the mountain with Rob Hall and Adventure Consultants. By morning only Hall was left, and he knew he was in deep trouble. By the wonders of modern communications he was able to talk with his wife, Jan (who was seven months pregnant) in New Zealand. She had climbed Everest with him previously and immediately understood that death was clawing at her partner's back. Two sherpas attempted a rescue in bone-chilling conditions and climbed to 200 vertical metres below Hall before being driven back. Hall, by this stage was badly frost-bitten and even oxygen and dexamethasone weren't enough. He died by the south summit.

Scott Fisher and a reckless Taiwanese, 'Makalu' Gau, made it further down the ridge to approximately 400 vertical metres above the South Col before giving up. When sherpas found them the next morning, although both were alive, only Gau revived. The sherpas, who could only manage one person at this altitude, had to leave Fisher to die.

The deaths may have shocked the world but in fact that season climbers got off relatively lightly, as John Krakauer in *Into Thin Air*, his first-hand account of the disaster, points out. Historically, approximately one in four summiteers have died, whereas in 1996 only one in about seven summiteers died.

Recent attempts on Everest

The desire to summit Everest has not faded. In 1970 an intrepid Japanese adventurer skied part of the way down using a parachute to slow himself and in 1988 Frenchman Jean-Marc Boivin jumped off the summit with a paraglider. New routes have been climbed, such as the south-west face in 1975 and the west ridge from Lho La. Different mountaineering methods have been applied and in 1978 Reinhold Messner and Peter Habeler reached the summit without the use of bottled oxygen, the first to do so. Messner went on to make a successful solo climb without oxygen in 1980 and has since soloed all 14 of the world's 'eight-thousanders'. Recently Hans Klammerlander repeated Messner's climb solo from 6400m to the top in a staggering 17 hours, and without oxygen. Partly using skis, he managed to return to his high base camp in less than 24 hours total. However, the first all-ski descent was made by Davo Karnicar in autumn 2000 and six months later in 2001 Marco Siffredi snowboarded from the summit in impressive style, jumping rocks and carving slopes that climbers use ropes on.

Sadly Babu Chiri, ten times a summiteer, died falling into a crevasse while photographing around Camp II (Advance Base Camp) on the Nepal side in May 2001. He was the first Sherpa to break out of the high-altitude guide/porter mould, being a Mountain Hardwear-sponsored climber and having set records for spending the night (21 hours) on top of Everest and climbing from Base Camp to the summit in under 16 hours (!). Self-assured and on the point of what could be called 'tubby', he occasionally delighted in teasing Western notions of what one of the greatest Sherpa mountaineers should look like, asking people what they thought he did. Until his picture was splashed around the world, few people would believe on sight this heavy man was the fastest high-altitude climber in the world.

As of 2008 the record for the most successes on Everest was Apa Sherpa, who has summitted an amazing 18 times.

THE EVEREST REGION

The first Nepali woman to summit Everest, Pasang Lhamu, died on the descent, becoming a posthumous national hero, and there are now stamps with her image, a mountain and a climbing centre named after her.

The rise of commercial climbing

Since the turn of the millennium, commercial expeditions (see box below) have ever more dramatically changed the dynamics of climbing Everest. Now with just a couple of months spare and for around US$10,000 to $60,000 you too can join an expedition.

Some companies provide a huge amount of support, giving the climber the best possible chance to summit, though it must be said that others don't even provide an acceptable minimum. In 2006 this was dramatically demonstrated with David Sharp, an Everest-experienced climber, dying partly from the lack of a walkie-talkie, and Lincoln Hall (another climber with prior Everest experience) surviving only by having a little more luck and also a strong support team of sherpas.

Many people debate the merits of commercial expeditions but, like trying to turn back the clock to the days before email, it's all but impossible to reverse the trend. After all, there is only one highest mountain on the planet. However, it is not just a case of paying your way to the top, Everest is still an extremely tough and dangerous climb, with several deaths every year. As you pant up Kala Pattar or Gokyo Ri, imagine what it is like over 3000m higher, or check the temperature outside the plane when climbing to 8800m/c28,800ft; furthermore, consider how pleasant acclimatizing at Gorak Shep and higher for more than a month might be.

Well over 3000 climbers have now summitted Everest and with all commercial teams the main keys to success are bottled oxygen and high-altitude climbing sherpas. If there were no climbing sherpas carrying the supplies (especially the oxygen) there would be no industry. Most come from the Solu-Khumbu, from areas near Phaplu up to Pangboche, as well as from the Rolwaling and Makalu regions; more recently, Tibetans trained in Lhasa have also started working on the expeditions. The climbing sherpas are all the real heroes of Everest – and you will meet them while trekking.

 The Everest industry

During the main season, counting both sides of the mountain, around 500 foreign climbers attempt the climb with around 1000 support staff, not to mention computers, satellite phones and cappuccino machines. Historically, approximately 10% of climbers attempting the mountain actually succeeded, although with the advent of commercial expeditions this ratio has increased to around 20% (for foreign climbers), so each year around 300 people summit, including sherpa climbers. Over 3000 people have now climbed to the summit and over 200 have died.

CHO OYU (8201m/26,906ft)

The name Cho Oyu is almost certainly Tibetan in origin and is transliterated in several ways. My favourite is Chomo Yu which means 'Goddess of Turquoise', the colour the mountain often assumes at sunset when viewed from the Tibetan side.

The 1952 British attempt

In 1952, while the Swiss were attempting Everest, Eric Shipton led a British expedition to Cho Oyu. They failed to reach the top probably because Shipton was unwilling to build a supply line up the mountain on the Tibetan side. Tibet had recently fallen into the hands of the Communist Chinese and Shipton was wary of doing anything that might jeopardize the planned 1953 Everest Expedition. In 1951 he'd been caught by the Tibetans on the wrong side of the border. Quite prepared to hand over everything he possessed (Rs1200) when they brandished their swords and demanded a ransom, he was soon amused to discover that his ever-faithful Sherpas had bargained the final sum down to a mere Rs7!

1954 – Austrian success

An Austrian attempt on Cho Oyu was launched in 1954, led by Herbert Tichy. The decision to climb was made on the spur of the moment after a conversation with a Sherpa, before Tichy had even seen the peak. The team consisted of three Austrians and seven high-altitude Sherpas but their prospects did not look good. One of the Austrians had previously been shot through the lung, another suffered severely from sciatica and Tichy admitted to smoking a lot and drinking 'without reluctance'. In addition, the attempt was launched after the monsoon, without oxygen, with little equipment and less than Rs1000-worth of food. At that stage in the history of Himalayan mountaineering, success had occurred only on well-equipped pre-monsoon expeditions.

On the walk in, Tichy soon noticed that changes were afoot in the area: 'We followed in the tracks of other expeditions – notably Everest expeditions. They had rubbed off the bloom which I was still able to enjoy in the west of Nepal the year before: they had also spoilt the market (four eggs for a rupee instead of ten) and the villagers treated us with that mixture of interest and condescension people bestow on a travelling circus' (*Cho Oyu by Favour of the Gods*).

Tichy's relaxed approach to climbing left much time for merry-making with friends in the Khumbu. On one such occasion he notes that the Sherpa porters had done full justice to the parting from their friends and their families and when 'we overtook our proud array we saw that some of our Sherpanis were so drunk that their male companions had to carry them and their loads as well. This predicament was taken as a great joke' (*Cho Oyu by Favour of the Gods*).

The walk up to Base Camp, slightly north of the Nangpa La (just inside Tibet), was accomplished with only 27 porters. Camp IV was established at 6980m/22,900ft, ten days from Base Camp, but then disaster struck. In savage winds with the temperature below -35°C Tichy made a desperate dive to save one of their tents and suffered frostbite on his fingers. The climb had to be temporarily abandoned. Nevertheless, nine days later he and his companions set off again, spurred on by meeting a Swiss expedition that had been rebuffed by Gauri Sankar and had just arrived with the similar intention of attempting Cho Oyu. A storm pinned the Austrians down for two days before they could return to Camp IV. However, on the following day, 19 October 1954, Tichy, Sepp Jochler and Pasang Lama made the summit.

For Pasang Lama the ascent was all the more remarkable, indeed the stuff of legends. Having returned to Namche to pick up more supplies, at Marulung (4150m/13,615ft), a day's walk from Namche, he heard of the Swiss plans and so raced, heavily loaded, in a day up to Base Camp. Then, even more remarkably, the next day he ascended with a load to Camp IV and on the following day climbed to the summit.

MAKALU (8475m/27,805ft)

British/American 1954 Expedition

In the line-up for attempts on Everest, the French had been allotted the year following the British. The same order was established for Makalu (8475m/27,805ft), with the British and Americans given permission for the spring of 1954 and the French scheduled to follow them. The French were naturally not keen to follow in the wake of a British success (as on Everest) and the results were anxiously awaited. With a strong team that included Hillary, it looked as if success on Makalu was likely. However, the summit was not reached. Interestingly the expedition took approximately 250 porters over the Mingbo La, West Col and East Col to Makalu Base Camp.

1955 – French success

The French were spurred into action with an autumn reconnaissance and gear-testing trip. Chomo Lonzo (7790m/25,557ft), just inside Tibet, and Makalu II (7640m/25,065ft) were both climbed from the Nepalese side.

The 1955 attempt was a classic assault of the mountain, superbly organized, kitted with the best of equipment and conducted as if the pride of the country was at stake. They were prepared for the worst and ready to make repeated attempts. However, perfect weather allowed all the expedition members, as well as some of the Sherpas, to reach the summit of Makalu between 15 and 17 May. Now around 100 foreign mountaineers pass through Tashigoan to attempt Makalu, Makalu II, Baruntse or Chamalang each year.

LHOTSE (8501m/27,890ft)

Lhotse was so named by one of the British expeditions in the 1920s; no local name for it could be found. It is Tibetan for 'South Peak' and Lhotse Shar is the south-east peak of Everest.

The 1956 Swiss Expedition

In the spring of 1952 the Swiss had climbed to 250m/820ft below the summit of Everest before being forced back. In 1956 an expedition was mounted with permission for Lhotse (at that stage the highest unclimbed mountain) as well as Everest. It was a very well planned and provisioned expedition and the team worked well together. A cautious acclimatization programme was followed, with many rest days at Tengboche and Pheriche. It's interesting to note that in an effort to make the route through the Icefall safer, explosives were used.

Success came on 18 May, when Ernst Reiss and Fritz Luchsinger, using oxygen, fought their way up the steep slopes in unsettled weather to the summit. The second goal was also attained and four climbers reached the summit of Everest on the same expedition.

The people

THE SHERPAS

Years of living in their villages left me well aware that Sherpas are no more strangers to greed, pride, love of power, jealousy or pettiness than other mortals. They seem still, for all the close familiarity, a singularly appealing people.
   Stanley Stevens *Cultural Ecology and History in Highland Nepal* (Univ of California)

The mountaineering exploits of the Sherpas on foreign expeditions since the 1920s brought them clearly into the world spotlight. Sherpa Tenzing's conquest, with Hillary, of Everest in 1953 was a fitting tribute to the part played by Sherpas in the history of mountaineering, not just in the Khumbu but in many parts of the Himalaya. Although the lure of Everest has brought crowds of foreigners to their land, they seem to have weathered the cultural invasion surprisingly well. Theirs is an ancient culture which Westerners have learnt to respect, indeed admire, for its tolerance, comradeship and many other positive values.

Origins

Shar-pa is Tibetan for 'Eastern People' and the first Sherpas were almost certainly migrants from 1300km away in Kham (north-east Tibet) possibly fleeing from Mongol incursions. It's thought that they tried settling in a number of places en route but were consistently driven on, crossing the Himalaya about 500 years ago over Nangpa La. Migration occurred in several successive waves with large numbers of people arriving in the late 1800s and early 1900s and another major migration in the 1960s after the Chinese invasion of Tibet.

Settlements first appeared in the mid-1500s on both sides of Lamjura La (Junbesi and north of Kenja), where Sherpas still live today. The Thame and Pangboche gompas were established later, possibly during the 1670s, though it's likely that the area had been populated previously. It's thought that the

Khumbu was used for pastures by Rai shepherds before the Sherpas arrived; the Dudh Kosi is known as 'Khambu' by Rais today. The Sherpas have always considered the Khumbu a *be-yul* (hidden valley), free from the troubles of the outside world.

Agriculture

The crop with the highest yield in the Khumbu is the humble potato and about 75% of the cultivated area is planted with them. Growing enough, however, is not easy and most families have always supplemented their income, originally by trading with Tibet and now mainly through tourism. Their agricultural methods are quite sophisticated even though their tools may be primitive. Land holdings are scattered and several crop varieties are used in order to minimize the risk of blight and other diseases. The soil is not naturally very fertile but large quantities of organic fertilizer (compost, human waste and animal manure) have worked well, according to soil scientists. Women and children do much of the work but the roles aren't rigidly defined.

Up until the 1950s all ploughing was done by hand with four men to a plough but now animals are used. The men tend to the animals and are also occupied with trade, often leaving their wives to manage the entire affairs of the household.

A year in the Khumbu

Many trekkers have mistakenly come away with the impression that Sherpas don't seem to do anything in the Khumbu apart from looking after trekkers. This is not the case. The Sherpa calendar of activities is governed entirely by the seasons with a short cultivation period. It's most fortunate that the main trekking season occurs at the end of the harvest.

● **April-May** After the fields have been prepared, the potatoes are planted, followed by barley and buckwheat; these are labour-intensive activities.

● **May-June** Traditionally, this is a time of trading. The high passes to Tibet are open for a short while after the winter snows have melted and before the snows of the monsoon arrive. It's also the season of yak-shearing and calving.

● **June-July** The fields are weeded: a laborious job that may have to be done several times.

● **June-September** After calving, the yaks and naks are herded up to the high summer pastures to protect the crops and save the grass lower down for the spring. Summer is the time of butter, cheese and curd production.

● **September-October** These are the busiest months. At the high pastures hay is cut, while in the villages the potatoes are dug up and the barley and buckwheat harvested and threshed. Once this is completed the cattle can return to the villages. It's also the breeding season for cattle and the beginning of the trekking season.

● **November-March** The long, cold winter months are filled with spinning and weaving, collecting firewood and feeding the animals by hand. It's also a time for trading, not only with Tibet but also Kathmandu; trips to the capital are also made to beat the cold and visit friends. Losar, the Tibetan New Year which usually occurs in February, is the main festival.

The Sherpas of Pharak and Solu live at lower altitudes and the milder climate enables them to grow a wider range of crops. In Junbesi, many of the vegetables served to trekkers are grown locally. Apples thrive in this area and apple pies and jams are on every lodge menu. Yaks, *naks* (female yaks) and crossbreeds are kept high in the mountains away from the villages. Their milk that was once made into butter and traded with Tibet to keep the monastery lamps burning is now sold to local cheese factories. Sherpa trade in this area is now mainly with passing trekkers.

Diet
As one might expect, potatoes are eaten at almost every meal, though the well-off also eat rice. Potatoes are usually boiled and once they've been peeled (the skin is never eaten) they're dipped in salt and a chilli sauce. Savoury pancakes made from a mixture of buckwheat (the non-sweet variety) and grated potatoes are eaten with butter and chillies. However, the great Sherpa favourite is *shakpa*, a thick soup made with whatever comes to hand – usually potatoes(!), a few other vegetables and sometimes chewy balls of wheat flour.

With potatoes being a staple, it's not surprising that the Sherpas are connoisseurs of the varieties that are suited to the Khumbu. Trekkers also consume huge quantities of potatoes, not because there are no alternatives on the menu but because they're surprisingly tasty. If you show an interest, the lodge owner may show you the different types. The highest yielding variety (commonly served to trekkers) is not considered quite as tasty as some of the older types.

The Sherpa diet is fairly healthy. Naks and *dzums* (a yak/cow crossbreed) provide dairy products and meat is occasionally eaten, dried or fresh. In the past the diet lacked only iodine, a deficiency that can cause goitres and cretinism. The situation was quickly solved by the first doctor at Khunde hospital. Now the majority of salt in Nepal, instead of coming from Tibet, is naturally iodized sea-salt from India.

The Sherpa house
Unlike the Tibetan house, which is flat-roofed and built around a courtyard, the Sherpa house features a roof adapted for the monsoon rains and has no courtyard. Although it does bear a superficial resemblance to the Tibetan house, the Tibetan architectural style is reserved for gompas.

The size of a house is a sign of prosperity. In the Rolwaling there are still many single-storied houses, whereas in wealthy Namche there are now even some four-storey hotel 'sky-scrapers'. However, traditional Sherpa houses consist of two levels. The ground floor is for stabling cattle and is a storage area for grain, animal fodder, firewood and tools. It's also where the *chang* (home-brew made from rice or barley) is fermented. The upper level of the house is usually an open living-room, sometimes with the kitchen partitioned off.

Roofs are made of slate or wood, though slates are now being replaced by corrugated iron sheets. Walls are usually stone with huge wooden beams running between them to support the floor. In some of the older houses, the beams can be up to 25 metres long which gives some idea of the size of the trees in the forests that once covered this area of the Himalaya.

The layout of the interior is dictated by tradition. The west wall is for a shrine with Buddha images, candles or butter lamps and pictures of the Dalai Lama and perhaps the former King and Queen of Nepal. Beneath the sunny south-facing windows are long benches, often covered with thick Tibetan rugs. The south-east corner is for the master bed, usually the only bed, in which the whole family sleeps. If there are visitors for the night, they sleep on the carpeted bench seats. The sunless north wall is windowless and lined with shelves displaying the valuable kitchenware. The long tea-churn for making salt-butter tea should always be near the stairway. Many tea-churns are cherished family heirlooms, passed down from generation to generation.

The Sherpa view of life

Most Sherpas are followers of the Nyingmapa ('Red Hat') sect of Tibetan Buddhism (see p82), the most ancient and least reformed of the four major Tibetan sects. It developed out of the Tantric practices introduced by the Indian Padmasambhava (Guru Rinpoche or 'Precious Teacher') and is combined with the older beliefs of the Sherpas: the Bon-po religion and animism. Spirits and demons (*lu*) inhabit the springs, trees and rocks, and there are detailed rites for protection and exorcism.

As Buddhists, Sherpas view life as an endless cycle of rebirth into a world of suffering. Escape (*nirvana*) is possible only by accumulating a series of 'good' lives. The measure of good and evil is *sonam*. By carrying out virtuous deeds you gain merit, but sinful acts reduce the total at a rather unequal rate. One sin is far more powerful than a few good deeds so constant work is required to keep ahead. If you fall far behind you may not even be born human again:

Prayers for the world

In addition to general good conduct, repeating *mantras* (prayer chants) is an important means by which to gain *sonam*. Most common is the mantra *Om Mani Padme Hum*, meaning 'hail to the jewel in the lotus', the jewel being the Buddha.

The more times a mantra can be repeated the better, so Tibetan Buddhism has evolved many ingenious labour-saving methods to mass-produce these prayers. **Prayer wheels** are filled with a long paper roll inscribed with mantras that are activated by turning the wheel. They come in many forms, from the portable hand-held device so admired by tourists to huge wheels that with a single turn repeat astronomical numbers of prayers. There are also water-powered prayer wheels and multi-coloured fluttering **prayer flags**, printed with mantras which infuse the winds with prayers to travel the world. The mantra may be carved onto a **mani stone**, which benefits both the carver and the person who has paid for the work. Large numbers of these stones are piled up into the mani walls you see along the trails.

Note that you should always pass to the left of a mani wall and walk clockwise (the direction in which prayer wheels must always be turned) around Buddhist shrines and monuments.

monastery dogs are jokingly considered reincarnations of the not-so-studious monks. The meritorious who have finally escaped may return to assist their brethren as reincarnate head lamas, such as the Rinpoche at Tengboche.

All forms of life are treated with respect since to kill something is regarded as one of the greatest demerits. However, Sherpas relish meat and to eat it is no sin as long as the consumer was not responsible for the animal's death. The Sherpas' approach to life is remarkably unpuritanical and considerably more liberated than that of the Hindu Nepali. There is no caste system and women (Sherpanis) are treated much more equally. In most cases it is the Sherpani rather than the Sherpa who controls the family finances.

Mountaineers, sirdars and porters

Sherpas are well known for their dedicated service to mountaineering expeditions, first as porters and sirdars and later also as participating climbers. The part they have played in many expeditions has often been behind the scenes but it is nonetheless crucial for that. On the 1922 Everest attempt, six Sherpas climbed to Camp VI (8170m/26,800ft) from Camp V 800m below, merely to deliver thermos flasks of beef-tea to the sahibs after a storm.

Shipton, who always took Sherpas on his long and wild treks in the Himalaya and Karakoram, thoroughly admired them:

One of the most delightful things about the Sherpas is their extraordinary sense of comradeship. During the six months we were together, I never detected any sign of dissension among our three ... This quality of theirs is due largely, I imagine, to their robust sense of humour. It hardly ever failed. Each enjoyed jokes against himself as delightedly as those he perpetrated. Two of them would conceal a heavy rock in the load of the third and when, after an exhausting climb, this was discovered, all three would be convulsed with mirth ... They were forever laughing and chatting together as though they had just met after a prolonged absence. **Eric Shipton**, *The Six Mountain Travel Books*

Today, Sherpa high-altitude porters and climbing guides play a vital role in many, many expeditions and the opportunity for mountaineering training has spawned local heroes. The majority of Sherpas who work for expeditions do so for money, however, and consider the risks a trade-off for income. Apa Sherpa, 18 times Everest summiteer, says simply that expeditions keep paying him more and more so he can't refuse. Most admired now, apart from the mountaineers, are the sirdars, now trekking company directors who have broken through caste barriers to become some of the most successful businesspeople in Nepal.

Coping with development

The Sherpas' liberal and positive outlook on life combined with the head-start they were given through the Himalayan Trust (see p172) have enabled them to develop and adapt at a far quicker rate than most peoples in Nepal. Although community spirit is strong, individual endeavour and achievement through hard work are respected. There is little resistance to change that is obviously beneficial. If a new strain of potato, for example, proves to be an improvement on a previous type, it will be widely adopted.

Change in the Khumbu has been rapid but not overwhelming. Houses are bigger, smarter and less picturesque but their basic design and the style of construction are still close to time-honoured methods. The diet is generally healthier and more varied but an increase in sugar consumption has led to a greater incidence of tooth decay, especially among children. The worldliness of the Sherpas has undoubtedly increased with the steady stream of visitors and with themselves travelling overseas but they are still delightful people nonetheless and can be entertaining hosts if you have time to spend with them.

THE RAI

At Namche's Saturday market (see pp175-6) the squat, almond-eyed people are Rais. A surprising number work in the fields and even in the lodges of the Khumbu. Trekking via Salpa-Arun you pass through many Rai villages.

Rai can be easily distinguished by their attire and accessories. The women wear a large round nose ring through the left nostril, while another ring hangs from the middle of the nose over the mouth. The musical clang of this ring with the tea cup is a constant melodic reminder of her wealth. They favour a wrap-around patterned *lungi* (tight skirt). The men often wear a wool vest called *luku-nis* and always carry a *khukri*, a large knife used for cutting firewood, splitting bamboo and cleaning fingernails.

Origins
Rai, along with the similar Limbu ethnic group, are collectively referred to as Kirat. They are considered the original inhabitants of Nepal. Having first lived in the Kathmandu Valley these people moved eastward – possibly from the second century on. Once in the east, the Rai were later confronted by the Sherpa, and were pushed still further east. However, mythology also relates how the mongoloid (Tibetan-style people) descended from seven brothers: Sherpa, Rai, Limbu, Tharu, Tamang and other Tibetan groups.

There are many Rai sub-tribes but the Kulung Rai consider themselves the original inhabitants of the Majh-Kirat area (what is now called the Makalu-Barun Conservation Area). The main concentration of this sub-tribe live in Bung (see pp257-8) and Gudel (see pp255-6).

Religion
The religion of the Rai ethnic group is called Mudum; although somewhat influenced by Hinduism and Buddhism it retains much of its originality in its animistic heritage through oral myths, ceremonial dialogues and ritual recitation. Oral myth transmission is preserved by priests, shamans and elders. Natural spirits form the basis for the Mudum religion, including the 16 gods of the forest. Mudums worship in the home whereas Sherpas worship in gompas and Hindus in temples. For the Rai, the cooking area is considered one of the most sacred places in the home where three stones are placed to represent the stages of marriage. One stone looks in the direction of where the father sits (called Pakalung), one stone looks in the direction of where the mother sits (Makalung)

and the third stone looks outside the house (Sabelung). A bowl (dampay) is kept on a shelf near the cooking area; it is filled with local beer (chang) four times a year and is used to bless the stones. If a new stove is built in a home, the original is not destroyed but kept as the place of worship.

Another important divinity resides in the main pillar of the house – a myth relates how a god or goddess became very angry with their child and tried to kill him first by the fireplace in the courtyard and then by the bottom of the door but was unsuccessful. Finally they tried by the main pillar and the child died. Filled with deep remorse for killing the innocent child in a fit of rage they blessed him to become the protector divinity of the house.

A Rai family has one major ceremony (*puja*) a year which takes place in the autumn. A holy man (*dhami*) is hired for one full day to bless the home. The puja begins outside during daylight hours. The dhami sits and chants next to offerings of food, alcohol and tree branches while a feast of chicken and millet is prepared. In the evening, the ceremony is moved inside to the cooking area where the family is blessed and another chicken, also blessed with rakshi and rice, is sacrificed for the second feast of the day.

Agriculture and work

The life of the Rai is deeply rooted in their natural surroundings. Living at a lower elevation than the Sherpas, Rais have access to a greater variety of natural resources, such as bamboo – seven different species are found in the surrounding area. Being strong, versatile, and fast growing, it is highly valued and can be made into over 50 different domestic articles. A keen eye can spot some of these items including mats, vessels, hunting and fishing implements, toys and musical instruments.

Economically, the needs of locals are not met by subsistence farming, forcing many young men to seasonally migrate to other regions for additional work. Some men work in the Khumbu or on farms in the Tarai (Terai), while others go to fruit orchards in Bhutan or join the Indian army. Many also join the forces of the trekking business. Being less of a celebrity than the Sherpas, most Rai are left with the less glamorous job of porter where a day's work often earns only the day's food. Still, mixed groups of them often treat the work as a non-stop party.

Values

A study of the Rai reveals an appealing culture. They have a long tradition of reciting *mandhums*, poetic expressions of legends, mythology, history and stories. Some explicitly deal with various taboos: promiscuity after marriage, incest, and bad/unequal treatment of women – the problems that every society faces. Several stories altruistically tell of the dangers of polluting the environment, especially the water in the lakes. They share community values and are gentle people but they are also said to have a quick temper and to be fast with a khukri without caring about the consequences. Similarly their relaxed attitude – spend and enjoy today, forget about tomorrow – is a minor cultural impediment to long-term development.

National parks

SAGARMATHA NATIONAL PARK

Set up to control the environmental impact of the increasingly large numbers of tourists visiting the Khumbu, Sagarmatha National Park was officially gazetted in July 1976. For the first six years the New Zealand government, through the National Parks Service of New Zealand, provided training, management and guidelines. In 1979 it was declared a World Heritage Site by UNESCO in recognition of its rich cultural heritage and magnificent scenery. The park's area is around 1200 sq km, encompassing the entire watershed of the Dudh Kosi with the boundary being a virtually impenetrable ring of mountains.

The number of foreign visitors has been steadily increasing: from around 5000 people in the 1981-2 season (Nepali calendar year) to around 10,000 during the 1990-1 season. During 1996-7 approximately 17,500 foreigners visited the park and in the year 2000 the figure again jumped dramatically to approximately 25,000, only now to be exceeded in 2008. Aside from these temporary visitors in the park, there is the local Sherpa population whose numbers are now approximately 3500, and several hundred civil servants and army personnel living in the park.

Policies

Initially, there was local resistance to the park owing to worries that the people might be forcibly resettled, as had happened when Rara Lake National Park (west Nepal) was created. To allay such fears village areas were excluded from the park. Inevitably, this has led to a clash of interests between villagers and park management: villagers are unhappy at not being able to farm new land or even work existing terraces that had previously been abandoned, while the park authorities take the view that land is a resource that is becoming more and more valuable, and as such that which can be protected, should be protected. In the Khumbu this clash has been less severe than in other parts of Nepal: the relatively well-educated people of the Khumbu have a slow rate of population growth and the land that they are presently allowed to farm is already enough to generate a surplus of crops.

Other policies have also gradually been accepted by the villagers, particularly once they've been seen to show positive returns. The management of forest resources is a good example. Local forests were once protected by the collection of firewood in different sections on a yearly rotation. The nationalization of forests partially broke this system down, then the influx of starving Tibetan refugees escaping from the Chinese invasion took a heavy toll on the forests and the environment in general. After that, large expeditions turned firewood into a valuable cash crop, all adding up to a devastating result. To try to combat the rampant deforestation that was taking place, when the park came into being the authorities immediately placed a complete ban on the cutting down of trees. Though unpopular at the time, this ban has since been accepted by the villagers as the most sensible course of action and, although not proven definitively, it seems that overall there is now more forest cover in the Khumbu than when foreigners first visited in the 1950s.

Problems facing the park

For a number of years the national park functioned reasonably well. Then the central government cut the budget to a minimum and slowly the cancers of corruption and laziness began to permeate the park system, just as they had in almost every other park in the country.

The park today is also in something of a crisis when it comes to visitor numbers, which are growing alarmingly: every October more than 7500 trekkers enter the park. Although the problem has been studied and is understood, what to do about it is as yet undecided. Currently the International Centre for Protected Landscapes, funded by the British Government, has come up with a comprehensive strategy that involves developing a new management plan for both Sagarmatha National Park and the entire Solu-Khumbu district. Convoluted though their proposals may be, with so many parties taking an interest in the future of the park – including not only the authorities and other relevant government bodies but also the United Nations Development Programme (UNDP), various other NGOs and, of course, the local people whose livelihoods depend on the park – a long-term solution that would satisfy everybody was always going to involve some serious and complex planning. Whether it will eventually prove to be successful, only time will tell.

MAKALU-BARUN NATIONAL PARK & CONSERVATION AREA

Makalu-Barun National Park and Conservation Area (MBNPCA) was gazetted in 1991 and formally inaugurated in 1992 with a total area of 2330 sq km, of which 830 sq km was a conservation or buffer-zone area. Encompassing a region that stretched from near the Arun River all the way up to the Sagarmatha National Park, including the Hongu/Hinku or Mera Peak area, the park was initially formed to set up an environmental protection system in case the planned 'Arun III' hydro-electric scheme went ahead. This truly massive project would require an access road that would open up a previously isolated area. The hydro-electric project has come close to being realized several times, including once by the now-bankrupt Enron corporation, but each time the proposals were cancelled in a storm of controversy.

Nepal desperately needs more power but there are no 'zero environmental cost' solutions. So instead one has to look at 'the least cost'. India is also desperate for power, especially during the monsoon when Nepal's production is highest. Furthermore, Nepal's peak-power needs are the winter and early spring, which is when India's need is at its lowest. Many experts see hydropower as vital to the development of the economy, and one that could earn more money than tourism. So Arun III is not yet officially dead.

Facilities for the trekker

ACCOMMODATION AND FOOD

Our travels in Solu-Khumbu depended on Sherpa hospitality. When we arrived at a village where we wanted to spend the night, we would yell up at the window of any convenient house and ask to spend the night there. Permission was invariably given, whereupon we went upstairs to the main room, cooked our meal on the family fire, and went to sleep on whatever flat surface was available, usually the wooden floor. The host typically gave us any extra pillows lying around. We paid for food but, from Junbesi east, not for firewood.

James Fisher, in the 1970s.

The development of lodges

The hill peoples of Nepal have traditionally provided food and accommodation for the many travellers passing through their villages on the trade routes that cross the country. These small family-run establishments were nothing like hotels in the Western sense: guests were traditionally charged for food but not for their lodging, which was very basic. Not so long ago these teahouses were providing the same level of facilities as they had for the first foreign trekkers: little more than dal bhaat or a plate of potatoes and a hard bed. As the flow of trekkers grew, however, it was soon realized that these foreigners were prepared to pay more for better accommodation and a choice of food.

Development was slow at first. In 1985 Kenja, Junbesi, Kharikhola and Monjo were the only places below Namche that had proper lodges. In the 1990s, however, many new lodges were built and teahouses upgraded in a building spree which continues to this day. Double rooms gradually replaced dormitories, showers and toilets were added and chimneys installed, so that the traditional smoky lodges are rare these days. Extensive menus catering to Western tastes are now provided too (most Nepalis have just two main meals a day, both dal bhaat). Perhaps the biggest change of all, however, is that lodges are now run as businesses, very different from the teahouses of yesteryear with their hosts eager for news of the world beyond the village.

Nepal now has well-developed mountain lodge systems in the Solu Khumbu, Annapurna and Langtang areas, and on average the lodges of the Khumbu are the best in the country. This is, however, a developing country and still one of the world's poorest, so the lodges are not as grand as those you might find in the European Alps – but nor are they as expensive. Each lodge is, for the most part, owned and managed by a single family. Supplies are purchased or grown locally where possible, or carried in by porters if not; by staying in lodges, therefore, you are supporting the larger local economy. As long as you don't expect star-quality facilities, you should be pleasantly surprised and happy with both the food and accommodation along the main trekking routes.

Hygiene

Once you could almost be guaranteed to get sick on a trek in Nepal. Now, although there is still a reasonable chance of a real stomach upset from Kathmandu, out on the trek there is a good chance you won't get sick at all. Remember, too, that if you do get sick there are a number of possible sources, including your own hygiene, so don't automatically assume that the lodge food is to blame.

Eating in well-established lodges is now probably safer than eating a cooked meal on an organized group trek, and getting sick from lodge food is becoming rarer, especially since Namche changed its water supply. Basic hygiene measures such as washing hands and boiling water have been learnt from courses in Kathmandu and while kitchens may lack stainless steel sinks and running water they are, nevertheless, cleaned frequently. The style of cooking (frying or boiling) renders much of the food safe and salads are rare. Hot drinks are safe, too, but local drinks such as *chang* are not always so hygienically prepared.

Lodges on the main routes

Food A typical lodge in this area offers an extensive menu based on noodles, rice, flour, potatoes, eggs and the sparing use of vegetables.

Breakfast offerings include muesli, a variety of porridges, pancakes and bread with jam or eggs. If you have a large breakfast (fried eggs on toast, yum!) do allow at least half an hour prior to walking.

For **lunch** it is worth considering what can be quickly prepared, with veg noodle soup being popular. Pancakes and Tibetan bread are also relatively quick to make. Increasingly toasted sandwiches are on menus too. A variety of dishes will take time to make.

Choosing a lodge

Most trekkers tend to head either for the biggest and best-looking lodge or for the one where other trekkers are staying. Lodge-owners are well aware of this and will sometimes try very hard to attract the first trekkers arriving in the village, occasionally even trying to seat them outside (on seats provided for this very purpose) in order to attract more. Overcrowding can be a problem in the most popular lodges. At dinner there may be 30 trekkers ordering 12 different dishes, all to be cooked on two stoves, although most lodges do seem to cope remarkably well.

Look around at a few places before deciding where to stay. Except at the height of the season, you may find an empty lodge that is just as good as the one the other trekkers are crowding into. It's also worth trying out some of the smaller lodges and teashops, at least occasionally. This can be a rewarding cultural experience that gives you a better chance to see how the family lives. Expansion and competition with the big lodges is beyond the means of many of these small lodge owners, their money going to support relatives and pay school fees.

Many lodges prefer that you order **dinner** at least an hour ahead so that they can plan. Popcorn is a good snack, and goes rather well with a beer. Most soups will be from a packet and few cooks read the instructions for adding milk, so don't expect cream of tomato soup to be that. Chips are a favourite but do check the quality of the ketchup. Fries' addicts might be better bringing their own sauces.

'Yak' steaks are increasingly available, although are without exception, actually buffalo. Chicken doesn't travel well and so is not generally available. In some places the pizza and pasta is good, but in less competent lodges, pasta sauce made with ketchup is generally disgusting. The vegetable spring rolls would be out of place in a Chinese restaurant, but are usually tasty even if the green vegetable is generally a bit salty.

Apple pie is generally delicious, deep fried in the same way as the spring rolls are. Custard and chocolate puddings often suffer lumps and not everyone knows they should be made with milk (powder).

Most meal choices are carbohydrate-heavy; exactly what trekkers require. All lodges serve tea, coffee, hot chocolate, hot lemon, soft drinks and beer (check its temperature first) and some places even offer wine.

Bathroom facilities Below Lukla and at more simple places these are still developing. Most lodges now offer hot showers and in the ones that don't a bucket of water is usually available. Above Lukla there are many Western (ie sit-down) toilets and an increasing number of lodges offer rooms with an attached bathroom. In other places, toilets are usually just the Asian squat type, so watch your ankles. The rural Nepalese have land that needs fertilizing so before foreign trekkers took to the mountains there was no need for toilets.

Rooms Most modern lodges offer twin rooms. If they have a dormitory it is more usually for trekking crews. While mattresses have become thicker, beds still tend to be narrow and the room partitions are still thin enough for a snorer to be heard throughout the lodge. While bed sheets are not changed each day, they are still usually clean and the mattresses are regularly aired out. The fussier may still want to bring a pillow case, or at least drape a towel over the pillow. Hard pillows are best replaced with clothing, with a down jacket on top. Very few lodges have double beds but in many places you can push the two single beds together; in smaller rooms this will probably also block the door so check this in advance if it bothers you.

Below Lukla facilities tend to be homelier and more basic. It makes sense to always use a sleeping sheet and your own sleeping bag, though relatively clean blankets are often available too.

Seasons Some lodges remain open year-round, even at Gokyo, Lobuche, Gorak Shep and Chukhung. They also never seem to suffer the problem of being full to the extent that trekkers are stranded without a bed, so you'll rarely be turned away. There are, however, a few busy places (Tengboche and

Lobuche especially) that during October-November are filled almost to bursting. Sometimes this is because people on a group trek inconsiderately decide a lodge is more attractive and warmer than their tents. The national park has been reluctant to allow the building of new lodges or the expansion of old ones in this area so it pays to arrive early at these places during peak season. Elsewhere, the law of supply-and-demand seems to work well.

Accommodation off the main routes

In general, wherever there is a village, accommodation can be found. There may not be a lodge as such but people will often invite you to stay. If this does not happen try asking around (this is not considered rude by Nepalis) and something will turn up. Conditions can be extremely basic, however, and very different from the lodges on the main trekking routes. In strongly Hindu areas your presence may be considered *jutho* (polluting) so you may have to eat alone and perhaps even sleep on the porch.

Wilderness areas and base camps offer no shelter other than the occasional overhanging rock. You should also be aware that on detailed maps the dots marked in *kharkas* (high-altitude pastures) are usually just roofless stone buildings occupied only in the summer. Even then they are rarely able to offer food or shelter.

SERVICES AND FACILITIES

Most lodges run a small **shop** offering canned drinks, Nepali and sometimes imported biscuits, chocolate, Mars Bars and some sweets. Often tins of fruit or fish can be found, along with noodles, coffee, drinking chocolate, tea, muesli, porridge, milk powder, jam and batteries.

The Khumbu shops, especially in Namche, are well stocked. If you're not choosy it's quite possible to assemble enough food for a few nights' camping from the better shops in almost any village.

There are **banks** for foreign exchange at Namche (reliable), Lukla, Salleri and Khandbari. **Post offices** are also found in these three places, plus Junbesi. All are closed on Saturdays.

There is reliable **internet access** in Lukla and Namche and, by the time you read this, probably a number of other places too. Charges are around $10 per hour.

GSM mobile phones now work in and around Namche, even up to above Dingboche and the service area is likely to expand to Lukla and other areas. Other centres such as Phaplu have services too, but often only CDMA services, which are expanding rapidly in rural Nepal.

THE EVEREST REGION

Minimum impact trekking

Take nothing but pictures, leave nothing but footprints (Motto of the Sierra Club)

It is undeniable that trekking has had a significant impact on the environment, the culture and the economy of the Solu Khumbu, with both negative and positive effects. The opinions of experts as to the extent of the damaging effects of trekking on this region vary. Awareness of the problems has been raised, however, and solutions are being effected far more rapidly than elsewhere in Nepal. What is important to realize is that Lukla and north of there are at quite a different stage and in quite different circumstances to the Jiri and Arun regions.

It was most fortunate for the people of the Khumbu that the trekking industry started just as the vital trade links with Tibet were being severed by the Chinese. The industry has now developed into the single most important force in the economy and the Khumbu has become the richest area in rural Nepal. Many schools, hospitals and bridges, the obvious benefits of development, have been built.

Many people search for the negative aspects of the tourist industry before they begin to understand and balance the benefits. While tourism has negatively impacted the environment, perhaps the biggest damage to the forests of the Khumbu occurred when thousands of Tibetan refugees, fleeing the Chinese 'Great Leap Forward' and the continuing 'peaceful liberation' of Tibet, arrived and stayed in the Khumbu for months before moving down to other regions. However, the area seems to have recovered from the environmental damage this caused. Local villagers and lodges still use plenty of firewood but I have not read or been told that the current usage is unsustainable; after all, thousands of tonnes of firewood still grow in the region each year. The biggest user of firewood was Namche–Khumjung–Khunde who now have enough electricity to cook with. The burning of juniper and moss has mostly stopped too.

As far as trail litter goes, Khumbu villages are for the most part clean, with locals organizing clean-up campaigns, often several times a year. Mostly it is the porters brought by trekking groups that litter with abandon and there is still a need for an attitude change there. Glass was a major problem years ago but since then the locals have resolved to use cans only. Probably the biggest litter problem now – aside from toilet waste – is the plastic mineral water bottles (see p152) that trekkers insist on using. Admittedly it is bottled locally so there are some benefits but there are more environmentally sound alternatives. It is paradoxical that the water in these bottles is in fact Namche town supply water, which is 100% clean.

Then there is the tricky question of the cultural impact that tourism has on the region. The question is, should the area be closed to avoid Western influences from seeping into the local culture, or should we let cultural 'imperialism'

> **A plea to trekking groups**
> Please make voluble complaints to trek leaders and trekking company direc-
> tors if any of the environmental recommendations noted in this section are not
> carried out. The entire group's unburnable litter must be taken out right to the end of
> the trek. Kerosene must be provided by the company not just for the trekkers but for
> porters' use also. They may not use any firewood either in the national park or en
> route to Mera Peak. The police of the area are lackadaisical and although the park
> staff have authority there are no penalties for contravening park rules. The trekking
> companies and sirdars do not yet care, seemingly motivated by personal gain only.

take its course? Personally, although I was apprehensive at first, I now know
that the Khumbu Sherpas can handle the world with greater aplomb than most
Western cultures. Theirs is a close-knit and united community and the bonds
that keep them together seem as strong as ever; indeed, in many ways it is us
that have lessons to learn from them.

As a trekker you can still minimize your impact on the land and culture.
Here are some suggestions.

ENVIRONMENTAL CONCERNS

Pack it in, pack it out
In national parks in the West, visitors are encouraged to take out all their litter
when they leave (and indeed anything they bring into the park with them). In
Nepal the situation is not so straightforward since many of the national parks
contain villages and much of what you consume is purchased locally.

Litter
The most worrying and obvious litter problems in the Khumbu and Hinku
(Mera Peak area) are directly related to the activities of expedition-style
trekking and climbing groups. Tinned food and bottled sauces are served at
every meal. The members may be careful with their litter, putting it in the bins
set up in the camp, but what then happens to this rubbish? Sometimes it is burnt,
with the remains left sitting in the embers. Sometimes it is buried in the toilet,
covered by little more than an inch of dirt or it may be dumped at the nearest
village or simply left in the snow. The problem goes virtually unnoticed by
group members because the kitchen crew are the last to leave a camp or lunch
spot. Despite constant clean-up campaigns, litter left by groups is still a serious
problem. Park rules specifically state that all rubbish generated by trekking
groups must now be packed out and not dumped in village garbage pits which
were dug for the needs of the villagers.

The problem of litter generated by individual trekkers is not so serious.
There is little non-burnable litter that is not recycled apart from plastic mineral
water bottles which are a definite and unnecessary problem. Flour, sugar and
rice come in sacks, the cardboard from egg-boxes is reused, oil comes in tins

that are prized for roofing and, besides, very little tinned food is on menus. Most lodges now burn the burnables and villages have locally managed rubbish pits. Soft-drink cans should be crushed flat.

Don't use mineral water Since mineral water is sold in non-returnable, non-biodegradable plastic bottles and is now widely available in the Everest region (and the rest of Nepal) the empty bottles are becoming a serious litter problem. There are quite a few alternatives, of which using iodine compounds is the best, see p289.

Put litter in bins There is absolutely no excuse for dropping any litter along the trails, yet many trekkers are guilty of this, even if it's only the odd sweet wrapper. However, one piece of paper multiplied several thousand times becomes a significant problem.

Tissues, film cartons and biscuit wrappers are all easily stuffed into a back-pack mesh pocket for disposal in a bin at a lodge. You could also help by picking up a few bits of litter generated by other people.

Dispose of excess packaging before arrival Today virtually everything comes wrapped in multiple, sometime unnecessary layers.

Other pollution
Use the toilet facilities provided Most lodges have toilets which individual trekkers should use. Group trekkers should ensure that the toilets that are dug in their camps are of a sufficient depth and are properly filled in and covered with large stones when the campsite is left.

Bury or burn used toilet paper Nepalis use the 'water method' rather than toilet paper so all the white streamers beside the track are generated by trekkers. Used toilet paper can easily be burnt, concealed under a rock where it will decompose, or put in a bin that has been provided specifically for this purpose. Some toilets double as compost heaps, their contents, when mixed with leaf matter, eventually being spread on the fields. As such, don't put tampons into these, but instead wrap them and put them into rubbish bins.

Don't pollute water sources In the West the provision of clean drinking water has reduced the incidence of diarrhoea-related diseases to a negligible level. Nepal still has a long way to go but efforts are being made to provide villages with water from uncontaminated sources.

If bathing in streams, don't use soap or shampoo. Do not defecate close to the trail or a stream. If there is no toilet ensure you are at least 20 metres away from any water source and bury your waste and used toilet paper.

Fuel conservation
The total consumption of firewood by trekkers may be less than 0.1% of all the firewood consumed each year in Nepal but its effect is concentrated in a narrow ribbon along the main trails. Not only is wood used directly by lodges but also by all the porters who carry supplies for the markets. It is true that these porters

would, like other Nepalis, use firewood anyway but the majority would do so in their villages away from these busy main trails. Depletion of the remaining forest cover compounds the already serious erosion problems.

For villages on the Jiri to Namche trail there is no instant solution. Kerosene has to be imported and is not entirely practical for lodge use. The micro-hydro-electric schemes cannot, so far, generate enough electricity for cooking and the establishment of an extensive national rural electricity grid is beyond the thinking of mainstream politicians. Tree replanting and community forests are, however, now well established and are showing returns.

The best news, however, is that Namche now has the most advanced hydro-electric system in rural Nepal, a 630kw medium-size hydro-scheme. The lodges and the local people of Namche and the surrounding villages are adapting to cooking on electricity because it is cheaper than a wood-fired stove. One hopes that this admirable project will serve as a pilot scheme for others.

Accelerated erosion

Erosion is a natural phenomenon that creates river deltas and shapes mountains. In some parts of the world, however, it may occur at an accelerated rate that has serious consequences. The Himalaya are a young range of mountains, still in the process of formation, and erosion has always been considerable here. In the last few decades the problem has been exacerbated by rapid deforestation. The natural ground cover is being stripped away for firewood or animal fodder allowing rain to erode the essential topsoil. The problem is very serious: Nepal's forests are disappearing at the rate of 3% per year. One hectare of cleared forest loses around 50 tonnes of soil annually and approximately 400,000 hectares are cleared each year in Nepal.

Don't damage plants and stick to the trails In the alpine areas, above the tree line, plants battle to survive in a harsh environment. Trekkers can have a negative effect on these areas. Big boots and yak hooves disturb the topsoil and sliding down a slope can leave scars that never heal.

CULTURAL CONSIDERATIONS

There is no return to the time of traditionality for those who have abandoned it because the first condition for belonging to a traditional culture is that one does not know it
Al Ghazale, 12th-century philosopher

One of the great attractions of Nepal for the first visitors was the fact that the cultures of the many different peoples living here had evolved independently of Western 'civilization'. Day-to-day life for most people had remained virtually unchanged. Sudden outside influence, however, has brought profound change, particularly in the rural areas popular with tourists.

There is no denying that the West is a technologically advanced society but its superiority over less 'developed' cultures does not, necessarily, extend beyond this. A visit to a country like Nepal can be a particularly rewarding experience, especially if you have not travelled much outside the West. Many things are done differently here but this does not make the methods any less valid and in some cases they may be better.

The Nepalese way of solving problems, for example, is to avoid confrontation which starkly contrasts with the head-on 'Rambo' style of the West. The incidence of murder, theft and rape (outside of the family) in Nepal is negligible in comparison to most nations.

Although probably the biggest cultural influences are from Western television and Hindi movies, here are some ways that you can minimize your impact, especially out of the main tourist areas.

Dress decently Dress standards are important despite the fact that they are overlooked by many trekkers. Whilst men may go around without a shirt in the West, this is considered indecent in Nepal. Women will find it more comfortable not wear short shorts or singlet/vest tops. See box p51 for further information.

Respect people's right to privacy Ask people before you take their photograph and be considerate when looking for subjects.

Don't flaunt your wealth By lowland and normal Nepali standards, even the poorest foreign trekker is unimaginably wealthy. Nepalis often ask how much you earn; by all means tell them the truth, but qualify your answer by giving them some examples of the cost of living in your country. Don't leave valuables lying around as this is further evidence that you have so much money you can easily afford to replace them.

Respect religious customs Pass to the left of mani walls and chortens where there is a good path. Prayer wheels should be turned clockwise. Remove your boots before entering a gompa and leave a donation; there's often a metal box provided.

Respect traditions There are a number of other customs and traditions that you should take care to respect. Not to do so is to insult your hosts. The left hand, used for washing after defecating, is not considered clean so you should never touch anyone with it, offer them anything with it or eat with it. The head and top of the shoulders is considered the most sacred part of the body and you should never touch anyone there. Avoid pointing the soles of your feet at a person's head. If you're sitting with your legs outstretched and a Nepali needs to pass, he or she will never step over you. Move your legs out of the way.

Encourage pride in Nepali culture Express an interest in what people are doing and try to explain that everything is not as rosy in the West as some Nepalis might believe. In restaurants don't consistently shy away from Nepalese food. Local people are being taught by insidious example that packaged sweets, biscuits, noodles and chocolate are more desirable than local equivalents but in most cases they are actually less nutritious.

ECONOMIC IMPACT

The initial effect of independent trekkers using local lodges was an increase in prices for many commodities along the major trekking routes. The villagers, naturally enough, sought the best prices for their produce and the highest bidders were the trekkers. In the short term this created a problem because villagers were more willing to sell scarce commodities to trekkers. It should, however, also be considered as a stage in the long development process: demand encourages production where previously there was no advantage in producing more. If the commodity is not available locally it must be carried in by a porter who possibly comes from a remote village far from the trail, thus creating work in areas where there may be few employment opportunities.

Teahouse trekking stimulates the local economy. Money from individual trekkers enters the local economy via the shops and lodges but it can have an effect on the whole area. Porters carry in the additional goods, new buildings may need to be constructed requiring local resources and labour, staff are required at the lodges and local producers have a new market. Collectively these factors provide more jobs and can lead to a higher standard of living, not just among lodge owners. This is immediately obvious from visiting areas frequented by trekkers and comparing them with villages without this stimulus. Namche probably has the highest per capita income in Nepal, ahead even of Kathmandu. It has often been said that only 10% of the money stays with the lodge owner, but then the other 90% is spread between the manufacturer/local growers, porters and middlemen, so there are many others who benefit.

Don't bargain for food and lodging These prices are fixed and in most cases are surprisingly reasonable. Wisely, few Khumbu lodge owners will put up with hard bargaining and most will simply suggest politely that you look elsewhere.

Don't give to beggars Some trekkers, embarrassed at the disparity in material wealth between their country and Nepal, have given money to beggars and sweets and pens to children. They may have thought that they were helping but the opposite is probably true. As well as fostering an unhealthy dependency attitude, begging can in some places be more profitable than earning money by portering or working in the fields. Giving sweets to children not only encourages them to see Westerners (and hence the West) as bringers of all good things but also leads to tooth decay, once quite rare in Nepal. See also box pp98-9.

PART 5: ROUTE GUIDE & MAPS

Using this guide

Route descriptions
All the main routes for the greater Everest region are described and each route description is accompanied by detailed trail maps. There is no day by day description; instead, all the lodges and possible stopping places are marked so you can decide where to stay. However, to aid planning there are sample itineraries in the Appendix (pp282-4). Information relevant to walking in the reverse direction is also given: this is marked by ▲.

The main route sections are as follows:

Village and feature names
Most of the Sherpa villages have both a Nepali name and the traditional Sherpa name; a few even have a name exclusively used by trekkers. All the familiar names of a village are mentioned in this guide, with the one most commonly used by trekkers and guides repeated in the text. For the purpose of this guide I have also tentatively named a couple of hills and passes that didn't appear to have a local name.

Trail maps
The main geographical features shown are major ridges, rivers and streams. Being the Himalaya, you are surrounded by huge mountains and steep gorges but the ruggedness of this terrain is not depicted.

For working out which mountain you are admiring, a detailed colour topographic map (see pp60-1) is invaluable.

ROUTE GUIDE AND MAPS

The maps in this guidebook are drawn to a scale of roughly 1:100,000 (ie one centimetre is equivalent to one kilometre). The maps of the Rolwaling Valley are at 1:250,000. Features have been stylized so that roads, rivers and villages appear larger (easier to read) than on a true topographic map.

Following trails

Unlike many tracks in developed countries the trails in Nepal are unmarked. Paths lead off the main route to grazing areas, firewood-collecting areas and water sources. However, the main trail is usually larger and travels in a consistent direction so is easy enough to follow. If you think you have inadvertently taken the wrong path look carefully at the size of it: on a main path you don't usually brush against branches and undergrowth. Is it still heading in the right direction? If you must climb to the village and the path has been contouring for a while, don't be afraid to turn back. Occasionally trails divide and rejoin a little while later, especially around *mani* rocks (ie rocks with prayers carved on them).

The paths across glaciers and other difficult terrain are often littered with stone cairns (stone men). The majority mark the correct route but a few merely show that it is possible to climb a point. Occasionally cairns are toppled by snow, wind or animals. If you are sure you are on the correct path, don't hesitate to rebuild these guides or add new ones. Locals take pride in the art of constructing ones that are surprisingly well balanced and in just the right spot so that they are visible from afar.

Walking times

The hills render measured distances in miles or kilometres virtually meaningless; walking times are far more useful. These are given along the side of the maps, with arrows indicating the villages they refer to. While I have tried to be consistent as to the times quoted, inevitably there is some variation. The walking times on the trail maps give a wide spread. Hiking briskly and steadily with few stops should approximate the lesser time while ambling along admiring the scenery and spotting wildlife, or following a guide who sets a slow pace, should approximate the longer time.

The times are not meant to performance-orientate you: fast walkers, especially when heading downhill, could easily come in under the lesser times. In fact, my fervent hope is that trekkers mainly use them to help lunchtime and end-of-the-day decision-making (for example, if it is 3.30pm and you are wondering how far away the next lodge is and whether to stay or to go on). Once at Namche the pace is dictated solely by the altitude gains so involves rest days and half-day walks only.

When taking **day trips** uphill you can assume that the return downhill will take you half to two-thirds of the time it took to ascend. Don't forget to allow time for relaxing and exploring too. On a fine day there is no more satisfying place to bask in the sun than atop a hill with a glorious view.

Altitudes

These are given in metres on the maps and in the text they're also quoted in feet. Altitudes are approximate and rounded for villages since there are very few

> ◈ **Trail etiquette**
> Heavily loaded porters spend most of their time looking at where they are put-
> ting their feet so it is best to make way for them. With dzopkio or yak trains
> be especially careful to stay on the inside where you cannot potentially get knocked
> off the trail, and on a narrow section of trail or bridges, check that a caravan won't
> meet you in the middle.
>
> As with the Kathmandu traffic, there are no real trail rules, and a friendly
> 'Namaste' often opens up a little more space from Nepalis.
>
> Many people use trekking poles, and these are particularly useful for going
> steeply up or down. There is not yet a rule that they must have a rubber foot.

truly flat bits of ground. Altitudes have been quoted from the most accurate
source available for the area: the National Geographic map for Pangboche and
up, the Schneider series of maps and, where these were not available, Nepali
topographic maps combined with an altimeter. In general, GPS measurements
agree closely, although I have yet to double-check them all.

Don't get too worried about the sometimes huge differences in altitudes
between some villages. Trekking in Nepal involves crossing mammoth ridges all
the time. Simply go at a pace that suits you, stop frequently and you'll soon get
used to walking uphill and downhill. On the Salpa-Arun route there is one
absolutely flat stretch near Tumlingtar but, strangely, instead of being pleasant it's
hell. You seem to be getting nowhere, the ground is hard and it's tough walking.

Main ridges and mountains are shown as **thick lines** on the trail maps.

Facilities

The facilities available along the trail are indicated by symbols on the trail
maps. **Large lodges** (❑) are the bigger and better establishments that will have
a comprehensive menu and twin-bedded rooms. Simple **lodges/teahouses** (❑)
may have a dormitory and a few twin-bedded rooms, and are generally smaller
and simpler. Some are in locations where trekkers stay less frequently, stopping
at them only for tea or a meal. **Teashacks** (▽) are the simplest places, and are
not marked in the Lukla and above section. In the lower country they are often
just a few bamboo mats over a wooden frame and generally don't look too
hygienic. In the most basic, for example in the Arun Valley, there are no beds
for guests, only room on the floor.

If there's just one lodge or teahouse it'll be shown as an **outline**, a few will
be shown **half blacked-in** and if there are many lodges or teahouses they'll be
shown with a **black symbol**.

For the majority of villages there is a village plan. This shows the names
and locations of the lodges, with the words lodge, hotel, restaurant and guest
house omitted. No doubt a few names will change and a few new lodges will be
built too, so don't be surprised if the map is not entirely accurate.

❑ **Map key** See p309 for the route map key

Trekking from Lukla

INTRODUCTION

For the majority of trekkers and climbers Lukla is where the Everest trail now begins. Surprisingly though, Lukla wasn't built with tourists in mind. Sir Edmund Hillary and friends' intention when they constructed the airstrip in 1964 was to make it easier to bring building supplies in for the ever-growing number of development projects they were undertaking. The late Sir Edmund Hillary regretted that it was ever built, and (unfairly) blamed himself for the volume of trekkers now arriving in (assaulting, he thought) the Khumbu. Undoubtedly the Lukla airstrip has made access easier and so, too, has the increasing standard of the lodges. Now the Khumbu isn't the exclusive domain of mountaineers and tough trekkers; instead it is enjoyed by a surprisingly broad spectrum of people.

It can take a few days to discover your trekking legs and settle into the rhythm of the days. It can even take a while before you begin to look around with a true appreciation of the surroundings, which is a pity, because the trail to Namche sits in a magnificent gorge with views before Cheplung of the softer hills. There is no race to Chomolungma (Everest).

The region is a fascinating study of how rural towns and villages blend the demands of tourism with their own traditional way of life. Canned beer is drunk alongside *rakshi*, the most basic of spirits,

Mars bars sit alongside *chirpee*, a dried cheese as old as yak herding itself, and from now on the only wheels you'll see are prayer wheels.

It can be instructive to look inwards and not pre-judge the things you see too quickly; the way of doing things here has been refined over time and is generally more sensible than a critical eye first appreciates. It's tempting to stay at the biggest lodges which are mostly run by friendly owners and are certainly well set-up for trekkers, but understand your decision-making process. Staying in smaller lodges, particularly during peak season, enables you to sit around the kitchen fire and chat with the owner. Trekking is enlightening: a window into the contrasts of the rural third world; see also box p160.

Services & facilities in the Khumbu

Both Lukla and Namche have a **post office** and a **bank** as well as **moneychangers**; if you are stuck the occasional lodge owner will also change US$ cash though at less than favourable rates. Visa and other credit/debit cards are **not** accepted anywhere for payment of services, and a cash advance involves a hefty fee: only use a card in an emergency.

The Khumbu is well endowed with **medical facilities**. The Western-staffed Khunde hospital is open year-round, Western doctors staff the HRA clinic at

---

Mountain madness
A number of lodge owners laugh at this phenomenon. We at Khunde Hospital cry over it. Some of our patients with serious AMS have been so goal-orientated that their trek, instead of being the experience of a lifetime, has turned into the journey from hell, with the one objective of seeing Everest close up over-riding all else. The Khumbu has so much more to offer than Everest. If your only focus is to see Everest, why not take a scenic flight instead?

Sue Heydon, ex-Khunde Hospital

> ### The art of trekking
> Oh, to be trekking. Trekking is a process, not a goal. The joy could be a well-balanced pack, the freedom to stop and chat, to sit and wonder at a waterfall, or time for the perfect photo, to revel in pushing up a long hill or to sit around the kitchen fire. It is all of these things and more. There are a few things to be aware of:
> ● It is too easy to stop walking then not bother putting on an extra layer or changing into a dry one. Then you wonder why that cold got hold of you and not others ...
> ● You should be aware when you are getting close to your physical limits. Many people have limited experience with this. If you are tired on the trail eat some snacks and drink (see below) but don't just push on until you are hypoglycaemic; see p299.
> ● Take care to drink enough. Mild dehydration makes people surprisingly irritable and intractable. Don't drink only sweetened drinks or caffeinated drinks: try plain hot water as it sits well in the stomach and definitely sits better than a very cold drink. Cold drinks have an immediate, more-ish quality; warm or hot drinks have a more enduring, more gentle satisfaction.
> ● Trekking is not a competitive sport. Don't always push to be the first in, the first up the hill, even though it is sometimes satisfying. Many Americans, in particular, come from intensely competitive environments. For some people, pushing hard at altitude is dangerous.
> ● You will feel the altitude. Anyone who says otherwise is either kidding or a Sherpa. Drink a lot and consider what is best but don't worry unnecessarily about it. The occasional mild painkiller can make being at altitude so much more comfortable – expect to take a tablet every now and then (see p296).
> ● Take time out for the little details too. That annoying pack strap? Stop to fix it. Don't feel so rushed that you don't have time for that shower, that extra cup of tea.
> ● And finally, the more you ask the more you learn!

Pheriche during the peak trekking seasons and a clinic at Everest Base Camp in April and May, while Lukla has a health post with a capable health assistant who can contact Khunde if needed, and a second small hospital. Cheplung has a new government health post as does Namche, although don't rely on these services: Namche even has a private dental clinic.

Once again Namche has the best **communications systems** in rural Nepal with fast internet cafés, wifi spots, satellite television and all mobile phones work here, although currently Mero Mobile has the most extensive coverage. Elsewhere services are expanding, and internet cafés are sprouting in Lukla, Phakding, and even Dingboche. There are landline **phones** in Lukla, Namche, Khumjung, Khunde and Tengboche: many

places also have satellite phones which are especially handy in emergencies.

Toilet facilities
All lodges for tourists have toilet facilities. In the older ones this may be a pit toilet but increasingly there are flush toilets, some Asian squat style, and others in the sit-down Western-style. Many lodges even have both. In all cases it is BYO toilet paper. Increasingly there are wash basins outside the better toilets as well.

LUKLA (2850m/9350ft)
Getting to Lukla is covered on p26 and p122. A quick squeal of rubber and once outside the bustle of the airport you can suck in the sharp, clean mountain air and feel the tensions of Kathmandu melt away.

(Opposite) Top: Namche (see p171). **Bottom left**: The Saturday market in Namche. **Bottom right**: The bridge below Namche, like most in the region now upgraded to a strong steel bridge.

Altitude awareness
Most people who fly into Lukla claim not to feel the altitude at all, but then most people seem to be afraid of admitting 'weakness' here on their very first night. The air feels noticeably sharper, fresher and drier and this isn't just the lack of pollution: it is actually thinner. It is quite normal to get breathless climbing stairs and it is also common to have a light headache in the evening. Even people who have previously been to high altitudes can experience this and it shows that your body needs time to adapt: it doesn't mean you are particularly susceptible to AMS or that you will have trouble later. Be kind to your body by drinking plenty of fluids and taking it easy.

Relax! For many people this is the real beginning of their holiday.

Lukla means 'sheep corral', which is all it was before the airstrip was built. Now it's more like a tourist pen operated by a mishmash of peoples: many Sherpas but also Rais, Brahmins and Chhetri shopkeepers. It has become a trekking focal point with group porters waiting for work, supplies being collected, trekkers staying for their flight out and, in the midst of it all, endearing and snotty-nosed kids. For the children of the local people, Lukla boasts one of the few schools in the area that was not initiated by the Himalayan Trust (see box p172). It's only a primary school so the middle- and high-school children must go to Chourikharka or to boarding school in Kathmandu.

By 2009 Lukla should have a comprehensive (100kw) electricity system, enough at least to light all the buildings and to allow some to cook with electricity, power internet cafés and allow mobile telephone services. A sewerage project is also planned.

Arrival

Introduce yourself to Lukla: wade through the throng of porters looking for work, go left uphill and be tempted by the bakery only a moment later. Continue around the top of the airport with its wire fence, down past the wire-protected control tower and cross the steel grating bridge, just before Paradise Lodge. You are now on the main trail through Lukla, watch out for dzopkio dung!

Want some breakfast or lunch before you start? There are several cafés in the centre of Lukla but equally most lodges will be happy to serve you; wander into the dining room and see if anyone is around.

ROUTE GUIDE AND MAPS

Lukla airstrip
The airstrip was constructed by local Sherpas under Hillary's supervision. It took a month and cost US$2650 but being quite short it could only safely handle planes with eight passengers. Subsequent improvements, the last one in 2000-1 with funding from the Asian Development Bank, have reshaped and tar-sealed the runway and added an airport building to cope with the increasing traffic.

Although the runway requires a steep approach, it is much less hair-raising than it used to be and much smoother, enabling not just the sturdy Twin Otters to land but also the STOL (Short Take Off and Landing) Dornier 288s. The Lukla landing is one of the best of Nepal's alarmingly rough rural airstrips and there have been no major accidents here, though in 2004 a Dornier pilot rather embarrassingly forgot to lower the plane's undercarriage.

(Opposite) Top: Chourikharka (see p165) is a picturesque middle hills village, probably the only real view you'll get of this type of terrain if you flew in to Lukla. **Bottom**: Landing at Lukla airstrip is an exhilarating experience.

Drinking water
Bottled water may be convenient but plastic bottles are an environmental nightmare. A better alternative is to ask for boiled water, all lodges have stacks of large thermoses. Higher up you will be asked to pay for this water. Even water that has barely been brought to the boil is in fact safe.

Some places also feature filtered water, a great alternative, and usually cheaper. In fact many of the water supplies are clean, including the tap water in Namche.

You will soon be able to work out the places that are set up to serve you quickly. Alternatively, eat at Cheplung, the first lodge-village around 25-45 minutes away.

If travelling with a group you are likely to be led to your lodge while the crew finish preparations.

Before you leave Lukla you should register with the **police post** by the exit of the town, right beside the trail.

Lodges
There's a wide variety of lodges, most of which are along the main street with another cluster on the other side of the airport. The most luxurious are *Everest Summit*, *Villa Sherpani*. *North Face Resort* and *Khangri*, where rooms with attached bathrooms go for $20-60 a night. At the other end of the market are basic lodges for the porters and guides who hang around for another job; and, of course, there's everything in between.

Planning the first night
Most people who fly into Lukla stay the first night at Phakding where there are plenty of big, good lodges. However, there are plenty of other places to stay between Ghat and Jorsale, where you will often have the lodge almost to yourself.

The next night you should be staying at Namche, which can be reached quite easily from all these places.

LUKLA TO NAMCHE   [Map 1, p165]
This is a trekkers' highway with *teashops* and *lodges* lining the route and, other than while ascending the hill to Namche, teashops are never more than 10 or 15 minutes away and lodges are never more than half an hour apart.

Flying out of Lukla
Flying from Lukla to Kathmandu you are supposed to **reconfirm your ticket** the afternoon before you fly. Most offices are open from around 2 to 4.30pm but in practice tickets can usually be reconfirmed any time up to around 5pm; talk with your lodge owner if you have problems.

Should you reconfirm? Yes; if you are walking from Namche to Lukla this is particularly relevant since you are likely to arrive quite late. You are much better off reconfirming and should try to arrive in Lukla at around 4pm. If you are trekking out of peak season you can usually get away with seeing the airline staff first thing in the morning or enlisting the help of your lodge owner to track down the airline representative.

Amazingly enough, peak season or otherwise, **if you need to buy a ticket** you stand a good chance of being able to arrive one afternoon and leave the next day. With the number of airlines and flights it is a bit unusual not to get a seat, though sometimes it can be very last minute and on the last few flights of the day. To make the process easier ensure you have dollars to pay for the ticket, preferably the right amount, and don't have too much luggage. In general avoid NAC, the national airline, and don't be disappointed if you do have to stay another day.

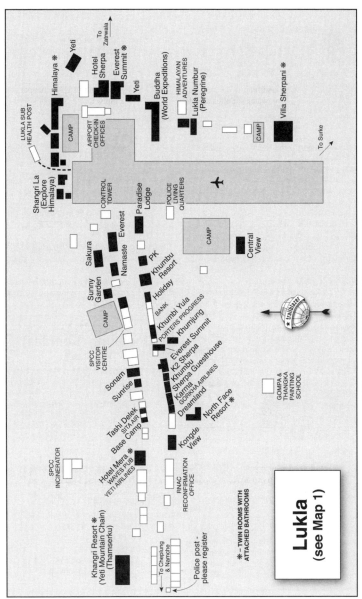

To Zatrwala

Himalaya *
Yeti
Hotel Sherpa
Everest Summit *
Yeti
Buddha (World Expeditions)
HIMALAYAN ADVENTURES
Lukla Numbur (Peregrine)
Villa Sherpani *

LUKLA SUB HEALTH POST
CAMP
AIRPORT CHECK-IN OFFICES
CAMP

To Surke

Shangri La (Explore Himalaya)
CONTROL TOWER
Paradise Lodge
POLICE LIVING QUARTERS

Everest
Sakura
Namaste
PK
Khumbu Resort
CAMP
Central View

Sunny Garden
CAMP
Holiday
BANK
Khumbi Yula
PORTERS PROGRESS
Khumjung

SPCC VISITOR CENTRE
Sonam
Sunrise
Everest Summit
K2 Sherpa
Khumbu
Sherpa Guesthouse
Karma
GORKHA AIRLINES
Dreamland
North Face Resort *

GOMPA & THANGKA PAINTING SCHOOL

Tashi Delek
SITA AIR
Base Camp
Kongde View

SPCC INCINERATOR
Hotel Mera *
WAVES PUB
YETI AIRLINES

RNAC RECONFIRMATION OFFICE

* – TWIN ROOMS WITH ATTACHED BATHROOMS

Khangri Resort *
(Yeti Mountain Chain)
(Thamserku)

To Cheplung & Namche

Police post – please register

Lukla
(see Map 1)

> ### Relative loads
> For new trekkers, the first talking point is the size of the loads the local porters carry. Group trekkers may feel guilty seeing their porters loaded with three trekkers' kitbags (35-40kg total), but porters working for themselves are almost superhuman. A box of water or bottled beer weighs 12kg and often five or more boxes are carried – a very real 60kg! Boxes of noodles are much lighter but hidden underneath is probably a 30kg bag of rice or flour; the heaviest loads will come in at around 90-120kg (200-264lbs). And all carried for a few dollars a day. They have my respect.

Resist the temptation to put your head down and walk hard. There are many rewards for focusing on the surroundings, particularly 15 minutes out of Lukla where there are some of the most beautiful rural scenes on the entire trek. Photograph the views now, if the weather is good!

Between October and mid-November the trails are clogged with trekkers tripping over and dzopkio bulldozing their way through. Don't despair as these crowds divide a little above Namche between the Gokyo and Kala Pattar trails.

Trekkers who have been here before will notice there are more painted mani stones and prayer wheels to spin and of course the lodges are getting ever bigger and even getting a regular coat of fresh paint. Below Namche there are more people of other ethnic groups attending shops and lodges or working as helpers further up.

A local speciality worth trying here and in Namche is apple pie. Bakeries serve the traditional style of apple pie while lodges serve a freshly made version of apple in a deep-fried pastry, deliciously flavoured with cinnamon or even a little chocolate powder. Most of the vegetables for Namche and above are grown along this stretch of trail; enjoy fresh *saag* (pronounced sarg), a type of spinach, and carrots and tomato achaar, a local sauce for dal bhaat.

If you are after a quick lunch on the trail consider carefully what to order. If the rice is already cooked, fried rice variations will work. Veg noodle soup is delicious and especially quick when made with instant noodles; chapattis, Tibetan bread and fried noodle dishes also come out smartly. Dal bhaat tends to take longer and is better

ordered for dinner. To be kind to the lodge owner, order dinner at least an hour in advance so they can plan the various combinations ordered. Ordering similar food helps but it isn't necessary any more except in the most simple lodges.

Information relevant to walking in the reverse direction is given, marked by ▲.

Cheplung / Lomdza (2660m/8727ft)
Here the trail from Lukla meets the main trail from Jiri and Salpa-Arun.

Three of the **lodges** burnt down in 2006, apparently by carelessness in a

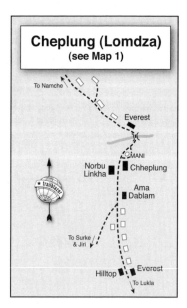

Cheplung (Lomdza)
(see Map 1)

To Namche

Everest

MANI

Norbu Linkha   Chheplung

Ama Dablam

★ trailblazer

To Surke / & Jiri

Hilltop   Everest

To Lukla

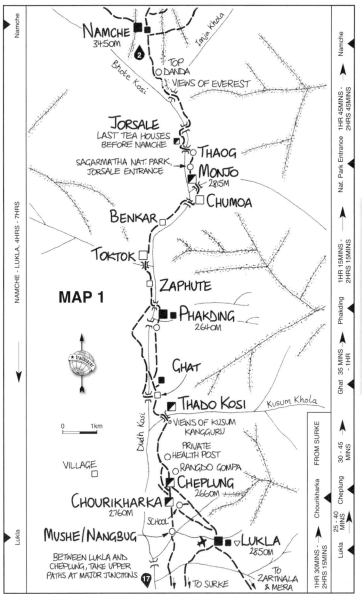

Sherpa dos and don'ts
(Compiled with the assistance of **Urken Norbu** of Dole). You are now in Sherpa country. They are a relaxed people whose favourite pastimes include gambling with dice, drinking chang, joking and kidding around, then repenting in the gompa.

Do:
- Treat them as equals
- Smile, be friendly and take time to say hello or chat
- Joke with the right people for you can't offend them
- If offered a drink with refills, accept a minimum of two refills
- Ask about culture and explain your own realistically: once this might have been a delicate subject, but now it isn't – most sherpas aren't the least bit naive
- Ask about caring for the environment and mostly you will be surprised – they *do* care, do sometimes spend their own money on conservation and, furthermore, often complain that the government doesn't do anything
- Hand over money or things with your right hand or both hands
- Accept with your left hand or both hands
- If someone (usually a good friend) shakes hands with both hands, reciprocate

Don't:
- Sit in the head of the house's place by the fire (usually the right-hand side, the warmest spot)
- Stretch your legs out so that people have to walk over them
- Throw rubbish on the fire, unless you are told it is OK
- Put your feet or boots up on the fire
- Whistle inside the house
- Put your feet or bum on a table
- Touch anyone (children or adults) on the head or top part of the shoulders

kitchen: so far only one, the *Norbu Linkha*, has been replaced. Luckily there were no injuries or deaths.

▲ Coming down from Namche, the straight route up some gentle stairs out of Cheplung leads to Lukla, while a smaller trail drops for the real walk out, a little past *Ama Dablam Guest House*.

Rangdo Gompa Stunningly set into the rock wall, this gompa is usually closed. Ask at the lodges for the key and usually a child will accompany you up. It is customary to leave a donation for the upkeep: Rs100-200 is appropriate, but any donation is appreciated. A village gompa promotes community spirit and pride and is a meeting point during festivals.

Thado Kosi Here an elegant bridge crosses the Kusum Khola and there are impressive views of Kusum Kangguru. This

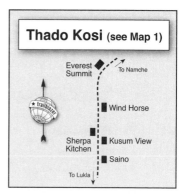

Thado Kosi (see Map 1)

Everest Summit — To Namche

★ trailblazer

Wind Horse

Sherpa Kitchen
Kusum View

Saino

To Lukla

mountain is revered by local people; its name means the 'White (or Pure) Mountain House of the Three Gods' and indeed from around Namche three individual peaks can be seen. Although there are plenty of places in the area offering snacks/lunch Thado Kosi is popular and the views mean it is a good place to eat outside.

Ghat/Nynyung This is the next settlement, just around the corner. *Ghat* means 'bridge' in Nepali and the bridge here was once important because it was one of the alternatives to the bridge at Jubing that was often washed away. With the advent of strong steel-cabled suspension bridges that route has lost its importance. The direct route to Namche does not cross the bridge but instead follows a trail lined with *lodges* a few metres apart. Few trekkers stay here but there are some friendly lodge owners, even if the lodges themselves aren't so fancy. It is often possible to have a look in the **gompa** at the top end of town.

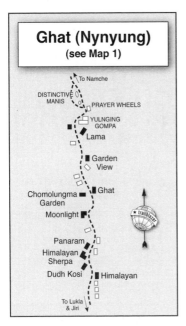

Ghat (Nynyung)
(see Map 1)

To Namche
DISTINCTIVE MANIS
PRAYER WHEELS
YULNGING GOMPA
Lama
Garden View
Chomolungma Garden ■ Ghat
Moonlight
Panaram
Himalayan Sherpa
Dudh Kosi ■ Himalayan
To Lukla & Jiri

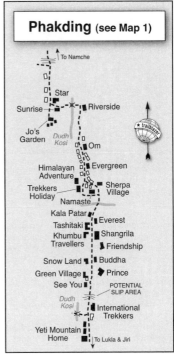

Phakding (see Map 1)

To Namche
Star
Sunrise ■ Riverside
Jo's Garden   *Dudh Kosi*
Om
Himalayan Adventure   Evergreen
Trekkers Holiday   Sherpa Village
Namaste
Kala Patar   Everest
Tashitaki   Shangrila
Khumbu Travellers   Friendship
Snow Land   Buddha
Green Village   Prince
See You   POTENTIAL SLIP AREA
Dudh Kosi
International Trekkers
Yeti Mountain Home   To Lukla & Jiri

ROUTE GUIDE AND MAPS

Phakding / Rhanding (2640m/8661ft)
Welcome to lodge-city. A two- to four-hour walk from Lukla, Phakding is the usual overnight spot for groups who've flown in to Lukla and as a result has a multitude of big, high-standard *lodges*, which may come as a shock to Jiri and Salpa-Arun walkers.

Despite the size of the lodges the *sahuni* are friendly, when not run off their feet. However, it is not necessary to stay here and there are plenty of alternatives further up, although the lodges are not quite as big.

If you arrive with time to spare there are two **gompas** on the west side of the river, half an hour from the main part of Phakding and visible from there. Another ten minutes further on is the village of **Gomila**, which is rarely visited by trekkers.

Feeling cold here? Don't be alarmed: in the steep-sided valley, afternoon cloud

❏ Sherpani dress

English	Sherpa
wraparound dress	*ungi*
front apron	*dungdil*
back apron	*giptu*
blouse	*ratuk*
necklace	*zikur*
black and white stone	*zi*
coral	*churuk*
turquoise stone	*yu*

often results in a penetrating, damp cold and a chilly evening here will compare with anything else the trek throws at you. Similarly a sprinkling of rain here is not indicative of what to expect higher up.

For those who have flown to Lukla, the first suspension bridge of the trek lies at the end of Phakding. Built in 1999, it's a long one but don't worry about having to cross one at a time as it was designed to handle yak trains. Just beyond Rhanding the trail traverses a steep section that periodically collapses and falls away through erosion.

Zaphute, Toktok and Benkar/Benkora Between Phakding and Monjo, a leisurely couple of hours' walk, are many *teahouses* and small shops and the occasional proper *lodge*.

From Toktok the sheer face of Thamserku comes into view to the northeast. **Benkar** has a set of homely *lodges* beginning above the waterfall pool.

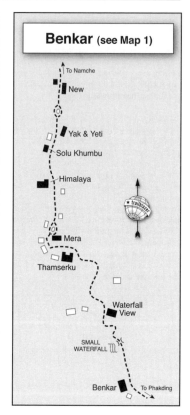

Benkar (see Map 1)

To Namche
New
Yak & Yeti
Solu Khumbu
Himalaya
Mera
Thamserku
Waterfall View
SMALL WATERFALL
Benkar — To Phakding

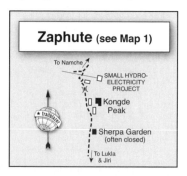

Zaphute (see Map 1)

To Namche
SMALL HYDRO-ELECTRICITY PROJECT
Kongde Peak
Sherpa Garden (often closed)
To Lukla & Jiri

❏ Timbore

Beside the trail between Lukla and Namche you might notice a bush with large thorns similar in shape to rose thorns. In September this bears red berries, from which a black seed emerges as the berry dries. The flesh (rather than the seed) is crushed to make the spice timbore. It has a sharp distinctive taste and numbs the tongue and gums so is widely used for toothache.

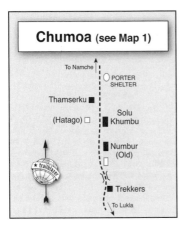

Chumoa Passing through, on your left are the ruins of Chumoa Lodge Hatago. This was one of the first high-standard lodges between Lamosangu (before the days of the road to Jiri) and Namche and was really a place to be looked forward to after the basic places on the long walk in. Unfortunately, the Japanese man who ran it was eventually deported and ownership of the land is in dispute.

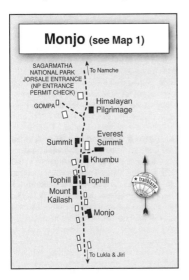

Monjo / Mimzok (2815m/9235ft) I guess that Monjo is a trekker corruption of the original name Mimzok, which means gathering or meeting place, being halfway between the older villages of Chumoa and Jorsale.

There are a handful more *lodges* here, some quite large and a few simple inns and *teashacks*.

Signs welcoming donations herald the **gompa** (monastery), situated a hundred metres or so off the main trail. Strangely, despite ten years of donations, not much has materialized and locals now support another gompa. A minute later you reach the gateway to Sagarmatha National Park.

Sagarmatha National Park (Jorsale entrance) At the grand new (2006) building, the entrance to the park, your **national park permit** will be checked; alternatively, show your passport/copy and pay the Rs1000 permit fee.

Your **TIMS permit** (see pp83-4), if the system is still in operation, will also be checked and you have to check out with both on the way down.

Porters and guides must also register and sometimes their loads are checked, partly due to endangered species protection, and preventing the smuggling of medicinal plants.

Jorsale / Tha Og (see map p170) Leaving the park entrance the path drops steeply to the long suspension bridge, built in 1995, across the Dudh Kosi.

The *lodges* and *teahouses* on the other side are the last lodges until Namche, as some of them indeed announce. Namche is still a minimum of 90 minutes away and closer to three hours if you are particularly slow so ensure you have enough snacks and water to get you there.

Soon you recross the river and sharp eyes may notice the Helvetas brass plaque; the Swiss have been assisting Nepal since the 1950s (see the box on p238 to find out why) and helped set up 'His Majesty's Suspension Bridge Division', now the Government Suspension Bridge Division, the builders of most of these fine bridges.

ROUTE GUIDE AND MAPS

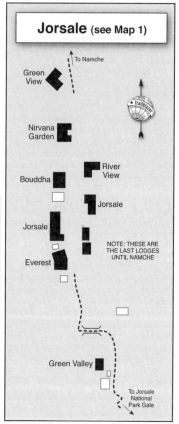

Jorsale (see Map 1)

To Namche

Green View

Nirvana Garden

Bouddha

River View

Jorsale

Jorsale

Everest

NOTE: THESE ARE THE LAST LODGES UNTIL NAMCHE

Green Valley

To Jorsale National Park Gate

trailblazer

High bridge over the Dudh Kosi The trail turns rocky with some short, steep sections up stone steps – beware of dzopkio coming the other way, stay on the inside – up to the 1989-built kata-bedecked suspension bridge denoting you are entering the Khumbu proper. Apparently designed with catastrophes in mind, it is indestructibly high above the river. After the nasty concrete steps the path is broad and pleasant, having been widened and tidied up to lessen erosion. It is still quite a hill, so it's hard on your legs and lungs if you flew in

to Lukla and the rapid gain in altitude may induce a headache that comes and goes.

Up a few bends is the first of several relatively uninspiring views of Everest: it is mostly hidden behind the Lhotse-Nuptse wall and is now partially obscured by trees too. The view from the next bend is better and it is also visible from Top Danda.

Top Danda is the halfway point up the hill from the bridge. Its stone load-resting places are popular with porters and it also has a view of Everest and is 35-60 mins from Namche, though there is a snack shop about 20 mins away. Until sometime in the 1800s this was the Tibetan border. Yes, Namche was in Tibet, and 'top' means a small-wheeled cannon, the protection for Namche, as were the piles of rocks collected there. Top Danda is the perfect spot for a teashop but this isn't allowed by the national park.

Interestingly, during the 1855 war with Tibet it is said that the Nepalis came up the valley and at night they attached burning branches to sheep, thus tricking the Tibetans into believing there were many more soldiers, and luring them into the valley where the Nepalis rolled rocks down in a neat ambush, winning the battle.

As you near Namche, with occasional views of the town ahead and above, you reach some lodges used by porters followed by water taps, a **police post** where you must register and a junction. The pious entrance to the town is via the lower path through the *kani* (to remove any bad spirits), around the stupa and up past the spring but local shopkeepers prefer you to take the upper route along the trail that passes the Saturday market area into the shopping heart of Namche.

▲ **Leaving Namche (for Lukla)** Heading down, especially in peak season, use the old but good path down to avoid traffic jams and as a bonus walk around the old manis the correct way. The path begins about 80 metres past the small snack shop a few minutes below the last of the teahouses out of Namche. The first five metres are a rough and small trail but from then on it is a good trail that rejoins the main one a minute or two before Top Danda.

Geography in action

In September 1977 a huge avalanche peeled off Ama Dablam and crashed into a glacial lake. The lake burst and sent a great wave of water down the valley. A number of bridges which were normally unaffected by monsoon floods were wiped out as well as some sections of the trail.

It has taken a long time, but the washed-out bridges have virtually all now been replaced. The next calamity, however, cannot be far away. There are many forces that shape the landscape, and these waves of water are not only monumental in scale, but common too. Their causes are numerous: sometimes it is a lake that bursts; often it is a landslide that blocks a river, causing it to bank up before releasing a devastating wall of water that cuts into the river bed, undercutting the banks and providing the instability for yet another hillside to collapse and block the river again ... and so the process starts all over again.

Namche and around

NAMCHE/NAUCHE (3450m/11,319ft)

Welcome to the Namche bowl. Looking across to the huge face of Kongde and with sharp peaks glistening above, you really know you are in the mountains.

Since all routes upwards pass through here, and it's an essential acclimatization stop, the facilities are well-developed and the village bustles with trekkers most of the year.

Called Nauche by all Sherpas and Naboche by Tibetans, the village is more widely known as Namche, a century-old Nepali mispronunciation. It's also long been referred to as Namche Bazaar, inaccurate since at the time all trading was con-

Rubbishing rubbish

In previous editions I discussed problems with litter and now I am pleased to write that there are bins along the route for trekkers' rubbish and in general the Khumbu is far cleaner than the media thinks.

The locals were first prodded to keep their villages tidy and rubbish-free for tourism but now keep them clean for themselves. The Namche and Khumjung youth groups clean trails several times a year and lodge owners often sing in groups cleaning the trails too, so if you do see rubbish it is usually of recent origin. If everybody picked up the occasional piece there would be none at all...

Glass used to be the biggest problem. However, sensibly, in 2001 Khumbu lodge owners united and resolved to stop selling beer and soft drinks in glass bottles. Cans should be crushed: bottled water is better not used, but if you do, crush the bottles.

Porters and camping group crews are by far the worst offenders when it comes to rubbish as many of them don't feel any responsibility to the region. From this point on no firewood is allowed to be cut so all groups must use kerosene for themselves and also for the porters: check that this is the case.

All that said, the only real blot on this good record is around the entrance to Namche and below the Saturday market, where rubbish is strewn down the hillside.

The Himalayan Trust and Sir Edmund Hillary

The Himalayan Trust is a charity that has helped local people set up almost thirty schools, several hospitals and construct many bridges and runways in the Solu Khumbu. Many years on, the positive results are obvious and the region is far ahead along the development road compared with the rest of rural Nepal. Its phenomenal success is the result of sound principles and dedicated staff. The late Sir Edmund Hillary deserves the highest praise for his selfless efforts: almost every Himalayan Trust school, bridge and hospital bears the stains of Hillary's sweat and until his death in 2008 he returned to Nepal virtually every year to continue the work. Villagers saw him as the one person who could realize their local projects.

It is the fact that these were projects initiated by the people themselves (rather than imposed by the government) that has been the key to their success. Development has happened at village pace. As far as possible, villagers must provide land and labour although the Trust provides the bulk of finance required for materials. This degree of local involvement ensures that bridges, hospitals and schools are well cared for. In addition, more than 50 scholarships are awarded each year for further education, with priority for girls.

ROUTE GUIDE AND MAPS

ducted in private homes; the weekly market (see pp175-6) started only in 1965. The Sherpa name, Nauche, is in fact only a short form of an older name, thought to be Nakmuche or Nakuche, meaning 'big dark forest' – unfortunately now an inappropriate name. However, the couple of walled-off areas on the hillside above the village are remedying this and, slowly but surely, forests of pine are returning.

This thriving village has grown up around a magnificent spring in its centre though it was only recently realized that this spring water is not clean. Now the drinking water is taken from a clean source: it's another step in the ongoing development of the village.

Namche now has a mountain resort feel with down-jacket-clad locals and several helicopters a day flying in to Syangboche above. The lodges have invested in ever-better facilities, many boasting rooms with attached bathrooms and the varnished wood panoramic dining rooms with traditional sherpa features and pot belly stoves really lend a cosy alpine experience.

For trekkers who visited in the last millennium the 'new' Namche can seem over the top but all of this has been driven by demand, and the fancy lodges are not going out of business. In many ways it is best to think of it as a new-style mountain-resort town, rather than a Sherpa village. It is still all Sherpa owned and managed, even if increasingly the workers are Rais from below the Khumbu. The 'yak steak' buffalo meat also comes from there, and vegetables from near Lukla and below, so it is not just the people of the Khumbu who benefit.

Acclimatization

It is important for all trekkers to spend at least two nights acclimatizing here and, if fresh from Lukla, spending three nights here may be advisable if you spent only one night on the trail between Lukla and Namche. However, even if you do adhere to this advice it's not unusual to suffer mild altitude sickness at Namche and some people have trouble sleeping.

If AMS symptoms do occur or are worse on the second night, staying three nights or taking Diamox (see p295) is a good policy: you will only invite further trouble higher up if your body is not given a chance to cope adequately here. A sound alternative is to spend the third night at Phunki Tenga which is slightly lower and may give your body a chance to recuperate. The fact that the next night will be spent 600m higher should not matter if you have already spent two nights at Namche.

If you have plenty of time, an extra night's stop in Thame or Khumjung/Khunde/Kyangjuma/Phortse would be rewarding and further aid acclimatization. Since these villages are at an equivalent altitude to Tengboche they are also excellent alternatives to spending two nights there.

Note that it is possible, although rare, to develop serious altitude sickness at Namche: several trekkers have even died in Namche because people did not consider they could be sick with AMS. If you feel bad tell somebody responsible.

Drink plenty here, and I am not talking about beer!

Lodges

In and around Namche there are about 50 lodges with the most popular being the group in the centre of town, simply because of their location, but all the lodges are good and a number are run by locally renowned sirdars and high-altitude climbers.

It is now easier to find a room with attached bathroom than dormitories, a sign of how the trekking market has changed. However, most people stay in standard double (twin-bedded) rooms. As is common further up there is a two-tier pricing system: the bed charge is nominal if you eat breakfast and dinner at the lodge. If, however, you are in a group with your own cook or wish to eat at other lodge restaurants the bed charges climb to cover this loss. Room prices are now fixed and uniform: Rs200 for a double and a double with attached bathroom costs the equivalent of $20. Don't try to bargain.

Food and drink

Lodge menus tend to be extensive and one of Namche's specialities is **yak steaks**: sufficiently tenderized and with a fried egg on top, they are delicious. Namche is also a good place to try **fried meat**, sometimes called *sukuti*, strips or cubes of meat with chilli, garlic and tomato.

Will this be you?

At Khunde Hospital we see too many cases of severe altitude sickness. Many people arrive close to death, and all need not have got so dangerously sick if they had followed altitude advice and guidelines. For example, a trekker in his early twenties arrived dying from HACE. From Monjo he had climbed to Gokyo in three days and had attempted Gokyo Ri. He said he knew there were warnings about altitude sickness – his English was excellent – but 'who ever reads them?' As you can guess, he did live to tell his story.

Our sickest patient who lived was a lowland porter but he was in a coma for five days. The Nepalese, especially Sherpas, have the completely untrue belief that Nepalese don't suffer from altitude sickness; they consider it a foreigners' disease, yet lowland porters are just as susceptible as foreigners, if not more so because of the load they carry. Ensure your sirdar is aware of this and ask the company to hire only altitude-experienced porters: it is false economy to hire young, inexperienced and therefore cheaper, porters as some will get sick and there have been cases of them being set down without companions and nearly dying. Watch your porters if you don't trust your sirdar and if they ask for aspirin it may be because they haven't drunk enough, but this is also a sign that they may indeed be suffering AMS.

One British trekker's porter became very sick at Lobuche. He had probably been suffering altitude sickness for a while but either didn't know what it was or didn't tell anyone. As soon as the trekker realized what was up, he helped him down but the porter died on the trail while still a day's walk from Khunde (Pheriche was closed). He was in shock and will suffer regrets for the rest of his life.

Sue Heydon, ex-Khunde Hospital

Facilities for porters
Namche's superior facilities may delight the trekker, but for porters it has become more difficult, a fact recognized a while ago. Now there is a porter shelter with toilets and showers, both for porters with trekking groups and also for market porters, with a large area to sleep in and a kitchen area, and even dal bhaat served for reasonable prices. It was partly financed by Sagarmatha Buffer Zone to the tune of around 1.5 million rupees and is run by the local community. The solar shower is for both porters and for the civil servants who don't have particularly good facilities.

Despite the drive for convenience, the local community still adheres to the principle of 'no killing of animals' above the bridge into the Khumbu. So all the 'yak steaks' are in fact buffalo meat, carried up by porters (did you pass any?) from villages several days walk away – well aged.

With the installation of electric ovens and microwaves new varieties of **cakes and pies** are appearing on menus. *Namche Bakery* has great cakes: try the pizza or apple strudel at your peril!

Milk coffee has been replaced with **cappuccinos** and coffee machines, and both **beer** and **wine** are available in lodge restaurants. Namche produces its own **mineral water**. The seals don't always look professional but lodge owners are normally honest about these things. Amazingly enough for people that are used to the perception that even the water in the mountains is dirty in Nepal, Namche's town supply water is the same as the stuff they bottle, and has been tested many times. So why not save plastic and drink from the tap or drink filtered water.

Services

Although Namche feels important it isn't the district headquarters: that is to the south at Salleri. However, with a customs post, the National Park headquarters and an army post there are still rather too many government officials and the imbalance of income is often a source of low-level conflict.

The **post office** is open from 10am to 4pm daily except Saturday, though it's really just a filing cabinet and a box.

Namche boasts the only modern **dental clinic** out of Nepal's cities. Nawang Doka, the Namche Sherpani who runs it, is to be admired for staying in Namche because with three years training in Canada she could earn much more elsewhere. It was funded by the American Himalayan Foundation and money raised by the 1991 Everest Marathon. It's usually filled with local people: they treat roughly 70 patients a month and are obviously doing a good job repairing the damage caused by the candy-culture, for which trekkers are partly to blame. Charges for foreign patients start from US$20. Visitors are welcome but the running costs are high: donations are appreciated. They sell logo T-shirts and also basic medicines, which can save a trip to Khunde but are no substitute for a consultation. The clinic also carries out community work such as the distribution of fluoride tablets in schools, which help prevent decay and make teeth stronger.

There is a newly built **government health post**, which is being watched carefully: hopefully with better facilities it might perform better than the previous one. However, trekkers generally use Khunde Hospital, see pp180-1.

The region's **electricity** is more reliable than Kathmandu's: see box p184 for how the project was set up. You can charge cameras etc although it is best to bring your own adaptor to fit the local plugs.

Yet another benefit of having a good water supply and electricity are washing machines: it is an easy place to get clothes washed. Some lodges offer a **laundry service**: there are also several people in the centre of town who pile load after load through their machines and driers. Impressively, Namche had washing machines before I ever saw any in Kathmandu.

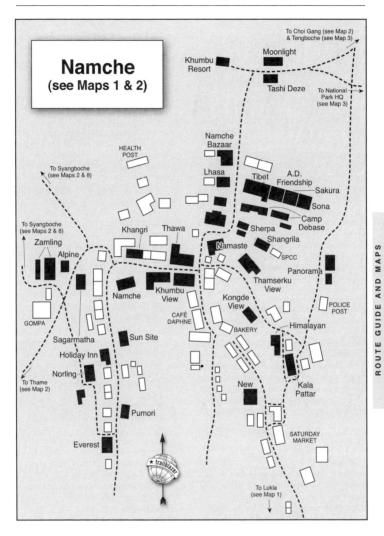

Namche
(see Maps 1 & 2)

To Choi Gang (see Map 2)
& Tengboche (see Map 3)

Khumbu Resort

Moonlight

Tashi Deze

To National
Park HQ
(see Map 3)

HEALTH POST

Namche Bazaar

To Syangboche
(see Maps 2 & 8)

Lhasa

Tibet

A.D. Friendship

Sakura

Sona

To Syangboche
(see Maps 2 & 8)

Khangri

Thawa

Sherpa

Camp Debase

Zamling

Alpine

Namaste

Shangrila

SPCC

Panorama

Namche

Khumbu View

Thamserku View

GOMPA

Kongde View

POLICE POST

Sagarmatha

CAFÉ DAPHNE

BAKERY

Himalayan

Holiday Inn

Sun Site

Norling

To Thame
(see Map 2)

Pumori

New

Kala Pattar

Everest

SATURDAY MARKET

To Lukla
(see Map 1)

★ trailblazer

ROUTE GUIDE AND MAPS

You can't escape the modern world up here any more: plenty of places offer **internet access**. Charges are Rs10 a minute: Western rather than Kathmandu prices, but think where you are.

The Saturday market

At this popular weekly gathering, Sherpas meet friends, catch up with the gossip and of course trade supplies. Surprisingly, this famous market does not date back centuries but only to 1965 when it was started by an

Blue roofs
Why are most of the lodge roofs blue? Simple, there are only three colours of roof paint available, and blue is normally the only one stocked by shops. However, this might change in the Khumbu as the Buffer Zone National Park authority is recommending green roofs to blend in a little more.

army officer to cater for the increasing number of civil servants the village was attracting. Shopkeepers and throngs of lowland porters offer food and goods arduously carried up to Namche. Most supplies originate from the roadhead at Jiri, with some reaching Lukla after being flown by helicopter from Jiri, but there are also *suntala* (mandarins) and rice from the Hinku, vegetables from Solu and eggs from Salleri. Lodge owners from up valley can often be seen with wads of rupees collecting yak-loads of goods.

Being one of the tourist highlights, the market determines many group schedules but, especially in peak season, it is actively worth avoiding this period because of the trail congestion it causes. Porters begin arriving late Friday afternoon so the Phakding–Namche trail becomes busy with both trekkers, their zopkios, and heavily laden porters. Heading down from Namche on Friday can slow you right down.

By Saturday afternoon the trail down from Namche is busy with unladen porters racing down to warmer climes while the trails heading up out of Namche are clogged with trekking groups, their yaks and lodge owners' yaks, all kicking up considerable dust.

AROUND NAMCHE [See map pp178-9]
There are plenty of possible **day trips**. Visits to the picturesque Khumjung and Khunde villages can be combined with the pleasant walk to Everest View Hotel.

A longer scenic trek is to Thame, with its gompa on the hill and the hydro-electric power station below. Closer and well-worth visiting is the National Park Visitor Centre at Choi Gang. This is also easily visited the morning that you leave for Tengboche, though note that the centre is closed on Saturdays and Sundays.

Less strenuous is the walk to **Namche Gompa** which is better visited early in the morning or late afternoon, though it is open for tourists most of the day. A donation is expected. Other equally popular activities are clothes washing, apple-pie feasting, chocolate bingeing and chang sampling.

❏ **A multitude of pressures**
Because the air pressure at altitude is less there are other pressures you will witness:
● peer pressure from the lads – 'ah ya whofta, ya can't handle the altitude'
● group pressure – 'you can't be sick here, we have to go up to Xboche tomorrow'
● couple pressure – 'You are alright darling' – 'no I'm not' – 'yes, you are'...
● goal pressure – 'you can't give up now, we are nearly there'
● time pressure – 'but we have to back by Tuesday and I really want to climb the Ri'
    We had followed the same route as the couple from hell all the way from Jiri. She had been sickly all the way, he had been totally gung-ho despite her problems. By Pheriche she had heavy AMS symptoms and came to other trekkers rather than her partner for advice; he insisted she had a head cold, and they pushed on. Five days later we saw her being portered out, slurring her speech and blue in the face.
                                                                              Joel Schone

Choi Gang and the National Park Headquarters

With *choi* (or *cho/tsho*) meaning lake and *gang* meaning hill dropping into a valley or flats, the name commemorates the fact that there was once a lake here. Long ago it was the main trading area before Namche and Thame took over. Deserted until the '70s, it's now the Sagarmatha National Park Headquarters.

Built with New Zealand aid, the **Information Centre's** main building houses modest displays on the history and points of interest in the park. It's open 8am-4pm daily except Saturdays and public holidays.

There are superb views from the helicopter landing pad behind the centre. Early in the trekking scene this was a favourite camping spot offering from-the-tent views of Everest, the Nuptse-Lhotse wall, Tengboche and Ama Dablam. Even the addition of a toilet block in the foreground cannot detract from the magnificent views. With binoculars considerable segments of the route to Dingboche can be seen.

The pine trees that used to line the path up to the headquarters were planted in 1976 but chopped down in late 2001 so that the army had a clear view around their post there during the Maoist problems.

The huge traditional-style building is *Hotel Sherwi Khangba* (Sherpa's Old House), which is popular with expeditions and groups and is worth nosing around even if you are not staying since it has a library, occasional evening slide shows and educational plus historical photos.

The **Sherpa Cultural Museum**, beside *Hotel Sherwi Khangba*, is also worth visiting. A donation of Rs50 is expected.

Syangboche (3900m/12,795ft)

Directly above Namche, although out of view, is Syangboche. The short airstrip here is capable of taking only the small single-engined Pilatus Porter planes (of which there are none left in Nepal) and helicopters.

There are several **hotels** around here but the pick is the *Panorama*.

Everest View Hotel

This is a small, soulless, upmarket hotel situated on top of a hill. Although it blends in with the environment – and is hard to spot from most places in the valley – it boasts superb views, even from the bedrooms. This is fortunate, because with the dangerously rapid gain in altitude this is where many people spend their time initially. Additional oxygen is provided and is very effective.

Even though the hotel often seems cold and empty, it is sometimes fully booked in high season, mainly with Japanese visitors on package tours. The cost is around US$200/£135 a night. On a fine day trekkers often visit for tea on the terrace.

Khumjung (3790m/12,434ft)

This is a picturesque village set under the steep rock of Khumbui Yul Lha (see box p181) with many beautiful houses and grand views of Kangtaiga, Thamserku and Ama Dablam. It is quieter than Namche and worth staying if you have the time.

Even with relatively few trekkers staying here, Khumjung has always looked well off because of expeditions. While Namche people set up lodges, Khumjung and Khunde sherpas worked as climbing sherpas for expeditions, especially Everest expeditions. Now some of them own trekking companies. All bar four of the lodges from Dole to Gokyo are owned by Khumjung people. (cont'd on p180)

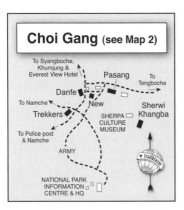

Choi Gang (see Map 2)

To Syangboche, Khumjung & Everest View Hotel — Pasang — To Tengboche — Danfe — To Namche — New — Sherwi Khangba — Trekkers — SHERPA CULTURE MUSEUM — To Police post & Namche — ARMY — trailblazer — NATIONAL PARK INFORMATION CENTRE & HQ

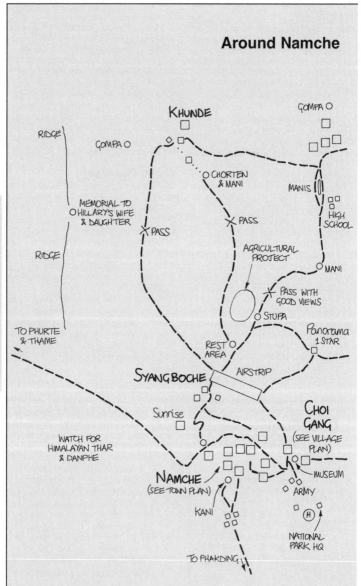

Around Namche

RIDGE

GOMPA O

KHUNDE

GOMPA O

MEMORIAL TO
O HILLARY'S WIFE
& DAUGHTER

RIDGE

O CHORTEN
& MANI

X PASS

X PASS

MANIS

HIGH
SCHOOL

O MANI

AGRICULTURAL
PROJECT

X PASS WITH
GOOD VIEWS

TO PHURTE
& THAME

O STUPA

REST O
AREA

Panorama
1 STAR

SYANGBOCHE

AIRSTRIP

Sunrise

CHOI
GANG
(SEE VILLAGE
PLAN)

WATCH FOR
HIMALAYAN THAR
& DANPHE

MUSEUM

NAMCHE
(SEE TOWN PLAN)

ARMY

KANI

(H)

NATIONAL
PARK HQ

TO PHAKDING

ROUTE GUIDE AND MAPS

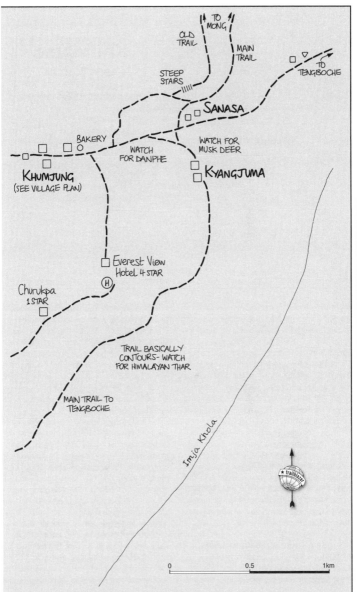

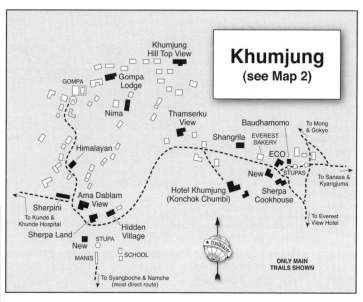

Khumjung
Hill Top View

Khumjung
(see Map 2)

GOMPA
Gompa
Lodge
Nima
Thamserku
View
Baudhamomo   To Mong
& Gokyo
Shangrila   EVEREST
BAKERY
Himalayan   ECO
New   STUPAS
To Sanasa &
Kyangjuma
Ama Dablam
View
Hotel Khumjung
(Konchok Chumbi)
Sherpa
Cookhouse
Sherpini
To Kunde &
Khunde Hospital
To Everest
View Hotel
Sherpa Land   STUPA
Hidden
Village
New
MANIS
SCHOOL
To Syangboche & Namche
(most direct route)
★ trailblazer
ONLY MAIN
TRAILS SHOWN

(cont'd from p177) In many ways it is a model village for Nepal with a good range of facilities, yet it has coped with development well and still has a strong sense of community.

Khumjung's **gompa**, which was established around 1831, is at the top end of town amid a pleasant stand of protected trees. The other major set of buildings is the school on the flats. This was the first built by Hillary and friends and has subsequently been expanded several times and is now a thriving high school.

Leaving Khumjung The track to Everest View Hotel begins by the chortens near the end of town and heads up the hill. The trails to Sanasa and Gokyo are initially the same, before dividing by a house a few minutes down from the stupa.

Khunde / Khumte (3840m/12,598ft)
Although Khunde virtually adjoins Khumjung the two villages are actually quite separate communities. The Khunde villagers have traditionally been associated with Pangboche Gompa, while people from Khumjung go to Thame for special occasions, despite the fact they have their own gompa. The village name is invariably pronounced Khunde or Kunde but originally it was Khumte: *Te* is upper, so upper Khum, while *jung* is lower flats. *Khum* refers to Khumbu, and Khumjung is considered the middle of the Khumbu.

Built in 1966 as a Himalayan Trust project, **Khunde Hospital** is staffed by dedicated locals and a volunteer doctor from either New Zealand or Canada. It offers exceptional services for a 'bush' hospital: there's even an X-ray machine. It's also one of the few places in rural Nepal where contraception and pregnancy testing are readily and reliably available. Most patients are local people who have developed a great respect for the service. Patients are asked to pay according to their means: from Rs20 for a destitute porter to US$40 (or rupee equivalent) for a foreign trekker. Additional charges for trekkers are $10 for

Khumbui Yul Lha
Rising almost sheer above Khumjung/Khunde is the very holy mountain, Khumbui Yul Lha. This hasn't been climbed and the locals certainly don't want anybody to disturb it. Apparently, despite the locals pleading with him not to, the late Sir Edmund Hillary tried climbing it many years ago, falling before getting to the summit and breaking his arm.

medicine, $100 for an overnight stay, while out-of-hours or Saturday consultations cost $80. All its earnings go towards the running costs. It's open from 9am to 5pm but is closed on Saturdays and on Wednesday afternoons except for emergencies. Previously fund-raising tours of the hospital were given but now the hospital is so busy they prefer to take people with special

medical interests only. Indeed, the hospital is now so busy there is enough work for two doctors much of the time.

The Himalayan Trust has always wanted a local doctor instead of the volunteers and offers scholarships and other incentives, and now after at least one doctor preferring the USA to home, there is a resident local doctor as well.

NAMCHE TO THAME [Map 2, p183]

Thame (see p182) is three hours from Namche. Since it's 350m higher than Namche, groups often stay the night here as part of an acclimatization programme before trekking to Gokyo – a sensible idea. As a day trip it is strenuous but it can help with acclimatization and the scenery is stunning.

If planning to stay at Thame the latest you can leave Namche is about 2pm, walking at an ordinary pace.

Leaving Namche Head up to the gompa and continue traversing up on the same trail which rounds the ridge enclosing Namche.

Soon you come to a forest, a favourite area for local women to collect *soluk* (leaves and vegetation that are mixed with dung and used to make fertiliser), singing as they work. It's also a good region to spot pheasant, especially the male danphe, the colourful national bird of Nepal. The female is a plainer spotted brown and similarly plump.

Phurte This is the first village you come to. It has a forestry nursery funded by the Himalayan Trust plus a few shops but no real lodges. The fields between Phurte and Samde/Samsing are known as *gunsas*: they

provide crops earlier in the season than fields at Thame, which is higher and cooler. The gunsas here belong to Thame Cho residents but several sons with their families have moved permanently to these sleepy hamlets.

At the end of the ridge after Phurte is a well-sited white stupa and from here, visible high above the main track, is a gompa. This is **Laudo**, a small monastic establishment built around 1970 as an arm of Kopan Monastery (near Bodhnath in Kathmandu). It is often used by foreign meditation groups. Also visible is the Gyajok (Kyajo) Valley, see p227.

Thamo / Thammu / Dramo In the centre of this village are the offices of Khumbu Bijuli Company who manage the Thame hydro-electric scheme. On the opposite side of the valley is a reminder to them of the damage a glacial lake outburst can cause: the first hydro-electric project was nearly completed in 1985 when a glacial lake burst and washed much of the river scheme away. The wall of water also engulfed many bridges and washed away farm land. The second attempt was far more successful (see box p184).

Scenic (normal) route to Thame

Immediately after the last houses of the village, climb the stone stairs on a track that slightly doubles back on itself. This climbs by a stream to Khari Gompa, then crosses it. The trail continues to climb until suddenly dropping slightly to cross the Nangpo Tsangpo (river).

A steel suspension bridge straddles a roaring tight gorge then the trail winds up and along to Thame.

Alternative route to Thame via the powerhouse

Continue straight ahead and across a temporary bridge to the Austrian hydro-electric project.

Thame (Og) (3800m/12,467ft)

Pleasantly nestled under a long rock wall, Thame has many slate-roofed houses and a quiet atmosphere. Thame is part of the group of villages called Thame Cho – Thame Og (lower), Thame Teng (upper) and Yulajung – and is an area noted for its potatoes.

These villages have traditional trading links with Tibet so when the Nangpa La is crossable Tibetans camp here and in Thame Teng. It is also home to a surprising number of Everest summiteers including Apa Sherpa who at the time of writing (2008) had climbed the mountain 18 times. Apa and his family now live in the USA.

Lodges There are now a handful of lodges which can offer lunch, snacks or a pleasant place to stay. They are mostly run by women since the menfolk are often away trekking or climbing.

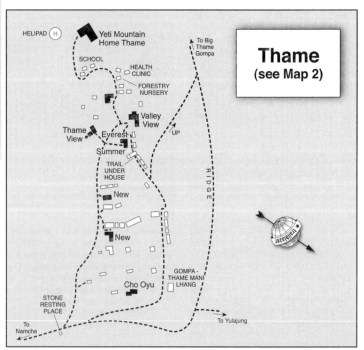

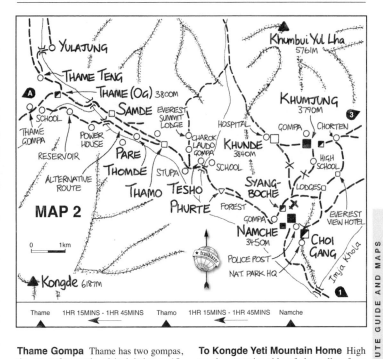

MAP 2

0   1km

Thame   1HR 15MINS - 1HR 45MINS   Thamo   1HR 15MINS - 1HR 45MINS   Namche

Thame Gompa Thame has two gompas, the most frequently visited being a 15-minute walk up the track that begins on the ridge to the north and heads west. It was established around 325 years ago on the advice of Lama Sangwa Dorje, fifth reincarnate Lama of Rongphu/Rongbuk in Tibet, who played an important part in the spiritual history of the Khumbu. It's said that some of the books here are over 300 years old.

The route description for the Nangpa La begins on p226, for the Lhenjo La (Renjo La) on p221, and the Tashi Labtsa on p263.

To Kongde Yeti Mountain Home High on the opposite side of the valley from Namche is a single isolated lodge with stunning views of the mountains including the Khumbu. There is a trail from Phakding, and also from Thame; ask at the Thame Yeti Mountain Home. It is about 6-7 hours on a small trail that can be impossible in winter and spring due to ice. There is only the Kongde Lodge up there at $185 per night.

ROUTE GUIDE AND MAPS

❏ **Map key** See p309 for the route map key

Thame Hydro-electric Project

The current project was set up with grant assistance totalling Rs124 million from the Austrian government and Rs14 million from the Nepal Electricity Authority (NEA): at the time a little under $2 million in total. An Austrian non-governmental organization (NGO) Eco-Himal carried out the installation and gave technical assistance and the project was officially opened in October 1995. The 630kw unit supplies around 500 households in Thame Cho, Namche, Khumjung, Khunde and the villages in between, plus enough power for all the lodges to cook with – a welcome attempt to counter the tourism-related problem of firewood use.

The generators are housed in a traditionally decorated building well below Thame and the two small turbines are fed by a pool, near and visible from Thame village, which collects glacier run-off from up the valley. A 600mm diameter pipe, one kilometre long, drops 200m to provide the head. A local technician, trained in Austria, maintains the plant. Luckily, underground cabling for the villages proved cheaper than overhead wires though unsightly overhead cables still run from the plant to the villages.

For a private house there are several fixed-cost payment schemes. Lodges use a meter system and for a large lodge during the busy months the bill may be Rs5000-10,000 a month.

One of the reasons for its overwhelming success is the structure of its ownership: each of the three main villages – greater Thame, greater Khumjung and Namche – owns a 28.3% share while the Nepal Electricity Authority has the remaining 15%. The power is sold on a profit basis but the profits are then used for maintenance and development. As with most assistance projects, the government in the form of the NEA was involved to spread technical know-how. However, although it is a model scheme, no other imitations have been set up yet.

To Lobuche and Kala Pattar

In this galaxy, which included a host of unnamed peaks, neither the lesser or the greater seemed designed for the use of climbers.   HW Tilman, *Nepal Himalaya*

NAMCHE TO TENGBOCHE
[Map 3, p187]

Leaving Namche There are two trails out of Namche which meet below Choi Gang. From the central intersection in Namche at Thawa Lodge, the first goes up the steps past lodges up to Moonlight Lodge where the angle lessens and the trail traverses to the National Park intersection.

The second heads away from Thawa Lodge, flat at first, then zig-zags up to the police post on wide stone steps to meet the National Park intersection. A moment up, walk around the big carved mani stone the correct way and now this is the main trail to Kyangjuma and Tengboche. The wide trail traverses with minor ups and downs to a large stupa, a good place to admire the extensive panoramas on a clear day. Beware of dust though, if there are many yak trains.

You are likely to see Himalayan tahr and, if you are lucky, danphe, especially early in the morning.

Kyangjuma (3600m/11,811ft)

This is the first set of *teahouses* you come to, about 1-1½ hours from the National Park HQ. There are a couple of good *lodges* with friendly owners and a decadent panorama.

Between here and Sanasa is virtually the only birch/rhododendron forest of the trek to Lobuche. Birch makes the best high-altitude firewood (oak is the best in the low country) and since it doesn't split easily it is often used to make mortars and pestles and wooden bowls, especially the traditional and ceremonial silver and wood bowls used for serving Tibetan tea. Occasionally you will see Himalayan tahr, pheasants and even musk deer here but it takes keen eyes to spot them.

Kyangjuma (see Map 3)

Route to Gokyo or Pangboche via Phortse

Route to Gokyo or Pangboche via Phortse After Kyangjuma and across the stream just before Sanasa is a signposted junction. The upper trail climbs in a couple of minutes to the main trail from Khumjung to Mong (see pp205-6).

Sanasa (see map p186; 3600m/11,811ft)

is five minutes beyond Kyangjuma. There are another couple of *teahouses* and more Tibetan souvenirs.

Continuing around the ridge are the *teahouses* of **Lawishasa** (see map p186; Tashinga). There is also a forestry nursery established by the Canadian Sir Edmund Hillary Foundation. Here the descent to the suspension bridge across the Dudh Kosi begins.

There are a few *teahouses* suitable for lunch along the way, and off the main trail is the large Everest Summit Lodge – ask for directions to it.

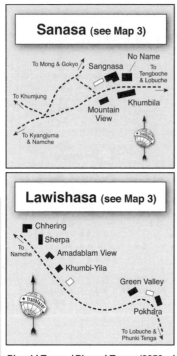

Sanasa (see Map 3)

No Name

To Mong & Gokyo / Sangnasa
To Tengboche & Lobuche

To Khumjung

Khumbila

Mountain View

To Kyangjuma & Namche

trailblazer

Lawishasa (see Map 3)

Chhering

Sherpa

To Namche

Amadablam View

Khumbi-Yila

Green Valley

Pokhara

trailblazer

To Lobuche & Phunki Tenga

ROUTE GUIDE AND MAPS

Phunki Tenga / Phongi Tenga (3250m/ 10,663ft) Down the hill just before you reach the bridge is *Evergreen Lodge*. Sometimes you can see musk deer around here, especially in the early evening. Across the beautifully situated bridge are more basic *lodges*. For those people suffering from the altitude, this is the lowest place north of Namche to stay the night.

The walk up the hill to Tengboche is pleasant, if sometimes hot. You pass through a blend of forest and shrub on a wide trail. Alternative trails are usually just so you can walk around a carved mani stone the correct way. It's also one of the better places for spotting pheasant, tahr and musk deer. They seem quite undisturbed by all the noise of passing trekkers and yaks. The end of the climb is heralded by an ornate kani, an arched entrance with ceiling paintings of deities and forms of Buddha.

Its function is to cleanse people of the many feared spirits before entering the sacred area.

TENGBOCHE / THYANGBOCHE (3860m/12,664ft)   [See map p188]
True we were awakened at 4 am by the din of horns and the clash of cymbals, but we were not expected to rouse out for prayer or meditation, or indeed do anything beyond reach out for a wooden jorum thoughtfully left in readiness. In this, of course, lurked what we called 'lama's milk', which was raksi flavoured with cloves.
    HW Tilman, ***Nepal Himalaya*** 1950

You may still be wakened by the clash of cymbals. And a snort of *lama's milk* might still be in order; during the cold winter months most Sherpas will down a shot of raksi before breakfast, sometimes even Sherpas who profess to avoid the demon drink. They firmly believe in its warming properties.

Tengboche is a cultural and religious centre for the people of the Khumbu region. It is unique in that all the other gompas of the region are associated with a village but Tengboche isn't. With the tip of Everest peeking from behind the Lhotse-Nuptse wall, and the impressive gompa it is the favoured overnight stop for all trekkers heading to Kala Pattar.

To the left (south) behind the gompa is a ridge pointing to Khumbui Yul Lha that affords superb views. From this viewpoint and higher to Pangboche is the classic view of Ama Dablam. Notice especially the spectacular high trail from Pangboche to Phortse on the opposite side of the valley. There are several origins given for the name Ama Dablam (Amai Dablang). One says that it refers to the necklace of turquoise or coral usually worn by married women. With a little imagination it's possible to visualize shoulders and a head, and the pendulous lump of blue ice (a glacier) is roughly in the right spot for a necklace.

There are only six **lodges**, five of which are owned by the gompa and are rented out, providing further income for the gompa. The sixth is owned by the National

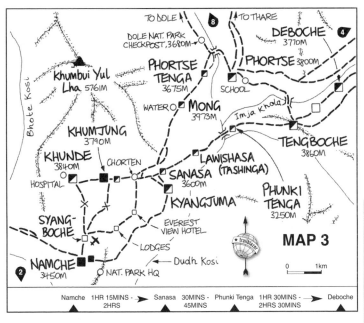

TO DOLE
DOLE NAT. PARK
CHECKPOST, 3680M
8 TO THARE
DEBOCHE 3770M 4
PHORTSE 3800M
PHORTSE TENGA 3675M
SCHOOL
Khumbui Yul Lha 5761M
Bhote Kosi
WATER MONG 3973M
Imja Khola
KHUMJUNG 3790M
TENGBOCHE 3860M
KHUNDE 3840M
CHORTEN
LAWISHASA
SANASA (TASHINGA) 3600M
HOSPITAL
KYANGJUMA
PHUNKI TENGA 3250M
SYANG-BOCHE
EVEREST VIEW HOTEL
trailblazer
MAP 3
LODGES
Dudh Kosi
2 NAMCHE 3450M
NAT. PARK HQ
0   1km

| Namche | 1HR 15MINS – 2HRS | Sanasa | 30MINS – 45MINS | Phunki Tenga | 1HR 30MINS – 2HRS 30MINS | Deboche |

Park. If the lodges are full Deboche (see pp188-9) is less than 15 minutes away. Most trekkers used to make Tengboche an acclimatization stop, staying two nights; now most stay just one and instead spend another acclimatization night at Khumjung (prior to Tengboche) or stay at Pangboche for the second night: Deboche and Phortse are less-used alternatives. Even so, with its limited number of lodges Tengboche is very busy in the high season.

Tengboche Gompa

This justly famous gompa is spectacularly situated under the mighty Kangtaiga ('horse saddle') and Thamserku ('golden door') mountains, in a commanding position with superb views up and down the surrounding valleys. You can see Everest View Hotel and the National Park HQ down the valley, perhaps now more easily spotted at night. With these as markers it's

easy to work out where hidden Namche and Khumjung are, and the path that brought you up here. The gompa is also the setting for the Mani Rimdu dance festival in late October or early November.

Surrounding the main gompa is the monastery. Boys are sent here from all over the Khumbu to study Buddhism. For the period of study they must remain celibate but they may (and most do) get married when they have graduated.

Although the area has long been considered revered ground, the gompa was established only in 1916, by Lama Gulu at the request of the Abbot of Rongbuk. In 1934 a disastrous earthquake struck the area, causing considerable damage to the gompa. Lama Gulu died of shock. It was rebuilt and headed by the present lama, Nawang Tenzing Zangbu. Tragedy struck again less than a year after electricity was installed: on 19 January 1989 a heater over-

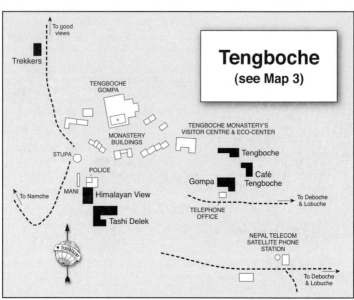

Tengboche
(see Map 3)

To good views

Trekkers

TENGBOCHE GOMPA

TENGBOCHE MONASTERY'S
VISITOR CENTRE & ECO-CENTER

MONASTERY BUILDINGS

STUPA

Tengboche

POLICE

Café Tengboche

Gompa

To Namche

MANI Himalayan View

To Deboche & Lobuche

TELEPHONE OFFICE

Tashi Delek

trailblazer

NEPAL TELECOM
SATELLITE PHONE STATION

To Deboche & Lobuche

turned burning the magnificent gompa to the ground. Not all was lost since some of what could be removed, including the priceless book collection, was rescued. The construction of the grand new gompa was considerably aided by the American Himalayan foundation (set up by Sir Ed) and donations from wealthy locals. The library has now been put on micro-film, and the hydro-electric system has been revived. The gompa is often flood-lit at night to great effect. The gompa is primarily a spiritual place and, so that the gompa itself is not disturbed too much, a wall was built around it and a modern **visitors centre** was set up. It is all self-explanatory. However, you are still welcome to visit the gompa through the imposing entrance gate. If you sit in for a ceremony, stay for the duration, a calm and resonate, absorbing experience. Do leave a donation.

Excursions from Tengboche

The forests above and below Tengboche are protected and are still considered to be owned by the monastery. It is pleasant to wander through the trees and there is a reasonable chance of seeing deer and pheasant. The rhododendrons are spectacular in April. For a longer half-day trip, the rock peak above Tengboche, often called Hamugon, offers better views of the awesome Thamserku-Kangtaiga glacier. It's an easy but breathless scramble to the top of the first peak. The higher peak requires some more committed scrambling. Listen to your body though, while ascending.

TENGBOCHE TO PHERICHE / DINGBOCHE [Map 4, p193]
Leaving Tengboche The trail starts beneath the Gompa lodge, on the right side of it and heads to the water supply.

Deboche (3770m/12,369ft)
Down through pleasant forest on a trail that is icy long after snowfall is a spread out series of four or five *lodges.* There are occasional superb views of Khumbui Yul Lha which looks formidable from here.

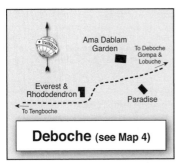

Deboche (see Map 4)

Deboche Gompa is slightly beyond the last lodge and is behind a barrier of trees: approximately 12 nuns live here. You are welcome to have a look around the gompa, which dates from 1925. The atmosphere is quite different from Tengboche.

After passing a few other hamlets you cross a spectacular little gorge on a steel box bridge. This is the junction for the trail to Phortse (see pp215-6). Follow the main

trail for Pangboche. About 20 minutes later the trail passes through a cleft in some rocks, with a mani wall virtually in the middle. Just after, the trail divides and is usually signposted, the upper trail heading to Pangboche Te Lim and the gompa, while the lower path takes a more gentle route through the fields to Pangboche Wa Lim.

Pangboche (4000m/13,123ft)

This used to be the highest permanently occupied village until trekkers created a demand in winter for accommodation higher up the valley. The lower village is now a popular place to stay and consequently there are quite a number of *lodges* in this pleasant place. From Lower Pangboche there's another trail which starts from the corner of *Himalayan Lodge* and winds up to the upper village.

In **Pangboche Te Lim** (Upper Pangboche) the houses are clustered round the old gompa and there are five *lodges* here. The surrounding juniper trees have

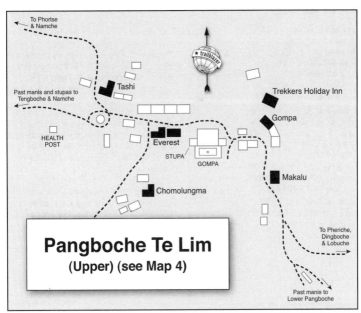

Pangboche Te Lim
(Upper) (see Map 4)

ROUTE GUIDE AND MAPS

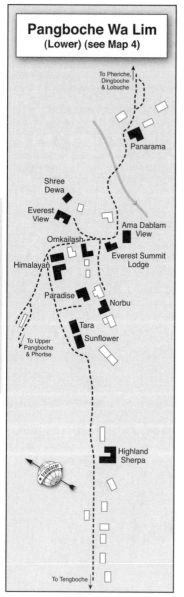

Pangboche Wa Lim
(Lower) (see Map 4)

To Pheriche,
Dingboche
& Lobuche

Panarama

Shree
Dewa

Everest
View

Ama Dablam
View

Omkailash

Everest Summit
Lodge

Himalayan

Paradise

Norbu

Tara

Sunflower

To Upper
Pangboche
& Phortse

Highland
Sherpa

To Tengboche

long been protected and are now very large. Legend has it that they were created by Lama Sangwa Dorje who tossed a handful of his hair into the air and it took root as juniper. Once the whole valley would have been thickly forested with trees this size.

The monastery is believed to have been founded around 1667, which makes it the oldest Sherpa **gompa** in the Khumbu. Many trekkers take the opportunity to have a look around: the lama (the 14th re-incarnate) or his wife are usually close by, and it is customary to leave a donation with them. This gompa was home to one of the Khumbu's famous yeti scalps until it was stolen under mysterious circum-stances in 1991.

Pangboche Wa Lim (Lower Pangboche; 3840m/12,598ft) was once just (big) grass fields, which is what the name 'Pangboche' means. It is now a settlement with at least ten *lodges* on the edge of the fields. Potatoes, radishes and a few vegeta-bles are grown here and there is often an abundance of wild mushrooms. Firewood collection in Pangboche is still well organ-ized; dead wood is collected from the oppo-site side of the valley from selected spots and when the supply thins another part of the forest is used. Yak dung, a valuable fer-tiliser, is now also used as fuel, something that started with the arrival of trekkers.

Now two lodges offer rooms with attached bathroom: *Om Kailash*, which charges around $20, depending on demand, and *Everest Summit Lodge*, which is part of a chain so prior booking is recommend-ed, where rates are over $100 a night.

For Mingbo and Ama Dablam Base Camp see p224.

Pangboche to Phortse (see also Map 8) The most direct route is a high and slightly wild trail that begins from near the gompa.

From the top of the gompa take the trail that contours west to two white chort-ens 100m away, then walk up to the bottom of *Tashi Lodge* and begin contouring. The path crosses fields and a stream. Once a lit-tle way out of Pangboche it is a large well-used trail. It takes a couple of hours to reach Phortse.

Pangboche to Shomare Leaving Upper Pangboche you can see Everest peeking over the Lhotse-Nuptse ridge and you can also see it from the trail between the lower and upper villages, from where there is also a good view back to Tengboche.

There are several small *chhusas* (yak-herding areas) en route. The first you come to is **Shomare**, owned by the villagers of Pangboche and used for growing potatoes. It is also a village that boasts many Everest summiteers. There is a growing collection of small *lodges* catering for lunch, although it is possible to stay. This is where trees fade away and the true alpine valley begins.

Further up are several more kharkas or grazing areas and a few scattered **teahouses**, also suitable for lunch or drinks, although they are only reliably open during peak seasons.

Looking up, the massive Lhotse-Nuptse wall dominates and the black jagged ridge below is Pokalde.

Shomare to Pheriche The track to Pheriche turns a few minutes out of **Orsho** (which means 'sunlight'). The trail veers left and climbs up to a small pass before descending on a wide trail to the bridge. It takes 30-40 minutes from the turn-off to Pheriche.

Despite being marked on even the most recent maps, there is no trail immediately after the bridge to Dingboche.

Pheriche (see map p192; 4280m/ 14,042ft)
To combat the afternoon wind, lodges here either have sun rooms or warm lounges. It is important to stop here or at Dingboche (see p195) for two nights (or more) to acclimatize.

There are nine or ten *lodges* and a few houses spaced along the track that runs through the village: there is also a HRA Post (see box p193). Pheriche can get quite crowded during the high seasons.

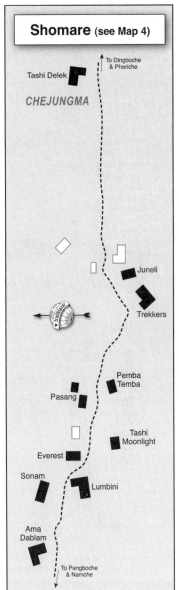

Shomare (see Map 4)

To Dingboche & Pheriche

Tashi Delek

CHEJUNGMA

Juneli

Trekkers

Pemba Temba

Pasang

Tashi Moonlight

Everest

Sonam

Lumbini

Ama Dablam

To Pangboche & Namche

ROUTE GUIDE AND MAPS

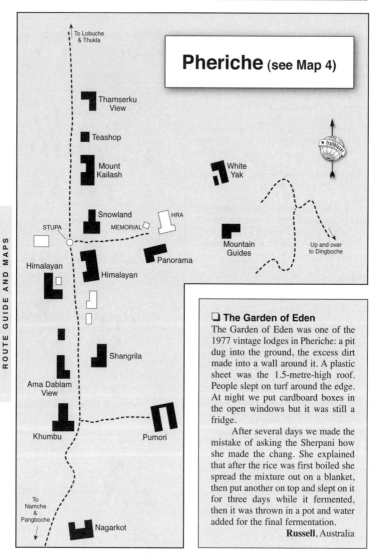

Pheriche (see Map 4)

To Lobuche & Thukla

Thamserku View

Teashop

Mount Kailash

White Yak

Snowland

HRA

STUPA

MEMORIAL

Mountain Guides

Up and over to Dingboche

Himalayan

Himalayan

Panorama

Shangrila

Ama Dablam View

Khumbu

Pumori

To Namche & Pangboche

Nagarkot

❑ **The Garden of Eden**
The Garden of Eden was one of the 1977 vintage lodges in Pheriche: a pit dug into the ground, the excess dirt made into a wall around it. A plastic sheet was the 1.5-metre-high roof. People slept on turf around the edge. At night we put cardboard boxes in the open windows but it was still a fridge.

After several days we made the mistake of asking the Sherpani how she made the chang. She explained that after the rice was first boiled she spread the mixture out on a blanket, then put another on top and slept on it for three days while it fermented, then it was thrown in a pot and water added for the final fermentation.

Russell, Australia

(**Opposite**) **Top**: Magnificent Ama Dablam (6828m/22,402ft) towers above Pheriche village just visible below. **Bottom**: On the path up to Lobuche, Pumori in the background.

(**Following pages**): From Mera (see pp274-9) there are spectacular views. In this picture Mera La is to the left, Makalu just left of centre and Kanchenjunga on the right.

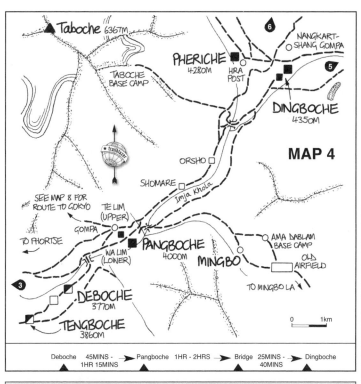

MAP 4

| Deboche | 45MINS - 1HR 15MINS | → | Pangboche | 1HR - 2HRS | → | Bridge | 25MINS - 40MINS | → | Dingboche |

ROUTE GUIDE AND MAPS

Himalayan Rescue Association (HRA) Medical Post

Built in 1976 by Tokyo Medical College, the post is staffed by two or three Western volunteer doctors. Available for consultations (US$50 or rupee equivalent, use of PAC bag $50 an hour, $10 per course of medicine), they also give a daily 3pm lecture on altitude sickness that's well worth attending; donations expected. Lectures are given every few days in Dingboche as well; look for a notice in the middle of the village. As part of the community service the consultation fee for Nepalis is less than a dollar, and group porters are particularly encouraged to visit since they are the least likely to complain of medical problems yet are the most likely to be sick, and with the loads they carry are more likely to suffer from altitude sickness than Western trekkers. The Pheriche post is open only during the peak trekking seasons (Oct to mid-Dec and March to May), when the donations and consultation fees are able to cover the running costs. They also sell HRA patches and non-prescription medicines, lip balm etc. They treat numerous cases of altitude sickness (and surprisingly, survivors often forget to donate). It is an extraordinary service, please don't take it for granted.

(Opposite) Top: Kala Pattar (see p202) is the most popular viewpoint for Everest, here the slightly darker central peak trailing a plume of cloud. **Bottom**: The Khumbu Icefall.

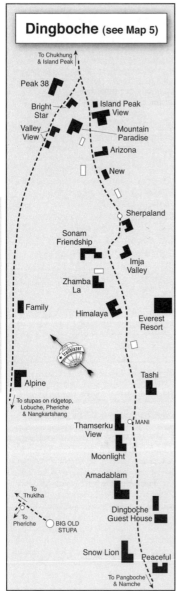

Dingboche (see Map 5)

To Chukhung
& Island Peak

Peak 38

Bright
Star

Valley
View

Island Peak
View

Mountain
Paradise

Arizona

New

Sherpaland

Sonam
Friendship

Imja
Valley

Zhamba
La

Family

Himalaya

Everest
Resort

Alpine

Tashi

To stupas on ridgetop,
Lobuche, Pheriche
& Nangkartshang

Thamserku
View

MANI

Moonlight

Amadablam

To
Thuklha

To
Pheriche

BIG OLD
STUPA

Dingboche
Guest House

Snow Lion

Peaceful

To Pangboche
& Namche

Orsho to Dingboche From Orsho follow the straight trail that drops to the small *teashop* then the bridge across the Lobuche Khola. Dingboche is still a hill and approximately 30-40 minutes away from the bridge. Approaching the village and walking through, the view of the Lhotse-Nuptse wall dominates.

Pheriche or Dingboche?

The villages are 45 minutes apart, separated by a ridge. Both have lodges and are at roughly the same altitude so it depends on your plans for the important acclimatization day as to where you stay. If the climb to Nangkartshang Peak (see opposite) appeals, or you plan simply to relax it really does not matter where you stay.

If planning a day trip to Chukhung it is more convenient to sleep at Dingboche. There's a trail to Lobuche from either village, and they are of equal distance.

❏ **Critical acclimatization**

Most trekkers spend two nights in Dingboche or Pheriche before moving on to Lobuche. However, even this relatively cautious approach leads to many people suffering altitude sickness at Lobuche. Now that it is possible to stay at Thuklha the best advice is to spend one (or two) nights at Dingboche/Pheriche, then a night at Thuklha, then stay at Lobuche. Breaking the 600m jump in altitude into two 300m gains will considerably lessen the occurrence of mild altitude sickness: as always, gradual ascent is the safest approach. Note that if you have slept at Chukhung (or Dzonglha) without problems you should be able to trek directly to Lobuche rather than stopping en route. If you want to stay at Gorak Shep, unless you have already been to Gokyo or Chukhung, staying a night at Lobuche before moving to Gorak Shep is the safest option.

Dingboche (4350m/14,271ft)

The houses of this summer village are dotted about the fields. The land is owned by people from Pangboche and Khunde so although Khunde sees few trekkers, the village is still very much linked with tourism.

As Dingboche has become more popular than Pheriche, so too the number of *lodges* has grown; there are nearly 20 of them now. Choose what you want from the lodges: peace or convenience. Some offer hot showers, satellite phones and battery recharging. A couple even show movies some evenings. Virtually all the lodges face Ama Dablam, which looks big and fearsome from here.

From Dingboche you can make the half-day trips described below, or head to Chukhung. If you suffered mild AMS on the first night here it may be a better idea to rest here or if you really suffered, trek slightly lower during the day (see box opposite). The bridge across the Lobuche Khola is the closest point that's easy to reach but often this small drop in altitude can make a big difference.

Half-day trips from Pheriche / Dingboche

For the amount of effort involved, a trip to **Nangkartshang Peak** (see Map 5) from either Pheriche or Dingboche offers some of the best views in this region – a perfect scenic lunch spot.

From Pheriche the path zigzags up directly behind the HRA buildings on the track heading to Dingboche. Some time before the steep descent, continue up the ridge past a stupa. From Dingboche any track heading up to the ridge will do. Then, from the stupa on top is a small trail that follows the ridge up, and up, and up. The top is marked by prayer flags and you are brought up short by a sudden drop. The views here are magnificent with Numbur, Chukhung, Makalu and Ama Dablam visible.

Among the moraine below **Ama Dablam** are two **lakes** at 4700m (see Map 5). Sometimes there's a bridge across the Imja Khola at the base of Dingboche and a track to Duroo, a small *yersa* (a summer crop-growing area, usually lower than the

> ### ❏ Tsampa
> The process of making tsampa (barley flour) is quite complex. Dark high-altitude barley is dried in the sun, then mixed with white barley. The grains are soaked in water and dried three times before being stored for a few days. Next the barley is roasted in sand. The grain explodes like popcorn and is ground up into a light fluffy flour. It can be eaten dry and washed down with *chang*, mixed with *solja* (salt-butter tea) to make a thick porridge or rolled into a doughy ball to be chewed. For trekkers, ordinary tea is used for tsampa porridge, rather than *solja*.

main village). The alternative is to cross the creek at the top of Dingboche and climb the steep hillside, or head upriver to Shangtso where there is usually a bridge and hook back on the trail heading up. The lakes are also a great place for lunch.

Opposite Pheriche is stunning **Taboche** (see Map 4, p193). Atop the broad ridge are a couple of small rock peaks that can be climbed, or a hidden higher valley to explore. Cross the bridge to Pangboche and from Tsuro Teng follow small steep trails up. It is quite a grunt up there. Don't forget to take lunch and snacks.

DINGBOCHE TO CHUKHUNG
[Map 5, p197]

By the top lodges in Dingboche the track continues between the hill and the upper fences and is easy to follow through the low, prickly scrub.

Further up the herding area of **Bibre** is above the main trail but below, beside the path at **Dusum** are a couple of shelters where people from Dingboche sell snacks during the trekking seasons. From here Imjatse/Island Peak looks awesome, a triangle of almost sheer rock and incredibly steep snow faces, steep enough to bring a lump to climbers' throats yet strangely at Chukhung its magnificence fades.

ROUTE GUIDE AND MAPS

Chukhung is perhaps 20-25 minutes beyond Dusum, but until you are almost on top of it, it remains invisible.

Chukhung (4750m/15,584ft)

Nestled between two streams, which is what the name means, this is traditionally a Pangboche herding station (or phu) used as a base to graze the rich and extensive grasslands of the valley. Viewed from above it is also surrounded by mountains, glaciers and their debris.

The views here are fantastic, even from the base of the valley, and they get even better the higher you explore. Looking down valley, Numbur, Khatang and Karyolung rise majestically above Kongde while Taboche (Tagouche/Tawouche literally means 'horse's head' but can be loosely translated as 'big ego') and Tsholatse (Cholatse – 'Lake-pass Peak') are closer to the right. Ama Dablam is quite something to see from here and the fluted snow wall above Chukhung Glacier is stunning, especially at sunset.

Chukhung now has four comfortable **lodges** with warm dining rooms and good

facilities including a satellite phone and battery recharging.

The *phu* makes a good base to explore the huge valley system with its many 'small' peaks that can be fun to climb. It is also at the perfect altitude between Dingboche and Lobuche, so a good acclimatization stop, though it is a long, tough trek to Lobuche in a day, whether you go over the Kongma La or around.

At the top of Chukhung is a memorial to Jerzy Kukuczka, Poland, one of the great mountaineers. He was the second person to climb all 14 of the 8000m mountains, and in each case climbed a new difficult route or climbed in winter. He had already climbed Lhotse, but this was the only mountain he had not climbed in that style (even though he had summitted previously), and he died climbing a new route on it.

Side trips from Chukhung

● **Chukhung Ri** An understandably popular excursion is to Chukhung Ri (5559m/18,238ft), involving an ascent of a ridge similar to Kala Pattar. The top cannot be seen from Chukhung but the paths are obvious scars ascending the side of the big pile of grass and dirt. At the saddle there's a choice: a lower peak (5417m/17,772ft) to the south or a trickier ascent on rock to the high peak (5559m/18,238ft). The views are staggering from both with Makalu dominating amongst a ring of mountains. It is possible to do this as a long day-trip from Dingboche but the altitude, for the unacclimatized (rather than the time), creates a problem.

● **Chukhung Tse** (5857m/19,216ft) This is the peak north of Chukhung Ri and is the highest hill in the Khumbu commonly scrambled by trekkers. The ridge between Chukhung Ri and Chukhung Tse is tricky to traverse in its entirety; take particular care on some short exposed moves and don't attempt it if it's wet or snowy. The safer route is a steep gully scramble on the east side directly to the summit. The ablation valley to the east provides access and/or an exit.

It is possible but strenuous to ascend both Chukhung Ri and Tse in a day, good

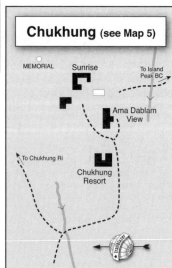

Chukhung (see Map 5)

MEMORIAL

Sunrise

To Island Peak BC

Ama Dablam View

To Chukhung Ri

Chukhung Resort

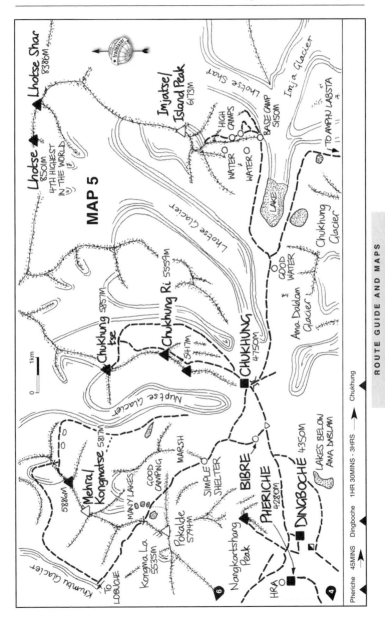

MAP 5

Lhotse Shar 8386M

Lhotse 8501M
4TH HIGHEST
IN THE WORLD

Imjatse/
Island Peak
6173M

LHOTSE SHAR

Inja Glacier

HIGH CAMPS

BASE CAMP 5150M

WATER
WATER

TO AMPHU LABSTA

LAKE

Lhotse Glacier

CHUKHUNG
GLACIER

GOOD
WATER

Chukhung 5857M
tse

Chukhung Ri 5559M

Chukhung 4750M

Ama Dablam Glacier

Nuptse Glacier

541M

0   1km

Mehra/
Kongmatse 5871M

5881M

GOOD
CAMPING

MARSH

MANY LAKES

SIMPLE
SHELTER

BIBRE

PHERICHE 4280M

DINGBOCHE 4350M

LAKES BELOW
AMA DABLAM

Pokalde
5794M

Nangkartshang Peak

Kongma La
5535M

TO
LOBUCHE

Khumbu Glacier

HRA

6

4

preparation for Imjatse/Island Peak or the Amphu Labtsa. An ice axe, or trekking pole would be handy. The views are staggering and include Chomo Lonzo (the white ridge extending north of Makalu and the 27th highest mountain on the planet) and Gauri Sankar.

● **Climbing to Imjatse/Island Peak Base Camp** This is an alternative to climbing hills around the place. The rate of ascent is more gradual, however it is quite a long way and is often windy and dusty. Take plenty of water, lunch and snacks.

Leave Chukhung by crossing the stream to the east on a bridge and ensure you are on the right trail at this point. From there the trail is reasonably well defined (look up on the moraine), though often breaks into two.

At the top of the moraine you may have the choice of the sheltered trail in the small valley, alternatively you can walk along the top of the moraine. Once in a larger valley with a sparkling stream (the last reliable easy-to-find water supply), note that you have to traverse right out of this around a shoulder, then in the sandy area, turn left still staying in the now broad valley. Take a map. See pp272-4 for further details.

Other routes Amphu Labtsa (see pp223-4); Kongma La (see p222); Pokalde and Kongma Tse (see p280); and 5886m Peak (see p222). A map will reveal more possible side trips to little-explored valleys.

PHERICHE / DINGBOCHE TO
LOBUCHE   [Map 6]
Route from Pheriche to Thuklha
Leaving Pheriche, the trail meanders up the open valley, beautiful when the weather's fine but muddy if snow or rain has recently fallen. It then cuts up a small but obvious valley. A smaller trail then branches off to the left and heads direct to the bridge over a few perpetually slippery boulders, while the main path heads up to join the trail directly from Dingboche just a minute before the bridge to Thuklha.

Route from Dingboche to Thuklha
Climb the ridge behind Dingboche on one of the many trails to the higher plain. There are then several paths to follow, all leading to the two bridges across to Thuklha (either will do, the lower trail crosses an unstable slide area).

Thuklha (4600m/15,092ft)
The translation of Thuklha is Ram's corral (uncastrated male sheep); tourist corral is perhaps a better name now.

This is a regular lunch spot but also a good place to stay to break the 600m gain in altitude between Dingboche or Pheriche and Lobuche, and there are a mixture of rooms and dormitories.

During the monsoon or heavy rainfall the bridge leading into Thuklha can be washed away: it is possible to recross the river below Pheriche and then follow a small trail up on the opposite side of the valley.

Leaving, the hill immediately beyond Thuklha is tough, especially if your pack is heavy. At the crest (4840m/15,879ft) among the many **memorials** for climbers who didn't make it back down are Scott Fisher's, from the 1996 disaster on Everest, and Babu Chiri, a particularly well-known Nepali climber who died on Everest in 2001.

From here the trail climbs more gently in the ablation valley and it's just over an hour to Lobuche. At this altitude, even in October there's ice on the streams; by December they may be frozen over. Once on the west side of the khola, although it is not obvious, you can see the horribly steep summit ramparts of Lhotse past Nuptse.

Lobuche (4940m/16,207ft)
Lobuche is set on the slopes of a pleasant ablation valley which, possibly because of the altitude, is very little explored off the path to Gorak Shep. Looking down valley, Kangtaiga and its rock face are striking. It is also well-worth climbing to the top of the moraine opposite the lodges or much higher behind the lodges for the sunset. Watch

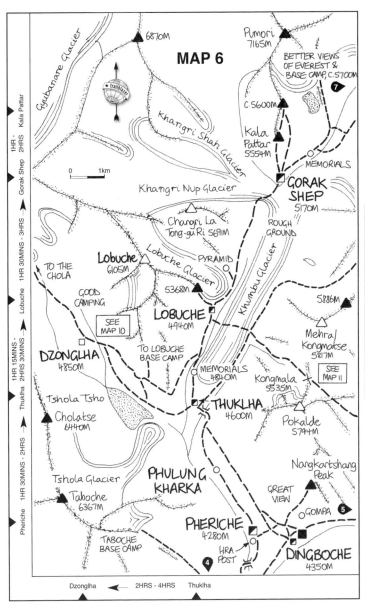

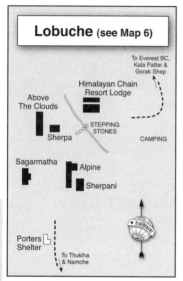

Lobuche (see Map 6)

To Everest BC,
Kala Pattar &
Gorak Shep

Himalayan Chain
Resort Lodge

Above
The Clouds

STEPPING
STONES

Sherpa

CAMPING

Sagarmatha

Alpine

Sherpani

★ trailblazer

Porters
Shelter

To Thuklha
& Namche

❏ **Toilet-paper trail**
There is far too much toilet paper littering the trail to Gorak Shep and it's all dropped by trekkers. Just because you might be trekking up in the early morning when it is dark, this doesn't mean toilet paper remains invisible. Toilet paper can be put in a bag and tucked under a flap or in a side pocket. If you have to go to the toilet make sure you are at least 10m off the trail and at least 30m from the stream, then lift up a rock.

Nuptse turn a photogenic orange then pink, and the alpenglow sky that remains dusky and captivating into the evening.

There is a real variety of standard in the **lodges** here: *Eco Lodge* (*Himalayan Chain Resort*, booking ahead suggested) is the best but the *Alpine* has been rebuilt with better rooms and the meals are good too. Be particularly careful with the water here: the supply is not always clean, although the lodges are now more aware of this and think they might have this once perennial problem solved.

The toilets (see box above) are also far too close to the water supply but at present nobody seems interested in rectifying this, which is a pity because Lobuche is in a sensitive alpine region.

Nights here from October onwards are invariably below 0°C and January temperatures are sometimes lower than -20°C/-3°F; only by April does it begin to warm up. However, the lodges are warm, if sometimes unhealthily stuffy.

Once the sun strikes Lobuche mornings are pleasant but the wind gusts after mid-day throwing dust storms around and when the sun leaves mid-afternoon it rapidly cools.

The Pyramid and the 8000m Inn Ten minutes further along, tucked in a side valley, is this futuristic pyramid. It was built in 1990 for research purposes and used to moonlight as a lodge but now is mostly full with high-altitude researchers. It is now also a registered rescue organization with trained staff, a welcome addition to the

How should you feel at 5000m?
The short answer is to expect to feel less than perfect. The air is thin and cold. Many people suffer sleeplessness (often through worrying about Kala Pattar, and altitude sickness), occasional breathlessness, mild headaches, anxiety, tiredness, disinterest in food or generally just don't feel 100%. And you thought you were on holiday!

These symptoms in mild form are quite usual. Minor suffering can often be relieved by drinking plenty, then drinking some more; and, consider taking Diamox or mild painkillers. The full discussion on AMS is on pp290-9.

region's services. They have a portable altitude chamber bag, portable oxygen, walkie talkie radios and are practised at using them. Expect to pay for any services and don't abuse their service.

The alert may notice 'K2' in the research post's real name: it was built at the time when K2 had just been remeasured and was thought to be higher than Everest. So Everest was also remeasured from around here, then a mistake in the K2 calculations was found and the old surveys were proved surprisingly accurate – in fact staggeringly so.

Short excursions from Lobuche

The small moraine towards Nuptse offers scenic sunset views if clouds have not rolled up the valley too far.

The moraine immediately north of the *phu* is a stiff climb that's a little longer than it first looks but it also offers a few surprises: the Lobuche Glacier is close and spectacular.

The grassy slopes behind Lobuche are also worth the climb. The sure-footed and energetic can attempt the three rock pinnacles, each harder than the last, for great views.

Changrila Tong-gu Ri

Want to climb something other than Kala Pattar for great views? From near the top of the ridge that swings around above the Pyramid you can see Everest Base Camp, the summit, the west ridge and south summit and it almost looks as if you are level with the Lho La (though you aren't: it is 6000m high). Through the gap is Changtse (the peak north of Everest) and, temptingly, the smaller mountains seem to fall away to reveal a ring of serious peaks behind. It also appears that you are standing at a higher altitude than Kala Pattar although, as any surveyor will tell you, this is deceptive. The first peak is in fact a similar height.

This summit was shown to me by staff from the Pyramid and not finding a name, I consulted with Sherpas there on something suitable and together we came up with Changrila Tong-gu Ri. Begin the walk at

the turn-off to the Pyramid and simply climb the ridge between the main trail to Gorak Shep and the trail to the Pyramid. Somehow you have to gain height – which can be a little tricky – but once on the ridge line it is as pleasant as can be.

Further along the trail steepens and turns a bit rocky and here, a little way up, there is a flat rock with a bolt (or a bolt hole) in it, and if you look up, you can just see the very top of Everest. This was one of the points used in 1992 to measure Everest.

Slightly further up, when you can see both the summit of Everest and Makalu, there is a memorial stupa for Benoit Chamoux, a famous French alpinist who died on Kanchenjunga with Rika Sherpa in October 1995.

From here the rock is substantially steeper and real scrambling is required. The first peak is roughly 5600m and a good place to stop. The farther peak requires scrambling that borders on rock climbing, and is more challenging than Gokyo's knobby view; however, it is a tempting 5691m high.

LOBUCHE TO GORAK SHEP AND KALA PATTAR
[Map 6, p199; Map 7, p203]

Early in the season when it's not really cold many groups leave Lobuche well before dawn to reach the top of Kala Pattar for sunrise. This is a rare and usually rewarding experience, at least once you've got over the shock of the early start. By late November, however, the low night temperatures make starting with the sun a more reasonable and safer proposition. From Kala Pattar the surrounding mountains usually display themselves at their absolute best from mid-morning until sunset, if the weather has been stable.

For a guide to the weather for your summit bid consider first the weather of the previous afternoon, and also ask lodge owners. Afternoon/evening cloud sweeping up the valley from lower down and **no** high cloud, or clouds hanging around lesser peaks, is a good sign. High cloud means the

ROUTE GUIDE AND MAPS

weather is harder to predict. In the spring season, during a patch where cloud forms regularly around or before lunchtime, a dawn start is advisable.

Some days a vicious cold wind picks up around 10 or 11am on the top while other days there is little more than a breeze on top for the whole day. Always take your warmest clothes (including a down jacket, if you have one), wind-proof clothing and a pack big enough to put it all in for the walk up. In winter, especially in snow, try to avoid getting your boots wet and beware of frostbite.

If the previous day was hopelessly cloudy don't despair. It could dawn perfectly fine the next day (but might not!). Being so far up a high valley system Kala Pattar is an unusually fine place and probably has one of the better weather records in Nepal. Even during the monsoon a day or two's patience will usually be rewarded with a stunning panorama. However, having two days set aside rather than just one will give you some peace of mind. Note that the majority of groups only allow a single day for Kala Pattar.

The walk to Gorak Shep takes only about one and a half hours for the fit and fast, or more than three hours for the less fit. Kala Pattar is one to two hours above Gorak Shep. Even for the slow, the round trip should take less than eight hours. Look out for furball pikas, the small Himalayan mouse-hare.

From Lobuche the path is clear and pleasant at first, gently wandering up the ablation valley. Then it climbs, twisting and turning, to thread its way onto the rough moraine of the Khangri Glacier. Here it's important not to lose the main track. The rough walking ends suddenly and the trail virtually falls into Gorak Shep.

Gorak Shep (5170m/16,962ft)

Here the Tibetan snowcock are so tame they will almost eat from your hands. For trekkers from Lobuche the lodges at Gorak Shep are merely places for a second breakfast or a late lunch after Kala Pattar but many acclimatized trekkers stay the night.

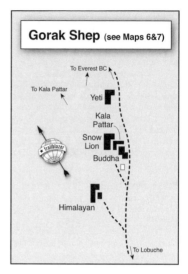

Gorak Shep (see Maps 6&7)

To Everest BC

To Kala Pattar

Yeti

Kala Pattar

Snow Lion

trailblazer

Buddha

Himalayan

To Lobuche

The *lodges* are amazing, considering where you are. The dining rooms are warm and there are plenty of small to tiny and sometimes cold double rooms and a few stuffy dormitories. They stay open all winter – the only time they may close is after a big winter storm, and perhaps only one will be open during the monsoon season.

If you intend staying here you must be confident that you won't suffer altitude problems so it pays to be well acclimatized before arriving. A few people cope with two nights at Dingboche/Pheriche, one at Lobuche then one at Gorak Shep but a better plan is Dingboche, Thuklha (or Chukhung), Lobuche then Gorak Shep.

If you have previously stayed a couple of nights at Chukhung or Gokyo then Dzonglha you are in a better position to go direct to Gorak Shep and bypass Lobuche. It is stupid to go directly from Dingboche/ Pheriche to Gorak Shep if unacclimatized.

Ascending Kala Pattar

Kala Pattar, which means 'Black Rock' in Hindi, is the most popular viewpoint in the area for Everest and the Khumbu Icefall.

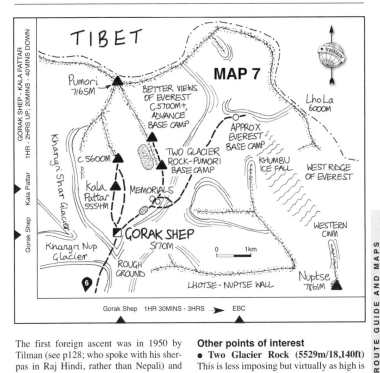

ROUTE GUIDE AND MAPS

The first foreign ascent was in 1950 by Tilman (see p128; who spoke with his sherpas in Raj Hindi, rather than Nepali) and Oscar Houston who rated it a 'subsidiary feature' without the extensive view of climbing access to Everest they sought. However, surrounded by a stupendous set of faces, peaks and glaciers, it offers a breathtaking arc of views.

From Gorak Shep a normal ascent time is 75 minutes but some people take as long as two laborious hours. Going fast but comfortably can take an hour, and a lung-bursting 45 minutes is about the minimum, while running down can take less than half an hour though it's more usual to take about an hour.

A dizzying thought is the fact that to climb Kala Pattar from Lukla you have had to ascend around 4800m/15,748ft, with a modest 2400m/7874ft of descents in total.

Other points of interest

● **Two Glacier Rock (5529m/18,140ft)** This is less imposing but virtually as high is the hill marked 5529m on the National Geographic Everest map and 5527m on the Khumbu Himal map. The 360° panorama is not as impressive but you can see more of Everest. Pick up a trail of sorts at the north-eastern end of Gorak Shep and head for the square cairn on the skyline. Over the other side is rough moraine and a small ridge, behind which, near the lake, is a flat spot often used as Pumori Base Camp. Pick up a rough trail somewhere around here that climbs to the eastern side of a minor rock spur (in reality a big lump of rock). A small trail leads to where the rock meets Pumori and a way up onto the spur.

● **Pumori advance base camp** For a better view of the Khumbu Icefall you can climb another of Pumori's spurs. Pick up a faint trail at Pumori base camp (the lake mentioned above) then pass by Two Glacier Rock, continuing a little north. Pick up, if you aren't already on, a small trail that soon begins climbing. The going gets steep and exposed but higher up you will come across a few tents/places for tents at an altitude of around 5700+m, Pumori advance base camp. From here it is obvious that to get any higher takes some rope and perhaps a fair amount of stupidity. Don't attempt these view points in anything other than perfect, snow-free conditions. Pumori was named by Mallory in 1921, it means 'Daughter Peak' or 'Sister Peak' (and is therefore pronounced 'Pumo-ri' or 'Pomo-ri' rather than the more common 'Pu-mori'. Incidentally, another mountain that is pronounced differently from when it was named is Everest: George's name was 'Eve-rest', not 'Ever-rest'.)

● Close to Gorak Shep are some more **memorials** to mountaineers who died on Everest, in particular to Rob Hall and others who died on Everest in 1996. To reach them walk the length of the Gorak Shep flats and continue a little further in the same direction. They are on the obvious minor ridge.

● While many people rate **Everest Base Camp** as a trek highlight, there are actually no views of Mt Everest. During the climbing season (late March, April and into mid-May) there are frequently yaks and sherpas on the trails but out of expedition season after fresh snow the trails can sometimes be hard to find or follow. To visit Kala Pattar plus the Base Camp in a single day is extremely tough – beyond most people. If you're going to visit one, Kala Pattar is the better choice.

The route to Base Camp follows the top of the moraine past the Gorak Shep flats for a considerable distance before dropping onto the glacier. The route sometimes seems rather roundabout since there are crevasses to avoid. Some expeditions don't mind the occasional visitor (especially when from their home country) while others prefer no distractions and would rather not run the risk of having sickness brought into their camp. It takes between ninety minutes and three hours each way.

HEADING DOWN

From Gorak Shep Reaching Pheriche or Dingboche is realistic, or pushing it Pangboche is possible, but it is difficult to reach Namche in a day; allow two. The Everest marathon is from Gorak Shep to Namche then slightly beyond to Thamo and back...

From Lobuche Most trekkers reach Pangboche, Deboche or Tengboche in a day. Groups tend to make for Deboche or Tengboche (making it more crowded). It's possible to reach Namche in a single long day, but it is long.

Alternatively, after climbing Kala Pattar some trekkers head down immediately. Pheriche or Dingboche are only a few hours past Lobuche, but can be a tough end to the day. If you have been suffering from the altitude, descending the short distance to Thuklha may offer some relief.

Phortse alternative A good alternative to the standard Tengboche route down is to go via Phortse and Mong, but allow more time – see p216. Note that the trail to Phortse starts from Upper Pangboche. Coming down the valley from Pheriche/Dingboche the turn-off is about 250m before the first houses, there are five small chortens and an X-shaped trail junction. The upper trail leads to Upper Pangboche, after passing more stupas, crossing the stream and rounding a spur with Mani walls.

Trekkers with more time can walk from Lobuche to Chukhung easily in a day via Dingboche or tougher but a more direct option is crossing the Kongma La (see p222). To Gokyo via the Tsho La/Chugyima La is covered on pp217-19.

Most people trek through or stay in Lower Pangboche.

Namche to Lukla This normally takes a day. Camping groups sometimes break this up: Namche to Phakding, then Phakding to Lukla. This then gives time for a special dinner and party in Lukla.

To Gokyo and around

INTRODUCTION

The Gokyo Valley offers great trekking and exploring but has always been overshadowed by the Lobuche, Kala Pattar and the Everest Base Camp area (see p204). While Lobuche and Gokyo are both in ablation valleys, its many glittering lakes and silky streams mean Gokyo is far more beautiful and offers more day-trip possibilities to appreciate the impressive surroundings.

From Dole upwards the majority of the lodges are run by Khumjung people. The main places have many lodges but there are also some delightful single *house-lodge* settlements where a meal and a dormitory bed can be found. In years past most trekkers would stay only two nights at Gokyo. Now lodge owners comment that most independent trekkers stay three nights or more – sometimes many more.

Acclimatization

Planning a sensible acclimatization programme is essential if you're heading directly to Gokyo. The helicopter rescue pilots used to call it 'Death Valley' because many people went up too fast, unaware of the consequences. This is partly because the walking days are short, tempting trekkers to go on past their acclimatization limits.

The minimum acclimatization programme is two nights at Namche, followed by one each at Khumjung (or Thame, Khunde, Kyangjuma, Mong, Tengboche or Phortse), Dole and then a night at either Luza, Machermo or Pangka. You can still get AMS following this but it is definitely better than two nights at Namche and a night each at Dole, Machermo and Gokyo.

A longer but rewarding itinerary would be Namche, Namche, Tengboche, Phortse, Dole, Machermo/Luza/Pangka, Gokyo. See pp28-9 and pp282-4 for sample itineraries.

The route

The first section out of Khumjung/Sanasa is a high open traverse; its highest point, Mong, is almost 4000m/13,123ft. The trail then drops abruptly through forest almost to the level of the river before climbing again. You may see deer and pheasant in this area. The countryside opens out offering great vistas of mountains on both sides of the deep valley and back to the stunning mountain wall above Tengboche. The climb up to the ablation valley beside the Ngozumpa Glacier leads you into a different world of azure lakes and golden alpine pastures beneath sparkling mountains overlooking the longest glacier in Nepal.

Facilities

Phortse used to be the last permanently inhabited village with only high *kharkas* higher up the valley. Now strategically placed *lodges* stay open year-round, including during the monsoon and winter.

The trail over the Lhenjo (Renjo) La has been upgraded and with several lodges in the Bhote–Thame valley, is now a tea-house trekking route, see p221.

There is a hospital at Machermo and satellite phones can be found at most places.

NAMCHE TO GOKYO
[Map 8, p207; Map 9, p209]
Namche to Khumjung See p176-7, 180.

Khumjung to Mong Either Khumjung, a beautiful village, or Khunde (see p180), is a sensible place to spend the night at the start of the Gokyo trek. Walk to the end of the village, then a minute down to a house with a blue roof by a junction, often marked with arrows painted on a convenient rock. Straight ahead is for Sanasa (see pp185-6); the left path is the more direct to Mong.

Rounding a ridge you come to a small valley where the trail divides again; although the upper trail is easy to miss, this isn't a problem since you will still be on the main trail. That upper trail leads up to a hair-raisingly steep stone staircase, the classic route. These days, however, it's more usual to contour on the better trail and head up the newer less steep stone stairs. Just beyond the main ridge the trail divides again, the larger trail for Mong, and the smaller trail to Tashinga.

Kyangjuma to Mong

A few minutes beyond Kyangjuma is a bridge across a small, sometimes dry stream, and almost immediately after is the junction beside a rock. Take the upper trail to climb in a few minutes to the main trail from Khumjung to Mong. Turn right for the gentle stairs, or left then right a moment later for the classic steep route.

Once through the rocks the trails cross the golden hillside gradually gaining height to a point overlooking Tengboche. It is well-worth keeping your camera at the ready and scanning the hillside, for it is common to see Himalayan tahr grazing here, and sometimes even musk deer in the gullies. Himalayan griffons and lammergeiers cruise the updrafts and, with a swoosh, often come amazingly close.

Near to Mong is a small stream: in dry times it's the only water supply for an hour in either direction.

Mong / Mohang (3973m/13,035ft)

The white chorten beckons and marks what is in effect a small pass. It is known to all Sherpas as the birthplace of Lama Sangwa Dorje, the patron saint of the Khumbu and founder of some of the gompas.

The views are stunning, especially of Ama Dablam, so if you haven't journeyed via the *Everest View Hotel*, this is a good substitute.

The track to Phortse Tenga is rather steeply down but with great views over to Phortse and the spectacular river gorge below, including an inaccessible natural rock-bridge.

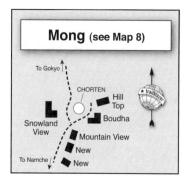

Phortse Tenga / Phortse Drangka (3675m/12,057ft)

Tenga means bridge but if heading to Gokyo you no longer need to descend to the river: a more direct trail contours from between *Phortse Tanga Lodge* and *Himalayan Lodge*. However, the better lodge is the *River Resort*, a few minutes down on the main trail, and not far from the river or *Drangka* in Sherpa.

For the village of Phortse and the routes to it see pp215-16.

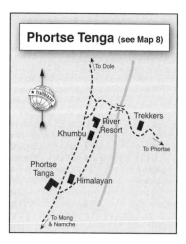

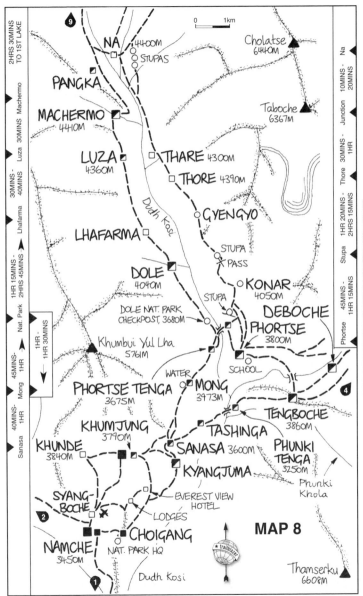

ROUTE GUIDE AND MAPS

2HRS 30MINS TO 1ST LAKE

Na

40MINS Machermo

10MINS - 20MINS

Machermo

Junction

Luza 30MINS

30MINS - 1HR

30MINS - 40MINS

Luza

Thore

Lhafarma

1HR 20MINS - 2HRS 15MINS

1HR 15MINS - 2HRS 45MINS

Stupa

Nat. Park

45MINS - 1HR 15MINS

45MINS - 1HR

Mong

Phortse

1HR - 1HR 30MINS

40MINS - 1HR

Sanasa

NA 4400M
STUPAS
Cholatse 6440M

PANGKA

MACHERMO 4410M

Taboche 6367M

LUZA 4360M   THARE 4300M

THORE 4390M

GYENGYO

Dudh Kosi

LHAFARMA   STUPA

PASS

DOLE 4040M   KONAR 4050M

STUPA

DOLE NAT. PARK CHECKPOST, 3680M   STUPA

DEBOCHE

PHORTSE 3800M

Khumbui Yul Lha 5761M

WATER

SCHOOL

PHORTSE TENGA 3675M   MONG 3973M

TENGBOCHE 3860M

KHUMJUNG 3790M   TASHINGA

KHUNDE 3840M   SANASA 3600M   PHUNKI TENGA 3250M

KYANGJUMA

Phunki Khola

SYANG-BOCHE   EVEREST VIEW HOTEL

LODGES

NAMCHE 3450M   CHOIGANG

NAT. PARK HQ

Dudh Kosi

MAP 8

Thamserku 6608M

> **How the Yeti Inn was named**
> In 1990 eight of us passed through the very basic lodges at Phortse Tenga and pushed on to Dole. Arriving in the gloom and stumbling across the stream at the meadow bottom, we saw a light at what looked like a stable. This was the Yeti Inn, really just a basic sleeping platform and a kitchen area: you ate sitting on the beds. As we ate the excellent food Urkien, the lodge owner, showed us a book full of sketches of the yeti that a foreigner on a yeti hunt had left. Apparently the Gokyo Valley is full of them ... **Joel Schone**
> (Update: the lodge is now run by Urkien's daughter.)

To Dole Continuing on, it is beautiful walking through rhododendron and birch forest with a few small wooden bridges crossing side streams. In winter the iced waterfalls are impressive but be very, very careful if these have iced over the trail. Particularly watch for musk deer in the forest. The now-abandoned army post and national park post were there to protect them. From them Dole is one to two hours, still with some climbing to get here.

Dole (4040m/13,254ft)
The name means 'many stones' but despite this it's a pleasant kharka with seven *lodges*. Here the yaks and naks are brought up in mid-June to graze and fertilize the soil with their dung, producing a rich crop of hay. If you arrive with time on your hands there are a couple of short exploration possibilities. Following the valley formed by the stream leads relatively gently up to a large grassy area in less than an hour. Alternatively follow the ridge from

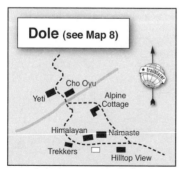

Dole (see Map 8)

Cho Oyu
Yeti
Alpine Cottage
Himalayan   Namaste
Trekkers   Hilltop View
trailblazer

Himalayan Lodge up a steep trail to a rocky viewpoint, in an hour or so.

Dole, and Lhafarma, Luza, Machermo get the sun early, making early starts easy, although there is little need with only a short day's walk between them.

The afternoon and sunset views of Kangtaiga and Thamserku from the hill behind Dole on the trail to Luza are most impressive. Up the valley are the first views of a high mountain wall, the left end of which is Cho Oyu, the sixth highest peak on the planet; the right-hand side is Gyachung Kang, a name that few people have ever heard of, though it is the 15th highest peak in the world and the highest below the 8000m mark, equal with Gasherbrum III in Pakistan.

Continuing towards Machermo the trail climbs out of Dole (past the Yeti Inn) and above the tree line to a chotar and small mani, and continues climbing up the ridge a short way before turning into a rising traverse with broad vistas.

Lhafarma / Lhapharma (4300m) has two *lodges* five minutes apart: first the pleasant *Mountain View Top Hill Lodge* with double rooms then the classically named *Holyday Inn* which is smaller. The mountain views both up, down and across the valley are extensive. From here the trail contours, about as flat as it gets in the region.

While walking the fragrant smell comes from the small rhododendron plants. There are two types that look similar but only one, sunpati, is burnt at offerings. Approaching Luza is a mani and just below

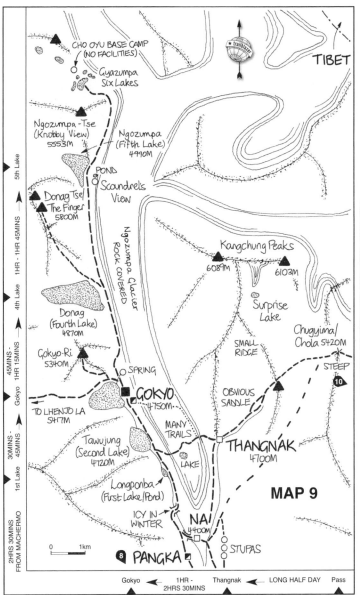

CHO OYU BASE CAMP
(NO FACILITIES)

Gyazumpa
Six Lakes

TIBET

Ngozumpa-Tse
(Knobby View)
5553M

Ngozumpa (Fifth Lake)
4990M

POND

Scoundrel's
View

Donag Tse/
The Finger
5800M

Kangchung Peaks

6089M   6103M

Ngozumpa Glacier ROCK COVERED

Surprise
Lake

Donag
(Fourth Lake)
4870M

Chugyima/
Chola 5420M

SMALL
RIDGE

STEEP

10

Gokyo-Ri
5340M

SPRING

GOKYO
4750M

OBVIOUS
SADDLE

TO LHENJO LA
5417M

MANY
TRAILS

THANGNAK
4700M

Tawujung
(Second Lake)
4720M

LAKE

MAP 9

Longponba
(First Lake/Pond)

ICY IN
WINTER

NA/
4400M

STUPAS

0   1km

8   PANGKA

5th Lake

1HR - 1HR 45MINS   4th Lake

45MINS -
1HR 15MINS   Gokyo

30MINS -
45MINS   1st Lake

2HRS 30MINS
FROM MACHERMO

Gokyo ←   1HR -
2HRS 30MINS   Thangnak ← LONG HALF DAY   Pass

is a memorial to an Italian trekker who died here, and not surprisingly. He trekked from Lukla to Phakding, then one night in Namche, the next in Dole and arrived at Gokyo not feeling too well. A porter carried him down later that night but he died in Luza.

Luza (4360m/14,304ft) is an hour or so from Dole and has several pleasant *lodges*. It is a good, and often less busy, alternative to Machermo, and although it is 50 metres lower this difference is insignificant. When leaving, immediately after crossing the stream continue up through the fields rather than taking the left trail. In winter, especially, Tibetan snowcocks cackle in the fields.

Luza (see Map 8)

Machermo (4410m/14,468ft) This is a relaxing spot with good views, especially of some little-known mountains. The grandest lodge is *Namgyal Lodge*, with some better than normal rooms for slightly more. There are a handful of smaller older-style *lodges* too. Since Lhafarma, Luza and Machermo are so close together and at a similar altitude it doesn't matter which one you stay at.

Most people head directly from here to Gokyo but if acclimatization is causing problems it might be wiser to stay another night at Luza or Machermo. Alternative places to stay are **Na** (4400m/14,436ft, see p214) where you can explore the surrounding area, or Pangka (see column opposite).

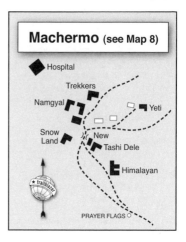

Machermo (see Map 8)

After an initial climb out of Machermo the trail is more or less level to Pangka.

Pangka (4480m/14,698ft)
This kharka has a chequered history. Two *lodges* opened in 1994. Then in 1995 one was hit by an avalanche during a freak snowstorm. Thirteen members of a Japanese group along with their Sherpas were killed. Now the simple *lodges* are built further away from the slopes above so that the same accident shouldn't recur.

There are trails around both sides of the fields. They rejoin by a small chorten

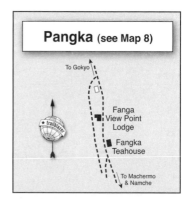

Pangka (see Map 8)

then briefly drop-traverse out of the kharka before climbing closer to the Dudh Kosi.

The massive slopes on your right (heading up) are the terminal moraine of the Ngozumpa Glacier (see Map 9), and less obvious, on your left, are the remains of a smaller terminal moraine.

You are now entering what is called an ablation valley, a usually narrow valley formed when a glacier lifts up moraine at its edges then retreats slightly, leaving this uplifted moraine to form a grassy valley.

Soon the trail meets the rock wall and traverses the steep side on a reasonable trail. The views down-valley are magnificent but don't walk and look at the same time. The trail continues climbing, always staying above the river to a water source that only the paranoid would purify. In late winter this area is often quite icy.

As you climb on the stone steps notice that there is one clear stream and one milky one. Unusually, the water draining from the glacier breaks through the terminal moraine here, rather than directly above Na. The clear stream comes from the first pond and is clear since much of the glacial sediment has settled in the lakes. A cold night, especially in winter, freezes the spray and sometimes even freezes the stream, diverting it onto the path which becomes treacherously slippery.

Longponba / the first pond A sudden change of scenery and hundreds of petite cairns introduce the first pond; it's really too small to be called a lake. It is beautiful up here, with a sparkling brook and tantalizingly close mountains.

Between here and the second lake/pond, one of the trails to Thangnak begins (ie for the Chugyima La/Tsho La) and, if you have time, the view from the top of the moraine or just over the other side is simply spectacular.

Taujung / Tawujung / the second lake (4720m/15,485ft) *Ta* is the word for horse and *Jung* means a grazing area, although it is now far more common to see yaks grazing here. It is worth soaking up the peaceful spaciousness here.

In winter here I was berated for walking on the frozen lake: a Sherpa said I would anger the gods of the area, for the second lake is considered the holiest of the region.

GOKYO
(See map p212; 4750m/15,584ft)
On the shores of the third lake is the **Gokyo kharka**. Given the distance from anywhere, the *lodge* facilities are really very good, the owners friendly and the prices reasonable, better than most of the Lobuche lodges. Most lodges offer camera-battery charging services. Note that a single large solar panel costs around $500, hence the charges for the service.

The Everest view from Gokyo Ri is only one of the many reasons for visiting Gokyo. Relaxing on the lodge patios or their sun rooms overlooking the rich turquoise, picturesque lake and the etched mountains above is considered reward enough by some; but it's the potential for far-ranging exploration that sets it apart from Lobuche. Climbing to the top of the Lhenjo (Renjo) La is exhilarating and walking up to the fifth lake and beyond can only be described as 'out of this world'. Many of the peaks around here require some steepish scrambling or bouldering. Recognize your limits and take account of the weather; rocks are slippery when damp: otherwise enjoy!

With everyone heading off exploring at all hours of the morning don't expect to sleep in undisturbed. At the same time plan ahead if you are leaving early: the kitchen may not be open so stock up the evening before on boiled eggs and chapatis or plenty of biscuits and chocolate.

Gokyo is indeed a wonderful place but it does have its problems. The toilets are potentially polluting the lake – without visible impact yet, perhaps, but it is hard to work out how to improve this situation.

Less seriously, the lodges specialize in tacky posters with Indian sayings written on them: *Love is only chatter friends are all that matter ...*

See pp214-5 for details of the **Na to Phortse route** as an alternative way back.

See pp218-19 for the route to Thangnak and to the Tsho La/Chugyima La.

ROUTE GUIDE AND MAPS

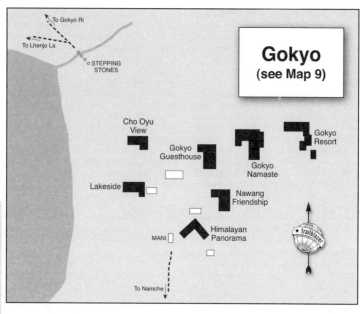

To Gokyo Ri

To Lhenjo La

STEPPING STONES

Gokyo
(see Map 9)

Cho Oyu View

Gokyo Guesthouse

Gokyo Resort

Gokyo Namaste

Lakeside

Nawang Friendship

MANI

Himalayan Panorama

★ trailblazer

To Namche

AROUND GOKYO   [Map 9, p209]
Gokyo Ri (5340m/17,519ft) A stiff one-and-a-quarter to three-hour climb on an obvious track brings you to the prayer-flag bedecked top of this viewpoint. The panorama stretches well into the distance, a blend of glaciers and grass, sheer rock, snow and ice.

The sunset on Everest and Makalu can be unforgettable here – as can be the descent afterwards if you forgot to bring your torch/flashlight. Sunrise is less worthwhile; only when it is fully light do the mountains look good.

Lhenjo La / Renjo La (5417m/
17,772ft)   [off Map 9, p209]
The trek to the top of this pass can be an exhilarating short day walk. In addition to some breathtaking new vistas, you end up in real alpine territory and pass within touching distance of a white glacier. Although it looks far from Gokyo, it's only two to three hours to the top. A reasonable

sense of balance and adventure is required as there are a few steep sections.

Begin by crossing the stream at the head of the lake, then follow the trail that contours, skirting the lake. At the head flats the views of Everest, Lhotse and, later, Makalu are interesting and quite photogenic. Cross the flats and stay to the right. The idea is to gain altitude up small stream gullies, eventually crossing the main stream that issues from high above. At the first crest the view is quite unexpected and looks substantially different from the view from Gokyo. Again, stay to the right on the flat area. From here note the position of the pass above (it's marked by at least ten large cairns) and pick your own route up.

It's best to ascend following cairns over glacier-rounded slabs to the top of these then skirt south a short distance at a point that looks as if it could be tricky, to find the dusty steep track up. Alternatively, walk alongside the glacier on rough rock and later there is a steep loose scree slope to the dusty track. For the route over the other side see p221.

Donag / Tonak / the fourth lake (4870m/ 15,977ft) Without crossing the stream, a track leads up the valley floor but a more scenic way is to follow the crest of the moraine as far as possible. In about an hour you reach the fourth lake. This is large and beautiful, flanked to the south on one side by monumental cliffs. The most exciting features, however, are the unnamed peaks north of the lake.

Donag Tse / The Finger (5800m/ 19,029ft) It's well worth scrambling up to have a closer look at these tooth-like towers, and the views are fantastic, even if you can't reach the true summit. The climb can be made in a day-trip from Gokyo but with the altitude this is **a trip for the fit and acclimatized only**. The route up steepens over large boulders, getting quite tricky. It looks as if there is no way on but it's possible to climb over the boulders to the point where you reach a drop to the next tooth, at around 5600m: it is not possible, however, to reach the true tops.

The wall between Cho Oyu and Gyachung Kang defies description from this distance and the web of glaciers is fascinating. There's also the most extensive view of Everest you'll get anywhere in the Khumbu without resorting to serious mountaineering. You can see part of the Geneva Spur (but not the Hillary Step), the South Col, the stunning Lhotse face and Nuptse. To the north is the famous North Ridge and the First, Second and Third Steps where Mallory and Irvine were last seen. The perspective from this point, although not as close as from Kala Pattar, is more realistic than elsewhere.

Ngozumpa / the fifth lake (4990m/ 16,371ft) This jewel is about one-and-a-half to three hours from Gokyo. Climbing the moraine, the pile of dirt to the east, to overlook the Ngozumpa Glacier also offers a '**scoundrel's view**' of Everest that is more extensive than from both Gokyo Ri and

Kala Pattar, and doesn't require climbing. Look out for furball pikas beside the trail. In the mid-morning light the view of Everest's formidable south face is the best of any viewpoint.

Ngozumpa-tse / Knobby View (5553m) From the true top this is simply the most outrageous trekking viewpoint there is; however, it is steep and exposed in places so only attempt it when the path is snow-free.

The only route that can be recommended is the spur that begins close to the fifth lake. Initially the ridge is steep but soon eases off. Closer to the top is a steep boulder field so pick your route carefully: there still isn't much of a trail here. Once on the main ridge and at the top of what looked from below like the summit is a surprise: the real top is still a couple of knobs away, but well worth the extra effort if your nerves are up to the traverse.

From the real summit you overlook Gyazumpa (six lakes) and the exploration possibilities unfold below. With the Cho Oyu/Gyachung Kang wall to the north, the lakes under your toes, glaciers, snow and ice everywhere, this is as alpine a scene as it gets, without climbing a major peak. For some giddy excitement poke your nose over the edge, drop a stone and watch it as it plummets down an almost 300-metre, truly vertical drop. You can even see Gokyo Lake and the lodges and ridge after ridge of hills. The two Kangshung peaks are spectacular from here and this is the best view of Lhotse (the mountain next to Everest) in the whole region.

It is possible to descend due east but this is dangerous. The terrain is very steep, there are a couple of places where you can be bluffed out, and there is a very real rock-fall danger. In summary, don't descend on this route. Ascending here would be even trickier, and it isn't obvious where you should go.

Gyazumpa / six lakes / Cho Oyu Base Camp (5150m) The scenery up here is so spectacular it's overwhelming.

ROUTE GUIDE AND MAPS

> **The Nup La 5985m**
> Viewing the icefall that leads to this pass from the peaks above Gokyo, one has to wonder why this was ever named, and whether it has ever been crossed. The name means West Pass, and was named by the 1920s' explorers to Everest, who also named Lhotse, which means south peak (because it's south of Everest). Amazingly enough, the Nup La has been crossed, and by none other than the late Sir Edmund Hillary and George Lowe, who in 1952, frustrated that the Chinese invasion of Tibet had stopped mountaineering attempts from the north, resolved to visit Everest's north base camp anyway. They also returned by the same route, without getting caught by the Tibetans or Chinese, which was better than Eric Shipton fared during the same period (see pp224-5).

It's a half-day trek from Gokyo but well-worth camping/bivvying here so that you can have more time to appreciate the region. North-east of the flat lakes area it is possible to climb several minor summits, only partially marked on maps, and there's a steepish (technical) ice route to the Sumna Glacier.

Despite being labelled Cho Oyu Base Camp, very few expeditions have used this as a base; as you might notice from here, Cho Oyu presents a formidable challenge. Instead the standard route is from the Tibetan side, accessible from just over the other side of the Nangpa La.

Cho Oyu is considered one of the least difficult 8000m mountains, if climbing on the standard route, but any 8000m mountain is a major challenge.

Pass 5443m (17,857ft) Between Gyazumpa and Ngozumpa is a minor pass, marked as 5443m on the Schneider map. The glacier to the north has an even set of crescent crevasses so stay on the edge or on the rock. It is a bit of a scramble to the top but the descent on the other side is pleasant, passing a small lake that begs to be camped by.

Pass 5493m (Ngozumpa) West of the Ngozumpa, the fifth lake, is a pass that has long been known to Sherpas (in contrast the pass 5486m, west of Donag, is unknown to them and requires a rope, if it is passable at all). Conditions have changed since it was regularly used and now the east face is steeper than it used to be. The difficulties are less on the west side. I am unsure whether or not is is still easily crossable.

Tsho La/Cho La/Chugyima La is covered on pp217-20.

Heading down
Leaving Gokyo, it is a full, fairly tough day's walk to Namche. Stopping in Kyangjuma can be sensible, and if you are feeling fit you can still make Lukla the next day. Alternatively explore around in the morning and head down in the afternoon to Machermo, Dole or Mong, breaking the trek down into two days, and this will give you an afternoon in Namche too.

With more time there are plenty of other options: so read on.

TO AND FROM PHORTSE
[Map 9, p209 & Map 8, p207]
Gokyo to Phortse
The quickest route down from Gokyo is via Dole and Machermo. However, rather than back-tracking, there's an alternative trail on the east valley wall direct to Phortse via Na. Note that during the monsoon often there is no bridge between Pangka and Na (ask locals) so the only way to take this route is to cross the Ngozumpa glacier to Thangnak and descend from there.

Na / Nala (4400m/14,436ft) This is a curious place, but has now joined the trekking world with a *lodge*, normally open during the peak seasons, and sometimes open at other times. The region is used by the people of Phortse, so ask there if it is open when coming up the valley.

Leaving Na To head down, aim for the small bridge. The trail is small. If coming up to Na from Phortse, half an hour before Na by a large rock is a distinct trail junction, the lower trail is for Na and the upper leads to the flats of Chugyima (no facilities there). **Thare** (4300m/14,107ft), **Thore** (4390m/14,403ft) and **Gyengyo** have quaint tea-houses, good for a lunch/snack stop and all possible to stay at. I have arrived during January and February snow storms, a monsoon downpour, as well as during the normal trekking seasons, to find at least one of these places open, and if the Tsho (Cho) La is closed, all of them are likely to be open. Leaving the last place there is a short climb which leads to the chorten at 4278m/14,035ft with magnificent views.

Konar (4050m/13,287ft) is deserted during the trekking season but with the increasing number of trekkers using this side of the valley expect a lodge here sometime. In summer it's a large hay-growing area and is the location of Phortse's hydropower plant. Around the corner all of the larger trails lead to Phortse.

Phortse (3800m/12,467ft)

Pronounced 'Phurtse' by the locals, *phurte* means flight, and it's supposed to have gained its name when the Khumbu saint, Lama Sangwa Dorje, landed here after a trance-induced flight. Apparently it was here that he attained enlightenment. It's a picturesque village, magnificently situated and defended by steep hillsides. The area is famous for its buckwheat but potatoes are also grown in large numbers.

The forests to the south-west and the north are protected by a ban on wood cutting that was made over one hundred years

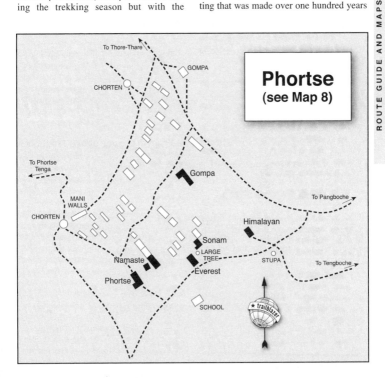

To Thore-Thare

GOMPA

CHORTEN

Phortse
(see Map 8)

To Phortse
Tenga

Gompa

MANI
WALLS

CHORTEN

To Pangboche

Himalayan

Sonam

LARGE
TREE

Namaste

STUPA

To Tengboche

Phortse

Everest

SCHOOL

★ trailblazer

ago by the lama who lived in the forest. In other areas, notably Namche, Khumjung and Khunde, when the government took over control of the forests and redefined the areas that could be cut, the pattern of use changed quickly. Here, the old lama's edict seems to have proved more effective. It is also a shelter for innumerable danphe, other pheasants and deer.

Late afternoon is good spotting time: only the blind would miss seeing a variety of wildlife and they would be likely to trip over them.

Phortse has several good **lodges** and a new (2005) electricity system. It's also home to many Everest summiteers, including Panuru (Phortse Guesthouse) and Tshering Lhakpa (Thuklha).

Above the village, at around 5600m, is **Look Ri**. In fact there are two rock peaks but one requires a rope, the other doesn't.

Phortse to Na From the top of the village head north (left) on a path that follows the walls but stays above the fields. If in doubt take upper trails.

Phortse to Phortse Tenga The trail starts behind the mani walls at the lower northern part of the village. It's a wide but sometimes slippery track passing through forest where there's a good chance of spotting pheasant and musk deer. It continues down until you reach the wooden bridge. Close by is a protected stand of trees that is set aside exclusively for bridge repair.

Immediately after the bridge there is a junction. Straight up a small path leads up to the main trail to **Dole** (p208). The route to the left goes to some reasonable camping spots and Phortse Tenga (p206).

Phortse to Pangboche or Tengboche
Walking without watching where you're going could be hazardous on this trail. If you're scared of heights and not happy walking along trails with steep drops beside them avoid this route.

The track starts from the top of the village on a gentle gradient with excellent views of Tengboche.

For the **gentle route to Tengboche/ Deboche** the turn-off for the bridge that crosses the gorge is immediately after the first small rock cleft. The path heads down steeply before continuing at a more gentle rate of descent. It's not always obvious, sometimes little more than an imaginary trail, and divides many times but it is not easy to become totally lost. Once close to the bridge the path heads up 100m or so to climb over bluffs below, crosses a stream, then drops to join the main Pangboche–Tengboche trail immediately above the bridge.

For **Pangboche** At the first rock cleft continue straight on the main trail as it winds and climbs in and out of bluffs. It finishes in Upper Pangboche.

For **Tengboche direct** From the southern corner of the village a trail drops to a small bridge for the steep climb to Tengboche.

▲ **From the bridge above Tengboche to Phortse** Climb up about 100m on goat tracks until you reach a point where it's easy to cross the little creek to your left. Follow the tiny trail on the other side down to the fields. Work your way across, taking the upper paths where possible until you reach the main Pangboche–Phortse trail.

ROUTE GUIDE AND MAPS

❏ **Map key** See p309 for the route map key

The Tsho La / Cho La / Chugyima La

INTRODUCTION

The 5420m/17,782ft pass between Lobuche and Gokyo is commonly called the Tsho La (or Cho La) on the Lobuche/Dzonglha side, which means very simply 'Lake Pass' while the people of Khumjung on the Gokyo side call it the Chugyima La, since it is above the grazing flats of Chugyima.

The crossing has become popular but it does traverse **a glacier which could be dangerous**. If it has snowed recently either avoid the pass or take great care descending/ascending the smooth slabs on the Gokyo side of the pass and the steep section on the Dzonglha/Lobuche side. If it has snowed heavily or the weather is unstable **avoid the pass** altogether.

The rock approaches are steep and exposed but present no real problems **in good conditions.** However, the glacier is sometimes icy and treacherously slippery. Porters are never provided with crampons, instead they tie thick string around their shoes at the ball of the foot. This concentrates the load at that point and provides more grip, a handy trick that everybody without crampons should adopt if it is icy. String can usually be found at Lobuche and Gokyo, as well as discarded near the pass.

Information relevant to walking in the reverse direction is also given: this is marked by ▲.

LOBUCHE TO GOKYO
[Map 10, p219, Map 9, p209]
Lobuche to Dzonglha

Follow the track towards Thuklha but do not continue across the creek: stay on the right (west) side. After a flat area (an ice sheet in winter) there's an obvious track that contours up around the huge spur to another flat area about an hour away. Up this broad gully is the route to Lobuche Peak Base Camp.

Continue straight ahead for the route to the Tsho La, climbing to the top of the ridge and then dropping down to an area with many streams. After jumping across the biggest stream the path heads gently up a tiny valley to hidden Dzonglha.

ROUTE GUIDE AND MAPS

 Khumbu passes
Linking the main valleys of the region are some short-cut passes or 'La', which means mountain pass in Tibetan and Sherpa. One old explanation of altitude sickness was 'poisonous vapours' at the pass tops, and chewing garlic while crossing was recommended. All these passes are very high (over 5400m/17,700ft) so ensure you have the appropriate acclimatization to cross them. They should also be approached with caution and only after sound preparation. Only cross in reasonable visibility and if you think you have lost the trail or the way, backtrack and start looking again. For the commonly crossed trekking passes (the Tsho La/Chugyima La, Lhenjo La and Kongma La) pack lunch and plenty of snacks, and carry plenty of water or a way of purifying water en route; there are no teahouses for refreshments.

Treat the true mountaineering passes (the Amphu Labtsa and the passes over to the Makalu region) as real climbing and if trekking with crew ensure they have the appropriate level of experience. Where possible avoid taking porters: instead take climbing-experienced crew.

Dzonglha (4850m/15,912ft) This is a summer yak-herding station on the left, or south, side of the miniature valley. There are two *lodges* here, at least one of which is normally open year-round. In difficult snow conditions or during the monsoon check at nearby lodges that a lodge is open. If **camping** there are suitable watered spots from here up to the beginning of the steep climb. Look out for Himalayan weasels nearby.

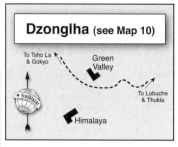

Dzonglha (see Map 10)

Approaching the pass There are two routes up the pass but one is disused now. Leaving Dzonglha the area is incredibly photogenic with Cholatse as one backdrop and the ridge extending from Lobuche Peak another.

Rounding a slightly rocky ridge, cross a stream and a small flattish area to the broad valley. Further up, as the valley tightens, the path crosses the main stream, which can sometimes be a little tricky to negotiate, then climbs a ridge on the southern side on a clear path. At the rock-face the trail virtually disappears. Head right, or north, and climb up big boulders and slabs staying close to the wall on your left (west). There are a few cairns to look out for and eventually a heavily cairned flattish area is reached. The route continues to climb still staying close to the rock which is now to your south since the trail has taken a 90° turn.

If you have crampons head for the glacier as soon as you can see a way onto it, otherwise continue up to where the rock meets an almost flat snowy area. From here the tip of Everest is just visible and down-valley Baruntse begins to look for-

midable. Little of this wild mountain is normally visible.

Take great care around here: when it is warmer rockfall can be a problem, when colder it can be dangerously icy.

The glacier Stay on the southern edge of the glacier on the trail (assuming there is one). Never cross to the middle. Sometimes the footprints stay high on the south bank and at other times they drop down a little. It's very important to keep a good look out for crevasses. Often none is visible, though if you do have to jump across one, be extremely careful. Also take care if you have to cross frozen ponds. The highest point of the pass is at the far end of the snow/ice.

Chugyima La to Thangnak Before continuing down, have a look at the route possibilities in the valley below. The main valley descends gently to the south to Charchung and Tshom Teng while the route to Gokyo crosses a couple of ridges via a shallow saddle with a large boulder with a cairn on top, the correct route. This saddle is apparently called Tar-Kure, or perhaps Targula, meaning 'like a horse's back'.

The descent is via rounded rock ledges, wide but often slippery. Staying on a track, or sometimes even finding one, is hard. Stay close to the southern rock wall. There are several vague trails and plenty of cairns around/over the rocky ridge to a camping place occasionally used by groups

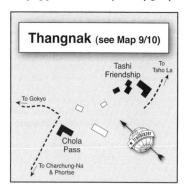

Thangnak (see Map 9/10)

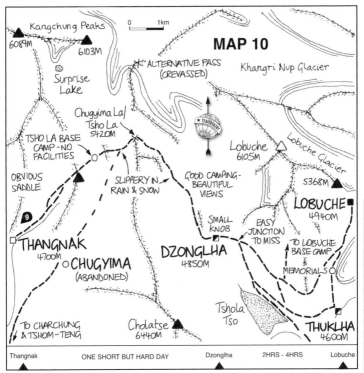

MAP 10

Kangchung Peaks
6089M 6103M

Surprise Lake

ALTERNATIVE PASS (CREVASSED)

Khangri Nup Glacier

Chugyima La/Tsho La 5420M

trailblazer

Lobuche 6105M

Lobuche Glacier

TSHO LA BASE CAMP - NO FACILITIES

OBVIOUS SADDLE

SLIPPERY N RAIN & SNOW

GOOD CAMPING - BEAUTIFUL VIEWS

5368M

LOBUCHE 4940M

SMALL KNOB

EASY JUNCTION TO MISS

TO LOBUCHE BASE CAMP

9

THANGNAK 4700M

CHUGYIMA (ABANDONED)

DZONGLHA 4850M

MEMORIALS

TO CHARCHUNG & TSHOM-TENG

Cholatse 6440M

Tshola Tso

THUKLHA 4600M

| Thangnak | ONE SHORT BUT HARD DAY | Dzonglha | 2HRS - 4HRS | Lobuche |

(called Base Camp). Once over the shallow saddle it's down, down, down, mainly on the north side of the khola.

Thangnak (Tagnag) (4700m/15,420ft)
The two *lodges* here have grown from being rather basic to having plenty of double rooms and good meals. They are normally open while the Chugyima La is passable. Gokyo is still an hour or two from here over rough ground.

Several guidebooks and maps have called this place Dragnag, Tagnag and other variations: the correct name is Thangnak.

Crossing the Ngozumpa Glacier
Follow a thin trail; up a little around the corner is a prominent cairn on the crest of

the moraine which you should head for. Scan the glacier and look for signs of the most direct route. The path across is well used but not always obvious: backtrack if you lose the path. The walking is tough for tired feet, but after climbing the moraine on the opposite side you drop to just above the first pond, a little below the second lake. Continue gently up to the third lake and the lodges of Gokyo (see p211).

Note that by the time you read this, the trail across from Thangnak to Gokyo might have changed; see below and check with the lodge owner.

▲ GOKYO TO LOBUCHE
Crossing between Gokyo and Lobuche in one day is tough: it's more pleasant to break

it up and now that there are lodges in Dzonglha and Thangnak (Tagnag) there are possibilities to suit everyone. Fit trekkers should, in good conditions, be able to make Dzonglha from Gokyo or vice versa, or Thangnak from Lobuche. Note that Dzonglha to Gorak Shep is a relatively easy day, and if you stayed at Gokyo for a few days, Gorak Shep's altitude shouldn't be a problem. For people equipped to sleep outside there are good camping spots between Dzonglha and the pass, and on the Gokyo side there is a huge area worthy of exploration.

Gokyo to Thangnak There are/were two routes: ask your lodge owner which is best. The old standard route starts from between the first and second lakes and crosses more or less in a straight line to Thangnak. The problem is lakes are forming on the glacier, almost certainly from global warming, and now crossing the stream from them is challenging. Any new route will have to pass to the north of these lakes. It is likely the route will change to climbing the moraine almost directly behind Gokyo, drop onto then cross the moraine-covered glacier, then climb up the steep moraine wall somewhere safe. Note that these steep moraines walls are very dangerous and always steepest near the top. Only follow a trail. At the time of writing after crossing the rubble-covered glacier, the trail travelled down on the (east) edge of the glacier to the normal way up the moraine very close to Thangnak.

Thangnak to Dzonglha Ascend the valley on the north side/left side of the stream. After 30-40 minutes follow the trail up a smaller valley on the left. After 15-20 minutes recross the main stream, leaving it behind, and head up to a minor saddle, another 12-20 minutes away, to a large rock. There are new views, including the Chugyima La, the steep rockface with a thin snowy saddle which looks particularly formidable from here. Descend on the trail, crossing streams, and traverse to a camping area sometimes used by groups and called

Tsho La Base Camp. From here the rough rock begins. There are several rough cairned paths – they are easy to lose – that lead to a flat area with a pond above it. Pick up a trail ascending a debris cone to the southern rock wall. This ascends moderately steeply and the trail is quite exposed. In deep snow this can be impossible or at least highly dangerous as this is in fact an avalanche cone. Thirty to seventy-five minutes later you reach the pass cairns, prayer flags and the glacier. Clamber onto the glacier and stay high on the southern side: beware if it is icy as it can be *very* slippery, and ice is very hard! Many people have bruised themselves.

Traverse the glacier, always staying on the southern side and once you reach the rocks descend on the difficult but short slopes to a set of cairns in a semi-sheltered area. Continue down on difficult ground, staying close to the rock wall to your right and look for the trail below. Once off the difficult ground at the ridge a clear path descends to the open, almost flat valley. The walking in this valley is pleasant and incredibly photogenic. Cholatse's face is utterly dramatic, Ama Dablam's triangle is stunning and Lobuche East peak looks particularly formidable and even surreal in some lighting. As the valley makes a bend towards Cholatse cross the stream and briefly climb-traverse to the trail. Don't descend further.

Dzonglha to Thukla / Lobuche
If you have reached Dzonglha and are contemplating continuing, Thukhla is about an hour away but involves a descent that would be tricky in half-light. Alternatively, 1½-2 hours of hard walking will bring you to Lobuche.

Heading out of Dzonglha to Lobuche, Cholatse steals the show with its awesome face. As you round the spur with your first views of Nuptse there is one of the best views of the uppermost parts of Lhotse's fearsome upper reaches that you get in the Khumbu.

The Lhenjo La / Renjo La

THE LHENJO LA

This 5417m/17,772ft pass has variously been spelt as Henjo and Renjo but the correct way is Lhenjo La.

With some lodges (built in 2004) and some trail building, it is now possible to teahouse trek between Gokyo and Thame – no camping. Previously the pass was steep and dangerous at the top but now it is easier to cross, which opens up the trekking possibilities significantly. You should still only cross in good weather though.

Virtually everyone crosses in the Gokyo to Thame direction so that is described here. In reverse you must be previously acclimatized, which is hard to do sufficiently around Thame. Plan on taking three days from Gokyo to Namche, although the quick can do it in two days. If you want to spend time in Thame, plan longer.

Times, on average:
- Gokyo to Pass top 3½ hrs
- Pass top to Lungde 3hrs
- Lungde to Maralung 45 mins
- Maralung to Thame 2½ hrs

Don't forget to pack some lunch and snacks and plan to leave early to get good weather up there.

From Gokyo to the top of the pass is covered on p212. Plan on around 3-5 hours to the top, depending on your acclimatization and how heavy your pack is.

One of the joys of pass-hopping is the sudden new views, more glorious mountain vistas. Amazingly there are stone steps down the other side, going down all the way to the first lake, and slightly beyond where it turns into a well-used trail to Lungden. Cross a small crest and drop to the wide valley on the right-hand side, passing several grazing areas. Pass a pond then the two lakes (pass on the right-hand side) to **Lhenjo (4720m)**, a grassy lake area that gives the pass its name Lhenjo. There is a sign for the turn-off to Arye (see below).

Lungde / Lungare / Lungden 4375m

There are three *lodges* here: two smaller ones and the first, the *Renjo Pass Support Lodge*, is just that, and is open for most of the year, as long as the pass is open. So far there are only dorm rooms here. If you don't stay here, plan where you will stay; it is still a long way to Thame, particularly if you are tired.

To Thame

Leaving, drop further, heading south, and soon after you reach the valley base, **Maralung** comes into view. This is a herding area with two teahouses: at the time of writing they were unsuitable for staying overnight but, by the time you read this, one of them might have rooms.

Do ask what the best way to Thame is. Usually after crossing the stream out of Maralung, you then cross the main river to the Thame side of the valley, but this could change.

Arye alternative

From the top of the Lhenjo La it is also possible to descend to Arye and the teahouse there, to explore further up the Bhote Valley. Heading down the pass, follow the main trail until near the grassy lake area near Lhenjo and look for the sign showing the way down. The trail is narrow. See the Nangpa La route description on p226.

ROUTE GUIDE AND MAPS

Khumbu side trips and pass-hopping

Some of these routes are distinctly adventurous so come mentally prepared. On one route, a couple of days from anywhere and on dicey ground, Tom and Vanessa's guide said 'I know a shortcut – did you bring a ladder?' Wisely, they decided to turn back.

Information relevant to walking in the reverse direction is also given: this is marked by ▲.

THE KONGMA LA   [Map 11]

Meaning 'Tibetan Snowcock Pass', the Kongma La (5535m/18,159ft) provides an interesting high route between Chukhung and Lobuche. It is a tough day-long walk and is longer than the lower route via Dingboche. If free of snow, it's a non-technical pass. It requires only a little confidence and steady feet for the last short section to the crest. A trekking pole may be handy. It's more pleasant to do in the Chukhung–Lobuche direction because the walk up is on grass, leaving the rock-hopping and loose scree for the descent. It's really worth camping by the high lakes for the stunning sunset and sunrise.

Chukhung to Lobuche Contour and cross the large stream issuing from the ablation valley just west of the Nuptse Glacier. Then there's a long climb up the huge grassy ridge. There are faint trails: aim for the point where the high, sharp rocky spur peters out into the grass. Pick up the track on the western side of this ridge at a high kharka which has some roofless **rock shelters** and a water source. There are two ways up, the left, or more westerly way, being more commonly used. It stays above the marshy/icy grass flats, then heads left (north-west), parallel to some bluffs where you may see Himalayan tahr nimbly cavorting over the sheer rockfaces. The track then curves and ascends right to round a big knob of rock (on the right side of it).

After a couple of climbs and short descents, **the lakes** are the next stage with the highest being the most beautiful. The sun arrives around here wonderfully early in the morning which makes up for the night temperatures (usually well below 0°C). Even when the lakes are frozen there's a tiny spring by one of the smaller ones.

The track to the pass goes to the right (north) of the highest lake to start the diagonal traverse of the steep face. The **Kongma La** itself is littered with cairns up each ridge, and 50m to the north up the ridge is a small ledge perfect for a single tent. Bring a block of ice up from the lake as there's no water.

The route down drops only a little while heading right (almost due north) for a long way before beginning a slide down scree. From the ablation valley, crossing the Khumbu Glacier takes another tiring hour before Lobuche appears.

▲ Lobuche to Chukhung

To locate the trail across the glacier from the Lobuche side, head downstream about 200m to a large rock right beside the stream. Perpendicular to the stream at this point there are a couple of tracks on the moraine that head for a small notch. Once across the glacier, climb grassy slopes on a small trail and once in the rock stay on the right-hand side of the valley. There are a few rocky stretches near the top without a trail across.

5886m (19,311ft) PEAK   [Map 11]

This peak is marked as 5880m on the Schneider map; the lakes below are unmarked. Accessed via the short north summit ridge from either the east or west side, it could also be used as a possible glacier pass-hop. There is the odd hole and step in the ice, and a sling plus 10m cord would aid retreat off the scenic lunch spot.

ROUTE GUIDE AND MAPS

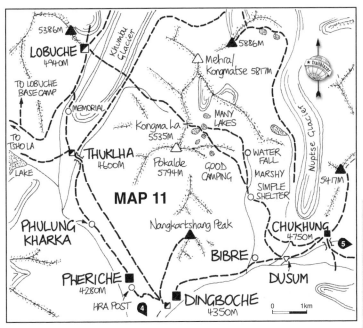

MAP 11

Since there are lakes on either side, camping here is easy. A good nose to follow and adventurous, steady feet are required.

AMPHU LABTSA (5787m/18,986ft) [off Map 5, p197]

Shipton was the first person (foreign or Sherpa) to cross this col, in 1951. The Amphu Labtsa is a tough and dangerous mountaineering proposition, nothing akin to the Tsho La or Thorong La (Annapurna area) and it leads into some particularly isolated country. You need a climbing-experienced guide who has crossed the passes many times, good equipment and a rope. Each year several porters get frost-bite and ill-prepared trekkers have died here.

The pass is well concealed: it's visible only as you near it or from Imjatse/Island Peak Base Camp. It's best attempted early in the morning to lessen the danger of avalanche and rockfall so this means camping below at Amphu, a short half-day's walk

from Chukhung where you start this walk. Unfortunately this grass/stone area gets very little sun, making it one of the coldest parts of the entire valley, and it also lacks water. The nearest easily accessible water is a clear spring just west of where the trail joins the Imjatse/Island Peak Base Camp path. Other possible sources are two small lakes above the faint trail and there's also glacier runoff or ice.

Routes to the top of the pass

There are two routes each with a sub-route or two. From both sides both routes look sheer but on climbing the route unravels. For the **snow/ice route** begin in Amphu and head up the glacier and across the big crevasses to the avalanche-smoothed diagonal gully – the route up. It is possible to stay mainly on rock for the first part even if at first this does not appear to be the case. Then there is a short exposed traverse before the final petit basin to the crest. If you're coming over from the Hongu it's difficult to reach the top of the pass in the correct spot and many lengths of rope testify to the number of parties that decided it was easier to simply abseil down a vertical wall than attempt to find the easiest crossing point. From a distance look for the two low spots. Between them is a small notch that is slightly higher – the pass.

If snow-free, the **higher rock route** (5900m/19,357ft) is an alternative. Pick up the trail on the way up; near the top one steep section often requires a short rope pitch. From the summit there is a tricky rock trail down. Sometimes it is possible to descend partly on the glacier beside, staying near the rock.

To Mera Peak
Along the shore of the larger lake of Panch Pokhari is a small trail that descends to the other lakes. The trail crosses briefly to the east bank of the Hunku/Hongu Khola to skirt the lake marked 5004m on the *Shorong Hinku* map. Otherwise the trail remains on the west bank. See pp274-8 for the Mera La.

KHUMBU TO MAKALU
Crossing between the Everest region and Makalu Base Camp is a route that requires serious planning (see the 1988 National Geographic Mount Everest map) and real mountaineering experience.

The route is via Sherpani Col (6146m/20,164ft) or East Col (6183m/20,285ft) over the large, almost flat, snow field to West Col (6143m/20,154ft) which drops down a glacier (multiple abseils) to the 5200m/17,060ft head of the Hongu Basin. There are several ways out of this. You can go over the Mingbo La (5866m/19,245ft), or over Amphu Labtsa (5780m/18,963ft) with its steep (or vertical, if your route-finding isn't spot-on) descent and couple of big open crevasses at the base. The third option is down the Hongu Valley to Mera La and one more pass to Lukla. These routes should only be attempted by well-

equipped, seasoned mountaineers. The survival rate among the inexperienced does not make nice reading.

THE MINGBO VALLEY [Map 4, p193]
Just above and opposite Pangboche, the Mingbo Valley is an infrequently explored but spectacular valley. Reaching a satisfying distance into it requires an overnight camp and some acclimatization.

Leaving Pangboche descend to the bridge, then follow the trail to the stream just before Mingbo. Here a trail branches off to roughly follow the stream to Ama Dablam Base Camp. The path straight ahead leads to Mingbo with its *goths* which are usually locked. Over the ridge from the Base Camp or ten minutes north of Mingbo is the outline of the old Mingbo airstrip which was used to ferry supplies to the Tibetan refugees leaving Tibet after China invaded. A glance at the approach will reveal why it is disused now, it was another 'Hillary job'. Several small paths continue up the valley and the keen can scramble to around 5700m on the larger of Ama Dablam's southern ridges.

Groups occasionally use the **Mingbo La (5866m/19,245ft)** rather than the more standard Amphu Labtsa after climbing Mera (see p278). The approach from the Hinku Valley up the Hunku/Hongu Nup Glacier is straightforward although crevassed. Conditions on the Mingbo side vary: sometimes the fluted face drops off at perhaps 60° and requires at least two pitches to reach the glacier proper, sometimes it is tamer, and occasionally it is virtually impassable.

▲ From the pass look for the small trail on the ridge descending from Ama Dablam. Once off the glacier you will have to cross some rough terrain and climb up to this.

THE UPPER BHOTE VALLEY
The upper Bhote Valley was officially opened to trekking only in 2002, although in fact nobody ever stopped you going up there previously. Now officially you need a

---

(**Opposite**) **Top**: The view from Gokyo Ri (see p212) of the Gokyo lodges and the first and second lakes. **Bottom**: Kangtaiga (left, 6685m) and Thamserku (6606m) from the second lake.

special permit, although in practice this is never checked. Currently there are no lodges above Arye-Lungde and no year-round occupied villages above Thamo Teng but there is some great wilderness trekking and several valleys deserve exploration.

Whatever you do though, **don't cross the border**, ie the top of the Nangpa La (pass), into China. Over the border you are in China and since you have just broken Chinese law, Tibetans have no problem robbing you because you can't go to the police, and they will hassle you. Secondly, there are border guards patrolling the area, normally situated past the end of the glacier, and to save getting blamed for assisting foreigners, many Tibetans will tell the Chinese patrol if they see anything unusual. If you are caught expect some real trouble. One story concerns two German brothers who were caught. The police simply locked one up and told the other to go back and return with $10,000 as payment for his brother's release.

Although the Chinese border police are now strict, until about 1995 this wasn't the case. Beginning with Shipton in 1952, Cho Oyu was attempted from the Nepal side by crossing the Nangpa La into Tibet. But even at that time Shipton was wary, and this is probably the reason the expedition failed: because of Shipton's concerns, their base camp was still in Nepal, just a little too far from the mountain. Herbert Tichy in 1954 had no such scruples and set a base camp up in Tibet. This pattern was followed by many expeditions who, strangely, usually had permits issued by the Nepal Government.

Suddenly in the mid-90s China realized the border was being crossed illegally and sent armed soldiers to confront a Spanish expedition, and the route was closed. Instead the multitude of expeditions that now head to Cho Oyu travel officially through Tibet to get to the mountain from the north.

Note that most maps don't actually mark the border and feigning ignorance with Chinese officials does not work. Note,

too, that Nepali law also forbids crossing the border, for the moment anyway.

If travelling with a company, ensure that they understand just how rough the last section is and that there are **no facilities for porters** up there; furthermore, it is savagely cold.

Part of the attraction of this trek are the **wild Tibetans**, who mostly are lovable scoundrels. Many of them will try to appropriate things from your pack or tent. Be careful.

Despite the fact that yaks are used to cross **Nangpa La** into Tibet, it is no ordinary trek. It's tough, even for yaks, judging from the number of carcasses along the track; the trek from Gorak Shep to Everest Base Camp is a trifle compared to the slog up to the Nangpa Glacier.

Facilities
Past Arye-Lungde there are no lodges, shops or teahouses. Don't underestimate how much you might eat on this trip, nor the number of days you might take and consider the altitude you will have to camp at. You will need to be self-sufficient for nearly a week and this doesn't allow for side trips.

Planning
Consider carefully where you might camp, especially if you seriously want to get to the top of the pass. In practice this at minimum means camping at Dzasumpa for the fittest and fastest trekkers, better on the uncomfortable, waterless, rubble-covered section of the glacier.

If acclimatized or crazy the best plan is to trek from Lhonak, Kangchung or Dzasumpa and camp on top of the pass, or near there. Be prepared for the cold though, I have slept out on top three times, twice it was -38°C, the last time also in December it was only -25°C but in the early evening I was charged by a rogue yak and danced about in socks and longjohns for half an hour until the Tibetan owners could rescue my yak-tossed gear.

(Opposite)   Cholatse (6440m) forms a stunning backdrop for the Dzonglha lodges (see p218) and the Tsho La trail on the Dzongbha side.

From Thame

This is covered in the Lhenjo La section, p221. Basically there are lodges at Maralung, Lungde and Arye.

Beyond Arye

From the teashops/lodge of Arye there are plenty of watered camping spots near the main trail. Stay on the upper main trail, don't descend down to the valley base level.

Sumna 4840m, where a major side valley joins, is one of the usual stopping points, about 2^{1}/$_{2}$ hours past Arye. Look around for the best camping spot, close water and for early sun.

Lhonak / Lunag 5005m

Leaving Sumna pick up the main trail that climbs up onto the rubble eventually crossing a stream and at a small kata-bedecked cairn descends into the sandy ablation valley on the other side. You have just crossed the Sumna Glacier. Climbing gently the trail leads past several more possible camping spots to the last comfortable one, Lhonak, 1^{1}/$_{4}$-2^{3}/$_{4}$ hours from Sumna.

Here are a couple of bleak stone shelters; camping is more comfortable. This is the last spot with plenty of grass, water, or lots of ice in winter and early morning sun. There are great views of the upper part of Kyajo/Gyajok/Kyazo Ri peak (6189m/ 20,300ft) in the distance, inspiring from this point, and in the middle distance the twin peaks are Machermo, a little over 6000m, all made trekking peaks in 2002.

From here the ground gets rougher; water can be hard to find, especially in winter. The scenery becomes wild. **Kangchung camp** is around the corner set down in a small dusty bowl with a small spring. Tibetans showed us where to get water here with a knife and ladle, even in real winter.

Dzasumpa The ablation valley ends in a huge semi-flat area and water runs off the glaciers to the east; no other water is easily accessible in dry conditions. It is a windy, exposed place to camp but you will have to camp here or on the glacier proper to have a chance of making it to the top of the Nangpa La and back in a **long day**.

The glacier

Pick up the only trail onto the rubble-covered glacier. This winds around finding a route through the lakes and ice pinnacles to the rough centre. If you lose the way retrace back to the last bit of trail. Take great care on any ice.

As you work your way up to the miserable waterless glacier camps (the first at 5271m) the surrounding mountains begin taking on mythical shapes. The rubble gives way to the most difficult section if without crampons, gaining the smooth white glacier (5500m) with contouring hair-line cracks every 10m or so. A bad slip here breaks legs as the carcass of the occasional yak proves and crevasses have, on rare occasions, swallowed a yak or even a person.

Nangpa La 5725m

The pass has a concrete border post (yes, on the ice) and is marked in true Tibetan fashion, and the view of the purple-brown hills is enough to inspire any explorer. In winter the sun leaves around 4pm and doesn't return until mid-morning.

Seracs collapse noisily but are unlikely to hit you on top. During late April in to May and September-early October you can see the colourful patchwork of tents of Cho Oyu expeditions on the other side of a glacier.

LUNGSAMBA LA (5615m)

Crossing between north of Sumna and the six lakes area is an unmarked (on all 2007 maps) route.

This is best crossed west to east as it is easier ascending the steep west slopes, than descending them, and only when there is some snow cover on the western side; the steep rock slopes are nasty unless covered in snow. Everyone in the party needs crampons or if with porters then climbing harnesses, jumars and 200m of rope that should be fixed.

From Sumna There is a thin trail on left side (true right) of the stream that goes up to a second camping area, and further up a third area.

Lungsamba 5080m

The best is still further up past a shallow lake/ice field, a huge magical grassy open area with an old expedition rubbish pit near the corner. The peak 5977m looks tempting from here and the area is worth a rest/acclimatization day. The grassy slopes behind continue up for a long way.

Continuing up the narrowing valley initially on the left side the grass finishes and the possibilities for crossing narrow. Climb on the edge of the glacier (northwest) to the reddish-ochre rock ribs and pick the least steep route up onto the glacier at the top, then swing south-east to the glacier-smoothed rock, marked with a small cairn. Stay high or on top along this rock ridge past the glacier to the north until finally you can see a single lake in a cold hollow a little below. From the south of this you can descend mostly on initially steep grass to the six lakes area, with its distinctive cairn in the middle, a memorial to a sherpa and Koreans who died on a peak visible from here. The best route to the fifth lake stays well away from the Lungsamba glacier moraine edge.

THE KYAJO VALLEY

The Himalaya and Tibet have many legends about mythical valleys accessible only to flying lamas. This is the real thing, **a hidden valley** that is an absolute delight to explore. The ability to fly at least for short sections would be appreciated: the routes into and out of this valley are adventurous even in the best of conditions. In poor visibility it is easy to lose the trail while in snow the thin trail with big exposure could be lethal. Yaks do occasionally graze up here but that says a lot about how agile yaks are rather than the quality of the trail. They are the sort of trails that unless you are standing directly on them you would have difficulty believing there is a trail at all.

If exploring, take three to four days' food; if climbing take supplies for at least five days, seven would be better and you increase your chances of success by camping as high as possible.

From Laudo Gompa (see p181) continue directly up the ridge. This turns into more of a steep valley that passes between some rockfaces. Then head right (at about 4200m) under one rockface on a more distinct trail and follow this up. From around 4300m the small trail begins traversing in and out of ridges to a **minor pass** at 4525m from where the route becomes more obvious, although is still small and little-used and there is little or no water along this stretch. The consolation is it's on the sunny side of the valley.

Finally traverse and descend to the valley floor at 4450m. Here the valley reveals its glacial heritage: impossibly sheer sides with a crystal creek meandering through. Looking back it feels as if you are looking over at the edge of the world.

The rock wall at the valley head looks formidable but a steep gully does lead to the next flat step. Not much lingers here except snow and ice. Ahead is the last step, topped by a glacier.

Exit via Khunde If you thought the trail in was fun you'll be happy to know the surprises don't end. A couple of short sections of this route follow little more than your imagination.

If coming from Khunde you might want to use a rope but heading up you can escape without one – just – if you have steady nerves.

The route drops under bluffs then climbs a short slippery gully at around 4230m, which is sometimes icy. It looks as if a ledge above this might go but it is even more difficult. These sections are the reason this trail is now barely used.

Traverse around then head up on a real trail up to a pass, 4410m, with views of the civilized world below. Pass by the water supply tank and piping.

Exit down valley If you are wondering if there is a trail down the valley; at first it looks like one might go, but later it is obvious that there is no way down without a rope.

Jiri to Lukla / Namche

INTRODUCTION

Jiri to Namche takes most people seven to nine pleasant days' walking, usually including a rest day at Junbesi and a shorter easy day or two. If you have more time and energy there are plenty of opportunities for side trips exploring little-visited villages and gompas. Several alpine valleys are also worth more thorough exploration by well-equipped parties.

For the extremely fit in a hurry, walking from Jiri to Namche in four days is possible – just. There are good lodges along the main route and since these are usually only a few hours apart it's not necessary to plan a detailed itinerary. Simply follow your instincts and the advice of other trekkers rather than sticking to a rigid schedule.

The walk is strenuous, following a route that goes against the grain of the land: all the rivers and ridges flow north to south and the trail runs west to east. You cross an unnamed 2700m/8858ft pass, the Lamjura Pass 3530m/11,581ft and Trakshindo Pass 3071m/10,075ft. Once across the Dudh Kosi (river), the trail climbs high up the valley sides skirting steep rockfaces before descending to recross the river several times before the final hill to Namche.

Following the standard route (not including side trips) by the time you reach Namche you will have climbed up almost exactly the height of Mt Everest, 8848m/29,028ft, and the corresponding descents to Namche total the height of Ama Dablam, 6828m/22,402ft. Since you have trekked the majority of the time between 2000 and 3000m this means you are well acclimatized to around 3000m and unlikely to feel the altitude at Namche. However, higher up you should take it just as cautiously as everyone else.

Jiri has been the end of the road into the hills in this region for more than 15 years. Now, however, the road is being extended, though it is unlikely to be completed particularly quickly. Currently sections are being built as far in as Bhandar but it is only driveable as far as Shivalaya. Some buses finish there, others at Jiri and with a local service going the rest of the short distance.

Information relevant to walking in the reverse direction is also given: this is marked by ▲.

Services

With the whole country in decline, facilities tend to be basic. For **medical facilities** ask local advice. Phaplu has a bush hospital, and there could be doctors at Jiri and perhaps Kharikhola. Between Jiri and Lukla there are no functioning **banks**. Jiri and Phaplu have **phone** services, then Lukla. The hill phones are normally CDMA, rather than the more common GSM systems.

KATHMANDU TO JIRI

From the old bus station in the centre of Kathmandu the first departure for Jiri/Shivalaya is at around 5.30am. Thieves

Homestay trek possibilities
There is plenty of good trekking out of Jiri through pleasant villages to high hills with superb views, and into the mountains and lakes to the north. The region is also culturally varied with six ethnic groups living close by, so locals want to develop these two concepts as 'homestay treks', with the help of some aid agencies. The internet will probably be the best place to find out more.

Asking directions

There's a certain art to asking the way on Nepal's trails. Naturally polite, the Nepalis don't like to cause offence by answering 'no' to a question such as 'Is this the way to Namche?' So an affirmative reply is just as likely to mean, 'Yes, I understand the question but I don't know the answer,' as 'Yes, it's the way to Namche'. You can try re-phrasing the question as: 'Which path is for Namche?' but rather than admitting they don't know, a Nepali may just take a guess at the answer. The solution is to ask again in a different way and ask more than one person. If you ask the way at a junction and then walk away down the wrong trail locals will usually shout after you that you're going the wrong way.

sometimes work the bus station and this route so **take great care of your luggage**. There are also occasional pickpockets at the bus station. Their favourite trick is to watch where you put your change after buying your ticket then hurry you onto the bus while their hand delves into your pocket. The police have been unhelpful in all cases.

The first part of this 10- to 12- (and occasionally up to 16-) hour bus journey is to Lamosangu (78km, 5 hours) along the Chinese-constructed Arniko Rajmarg or Kodari Highway that runs to the Tibetan border and Lhasa. Leaving Kathmandu you pass through the lower part of **Bhaktapur**, then Banepa where, until the early 1960s, the expeditions to Everest began.

There is a steep climb out of the Kathmandu Valley and from **Dhulikhel**, at the crest of the hill, there are views on a clear day of the Himalaya from Manaslu to Everest. The road drops to **Dolalghat** (*ghat* means 'bridge') and crosses the Indrawati River. The Chinese road had progressed this far by 1967 so the first commercial treks to the Khumbu started from here.

After crossing the Sun Kosi ('Gold River') the road follows the river to **Lamosangu** ('Long Bridge'), the buses usually stopping by the scruffy stalls by the bridge for dal bhaat.

From the bridge it's a further 110km to Jiri, marked by kilometre posts that start at 0km from Lamosangu bridge. This road was part of a Swiss aid programme, constructed as a model to demonstrate building techniques for mountain roads using appropriate technology. Rather than employing

expensive machinery it was decided to maximize the use of local labour. Rocks were broken with hammers and a lot of sweat, and all the wire netting was woven by hand, providing a vast amount of work. In addition to wages, food was sold in set quantities at subsidized prices to reduce the local impact of the hungry workforce.

The only heavy machinery used was a road roller. The result is a Swiss-quality road that has lasted longer with less maintenance than any other road in Nepal. Unfortunately, the technique and attention to detail hasn't been duplicated for the rest of Nepal's rural hill roads.

From Lamosangu it can be pleasant to ride on the roof of the bus (theoretically illegal) but take a jacket or wind-cheater. At the top of the first major ridge is **Muldi** where there may be another stop before continuing to **Charikot** (at the km54 marker). The turn-off to the left here leads to **Dolakha** (see p269), a few kilometres away. On a cloudless day the monumental twin-headed Gauri Sankar stands out for the next half-hour. The high peak slightly to the right is Menglutse in Tibet.

The descent to the Tamba Kosi ('Copper River') is steep. At the bridge the driver takes a break for a cup of tea or two. If you are on the roof it's a good idea to start putting on warm clothes because it is still several hours and 38km to Jiri. The plantations you pass are a Swiss reforestation programme.

After another pass the gradual descent to Jiri begins and at a stop at **Kot** you might have to register at the police checkpoint. **Jiri**

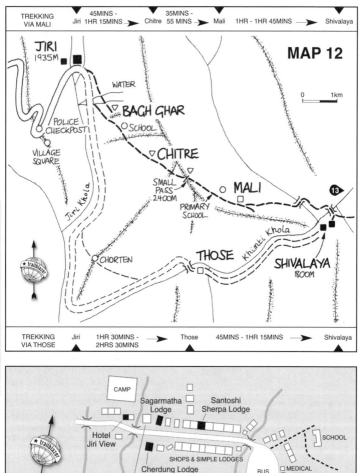

ROUTE GUIDE AND MAPS

Jiri — 45MINS - 1HR 15MINS → Chitre — 35MINS - 55 MINS → Mali — 1HR - 1HR 45MINS → Shivalaya

JIRI
1935M

WATER

BACH GHAR

SCHOOL

POLICE CHECKPOST

CHITRE

VILLAGE SQUARE

MAP 12

0   1km

SMALL PASS
2400M

MALI

13

Jiri Khola

PRIMARY SCHOOL

CHORTEN

THOSE

Khimti Khola

SHIVALAYA
1800M

TREKKING VIA THOSE   Jiri   1HR 30MINS - 2HRS 30MINS →   Those   45MINS - 1HR 15MINS →   Shivalaya

CAMP

Sagarmatha Lodge

Santoshi Sherpa Lodge

SCHOOL

Hotel Jiri View

SHOPS & SIMPLE LODGES

Cherdung Lodge

NEPAL BANK
(NO FOREIGN EXCHANGE)

BUS PARK

MEDICAL HALL

To Livestock Education Farm

To Hospital

Jeep trail to Those and trail to Shivalaya

Jiri (see Map 12)

is ten minutes further on, and Shivalaya a rough hour or so.

Note that in winter it's not unknown for a snowfall or sheet ice to block a high section of the road, which means a couple of extra days' walking.

JIRI TO SHIVALAYA [Map 12]
Jiri (see map opposite; 1935m/6348ft)
Nestling in a fertile valley and beyond the ugly materialism of the road, Jiri is a prosperous and tidy village. The people are mainly of the Jirel caste who originate, so the legend goes, from a Sherpa mother and a Sunuwar father. There are also some Sherpas and with the road (which linked Jiri in 1984) came the merchant castes, mainly Newars.

There are many *lodges* now mainly used by locals.

If you do end up trekking ask Jiri locals where the trail starts. It climbs to Chitre then further over a small pass before dropping to Mali then more steeply to a fine suspension bridge to Shivalaya.

Shivalaya
The good tar-sealed road ends and it is a rough and dusty ride to Shivalaya. This once sleepy village is now booming: there

are a handful of *lodges*, all simple, and in most cases it will be safest to order dal bhaat (see box below) or noodles. The small **shops** here are packed with cheap goods and supplies.

SHIVALAYA TO BHANDAR
[Map 13, p233]
The road is being pushed beyond Shivalaya and even at the time of writing sections of it went as far as Bhandar, though when it becomes navigable by vehicle is anybody's guess. The following assumes you are walking.

The trail out of Shivalaya is steep from the first step and will get the sweat flowing. The gradient relents only after the next village. The walking route is much more direct than following the road.

Sangbadanda
This is a mainly Sherpa settlement and has a couple of simple *lodges* with **shops**.

Deorali (2705m/8875ft)
Meaning pass in Nepali, Deorali is a common village name. The actual village is slightly south where the water supply is better so this is just a group of *lodges*. They are set in two neat rows divided by a set of

ROUTE GUIDE AND MAPS

The good dal bhaat guide
In those early trekking days of the 1980s and '90s there was very little choice for a meal: roll up at a lodge at 11-ish and there would be dal bhaat and little else. Now you'll rarely see dal bhaat, at least in high season on the busy routes, with the lodges dishing out apple pie and pizzas instead.

Out of season, however – or if you're with a bunch of friends and happen to catch the owner at the right time – providing you can wait 40 minutes you might be in for a surprise. In the low country in January, for example, we got a delicious spicy tomato chutney and an excellent potato soup instead of dal, with some fresh *mullah* (radish) on the side. Our smiling *sahuni* (female business owner) then produced a tiny steel plate on which was lovingly arranged a green, orange, and red chilli, the idea being that you take a bite of the chilli then shovel the food in afterwards, local style. The next day we got sticky rice, black dal, and some pickled mullah from some jars in the kitchen that would not have looked out of place in Frankenstein's lab (you may have to ask for this as they rarely give such delicacies to guests). For extra protein ask for *sukuti* – slightly dried buffalo meat usually found hanging over the kitchen fire, which is then fried up with chillies and sometimes garlic and ginger – or even pork, which is usually reminiscent of British pork scratchings. **Joel Schone**

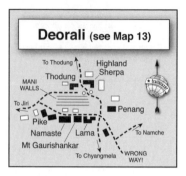

Deorali (see Map 13)

To Thodung
Highland Sherpa
Thodung
MANI WALLS
Penang
To Jiri
Pike
Namaste   Lama   To Namche
Mt Gaurishankar
To Chyangmela   WRONG WAY!

mani walls (see map above), the first real sign of Buddhist Sherpa country. You should pass to the left of a mani wall or a wall of prayer wheels.

From some rocks immediately above the lodges there are superb views into the distance on a clear day; you can see much of the route ahead, and the scars of the new road. Below, the hillside stretches down to where the twin chortens of Bhandar are clearly visible. Take the left fork a couple of minutes below the pass; the descent is initially steep.

Bhandar (2200m/7218ft)
The Sherpa name for this area is Chyangma. Immediately above the chortens is a small gompa and below, a group of *lodges*.

BHANDAR TO JUNBESI   [Map 13; Map 14 p234; Map 15 p235]
From the chortens the descent is gentle with simple *lodges* or *teahouses* evenly spaced a few minutes apart down the hill.

Kenja / Kinja (1640m/5380ft)
When the Jiri trek was popular this was a thriving village, but now it seems to be entering old age, gradually but gracefully in decline. However, the *lodges* are still pleasant and the owners friendly.

In October you might see something that looks like a prickly pear dangling from leafy creepers. The local name is *iskus* and it must be cooked to be edible and tastes like a slightly sweet potato.

The **side trail to Pike Peak** (pronounced 'pee-kay'), the home of the benevolent spirit for this area, starts from the bridge over the Kenja Khola. The trail goes up the ridge to the south, then skirts the peak to a ridge heading north. It finally drops to the main trail after the Lamjura Pass. Since there are no facilities along the way, it is a camping route only. The panorama from the top is stunning.

Sete (2575m/8448ft) There are a couple of ageing *lodges*. When you've got your breath back, it's around an hour to Dagchu.

Dagchu A settlement consisting of a handful of simple *lodges* atop the ridge. Out of the forested areas there are some

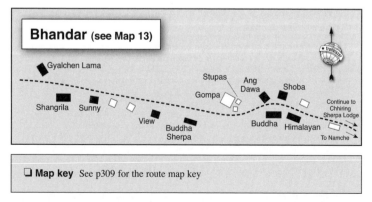

Bhandar (see Map 13)

Gyalchen Lama

Shangrila   Sunny
View
Buddha Sherpa

Stupas
Gompa   Ang Dawa   Shoba
Continue to Chhiring Sherpa Lodge
Buddha   Himalayan
To Namche

❏ **Map key** See p309 for the route map key

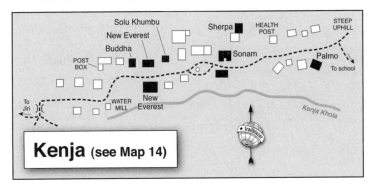

Kenja (see Map 14)

good views. To the south-east (right) you can see the twin tops of Pike Peak. The trail to the pass continues up the ridge; ignore all trails that lead off it. From some parts you can see the pass, well to the left of the ridge. Looking back you can see Deorali clearly with Bhandar below along with the scruffy road from Jiri.

ROUTE GUIDE AND MAPS

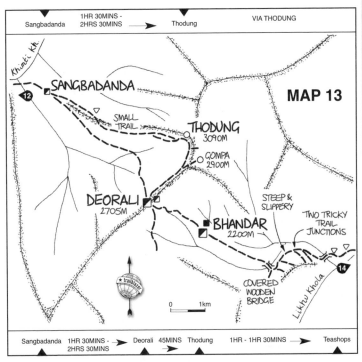

Sangbadanda — 1HR 30MINS - 2HRS 30MINS → Thodung   VIA THODUNG

MAP 13

SANGBADANDA

SMALL TRAIL

THODUNG 3090M

GOMPA 2900M

DEORALI 2705M

STEEP & SLIPPERY

BHANDAR 2200M

TWO TRICKY TRAIL JUNCTIONS

COVERED WOODEN BRIDGE

Likhu Khola

0   1km

Sangbadanda 1HR 30MINS - 2HRS 30MINS → Deorali 45MINS → Thodung 1HR - 1HR 30MINS → Teashops

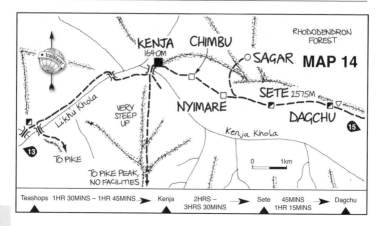

Goyem Another half an hour up brings you to Goyem with two groups of *teahouses/lodges* about five minutes apart.

A minute out of Goyem is an important junction: continue up on the ridge through forest on a somewhat scrappy trail avoiding the good trail that begins contouring on the south side of the ridge. That is the direct, steep route to Salleri. The forest here is magnificent. Demand for firewood, however, grows with each new lodge built – a negative impact of the teahouses.

In spring the rhododendrons put on quite a show with whole hillsides covered in blossoms that from late February spread upwards, reaching the crest of the pass by the end of April. The air is heady with their scent and with that of the many other flowering trees and shrubs.

Lamjura (3330m/10,925ft)

Soon the trail becomes clearer and you reach three basic *lodges* scattered along the ridge that call themselves 'Lamjura'. This is the point where the trail starts contouring to the north of the ridge. There are several junctions but each trail rejoins the main route a few minutes later.

Further along in what was once pristine rhododendron forest are three more *lodges*. Both settlements are above 3300m so are quite high places to sleep. It would

help if you had slept at Deorali, but don't be unduly worried if you didn't. Although you are high and may have an uncomfortable night's sleep, you are descending the next day so there is little chance of worsening altitude sickness.

Passing a few mani walls, it's around a slightly breathless half an hour to the top of the pass. Unless the weather is perfect this section can be very cold and windy, and in October even snow can fall with the patches shielded by the sun not melting for several days.

In winter there may be quite a bit of snow lying around making the track muddy and even icy – real down-jacket weather. The difference to the temperature that altitude makes is really driven home to you as you head up this pass.

Lamjura La (3530m/11,581ft)

The prayer flags and chortens mark the gateway to the Solu (sometimes called Shorong) Sherpa area. It's common to suffer some altitude sickness, especially if you stay up here for a while to admire the view. This does not mean you will not make it to the top of Kala Pattar, it's just a warning that ascending too fast has its consequences. You are in fact higher than Namche, where several nights are spent acclimatizing.

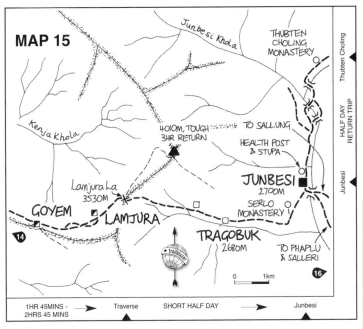

MAP 15

Junbesi Khola

THUBTEN
CHOLING
MONASTERY

Thubten Choling

Kenja Khola

4010M, TOUGH
3HR RETURN

TO SALLUNG

HEALTH POST
& STUPA

JUNBESI
2700M

HALF DAY
RETURN TRIP

Junbesi

Lamjura La
3530M

GOYEM

LAMJURA

SERLO
MONASTERY

14

TRAGOBUK
2680M

TO PHAPLU
& SALLERI

16

0   1km

1HR 45MINS -   Traverse   SHORT HALF DAY   Junbesi
2HRS 45 MINS

Heading down from the pass there are many paths weaving through the forest but luckily they all head to the same place: a few well-spaced *restaurants* an hour below the pass. Occasionally you may see monkeys in the forest here.

Tragobuk / Taktok (2680m/9383ft) is proud to have a new **gompa** which you are welcome to look around. As with all gompas, it is customary to leave a donation when visiting: Rs100 is appropriate.

Continue straight through the long village and at junctions avoid trails that descend; these go to Salleri and not Junbesi. The scenic trail stays fairly high and rounds a major ridge and a large rock, with views of Junbesi and its distinctive yellow-roofed gompa. While here, take a look at the trail options immediately across the river from Junbesi.

JUNBESI (see map p236; 2700m/ 8858ft)

This is one of the most pleasant Sherpa villages en route to Namche and has some good *lodges*. The **gompa** at the top end of town is old, perhaps founded in 1639. Ask your lodge owner if you want to see it.

Side trips from Junbesi

Thubten Choling is an active Buddhist monastery/nunnery with about 50 monks and over 200 nuns. Many are Tibetan; some are very recent arrivals. The murals were painted around 1970, a few years after the monastery was founded. The walk up is pleasant and, although it is little more than an hour away from Junbesi, with the friendly monks and beauty of the area do not count on being back for an early lunch.

Around Junbesi are a scattering of **gompas** perched atop hills, good alternatives to visiting Thubten Choling.

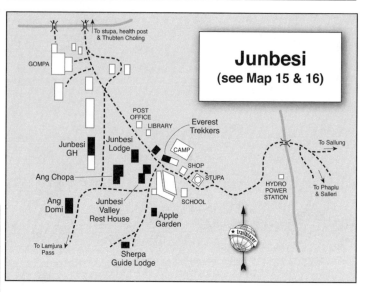

Junbesi
(see Map 15 & 16)

To stupa, health post & Thubten Choling

GOMPA

POST OFFICE
LIBRARY
Everest Trekkers

To Sallung

Junbesi GH
Junbesi Lodge
CAMP
SHOP
STUPA
HYDRO POWER STATION
To Phaplu & Salleri

Ang Chopa

Ang Domi
Junbesi Valley Rest House
SCHOOL
Apple Garden

To Lamjura Pass

Sherpa Guide Lodge

★ trailblazer

Rumbak, to the south above the track to Salleri, takes one and a half hours one way. Take something to eat and drink with you.

JUNBESI TO BUPSA
[Map 16; Map 17, p241]
Leaving Junbesi After crossing the Junbesi Khola the main track divides twice. In each case take the upper/left path which might be signposted. The lower paths head to Phaplu and Salleri, a good half-day's walk away. The section around this huge ridge is one of the most pleasant walks so far. Although the trail climbs in places, it's not steep. The track is set high above the valley floor, at first through open forest. Later the view extends across the valley to picturesque villages surrounded by terraces and divided by sparse woodland.

Phurtyang / Sallung (3000m/9840ft)
Early morning is generally the best time to spot Everest. If there's a single cloud in the sky a corollary of Murphy's Law says it will obscure Everest first and it usually

does. For the energetic even better views can be had by climbing part of the ridge behind.

Leaving Phurtyang The clear trail wanders gently downwards. After a few gullies you round another ridge for a change of view: the amazing knife-edge ridge of Karyolung whose ridge extends down to Ringmo and the Trakshindo La, the next pass.

The trail winds around ridges and streams to a bridge across the Beni/Dudh Kund Khola, whose waters originate from the glaciers in the impressive basin formed by Karyolung (6511m/21,361ft), Khatang (6853m/22,483ft) and Numbur (6959m/22,831ft). The twin peaks of Numbur and Khatang are the Shorong Yul Lha, where the Sherpa god for the Shorong area resides. It's possible to camp at the high grazing areas below their glaciers and stunning mountain faces although this is hardly ever attempted by trekkers.

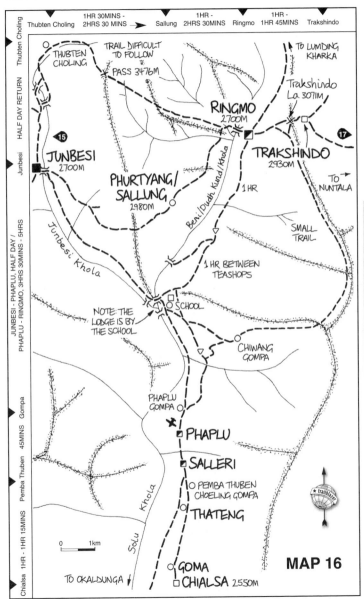

THUBTEN CHOLING

TRAIL DIFFICULT TO FOLLOW

PASS 3476M

TO LUMDING KHARKA

Trakshindo La 3071M

RINGMO 2700M

15

JUNBESI 2700M

TRAKSHINDO 2930M

PHURTYANG/ SALLUNG 2980M

TO NUNTALA

17

Ben: Dudh Kund Khola

1 HR

SMALL TRAIL

Junbesi Khola

1 HR BETWEEN TEASHOPS

NOTE: THE LODGE IS BY THE SCHOOL

SCHOOL

CHIWANG GOMPA

PHAPLU GOMPA

PHAPLU

SALLERI

PEMBA THUBEN CHOELING GOMPA

Solu Khola

THATENG

0   1km

trailblazer

GOMA

MAP 16

TO OKALDUNGA

CHIALSA 2550M

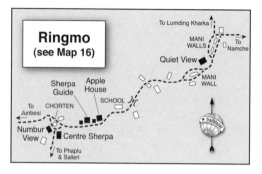

Ringmo
(see Map 16)

To Lumding Kharka

MANI
WALLS

To
Namche

Quiet View

Sherpa
Guide

Apple
House

MANI
WALL

CHORTEN

SCHOOL

To
Junbesi

Numbur
View

Centre Sherpa

To Phaplu
& Salleri

At the top of Ringmo
are two 50-metre mani
walls. After correctly
passing to the left of both
do **not** continue straight
on unless you're going to
Lumding Kharka (see box
below). The correct route
(often signposted) is to
the right. This is the
beginning of the ascent to
the Trakshindo La.

Trakshindo   La
(3071m/10,075ft) The
pass, marked by a white
stupa, divides the Solu

Ringmo (2700m/8858ft) From the
bridge the trail climbs, steeply at first, to
Ringmo and a major trail junction by the
stupa. The south/right-hand trail heads to
Phaplu and Salleri (see p243-4) on a beautiful, wide path. Straight on is the route to
the pass, the Trakshindo La.

Ringmo is a spread-out settlement set
among **apple orchards** and famous for all
things apple. Try their apple pie, apple
cake, apple juice, apple cider, and (or) their
pink apple brandy. Apples, peaches and
apricots are cultivated to such an extent that
half the crop has to be made into delicious
cider and fire-water brandies. This is also
the main source of fruit for the famous
Namche apple pies.

(Shorong) and the Pharak Sherpa areas.
There is a basic *lodge* and a handful of
teashacks where porters stop for a welcome
glass of tea. It's less than half an hour down
to the gompa at Trakshindo, on wide stone
steps, or what's left of them.

Trakshindo (2930m/9612ft)
There are two large but simple *lodges*. If
you arrive in cloudy weather and stay here
be sure to have a look outside upon waking:
the views are stunning. Trekking-peak fans
will enjoy the impressive pyramid of
Kusum Kangguru. In the coldest winter
months you may wake up to snow here and
ice on the trail.

Side route to Lumding Kharka

The path that continues straight ahead from the Ringmo mani wall leads to
high grazing pastures below Numbur and several isolated high routes into the
Dudh Kosi. There are **no lodges** or even villages until the Dudh Kosi, a two- to four-
day walk away (depending on which route you take).

The Lumding La route offers some good and unusual views of Everest, Lhotse
and Makalu. Interestingly, it was used extensively by Tibetans who, because many
yaks had died at Kharikhola in 1959 from the low altitude, it was thought, preferred
this high route (until the early 1970s). It was also the alternative route if the bridge
across the Dudh Kosi below Jubing had been washed out: this was why the 1952
Swiss Everest Expedition was forced to use it. Two porters died of the cold which led
to the Swiss providing the suspension bridge that now spans the Dudh Kosi. More
than that, they set up, and for many years funded, the government's Suspension
Bridge Division, the organization responsible for building many of the bridges across
the country.

Kayaking the Dudh Kosi

In 1976 a group of British kayakers lead by Dr Mike Jones paddled part of the river above and below Namche. Lou Dickinson filmed it producing *Canoeing Down Everest*. The kayakers' summary was 'A steep rock-infested ditch with only fame to recommend it'. In 2000 it was kayaked again and found to be much easier, mainly on account of the development of kayaks. The plastic boats are much more manoeuvrable and tougher than the fibreglass boats used in 1976.

The **gompa**, established in 1946 by the Tengboche Lama, can be visited and is usually open sometime early in the morning or around sunset.

Nuntala is visible from the gompa and when leaving the path contours around immediately below the gompa fence and past a house or two before descending. The route down continues to contour in and out of gullies with a steep descent or two on the way. You pass some camping spots popular with porters heading for Namche.

Babu Chiri (see p133), from here, was becoming a well-known mountaineer when, in 2001, he fell into a crevasse on Everest and died. A school has been built in memory of him.

Nuntala / Manidingma (2350m/7710ft) Primarily a Sherpa village with a few Rai inhabitants, Nuntala is pleasantly situated in a large valley. The bushes around and below the village are tea bushes. The views are better at the pass or

gompa but the snowy tip of Karyolung can still just be seen, above a ridge to the north.

The wide, paved street is lined with inns and a few *lodges* for travellers, and is the more usual overnight trekkers stop.

Jubing (1700m/5577ft) Half an hour uphill from the bridge, this is the only non-Sherpa village past Sete. It's a pretty Rai village, especially attractive in winter when the Khumbu appears brown and dry. Here plants thrive in the tropical warmth of the low altitude with flowers and vegetables growing year-round. It is a rice-growing area, although the higher reaches of the village can support only millet and maize, the monsoon crops, and wheat plus barley in the winter. There are a couple of *lodges*. Being warm year-round it's a good place to do a batch of washing – or at least a sock rinse.

Around ten minutes out of Jubing is a small but distinct trail junction. Continue upwards: **don't** take the path that cuts left through paddies and can be seen contouring around the next ridge.

Another ten minutes up the hill is **Churkha**, a group of three double-storied houses and another trail divide. Both forks end up at Kharikhola: the left path is slight-

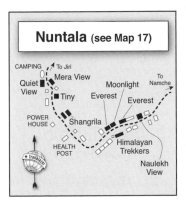

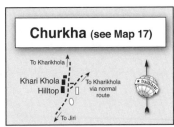

ly longer in distance but not in time and is a little more gentle on the legs. The right fork is the 'Nepalese way' (the shortest distance no matter how steep) and is always used by porters. It heads over a small pass which offers good views up the valley. Khumbui Yul Lha (see box p181) is prominent, and with a map it is easy to figure out roughly where Namche, Khumjung and Khunde are, though they cannot actually be seen.

The high snow and rock peak in the distance is Gyachung Kang (7922m/25,990ft), not Cho Oyu as guides will tell you.

Kharikhola / Khati Thenga (2050m/6726ft) If you spend the night here make an early start the next day, leaving well before the sun actually reaches Kharikhola, or the going gets hot and sticky. The chorten at Bupsa can be seen from Kharikhola but once over the small bridge there are several false crests that can be rather demoralizing on the slog up to Bupsa.

Bupsa / Gompa Danda / Bumshing (2350m/7710ft) Perched on top of the ridge, this is a welcome refreshment stop after the long climb. There are three *teahouses* in a cluster and, a few minutes further on, a couple more well-spaced *lodges*. Below, along the ridge, is a small **gompa**.

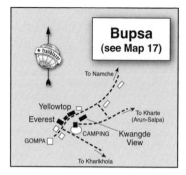

You may be invited to visit – donation expected, of course.

BUPSA TO SURKE [Map 17]
Route to Salpa-Arun and Tumlingtar
Take the trail straight up the ridge behind the lodges in Bupsa.

Khari The hills are not over yet: the trail continues steeply up, cutting into valleys, and there is a cluster of basic *lodges* where it is possible to stay.

After rounding more ridges you come to the **Khari La**, marked by a mani wall, a small *teahouse* and a lodge around 40 minutes before Puiyan. This isn't as much of a pass as it once was, for the original trail used to be much higher. From here, at

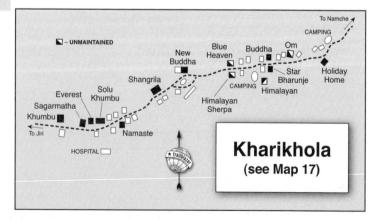

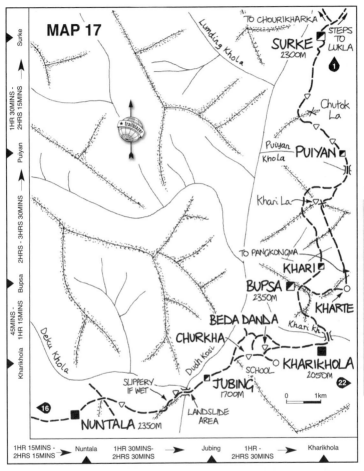

MAP 17

TO CHOURIKHARKA

Lumding Khola

SURKE 2300M

STEPS TO LUKLA

❶

Surke

1HR 30MINS - 2HRS 15MINS

Chutok La

Puiyan

1HR 30MINS - 2HRS 15MINS

Puiyan Khola

PUIYAN

Khari La

2HRS - 3HRS 30MINS

TO PANGKONGMA

KHARI

Bupsa

BUPSA 2350M

KHARTE

45MINS - 1HR 15MINS

Khari Kh.

Kharikhola

Deku Khola

BEDA DANDA

CHURKHA

Dudh Kosi

SCHOOL

KHARIKHOLA 2050M

㉒

SLIPPERY IF WET

JUBING 1700M

0   1km

❶⓺

LANDSLIDE AREA

NUNTALA 2350M

ROUTE GUIDE AND MAPS

| 1HR 15MINS - 2HRS 15MINS ▲ Nuntala | 1HR 30MINS - 2HRS 30MINS → Jubing | 1HR - 2HRS 30MINS → Kharikhola |

The perfect flower

Home dull? Plant marigolds! Besides brightening up even the drabbest of mud houses, marigolds act as a natural pesticide to nearby kitchen (vegetable) gardens. Every Dasain, along with freshly whitewashed homes, a new string of marigolds adorns all entrances. It is also the preferred flower for *mallas* ('disposable' celebratory necklaces). Take a close look next time you pass a marigold: you'll notice two different types of flowers – one is male and one is female – and they don't smell too bad either. No wonder Nepalis consider the marigold to be the perfect flower.

Suzanne Behrenfeld

2850m/9350ft, Khumbui Yul Lha and Gyachung Kang are visible. Looking down the valley you can really appreciate the scale of the middle hills. Continuing, the trail contour-climbs to a huge rock from where you can see Puiyan. There are a handful of *teashacks* on this corner.

Puiyan / Paiya / Chutok (2780m/ 9121ft) The surrounding area was once heavily forested but many trees were cut down to make charcoal. There are several *lodges* and, ten minutes later, two more just before the climb to the pass.

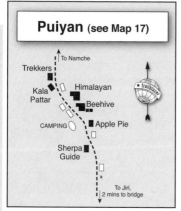

Puiyan (see Map 17)

To Namche
Trekkers
Kala Pattar
Himalayan
Beehive
CAMPING
Apple Pie
Sherpa Guide
To Jiri,
2 mins to bridge

trailblazer

Chutok La (Paiya La) The route passes 200m below the Chutok La, at 2780m/ 9121ft, but the views of Khumbui Yul Lha and Gyachung Kang are still good, though better just around the corner. The steep rock peak is Gonglha, above Lukla, and the bigger mountain is Kusum Kangguru. Part of Lukla airstrip can also be seen but this is difficult to recognize: it's no use looking for a stretch of level ground.

On a corner further down at a place called **Pakhepani** are a couple of aptly named lodges.

Surke / Surkie / Bua (2300m/7546ft) Local legend says that this area was once a lake: this would account for the fertile soil.

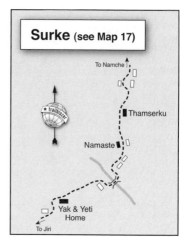

Surke (see Map 17)

To Namche
Thamserku
Namaste
Yak & Yeti Home
To Jiri

trailblazer

Bua, the Sherpa name for the hamlet, means 'damp', no doubt from the lack of sun, but in fact it's a pleasant-enough place. Just around the corner from Surke are the first good views of Nupla (5885m/19,308ft) which forms part of the spectacular Kongde ridge that rears up above the Bhote Kosi by Namche.

Route to Lukla About ten minutes out of Surke by a mani are some stone steps heading up; these lead to Lukla (see pp160-2) in about an hour. Although the trail starts off well-defined it breaks up into many confusing paths. You need to cross a bridge en route. If in doubt stay on main trails; going left at intersections usually works except around a carved mani rock. There are tracks up both sides of the runway.

Direct route to Namche This continues straight ahead from the mani wall out of Surke. A little further on is an impressive waterfall, so high and close that it defies most camera lenses, although over the bridge and up the hill there's a more complete view. The trail traverses some impressively steep hillside. In the past, in tough country like this, the trails tended to be precarious and narrow but to cater for tourists this has been blasted out to a safe width. Stone steps and a few cunningly constructed stone shelters herald Mushe, still a few minutes away.

Mushe / Nangbug   This is a pleasant place with a few *lodges*; since it is overshadowed by Lukla few people stay here. Many vegetables are grown in the area especially for the hotels in Lukla and Namche.

Chourikharka / Dungde (2760m/ 9055ft)
Meaning 'yak-herding area', Chourikharka is often mis-spelt Chaunikharka, although if you listen hard to a local person saying the name, the quietest of 'n's can often be heard. Dungde, the Sherpa name, means *dingma* or 'flat farming area': a more accurate name now. The village begins at the top of the short steep climb to the kani and has three well-spaced *lodges*.

Route from Chourikharka to Lukla
Thankfully Lukla is not visible from here but there are numerous small trails up. First head for the school, then from there a path leads up to join the main trail. The Hillary school was constructed in 1964 and has expanded to provide education to the final grade: grade ten. There is also a **health post** founded by the Himalayan Trust. Alternatively walk to Cheplung and take the main trail.

Direct route to Namche   If you're bypassing Lukla, the route description continues on p164.

Starting from Phaplu

INTRODUCTION
Beginning a trek from Phaplu is a great way to experience the middle-hills Sherpa culture. The main difference compared to starting at Jiri is that flying in saves the arduous road journey and shortens the walking by a couple of days. From Phaplu it is less than a day's walk to the main Jiri to Lukla trail, which you join at either Junbesi or Ringmo, so you have also skipped the Lamjura Pass, the highest on the Jiri trek. Note that flights here are not nearly as frequent or reliable as to Lukla.

While you can arrive in the morning and meet the Jiri trail in the afternoon, plenty of side trips, exploring around Phaplu and Salleri, are possible.

Information relevant to walking in the reverse direction is also given: this is marked by ▲.

PHAPLU
The short runway describes a gentle 'U' shape, a real 'Hillary job'. It was constructed to help build the Himalayan Trust hospital here. The hospital, now government-run, sits a few minutes' walk below the runway.

Phaplu is the airport that services Salleri, the district headquarters of the Solu-Khumbu district. It has a collection of dal bhaat hotels, houses and offices that could more properly be described as mansions and some shops that even stock chocolate. NAC and the helicopter companies have offices here. It has a strange atmosphere with the large buildings and a rubbish dump in the middle of it all. There are a string of *bhattis*, simple hotels where you can stay. The one real lodge is *Hotel del Sherpa*, which is more used to seeing aid workers than trekkers. It is set slightly off the main trail through a *kani* and ornate dragons guard the main door.

SALLERI
Salleri is the hustling, bustling district headquarters of the Solu-Khumbu Jila (or district). It has a strange atmosphere, lackadaisical almost to the point of being

unfriendly. They aren't used to trekkers but there are several Nepali-style *lodges* and *restaurants*. The path running through town has been widened with the expectation that the Okaldunga road will be extended to here. It is many years off though.

PHAPLU TO CHIWANG GOMPA
[Map 16, p237]

The main trail passes beside the airport. At Phaplu Gompa the lower trail leads to Junbesi while the higher leads to **Chiwang Gompa**.

On the path up it is common to see langur monkeys, squirrels and deer. The gompa is particularly old, being originally built at the time of Lama Sangwa Dorje, and is of an interesting design. Although there is no real lodge monks will generally invite you in to stay with them and expect a donation for the service. There is also a good camping place a little below the gompa.

PHAPLU TO RINGMO OR JUNBESI
[Map 16, p237]

From Phaplu you can either walk direct to Ringmo or make a worthwhile detour to Junbesi.

For **Ringmo**, take the wide trail beginning just above the end of the airstrip. There are a couple of basic places en route that could provide lunch, some snacks and even a simple bed. For **Junbesi**, head north and down to the valley floor. Follow the valley to cross the suspension bridge. This leads to the trail on the northern bank of the Junbesi Khola.

▲ Ringmo to Phaplu

The junction for the path to Phaplu is obvious at Ringmo but don't believe local assurances that Phaplu is only a couple of hours away. It'll take more than three hours and probably almost five.

The trail is well constructed and passes through some pleasant forest. An hour or so out of Ringmo another path branches off the main trail. This descends to the river

---

> ### ❏ Salleri to Bung
> Although little used by trekkers, the direct trail between Bung and Salleri is a main local route. Between the two is the Dudh Kosi, which must be descended to, and a high ridge close to Salleri, which must be crossed. It is normally a two-day walk.

---

and the bridges below to join the track from Junbesi to Phaplu. However, it's better to continue along the main trail, the branch that contours leading to Phaplu without any serious climbs. After many more bends the airstrip at Phaplu comes into view.

PHAPLU TO CHIALSA
[Map 16, p237]

Chialsa is commonly called a Tibetan refugee camp, implying a temporary nature. Now it is perhaps better called a sanctuary. Although the people are Tibetan they have adapted and more or less integrated with the surrounding region. For the trekker with energy or time and a desire to learn a little more about Tibet it is well worth a visit.

The route Slightly above the main trail leading through Salleri (see p243) is a parallel trail that goes to Chialsa, among other places. Perhaps the easiest place to pick up the Chialsa track is to trek south to the **Pemba Thuben Choeling Gompa** (in part funded by the Himalayan Trust and was completed in 1998) and climb immediately above that. The trail passes above a higher education college then passes through Thateng. About 40 minutes from the gompa climb to and pass another gompa. A further 20 minutes along, where the power lines end, is a stupa with prayer wheels – the entrance to Chialsa.

Chialsa The people are friendly here, although not much English is spoken. The *hotel* is simple and only has one room. The food is whatever you can think of that they

Tibetans in Nepal

Beginning in 1949 the Chinese built a road to Lhasa so as to 'peacefully liberate' Tibet. (They have also built friendship highways into Nepal and Pakistan, while with India they were more brazen, building a road through India's Aksai Chin that led to a border war in 1962.) This Peaceful Liberation, the Great Leap Forward and the Cultural Revolution resulted in the deaths of around one million Tibetans, perhaps a quarter of the population. In 1959 they plotted to kidnap the Dalai Lama, Tibet's leader. He escaped but the consequent fighting, in which the Chinese displayed merciless brutality, set off an exodus of Tibetans. It was estimated by the International Red Cross (IRC) that between 7000 and 10,000 fled over the Nangpa La alone. The IRC set up ten transit camps throughout Nepal but many Tibetans still died of hunger and disease.

In 1961, using thinly veiled threats, the Chinese forced the Nepalese to kick out the IRC, so the Swiss Red Cross stepped in (the IRC is based in Geneva), buying 40 acres of land in the name of the Nepal Red Cross. Tibetans, who were scattered throughout Solu-Khumbu, trekked there to establish new, hopefully temporary, lives. During the 1960s and 1970s over 1000 Tibetans lived there. SATA, a Swiss project, helped with agricultural and handicraft programmes: carpet-weaving, established in 1961, boomed and by the late 1970s some workers migrated to Kathmandu and set up business there. With intense competition from imitators in the Kathmandu Valley, however, Chialsa's carpet sales declined to next to nothing by the 1990s.

In 1993 the Germans dealt a further blow by banning Nepalese carpets because of concerns over child labour. Carpets are still made in Chialsa, however, and the quality is excellent, being 30% Tibetan and 70% New Zealand wool.

To make up for the loss of income five orchards were planted. After selling in the surrounding area the surplus is dried, and what is left after that will no doubt be made into brandy!

In 1989 the Nepalese Government no longer allowed Tibetans to seek refugee status in Nepal, although existing Tibetans are allowed to remain. Chialsa now covers 100 acres and around 250 Tibetans remain.

ROUTE GUIDE AND MAPS

can make: momos, *thukpa* (Tibetan soup), fried and boiled potatoes, *sukuti* (fried dried meat), roti, tsampa and the inevitable Tibetan salt-butter tea.

There's an extensive mountain panorama from the top of the ridge, an hour or so up. Apparently even Everest is visible. For less breathtaking views visit the **gompa** that is ringed by flags.

This gompa is one of four that His Holiness the Dalai Lama commissioned to face Tibet. The others are in India at Zanskar, Ladakh, Deurali-Gantok in Sikkim and Bumdila.

HEADING SOUTH

Okaldunga is around 36km away, a long day's walk for locals but two days for loaded porters and trekkers. A road from the Tarai (Terai) to Okaldunga is still under construction. Once the new Eastern Highway out of Kathmandu is finished as well, this could provide an alternative trekking route to Jiri and the Salpa-Arun. Those who hope this route might involve no hill-climbing, however, will be disappointed: there is still a 3000m ridge to cross between Okaldunga and Salleri.

Salpa-Arun to the Khumbu

INTRODUCTION

On the walk between the Khumbu and the Arun Kosi the differences between ethnic groups are probably more striking than on any other teahouse trek. Although the Sherpa and Rai peoples are both of Mongolian stock and speak Tibeto-Burmese languages, the fact that they live at different altitudes influences many areas of their lives.

The self-assured Buddhist Sherpas (see pp137-42) inhabit the higher regions, growing potatoes and barley or wheat, and have herds of cattle. Throughout the year they wear heavy dark woollen clothing.

In contrast the ancient Animist Rai people (see pp142-3) occupy land at a lower level, growing rice, millet and maize. It's warm enough for cotton clothes and they often harvest two crops a year in the frost-free climate. Although they mostly keep to themselves they are a pleasant, polite, community-orientated people with egalitarian views.

Also living in the perpetually warm low country are the traditional rice farmers, the Hindus: the lean Brahmins, Chhetris and other castes, a land of bodice tops, singlets and umbrellas. In the lazy heat there is a listless feeling in the small shops and the ways of the buffalo.

The walk is described in the Tumlingtar–Namche direction.

The route

Less experienced trekkers planning to walk in and out (rather than fly from Lukla) should still consider walking in from Jiri then out to Tumlingtar. The reason is the Salpa-Arun route is tougher than the Jiri to Namche section – the hills are steeper and the facilities more basic. Tumlingtar to Namche involves around 10,000 vertical metres of ascent (as well as 7000m of descent) and being fitter and more used to the trekking lifestyle definitely makes the going easier.

The most sensible place to begin this trek is from Tumlingtar airport. The other possibilities are Hille/Leguwa and Basantpur, which involve long bus rides.

From the flats of Tumlingtar the trail crosses the mighty Arun river then climbs over a spur to follow the Irkhuwa Khola up to Phedi (which means bottom of the hill). From here it is a long climb to the top of the first pass, the Salpa Bhanjyang (3349m /10,987ft), the highest pass en route. The Surkie La (3085m/10,121ft) then the Satu La (3173m/10,410ft) follow in quick succession but between them, of course, are deep valleys.

The route joins the main Dudh Kosi trekking route from Jiri between Puiyan and Kharikhola and it is a further two to three days to Namche.

> ### The first trekkers
> The first foreign visitors to the Khumbu were HW Tilman, Oscar Houston and his wife, Dr Charles Houston and a couple of other companions. This was perhaps the first true trek undertaken in Nepal; it was purely for pleasure rather than science or mountaineering. They trekked from Dharan to the Khumbu and back during November 1950. Their trek in via Salpa Arun was considerably more pleasant than the Everest reconnaissance of 1951, led by Eric Shipton, who trekked in during the monsoon. His party had great difficulty recruiting porters, had to avoid villages struck by bubonic plague, suffered leeches and was even attacked by hornets.

Rafting the mighty Sun Kosi
This is a fantastic six- to eight-day rafting expedition, at least during the September to November season. The rafting ends roughly where the Arun and the Sun Kosi merge so why not begin the Salpa-Arun immediately afterwards? Either hop on a bus to Hille/Leguwa or head to Biratnagar and fly to Tumlingtar. See p38 for further details.

The time needed

The amount of time required for this walk varies considerably. From Tumlingtar to Namche takes nine or even ten days at a moderate pace; faster, fitter trekkers are still likely to take eight days in, although doing it in seven days is possible. Using the Basantpur or Hille/Leguwa routes and including a leisurely drive, allow eleven or twelve days, although nine is possible.

▲ On the way out Namche to Tumlingtar is likely to take eight days at a moderate pace, although seven is also possible. Feeling strong? The fit and hill-hardened could reduce Namche to Hille to five and a half tough days, though a week is more realistic.

Facilities

Between the Arun and the Dudh Kosi there's a scattering of *lodges* and family homes masquerading as lodges that offer food and a bed. Their varied standards add to the pleasure of trekking along this route but because of this it is worth planning/asking ahead. Don't expect apple pie or pizza here; in fact, don't expect even a menu, just a share of what the family is eating. Prices are mostly very reasonable and often ridiculously cheap, and barely reflect the true costs of running a small lodge that sees only a low volume of trekkers. The majority of lodges have at least a dormitory and simple rooms are becoming more common.

Do get a good map and plan each day ahead. Always **carry plenty of snacks**, too, for when you get caught out. Change has been slow, so don't count on finding extra facilities that aren't already marked here.

Alternatively arrange this as a camping trek with a Kathmandu trekking company.

GETTING TO EASTERN NEPAL

Flying to Tumlingtar is by far the quickest way into the region but the new (2009) Sindhuli Highway has cut road distance and travel times drastically and now most road ends are accessible with less than 12 hours in a vehicle. Prior to this buses going east would make a five hour or so detour west to Mugling, halfway to Pokhara.

By air

There are several flights a day into **Tumlingtar**, both direct from Kathmandu, around $100 one way, and from Biratnagar around $75; the Biratnagar-Kathmandu sector costs $120 or so.

Biratnagar, Nepal's second largest city, is the air hub and trading centre for the east. Calling it a city is rather an exaggeration: rather it is a town trapped in the 1950s, and not worth a detour if you have visited another Terai town. The airport is well out of town, the bus station is in town and the few hotels are scattered randomly. There are frequent buses (8 hours) to Kathmandu and Dharan is perhaps two hours away.

By land

The Hille road now continues to Leguwa, and after one more bridge is built, will reach Tumlingtar and Khandbari, the district headquarters. There are direct buses from Kathmandu to Dharan, and also Dhankuta (a pleasant place to break your journey), and even to Leguwa Ghat. However, it often makes sense to take a bus to Dharan or Dhankuta and then change buses.

All buses leave from the main bus station. Since the new highway wasn't quite open at the time of writing I am not sure if there will only be soul-destroying night

> ### The chautara – 'the coolies' joy and the travellers' bane'
> 'In this pleasant land where all loads are carried upon men's backs, where the tracks are rough and steep and the days hot, various pious and public-spirited men – of which in my opinion there have been too many – perpetuate their names by planting two fast-growing shady trees and building round them a rectangular or sometimes circular stone dais with a lower parapet as a seat...
>   There is a Nepali proverb – or if there isn't there should be – that the sight of a chautara makes the coolie's back ache.' **HW Tilman**, *Nepal Himalaya*

ROUTE GUIDE AND MAPS

buses, which leave from 4pm onwards, or if the journey will be short enough for day buses, which would then leave early (from 5.30am).

TUMLINGTAR (515m/1700ft)
Approaching Tumlingtar by plane, the endless terraced hills, pretty villages and the distant Himalayan peaks are staggeringly beautiful. Arriving is mellowing. The runway is very 1950s, grass-covered with a simple fence to keep the cows and goats out. One day this will change: it is destined to be the eastern air hub once an all-weather road reaches here.

The two main **hotels**, *Kanchenjunga* (☎ 029 69120) and *Makalu* (☎ 029 69057) are immediately opposite the gate, and *Arun* (☎ 029 69062) is a few minutes north. They mainly cater to the locals arriving and leaving by plane but the dal bhaat is OK and the beer cold. If buying a ticket you are perhaps better off staying at the lodge concerned (see By air p247).

TUMLINGTAR TO BALAWA BESI
[Map 18]
On a clear day mountains rise surreally out of the heat haze. Chamalang is the left-most peak and Makalu is to the far right, often with a tell-tale cloud spinning off it: jet-stream turbulence. Beat the heat by starting early and **drink lots**.

The main path heads north from the hotels and passes to the left or west side of the brick pits. Follow the electricity poles. The track is straight, passing the occasional house and shop/teashop.

After an hour is **Gidhe** and the simple *Irkhuwa Arun Hotel*, with another hotel

beside it. The trail drops close to the river bank (but no swimming for a while) and uses every opportunity to follow the shore.

Assuming you stayed the night at Tumlingtar, **Chewa Besi** is the place for lunch although the quick may make Kartiki Ghat. At **Kartiki Ghat** a suspension bridge crosses the Arun. There are a few simple *restaurants* and it is possible to find a rough bed but the place, and Balawa Besi, are not particularly endearing, with a sometimes rude, laughing indifference that's thankfully found nowhere else.

Balawa Besi is a bridge across a sparkling khola plus a few houses and a shop that sometimes puts up trekkers. If you flew in and made it to either Kartiki Ghat or Balawa Besi that evening, aiming for Dobani, or for the fit, Tallo Phedi or Phedi, the next day is realistic.

The Dingla alternative
The standard trekking route (as described here) is the shortest trail: hence from Baluwa Besi to Charlissay you need to ask the way frequently. In fact the main trail detours via Dingla, a historic bazaar town. Although it is a main route, the Dingla to Salpa Bhanjyang trail isn't straightforward trekking.

BALAWA BESI TO JAU BARI
[Map 19, pp250-1]
Leaving Balawa Besi, cross the sturdy frame bridge and head right past **teashacks** and homes then head left climbing up and up. At first the trail is clear, but then climbs steep, slippery clay. There's a Nepali saying 'Rato mato, chiplo bhato' or 'red mud, slippery trail', and more appropriately in

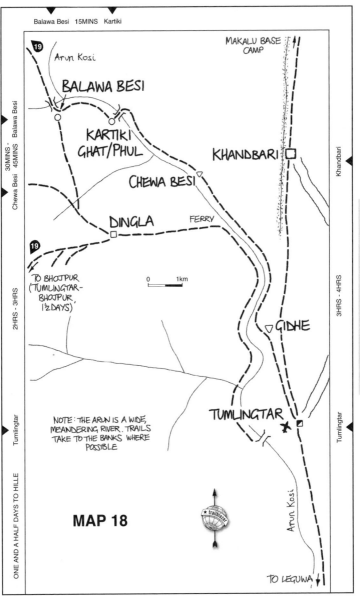

MAKALU BASE CAMP

BALAWA BESI

Arun Kosi

KARTIKI GHAT/PHUL

KHANDBARI

CHEWA BESI

DINGLA FERRY

TO BHOJPUR (TUMLINGTAR-BHOJPUR, 1½ DAYS)

0   1km

GIDHE

TUMLINGTAR

NOTE: THE ARUN IS A WIDE, MEANDERING RIVER. TRAILS TAKE TO THE BANKS WHERE POSSIBLE

MAP 18

Arun Kosi

TO LEGUWA

ROUTE GUIDE AND MAPS

Balawa Besi

Chewa Besi

Tumlingtar

ONE AND A HALF DAYS TO HILLE

30MINS - 45MINS

2HRS - 3HRS

Khandbari

3HRS - 4HRS

Tumlingtar

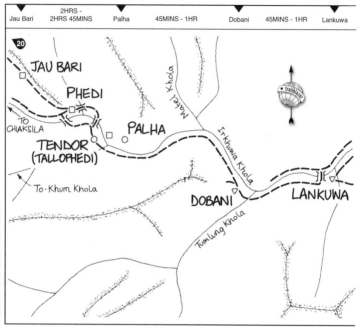

▼ Jau Bari	2HRS - 2HRS 45MINS	▼ Palha	45MINS - 1HR	▼ Dobani	45MINS - 1HR	▼ Lankuwa

ROUTE GUIDE AND MAPS

English, 'red mud, land with a thud'. Up the steep section, take a traversing right at a chautara with a small, off-centre tree.

You are beginning a 600m traversing climb with many trail junctions, although heading up most are obvious in the first stretch and locals point the way. If you reach *Sagarmatha Lodge*, on the ridge and the first real lodge set up for trekkers, you are doing OK. From here it is better to follow some porters or ask frequently for Phedi and Salpa Bhanjyang.

After the spur follow the most-worn track (ask too!) through terraced fields for about 20 minutes to **Marduwa**. Between Marduwa and Charlissay contour around a small bowl.

Charlissay This is the name of a Chhetri caste that lived in these areas generations ago. It is said that they now mostly live in the Kathmandu Valley. Villagers, usually older women or children, may invite you in to eat or stay.

From here the real main trail junction (ie the old one from Dingla) is around 20-25 minutes away. Contour and cross a small ravine. Once out of this head for two large **pipal trees** with a chautara and rejoin a larger clear trail here.

From the trees descend through dense semi-tropical forest to the Irkhuwa Khola. A few minutes along the bank, at **Tabutar**, is a *teashack*. Between here and Gothe (Gothe Bazaar) the trail – and the point where it crosses the Irkhuwa Khola – changes regularly: ask the locals for directions! Reaching Gothe is for those keen to put in a harder day.

▲ About half an hour after leaving Gothe there is a steel bridge across the Irkhuwa Khola. Above this is a pleasant, rising traverse through some forest. You want to be

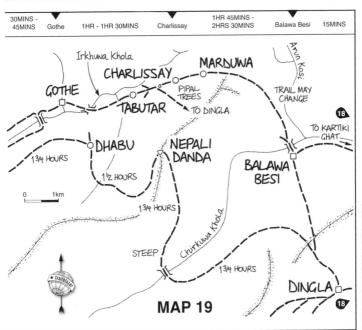

Irkhuwa Khola

CHARLISSAY

GOTHE

TABUTAR

PIPAL TREES

TO DINGLA

MARDUWA

Arun Kosi

TRAIL MAY CHANGE

18

TO KARTIKI CHAT

DHABU

1 3/4 HOURS

NEPALI DANDA

1 1/2 HOURS

BALAWA BESI

0   1km

1 3/4 HOURS

Chirkuwa Khola

STEEP

1 3/4 HOURS

DINGLA

18

MAP 19

ROUTE GUIDE AND MAPS

on this trail, no other; it leads to the two trees and chautara with the fields of Charlissay in view. You are now well above the khola. At the pipal trees people usually offer tea, dal bhaat and, during the right season, suntala (mandarin oranges).

About 100m past the trees the trail divides properly, the upper trail going up to Nepali Danda then Dingla while you want to head across the fields on a trail that then drops very briefly before passing through the village, where dal bhaat is on offer, and continues on its climbing traverse through fields to another pipal and bhodhi tree chautara. Soon after this you have to climb a stone wall, walk through the fields past a house and over a crude stile by a water tap, then head up.

Finally, within sight of the Arun, take the main trail up; rounding this ridge, you'll find three chairs with a view at the highest

point. Heading straight, and flat rather than down, sets you on the main way to another large chautara and porters shelter, and just below, the well-placed, simple *Sagarmatha Lodge*.

Gothe Bazaar / Tintamang / Membahang (775m/2550ft) After crossing the Irkhuwa and climbing a small hill you come to the delightful settlement of Gothe (pronounced Got-hey).

There is one *lodge* and a camping place before the khola, the Tintamang side, and a *teashop* on the Membahang side, and after a hot day's trekking the best place is in the middle, the sparkling khola. With the bamboo, airy lodgings, and the sound of water, one could almost be in Thailand.

The people here are apparently a mix between Gurung from the Pokhara region and local Rai.

> ### Cardamom
> Look out for cardamom (*elaichi*) plants in small fields in the cool shaded forest. In early October they are distinctive for having a red fleshy flower at the base of a 1-1.5m stem with well-spaced leaves around 30cm long. By the end of October the stem withers and all that's left is the thick red flower with mainly white seeds. Thousands of kilos of these valuable and fragrant seeds are grown in East Nepal then dried and carried down to roadheads. Kashmiri tea relies on the seeds' distinctive flavour, as do many masala-flavoured Indian dishes, and the plants are also valuable for soil conservation.

Lankuwa (875m/2870ft) Things haven't changed here for at least ten years. If you do have an urge or need to stay check the quality of the tea first, and then the price and arrangements. It is a curious place – some of the inhabitants even think they are still in Gothe.

Dobani / Thunglung Doban (975m/ 3200ft)
Doban means Confluence of Two Rivers. The 1999-built bridge and trail bypass the small cluster of buildings including a simple *lodge*. However, there might still be a bamboo bridge, if you want to stop for tea at the lodge.

Around this region paper is made by hand, destined for Kathmandu. Here and at Tallo Phedi you may be able to watch the process and buy some of the finished product. Leaving Dobani, the trail stays above the Irkhuwa Khola for a while.

Tendor / Tallo Phedi (1400m/4600ft)
Don't confuse Tallo Phedi (Lower Bottom of the Hill) with Phedi (which merely means Bottom of the Hill). There is a paper factory and immediately above, *Irkhuwa Rai Lodge*. Leaving, traverse into the gully and cross near, or on if you are game, the dodgy bridge.

At the next village, Tendor, there is a choice of two trails. One climbs the ridge to Chole then contours and descends to the suspension bridge. The other, more usual route stays low in fields, passing the school and crossing the river, before climbing a bit on the opposite bank to recross to Phedi.

Phedi (1700m/5575ft) Virtually at the confluence of two rivers, Phedi boasts three simple but developing *lodges*.

Trekking up through the village, if in doubt take two lefts and follow the stone steps. By this stage of the trek you have already gained 1400m, perhaps barely noticing it. But from here the real climb begins: the attack of the killer stone steps, sweatier and more real than any B-grade movie.

At the same time as cursing the never-ending steps one has to wonder who built them. Was it a labour of love? Was it for money? Or for penance? And how old are they? It's a very tough day from Phedi over the pass so an early start is useful. It's not a bad idea to see if you can find a porter to help for this stretch.

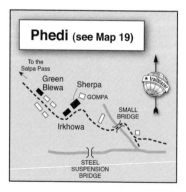

Jau Bari / Thulofokte (2300m/7550ft)

The trail to this spread-out small settlement is relentlessly steep and brutal at the end of the day. There are two simple *teashops* then, further up, two simple *lodges*, also well separated: **Saelpa Seharpa**, where donations for the gompa are sometimes collected (they can open it for you too) and, the higher lodge, **Kalo Patthar**.

▲ Prepare to fall off the end of the world.

JAU BARI TO SANAM
[Map 19, pp250-1; Map 20, p255]

After cresting the sharp ridge there is a flattish area with a sometimes **dry pond** and a **stone shelter**. The trail to Guranse stays on the south side of the main ridge and divides about 20 minutes past the pond. The other trail up the ridge goes direct to Salpa Pokhari.

Guranse (2920m/9580ft)

Guranse (pronounced Gurasé, light on the 'n') is a rhododendron (*laligurans* or *laliguras* in Nepali) region, but it is a somehow miserable place with tree stumps littering the cleared area. There are a couple of buildings, both *lodges*, although only one is generally open year-round, and they are set up for porters rather than trekkers – though it is possible to stay.

▲ The thin track passes though untidy grazing land to pass by a pond with a stone shelter then climbs to the crest of the obvious razorback ridge and descends steeply.

Salpa Bhanjyang / Khulophongko (Danda) (3349m/10,987ft)

A weathered chorten graces the top of the pass. Slightly better views can be had by climbing south a little way. The pass also marks the boundary of the Bhojpur district, which you have been in since Kartiki Ghat or Bhojpur, and Solukhumbu, which you stay in for the rest of the trek. You are now entering a Sherpa region.

The top part of the pass receives snow during the winter and the locals may wait several days after a fall before crossing. If snow-covered, the trail can be slippery and challenging to follow.

▲ Going down the other side is easy. Follow the stone track that curves left, and continue roughly in the same direction, eventually to Guranse.

Side trips

To Silingchuk (4156m/13,630ft) This is a difficult scramble on narrow, steep, almost non-existent trails. Don't attempt this climb in winter with snow lying around. There are no possible camping spots on or near the top. Locals swear there is a route from Silingchuk to Sanam and Gudel but the only way to find this would be to take a local guide, otherwise you will be bluffed out.

Paper-making Nepali style

A number of paper-making set-ups are found along this part of the Salpa-Arun trek. A plant called *lokto* is harvested from the forest; the outer layer is pulled off and the fibrous heartwood is carried down for processing. After boiling the lokto for two hours, it is smashed into a pulp with a rock and mixed with water. A wood-framed piece of mesh is then dipped into the soup which helps to evenly distribute the pulp. This frame is then set out in the sun to dry for a day.

The finished product is 'transportered' to Kathmandu, Hetauda and Biratnagar to be sold at approximately Rs10 per sheet. Once all official government documents had to be printed on this special paper but the advent of typewriters, and now computers, means this practice is changing, and now it is the export and tourist market that are the main consumers.

Salpa Pokhari

A long, long time ago a local Rai king and queen went for a vacation in the local hills. Unfortunately, at the time, the queen was suffering from a mental sickness, though upon reaching the lake she recovered – only to then be consumed by a large serpent living in the lake. The king spent the rest of his weary days looking for his beloved wife.

It's said that if a person comes to praise the lake, she/he will be successful in the future. So naturally enough to take advantage of this there are four main *mellas* (festivals) a year, each lasting four days and attracting thousands of people from the Solu Khumbu, Kotang, Bhojpur and Sankhwasaba districts. It is a time to eat, drink and be merry and many of the local *dhamis* (holy men) perform sacred ceremonies by the lake to ask the lake god (the snake) to protect all. During their long trance it is said that the dhami are able to see both the snake and the queen. Both Buddhists and Hindus visit the lake.

In the Hindu religion, the God Shiva is related to the snake with the snake being the symbol of water. So to worship the lake is to worship the element of water, and therefore the snake and Shiva. In Nepali, *serpa* means snake.

To Salpa Pokhari (3460m/11,350ft)
This trail begins on the right side of the large boulder, to the north of the chorten on the Salpa Pass. Traverse north-east, gradually ascending for 30 minutes and walk through a flat open area. A large stupa marks the beginning of the holy area (see box above).

Salpa Bhanjyang to Sanam The path down soon follows a small stream and passes a few old mani walls. There are three rock shelters (all leak in rain) before Whaka but none is particularly dry. In the main valley, well down, the track crosses to the north bank of the Lidung Khola. Later,

where the trail emerges from the forest, there's **Whaka/Orkobug**; here there are two *teahouses*, of which one is usually open, and a camping place. The usual place to stay after the pass is Sanam but everywhere can now support trekkers.

Sanam (2650m/8700ft)
Land of the Sky is the Sherpa translation of Sanam. The locals are keen for trekkers' business and all the houses there seem to be turning themselves into *lodges* or *home-stays*.

▲ The pass is a half-day's walk from Sanam and is not at the obvious head of the

Nature is God

In essence the Rai people worship nature, perhaps more so than any other ethnic group in Nepal. They work in a co-operative, community-based way unlike, say, the Brahmins, so development agencies find they are easy to work with, but there are a couple of projects that have been notably unsuccessful for cultural reasons. The design for more efficient cooking stoves was demonstrated but there was zero uptake since the three cooking stones are the holiest part of the house. It is hoped that a new design incorporating these three essential stones might be more successful. The new designs are much more efficient, using less firewood, and produce less smoke. A chimney can also be added. Many of the health problems throughout Nepal are caused by smoky homes.

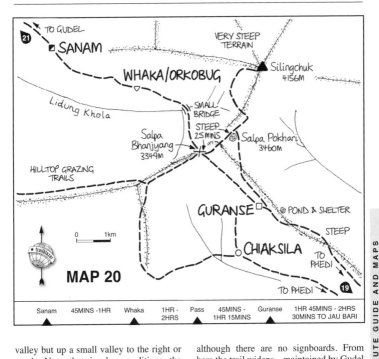

TO GUDEL

21 SANAM

WHAKA/ORKOBUG

VERY STEEP
TERRAIN

Silingchuk
4156M

Lidung Khola

SMALL
BRIDGE

STEEP
25 MINS

Salpa Pokhari
3460M

Salpa
Bhanjyang
3349M

HILLTOP GRAZING
TRAILS

GURANSE □   ● POND & SHELTER

STEEP

○ CHIAKSILA   TO
PHEDI

MAP 20   0   1km

★ trailblazer

TO PHEDI   **19**

| Sanam | 45MINS -1HR | Whaka | 1HR - 2HRS | Pass | 45MINS - 1HR 15MINS | Guranse | 1HR 45MINS - 2HRS 30MINS TO JAU BARI |

valley but up a small valley to the right or south. Note that in dry conditions the Lidung Khola is often the last source of water until well over the pass.

SANAM TO NAJING DINGMA
[Map 21, p256]
Tiu / Duire (2600m/8500ft) Meaning Horse Mare, the name commemorates the fact that once someone was silly enough to bring one up here.

There are a couple of simple **lodges**: *Tiue* and *Arun Valley*.

Nimtsola / Gompa The monastery here gives tutelage to a number of boys from the surrounding villages. Several of the people here offer tea and it is possible to eat/stay,

although there are no signboards. From here the trail widens – maintained by Gudel Village Development Committee (VDC) – and Sherpa country ends; lower down are Rai people.

The main trail leads to a mani (visible from afar) on the ridge that overlooks the large Rai village of Gudel. As well as Gudel and Bung the panorama includes the Naulekh mountains and, with good eyes, the Kiraunle-Chambaling (Boksom) Gompa.

Gudel (1950m/6400ft) There are three lodges, all basic: *Kulung* is right at the base of the village, *Namaste* is signposted in the middle and just above it is *Kopila*. Ask around to find them.

❑ **Map key** See p309 for the trail map key

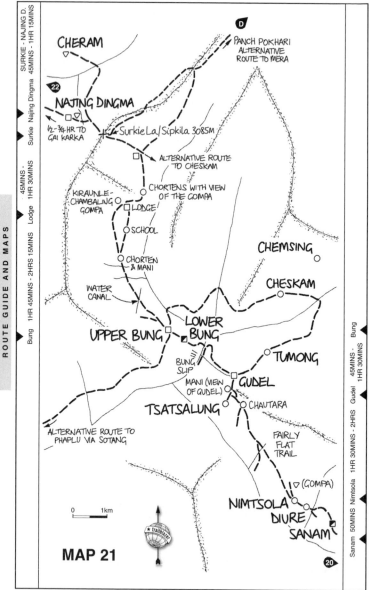

SURKIE - NAJING D.
Surkie Najing Dingma 45MINS - 1HR 15MINS

CHERAM

22 NAJING DINGMA

½-¾ HR TO
GAI KARKA

Surkie La/Sipkila 3085M

45MINS -
Lodge 1HR 30MINS

ALTERNATIVE ROUTE
TO CHESKAM

KIRAUNLE-
CHAMBALING
GOMPA

CHORTENS WITH VIEW
OF THE GOMPA

LODGE

SCHOOL

CHEMSING

CHORTEN
& MANI

Bung 1HR 45MINS - 2HRS 15MINS

WATER
CANAL

CHESKAM

LOWER
BUNG

UPPER BUNG

BUNG
SLIP

TUMONG

MANI (VIEW
OF GUDEL)

GUDEL

TSATSALUNG

CHAUTARA

45MINS -
Gudel 1HR 30MINS

Bung

ALTERNATIVE ROUTE TO
PHAPLU VIA SOTANG

FAIRLY
FLAT
TRAIL

1HR 30MINS - 2HRS

▽ (GOMPA)

NIMTSOLA

DIURE

SANAM

50MINS Nimtsola

Sanam

0   1km

MAP 21

PANCH POKHARI
ALTERNATIVE
ROUTE TO MERA

D

20

*For dreadfulness nought can excel
The prospect of Bung from Gudel
And words die away on the tongue
When we look back at Gudel from
Bung*
HW Tilman, *Nepal Himalaya*

From Gudel you can see the trail from
the bridge zigzagging up to Bung. Follow
the stream on a mainly stone path for a
while. The trail then veers right (or north)
away from the stream, and down towards a
beautiful waterfall before cutting back
south-west to the bridge that crosses the
Hongu Khola at about 1280m/4200ft. Bung
begins approximately ten minutes up. The
Dudh Kosi Schneider map marks the trails
in and out of Gudel inaccurately.

Note the large stream north of Bung:
for several hours the trail above Bung stays
approximately parallel to this about half to
one kilometre away.

▲ **Gudel to Sanam** Climb on one of several trails to the mani walls above Gudel on
the spur to the south. From here the wide
trail climbs gently but steadily, hugging the
steep valley wall. The trail abruptly narrows at Nimtsola.

Bung (Lower and Upper)
Meaning Beautiful Flower in Rai, this is the
largest village of the Maha Kulung (great
Kulung Rai) region. It spreads over a huge
hillside. There are two *lodges* close to the

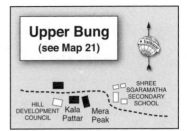

bottom of the village (Bung, lower; 1420m/
4650ft) with a second cluster in the upper
village at around 1800m/5900ft.

Bung is a particularly pleasant middle
hills village, it's clean and the kids barely
beg: joyful 'namastes' and 'hellos' are the
norm. See box p258.

▲ Just before Bung is a white three-sided
porters' shelter; the village is heralded by
clumps of huge bamboo. Soon there is a
trail junction: contour following the wall
rather than descending through the fields.
This leads to a pleasant bamboo-lined
gully. Once in the open again it is five minutes to the top set of lodges.

To Phaplu The trail starts at the top set of
lodges. The path to Sotang basically contours and is easy to follow.

▲ From Bung it's a short day's walk to
Sanam or one very long and tough day to
Guranse. It's possible to camp after Sanam
but not on top of the pass since there is no
water there. Leaving Bung, there is a maze
of paths, hopefully signposted. After some

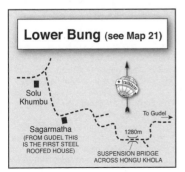

❏ **Allo**
Nettle fibre, called *allo*, was once the
main source for cloth. A few items,
such as vests, are still worn though
the importance of allo weaving has
greatly decreased due to the intensive
labour required and the ready availability of cotton clothes.

ROUTE GUIDE AND MAPS

> ### Bung
> This region is known for its *tungba*, an alcoholic brew served in a tall wooden vessel and drunk using a bamboo straw. Boiling water is poured over fermented millet to make this warming drink. If there's a really big celebration it's served in a barrel, everybody using their own straw. The more mature the millet, the smoother the taste with a special vintage (rarely served to tourists) being about a year old.
>
> The villagers are also big chang drinkers: usually a mix of corn (more) and millet (less) and raksi, distilled from the chang. The Rai culture has been surprisingly durable, and occasionally you will see the men wearing the traditional *phenga* sleeveless jacket made from *allo* (see box p257). The *phoria* or *lungi* wrap skirt is what the women wear, and, if it is raining, the *ghum*, which is a folding bamboo mat with either banana leaf or plastic sandwiched between to cover both the person and the *doko*.
>
> Many women still wear the traditional double nose piece, the *dhungri* which is round, and the hanging piece, the *jhamke*. Earrings (*maluwari*) complete the picture. Prior to marriage girls usually wear a *phulli* – a nose stud – and if they marry someone wealthy they receive gold earrings, necklace and other pieces. However, a love marriage without the trappings of wealth is also totally acceptable, and in this case no gold or anything else need be given. It used to be that most marriages were arranged, over lots of drinks and discussion, but now mostly the trend is for love marriages. Once married all work is generally shared.
>
> The houses are all still made from traditional adobe mud and, although steel roofs are arriving, most are either wooden shingles with bamboo mats over the top or thatched. Inside, the fire is always in the middle of the room so that in winter everyone, especially the guests, can all sit around it. As you can imagine, the Rais know their wood, and in many houses there is a wooden frame that sits over the fire to dry the wood but prevent it, one hopes, from burning. Most houses have a *janto* stone for grinding corn and millet. Although there are no chimneys and the ceiling is shiny and smoke-blackened, usually the interior is not too smoky, at least as long as you sit on the floor. Neatness seems to come in threes – sit in a Rai house and gradually you will see what I mean.
>
> The region exports ghee, eggs and quite a bit of meat to Namche, where the money and demand is. Bung, although a pleasant place, is a long way from any road, something that makes life less than easy for the locals.

clumps of bamboo there are many tracks and slips but most lead to the suspension bridge. Take the left fork after crossing the bridge for the steep ascent to Gudel.

Kiraunle-Chambaling Gompa (Boksom)
After an initial steep ascent out of Bung the trail eases to a continuous gently ascending traverse. It's easy to get lost as there are numerous trails, but all lead close to Kiraunle-Chambaling Gompa (several hours away) and its distinctive ring of large trees. The main trail is perhaps half a kilometre above this.

The friendly owners of a small *lodge* close to the gompa are intent on creating a new trail that passes through a school then on to the gompa and themselves. It isn't necessary to take this trail; the lodge is only five minutes off the main trail higher up, and is signposted. The gompa is being rebuilt and you are welcome to look around. Once on the main trail, just a little before the chortens is a simple *teahouse*.

The Surkie La / Sipki La / Betoma Cha (3085m/10,121ft)
Above the gompa on a ridge are some chortens followed by some mani walls and a beautiful, mainly old and moss-encrusted rhododendron forest. At two *teahouses*

there is a major trail junction: go up for the pass. This is an uneventful pass but for better views climb the trail to a sightseeing platform where you can see Khatang and Numbur, collectively called Shorong Yul La, the holy mountains of the region around Junbesi. The descent is initially quite steep (and icy in winter) through bamboo groves.

Najing Dingma / Naji Dingma is on a flat grassy knoll at 2650m/8694ft. Here, among the few houses are two *teahouses* and a small shop. These are run by people, often kids, from the Sherpa village of **Cheram** (Chereme on the *Shorong/Hinku* Schneider map). Although most trekkers take the shorter Gai Kharka route to Shubuche it is possible to go via Cheram. You can stay there, although there are **no real lodges**. People from Najing Dingma can show you the way.

GAI KHARKA TO PUIYAN
[Map 22, p260]
Gai Kharka This means Cow Pasture but now the area is under cultivation. Apart from a new water tap there are no facilities for trekkers and it is easy to lose the way. At first stay right on the trails then, once well down, join a path leading across a small stream that heads up. Three metres after crossing the stream another trail, only now visible, heads down. Take this down a minor ridge. In all it takes approximately 15 minutes to descend through Gai Kharka.

Bridge across the Inkhuwa / Inukhu / Hinku Khola (1850m/6069ft) The bridge is an impressive height above the river, and even more impressive are the hills on the western side. This is one brutal, unrelentingly steep hill.

Shubuche / Shiboche The fields begin as the hill relents in gradient, but it is still perhaps half an hour to the main *lodge*. This lodge is occasionally closed: either temporarily while the family work the fields, or sometimes completely while the family goes shopping. One other family sometimes offers to put up trekkers. There are great views of the Inukhu Valley and the peaks of Mera.

▲ The trail continues straight to the end of the ridge, crossing a fence or two before dropping off, turning slightly south. It's a very steep, knee-jerking descent.

Satu La / Pangum La (3173m/10,410ft) Atop the pass on the far side of the valley you may be able to make out the trail heading up to the Trakshindo La on the Jiri route. Looking behind you across the valley it's possible to see Najing Dingma, about two-thirds of the way up the previous ridge.

Pangkongma / Pangum (2850m/9350ft) The village has a wonderfully located 1970 Hillary school and a gompa. There are two *lodges*.

Pick up the trail at the parallel mani walls just below the lodges and head northwest. Bupsa can be seen on the ridge slightly north and Kharikhola (see p240) below on the southern wall of the valley. At first the trail is straightforward but further on are several junctions that can be confusing. Think about which trail you want: Bupsa (see p240), Kharte, or the old trail to Puiyan (in Nepali 'purano Puiyan ra Khari La bhaato'), then ask the locals for directions.

▲ **From the main trail to Pangkongma (Pangum)**
The main Namche to Kharikhola trail can be left at Puiyan, Bupsa (possibly the best option) or Kharikhola. It is about half a day's walk to Pangkongma from these places. At the beginning of Pangkongma after two approximately parallel mani walls walk to the left and head up to a group of houses and *lodges*.

If you're very fit you may be able to reach Najing Dingma from Bupsa in a day, or make Bung from Pangkongma or Shubuche. For most people, from Pangkongma or Shubuche to Najing Dingma is a long day. Carry lunch and snacks.

From Puiyan Ten minutes north of Puiyan is a big boulder that makes an attractive viewpoint. From here the several trails south of Puiyan are visible. You can also see the rocky gully that the main Namche trail traverses. Just visible above is

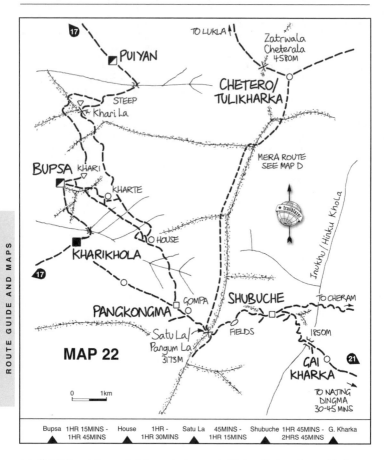

| Bupsa | 1HR 15MINS - | House | 1HR - | Satu La | 45MINS - | Shubuche | 1HR 45MINS - | G. Kharka |
| ▲ | 1HR 45MINS | ▲ | 1HR 30MINS | ▲ | 1HR 15MINS | ▲ | 2HRS 45MINS | ▲ |

a trail which can be reached by a short scramble up the rocks and a slip to the path. This is part of the old route between Puiyan and Kharikhola, via Kharte. Head over the ridge and the **Khari La (3081m/10,108ft)** and down to the distinctive two-storey white house (a couple of hours in total). Five minutes below is the main trail leading to Pangkongma, heading up the valley.

From Bupsa Ask locals, but basically go straight up the ridge from the village on a mainly mud trail. At the mani wall further up, just before the two-storey white house, turn right and contour or drop to the main trails ahead and below. The Bupsa–Pangkongma trail is narrow but well-used and contours with some real ups and downs. A couple of days before the Namche Saturday market the trail is crowded with heavily laden porters heading for the bazaar.

From Kharikhola The locals recommend going via Bupsa, although there is a direct trail from Kharikhola after the maze of fields. You pass by a gompa along the way.

The Rolwaling Valley

INTRODUCTION

Rolwaling means 'the furrow left by the plough', an appropriate name for this steep-walled valley. It's a rugged yet beautiful area inhabited by friendly Sherpas. Unlike their Khumbu cousins, they form a single isolated community with just one main village.

Above the inhabited area the valley divides into several little-explored glaciated valleys dominated by formidable 6000m/c20,000ft peaks. The highest mountain in the area is the holy Gauri Sankar, an ice-castle that can be admired even from Kathmandu.

Despite the dotted line marking the route on many trekking maps, the Tashi Labtsa (5755m/18,881ft) is a mountaineering challenge not a teahouse trekking route. It's far more dangerous than the Kongma La, Tsho/Cho La or Annapurna's Thorong La.

Safety

It would be insane to try to cross the **Tashi Labtsa** by yourself and several climbers have disappeared while alone in this area. Crevasses are a real danger and there are some areas in the icefall that may need an abseil. From Thame or Beding you will need at least three days' food and should carry reserves for two more days, plus enough fuel to melt snow or ice for water. For small parties ice axes and crampons are needed by all, plus a rope with a few ice screws and slings and gear for a short abseil. Conditions have changed considerably on the glaciers in Nepal; as recently as 1972 yaks were taken across this pass.

There is one section of the route that could quite possibly change, making traversing around the Tsho Rolpa even more challenging than it already is, if the lake isn't frozen. **You must** consult with someone who has crossed the pass that season to find out the exact situation.

� Are you prepared for the worst?

Where is the place that you would least want to be when it snows? I can't think of many places worse than being on the Drolambao Glacier between the pass (Tashi Labtsa) and Noisy Knob camp (Dza Bua). We set up camp in the icefall slightly off route and awoke to find snow completely covering our two tents. The three guys in the other tent were actually suffocating. It was a marathon three-hour job to completely clear around the tents (always take a snow shovel!) and they needed clearing again in the afternoon.

The next night the tents were completely covered again but this time we stayed awake keeping the air vent clear. Enough snow had fallen that the crevasses, some more than ten metres deep, were completely filled and in all probability we waded over a few. It wasn't more than 1.5km to Noisy Knob but it took us a whole day of laboriously breaking a trail then packing down enough so that the guys following wouldn't fall through to their waists too often. We crawled across many patches too. To cut a long story short it took us a further four days of the most torturous trail-breaking imaginable to make Beding, and that was taking a shortcut over the frozen lake. Everyone suffered frost-nipped toes and had wasted away but luckily we all lived, and with no permanent damage.

We survived the worst; but will you?   **Jamie McGuinness**

Route planning and acclimatization

The Rolwaling Valley is a destination in its own right but most trekkers combine it with a visit to the Khumbu. Commercial trekking groups usually approach the valley from Dolakha-Singhati, or rarely from Barabise, attempt the trekking peak Ramdung-Go for acclimatization, then cross the Tashi Labtsa. For proper acclimatization 12 nights should be spent between Simigoan (2000m/6562ft) and the first night above 5000m/16,404ft. Since the highest village (Beding) is at 3700m/12,139ft this means many days camping.

Independent trekkers will find crossing from the Khumbu to the Rolwaling makes more sense logistically than the other way around. From Thame (suitably acclimatized) it is possible to reach Singhati in just under a week. Extra time will allow exploration of the valleys that head the Rolwaling and the wall of mountains to the south.

There are two route possibilities for starting (or finishing) the trek (see Map B: p267; Map C: p268). Dolakha (near Charikot) is a few kilometres off the Jiri road and a very rough road extends now to Singhati with the walk to Simigoan two days following the Tamba Kosi. A road is being built up to the Tibet border, so the start point of this trek will be shortened at some stage. Already parts of the road are being constructed opposite Simigoan. Barabise is on the Arniko Highway and from here to Simigoan takes four to six days. Between Simigoan and Beding there is also a choice of routes.

Note that the route is described crossing the pass from Thame to the Rolwaling and on to the roadheads at Singhati and Barabise. Information relevant to walking in the reverse direction is also given: this is marked by ▲.

Facilities

Since it's usually groups with tents that pass through here, there are few trekker lodges but finding basic food and a place to stay at villages en route isn't difficult. Bigu Gompa and nearby have some lodges that opened in 2008.

However, there are a number of nights where camping is unavoidable and camping supplies are far more difficult to find than in the Khumbu. Don't expect them to stock things like muesli and milk powder, except perhaps in Beding. It's best to carry in all you need and it's worth considering employing porters unless you're approaching from the Khumbu.

Getting to the start of the trek

For both Dolakha-Singhati and Barabise, buses leave from the old bus station by the clock tower in the centre of Kathmandu. For Dolakha-Singhati, buses leave in the morning 6am, 8am and 10am, although this might change. If you miss these you can take a bus to Jiri and get off at Charikot, then try to catch a bus through to Singhati or walk down to Dolakha and stay there. There are plenty of buses heading to Barabise, leaving approximately every hour for most of the day, and all buses going through to Kodari, the Nepal–Tibet border post, also pass through Barabise.

THAME TO SIMIGOAN
[Map A, p265]

The trail leaves **Thame** (see p182) from the little *lodge* beside Thame Gompa (visible from Thame village).

Take the upper tracks at each of the main junctions and you pass several small *chhusa*, deserted except during summer.

Tengpo (4350m/14,271ft) is a couple of hours from the gompa. This large *chhusa* has a number of minuscule two-storey houses. It's overlooked by the spectacular south faces of Teng Kangboche. There's ample spring water year-round and plenty of places to camp. If, however, your party is well acclimatized it's a better idea to camp closer to the pass.

The track continues but is smaller now. Looking back there's an unusual view of Ama Dablam with the fluted cirque and glacier of the Mingbo La clearly visible and with Makalu almost hidden behind Ama Dablam.

There are good camping areas around the point from where the views of Ama

Dablam start to disappear. Further up the track stays above the valley base and heads to the black rock spur (the north-western side of the valley), where there are more camping places but these lack water after a spell of dry weather. Over and slightly down the other side of the moraine (the route does not follow the valley by the black rock ridge) there are several more rocky sites.

To the north is an icefall and to the left of this are several rough moraine ridges. Partially ascend one and head up, keeping to the left of the icefall. There should be a rough track to follow. Above are another two groups of campsites called **Ngole/ Mgole** (5100m/16,732ft) with windy and very cold overhanging rock shelters.

▲ Note that when coming down from the pass to Ngole/Mgole you must keep to the left and avoid descending to the obvious and large valley floor.

The Tashi Labtsa / Tesi Lapcha (5755m/18,881ft) Access to the pass involves passing areas of frequent rockfall so an early morning start is best. In the early morning the rocks may still be frozen in place but as the sun hits them they expand, loosen and come thundering down. On a winter's day things might be stable but on a warm October afternoon it's like Russian roulette. It's said by the Sherpas that Lama Sange Dorje crossed this pass and the name Tashi Labtsa bestows a certain protection on travellers.

Onto the glacier There are two obvious routes. You can head left, down and under an icefall close to a large avalanche cone from Parcharmo. However, the quicker and more popular route is simply to stay on the moraine-covered ice and head up the ice valley. This could also be totally snow covered. Once up here the lay of the land becomes clearer. To the left, almost on Parcharmo's flanks, is a small diagonal icefall that fails to meet the smooth, white, almost flat glacier below. The upper part meets a rock wall that stretches from the right of the glacier to above you. Make for

the point where the icefall and the wall meet, which involves an ascent of the steep unstable scree slope below the wall. Beware of heavy rockfall here. Sometimes stepping onto the icefall is easier. Groups often use a rope here although with crampons and good glacier conditions it may not be necessary.

Alternatively, right of the small icefall is a large avalanche cone which leads to a rock shelf that runs between it and the top of the small icefall. Consult locals as to which route might be easier and safer.

From above the small icefall the going is easier and it's a simple plod to the top of the pass. Crevasses are not normally a problem but if there has been a lot of snow recently then use a rope. Parcharmo's snow bulges rise to the left and you should watch out for falling rocks from Tengi Ragi Tau (6940m/22,769ft) to the right. Just before the pass is Tashi Phuk (Tashi's Cave), a few daringly placed camping spots sheltered by a slightly overhanging rock wall. These make a good base for an attempt on Parcharmo.

The pass (5755m/18,881ft) New vistas unfold at the pass which is a small flat rock rib running out from Tengi Ragi Tau/Kangi Tau marked by cairns and a few prayer flags.

The descent is steeper than the ascent and requires care – there are several crevasses and a bergschrund. Head directly down, to where the glacier flattens out and meets the white Drolambao Glacier, divided by a line of moraine rubble. Once down stay close to, or on, the nearest medial moraine. Most groups camp somewhere around here (Tolungbawe Nang) but if you're making good time you may be able to reach the next camp. Don't cross to the far side of the glacier – the route marked on the *Rolwaling Himal* Schneider map is the 1950s route, now out of use, considered too dangerous and impractical.

From this point several routes have been used. Some trekkers have crossed the Drolambao Glacier before it starts to break up (and off!), then descended against the wall of Dragkar-Go but this requires some

ROUTE GUIDE AND MAPS

abseils and appears to descend a very dicey ramp. On my explorations, after descending some distance, I could not find a practical way down that did not need several abseils. Much better is to continue following the moraine, then cross over the broken ice to the left to another line of moraine debris formed by a glacier entering from Bigphera-Go Shar. This begins under a distinctive striped rock face. It leads, sometimes easily, sometimes hazardously, off the glacier/icefall onto solid rock. Conditions vary tremendously just here and at times it may require an abseil of up to 25m. Below, perhaps slightly to the right, is a massive lump of rock with obvious camping spots perched on top of it.

Dza Bua / Dzenasa / Noisy Knob camp (5000m/16,404ft)

To reach this camp, either drop to the obvious wide rock ledge below or bear right and drop into it further along. Then drop down the small diagonal gully within view of Noisy Knob. Depending on conditions and your skill, a rope may be necessary here. The camp is a classic, perched almost under the falling seracs and above the Trakarding Glacier. A warm night will surround you with the roar of avalanches, the crash-tinkle of seracs and continual groans of the glacier ghosts.

▲ Dza Bua is situated on the large blunt knob of rock clearly visible projecting at the far end of the Drolambao Icefall, dividing it and the next icefall, and is shown or is visible on most maps. The route up the knob is from the Bigphera-Go Shar side.

The Trakarding Glacier

Continuing on, the most frequently used route is on the north side where there's a definite track but moving down on the south side is equally feasible. You could perhaps even head for the ablation valley early. If on the north side once you're well down, the glacier cairns lead to the south side, while a vague path continues. Don't follow this path unless the lake is frozen. You must cross to the south to traverse around the lake. The old northern route is extremely dangerous. Some of the steep moraines extend to sheer rock faces and are shelled with a virtually continuous hail of stones and rocks.

Once on the south side of the glacier, climb up on a rough track, eventually reaching the steep crumbling moraine (groups use a rope down here). Binoculars will help you spot a large cairn well above. There's grass and a big flat dust bowl with a track across it here. Then it's up again to avoid the huge bowling alley that drops into the side of the lake.

At the top, walk south-west a little before crossing among the boulders. The descent is steep but with great views of the **Tsho Rolpa** (4534m/14,875ft) and the mountains towering above it. This section of trail is getting more and more precarious each year. It is possible that the hillside might fall away meaning this route is no longer possible.

Down the ablation valley is **Kabug** with its small cave, water and pleasant camping area. **Sangma** and the areas below the lake are also pleasant camping areas, especially for a day or overnight trip up to Bombok (or higher) beside the Ripimo Shar Glacier. The bridge below Sangma is sometimes dismantled for winter.

Na (4183m/13,724ft)

After a few hours of pleasant walking down the valley, cross the bridge to Na. This is a large *chhusa*, a summer village set under an incredible wall of mountains on the sunny northern side of the valley. It's deserted soon after the potatoes have been harvested, the fields left for the yaks and naks to pick over and add their dose of fertilizer.

It's a short half-day's walk above the north bank to Beding, still with the spectacular Chobutse/Tsoboje (6689m/21,945ft) rising behind. The forests en route are striking for the size of the trees, even in areas that get very little sun. This is how the area around Namche, and even as high as Dingboche, must once have looked. As Beding becomes visible it is framed against one of the twin peaks of Gauri Sankar (7146m/23,445ft), or Jomo Tseringma (Chomotseringma) as the Sherpas call it.

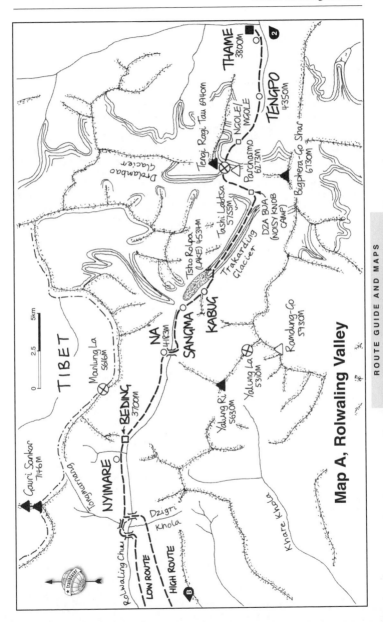

Map A, Rolwaling Valley

Beding (3700m/12,139ft)

Beding is a picturesque cluster of buildings centred around the gompa, with a well-kept stupa in the river bed. Although it's the only real village in the upper Rolwaling Valley, it's not permanently occupied. During the coldest winter months the entire population huddles down in the *gunsas* (Gyabrug to Nyimare). In the summer, some villagers move up to cultivate potatoes at Na and others roam higher with their grazing yaks.

The people seem to manage their village well without outside interference or government offices but there's no health post. There is a school opened in 1972 by Hillary and bridges erected with Japanese aid. The way of life here has changed less than for the Khumbu Sherpas in recent years. Trade with Tibet has been replaced with trekking-related jobs but since only groups pass through, there are no trekking lodges. (Nevertheless almost every resident will more than willingly put a few people up in local style.) Locals find employment as sirdars, cooks and especially as high-altitude sherpas on expeditions. Lots of Everest summiteers live here.

Trading with Tibet has virtually died out now that Indian iodized salt is so cheaply available. Previously salt, tsampa, yaks and naks, dried meat and Chinese-manufactured goods were traded. The route was over the Manlung La (5616m/18,425ft) which is reached up the impossible-looking slabs a little to the north of Beding. The glaciated pass affords amazing views of the mountain known to the Sherpas as Jomo Garu (Chomogaru: 7181m/23,559ft). This beautiful peak is more commonly known as Menlungtse, the name Shipton gave it in 1951.

Routes to Simigoan

There are two routes: the **direct lower winter route** via Gyalche, a short day's walk down but tough coming up, or the **high scenic Daldung La route** for which it's best to allow two days.

Snow in winter virtually precludes using the high route because the track is mostly in shaded areas where the snow is slow to melt. In addition, except in the early part of the season, this route is uninhabited until Simigoan.

To the Dzigri Khola, the boundary of the high Rolwaling Valley, both routes follow the same trail. The path is sunny and pleasant, always on the northern side, sometimes through forest, and, lower, sometimes in stunted bamboo. Prayer flags mark the wooden bridge (3200m/10,499ft).

The low route The trail, narrower now, continues on the north bank to cross the Tongmarnang, the stream with a view up Gauri Sankar's stunning face.

A little further down, the trail crosses to the south bank and starts its long roller-coaster ride to Simigoan. There are infrequent small *campsites* and perhaps one *teashack*.

The trail is different from that marked on the *Rolwaling Himal* Schneider map but is wide, well-used and easy to follow. It leads directly into Simigoan Gompa rather than heading via **Shakpa**.

▲ The **high route** is especially rewarding on the way in, with stunning views of Gauri Sankar and perhaps even a glimpse of Menlungtse. It's also an introduction to altitude, and a rather harsh one for many people, but relief should come when crossing the Rolwaling Chhu. For this reason it is preferable to stay at Shakpa (2650m/8694ft), rather than Simigoan, and it reduces the climb the next day over the Daldung La (3976m/13,044ft).

SIMIGOAN TO SINGHATI   [Map B]
Simigoan (2000m/6562ft)

This is a large agricultural village, spread way down the hillside: Sherpa in the higher parts and Tamang in the lower section. There are a couple of *campsites* (where it is also possible to stay inside and get a meal). Camping by the gompa offers superb views.

To leave Simigoan descend through the village and continue down. At the edge of a flattish cultivated area is a junction almost overlooking cliffs. It's worth asking someone around here to check that you're on the correct trail. Go right (north) here, descending steeply, writhing down a steep

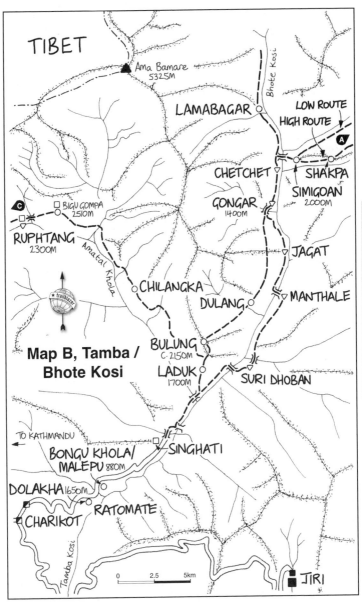

Map B, Tamba / Bhote Kosi

wide gully to the suspension bridge across the Bhote Kosi at 1520m/4987ft.

On the west bank, the trail to the north leads to Lamabagar/Chhogsham and the police post controlling traffic to Tibet. The trail to the south leads (in just a minute) to **Chetchet** and a *teashack*. The route down follows the impressive Bhote Kosi (Tibetan River) with the path, in places, held together by concrete. The tide marks on the river rocks show the height of the torrent that rages through during the monsoon. For this reason there's a second higher route to Gongar, used when the river is at its most dangerous, which branches up half an hour below Chetchet. Around here the waterfalls and the gorge are particularly impressive.

Gongar (1400m/4593ft)

This is just a small village but lodging is available. Around the corner, a few hundred metres upstream, is the bridge across the

Gongar Khola. On the main part of the far bank the trail divides: the lower path passing a huge house just below is for Charikot, while the upper path goes to Barabise (see opposite).

The trail roughly follows the river, sometimes traversing and sometimes with short climbs to avoid bluffs.

Jagat is approximately the half-way point to the old suspension bridge at **Manthale**. Here, particularly on the east bank, are some shops and frequently fruit, usually suntala (mandarin oranges), can be found.

The valley starts to widen out en route to Suri Dhoban.

Suri Dhoban / Dhovan (1020m/ 3346ft) has *teashacks* and *bhattis*. Across the fine suspension bridge up-valley is one of the trails for the route over the Yalung La, up the Khare Khola.

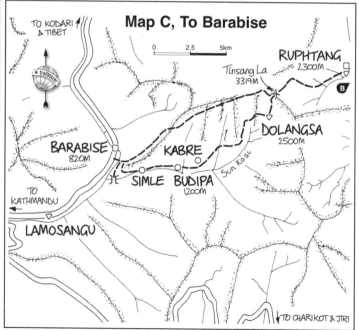

Map C, To Barabise

The route down passes a post office little bigger than a postage stamp. The trail continues more or less along the river bank and after a cluster of houses crosses to the west bank on a suspension bridge. At the Sangawa Khola is a small but often busy village with a *bhatti* or two.

Somewhere around here the name of the Bhote Kosi (Tibetan River) changes to the Tamba Kosi, or Copper River. The Tamba Kosi and the Sun Kosi, or Gold River are said to issue out of water spouts, one made of copper, and one of gold.

Singhati
This is where the road reaches, for now. It is a very rough 33km to Dolakha before the road improves, and in bad weather it may be impassable.

Dolakha (1650m/5413ft)
This is a beautiful and historic town with a few stupas and some flagstone-paved streets.

Once it was a main town on the trading route from Tibet to the Indian plains and it still has a **Saturday market**. There are at least three **buses** a day to Kathmandu at 6am, 8am and 10am.

Dolakha, sometimes also called Charikot, and the new Charikot further up the ridge share the title of headquarters for the Dolakha District, which stretches from here to the Tibetan border. Consequently there are a number of government departments. The latest addition is a modern **hospital** funded by Korea. The view alone is worth the visit.

GONGAR TO BARABISE
[Map B, p267; Map C]
This is one of the classic routes which has been superseded by the Jiri road, and is now almost redundant with the new road being built to Lambagar. As a route into the Rolwaling, it still has advantages because it offers a degree of helpful acclimatization. It's also little changed since the early days of trekking (apart from some lodge management training in 2008) and is very much a route suited to the expedition approach or to individual trekkers happy to eat dal bhaat and learn some Nepali.

Simigoan to Barabise is a pleasant four-day walk including perhaps a half-day rest at Bigu Gompa. It could be shortened to two-and-a-bit days by strong legs in a hurry.

Trekking peaks

INTRODUCTION
In 1981 the government of Nepal streamlined group climbing-permit applications for 18 mountains which it calls 'trekking peaks'. The name is not well-chosen: 'limited bureaucracy' peaks is more accurate because some of these peaks are actually challenging technical climbs but a handful are 6000m or c20,000ft peaks within the ability of the experienced hill-walker/hiker with a guide. The Nepal Mountaineering Association (NMA) handle the simplified paperwork and royalty (fee), although there are rumours this system might change in the next few years.

The idea behind the rules is that the expedition should be organized through a guide or better, a trekking company, and unless you are particularly independent and an experienced climber this is the better way. For many people the main decision is whether to go cheaply with a Nepali company or pay more for a Western-guided trip through an overseas operator.

Basically, unless you are an experienced climber who would prefer to lead and be responsible for everyone's safety you are better booking with a competent home-country adventure trekking company. The standard of Nepali mountain guides, even the NMA certified, is generally ordinary: only some 'guides' understand Western-standard safety practices and amazingly enough many Nepali guides, qualified or not, can't even belay, although they are generally skilled sirdars (organizers).

The best professional operators offer full expedition-style treks with experienced mountain guides and staff with medical training to ensure a safe trek. Expedition peaks are now also on a few company pro-grammes: Ama Dablam (6856m) is popular and so are the big peaks, Cho Oyu and Everest.

Expedition peaks could perhaps be called 'unlimited bureaucracy peaks': they require the completion of a lot of paperwork.

To climb or to explore

For climbers on a budget and on their first journey to Nepal the expenses of permits, getting gear over and getting it all to the base of the mountain add up. Realistically a climb with permits will add at least another $700-1000 per person. Then there is how to organize it. You will probably want some-one to haul all the gear to the last village and join you there but very few trekking companies will do this; naturally they pre-fer that you book a full trekking tour with them, sometimes lodge-based except for the climb, but mostly camping style. Even though the cost will be around $1500-2000 their service has a high chance of being ordinary. All this takes some setting up too.

For many people going exploring – rather than mountaineering – is a better option. There are lots of 5500-5800m peaks to scramble on and without climbing gear you can travel lighter. A few budget moun-taineers get a permit and simply take a porter or two from a company. To do this you should be confident of your organiza-tional and climbing ability.

Permits and costs

The procedure for obtaining a permit is streamlined in comparison to the peaks under the expedition system. It's possible to arrive in Kathmandu, organize a trekking-peak trip from scratch and be on the trail in only a day or two.

Expedition peaks – changes and charges

The expedition peak rules seem a work in progress and now royalties (fees) differ with the climbing season, with spring being normal, autumn being 50% cheaper (except Ama Dablam) and going in the winter saves 75%. Additionally there are now separate prices for a one-person permit, two-person permit etc all the way up to the once-standard seven-person permit.

For peaks in West Nepal there is no royalty and for peaks under 6500m no liai-son officer is required. This sounds ideal for smaller peaks but in reality the paper-work still amounts to an inch-thick file, and perhaps removing the royalty for peaks under 8000m, and simply putting a more simple congestion and garbage certification charge might be even more sensible.

Royalty costs – Spring

Number of climbers	6000-6500m	6501-6999m	7000-7500m	7501-7999m
1	$400	$1000	$1500	$2000
2	$500	$1200	$1800	$2400
3	$600	$1400	$2100	$2800
4	$700	$1600	$2400	$3200
5	$800	$1800	$2600	$3600
6	$900	$1900	$2800	$3800
7	$1000	$2000	$3000	$4000
Additional	$200	$300	$400	$500

For Group A peaks the royalty is a flat US$500 for up to and including seven members: each additional member is another US$100, up to a maximum of 12 on one permit. For the older Group B it is more complicated:

Group size	Rate	Additional rate per person
1-4 persons	US$350 only	–
5-8 persons	US$350	US$40
9-12 persons	US$510	US$25

Note: maximum number of members in team is 12.

An NMA-registered sirdar or climbing guide must accompany the group for the entire trek and climb.

Without a permit The new permit system means one or two people on a tight budget are hit for more money per person, yet joining another group of people who are probably also inexperienced is not the safest way to climb a mountain. The fine for climbing without a permit is double the climbing permit fee. Half of this goes to the sirdar who catches the illegal climbers, half to the NMA, so there is a powerful incentive for them to ask to see a permit. For a peak like Island Peak or Mera you will stand out from the other teams if you have just a porter or two; the climbing sirdars mostly know each other and know the companies everyone is working for. Climbing out of season on other peaks you are less likely to encounter trouble.

Ethically, lots of climbers disagree with a permit system, but you are guests in another country and they, of course, make the rules. The NMA's 'trekking peak' system is, however, at least better than India's and Pakistan's, where you have to take a liaison officer (LO) for any peak over 6000m. The money collected, too, has in the past sometimes been put to good use.

Nepal's **expedition peak system**, on the other hand, is run through the Ministry of Tourism and has similar rules to India and Pakistan. But whereas in India and Pakistan an LO does his/her job, in Nepal they don't, and the system is corrupt.

Equipment and safety
One man's prudence is another man's poison.
HW Tilman

If climbing as part of a trekking company group headed by a climbing guide, **harnesses and ropes** will be used on every one of the following peaks, whether for crevasse danger or steep slopes. If climbing without a guide, recognizing your **personal limits** is important. Some of these peaks are 'straightforward' but what this really means is that to be safe you don't need a shop's worth of karabiners, ice screws, snow-stakes and rock racks – just a partner, a rope, a few bits of protection, experience using this gear, good weather and an overriding urge to live.

The routes described below cover the least difficult way up some of the main trekking peaks in the region. For proficient technical alpinists none of the routes are particularly challenging under good conditions. For safety-conscious amateurs, they have potential to provide satisfaction and experience without excessive danger.

The officials involved with the permit system have always insisted that the procedures behind permits were for climbers' own safety, yet one of the best tools for increasing safety, **walkie talkies**, have ridiculous paperwork and fees surrounding their use. However, small cheap handheld radios are rarely noticed by the wrong people, so don't bother with the paperwork.

Itinerary planning
Heading straight up to high altitude for the first time, even if following the recommended guidelines, is usually a shock to everyone's system. The effort required for walking, let alone climbing, uphill at 5000m is much greater than you might think. By far the best approach to climbing trekking peaks or the mountaineering passes is to warm up first by heading high, say to Kala Pattar or the Gokyo viewpoints then down, sleeping a night or two much lower, eg Namche. Although this advice is not yet scientifically proven and the technique little-used, many climbers will attest to how much easier the next slog to high altitude is.

ROUTE GUIDE AND MAPS

Glacier preparation

Everyone on the rope should always carry prussik loops/jumars and be familiar with their use. If you fall in a crevasse and do the job properly, knocking yourself out, then rescue, particularly by only one partner, is an arduous, sometimes impossible, business requiring a pulley system and some gear. Crevasses can be completely invisible, especially in spring. Practise rescue moves and reacting quickly before entering dangerous territory and that worst-case scenario is unlikely to occur.

Avalanche danger

Just as the Himalayan mountains are the largest in the world, so too are some of the avalanches. They should be treated with similar respect. Debris cones are a tell-tale sign that avalanches are frequent. Try to avoid going within 300m of these. One of the most dangerous times for avalanches is early winter when there is a massive dump of snow. Parts of Island Peak Base Camp can be hit in these conditions. However, most of the avalanches in Nepal are not from snow, but from ice seracs and hanging

glaciers collapsing and worryingly, these can and do occur at any time, whether it has snowed recently or not. One would think that once a section has fallen, it is unlikely to fall again. This is usually wrong.

Technical climbing

Although some of the peaks are regularly climbed by groups many of the peaks are delightful technical mountaineering propositions. For more detailed information there's Bill O'Connor's dated and often less than accurate *The Trekking Peaks of Nepal*.

Trailblazer's new *Nepal Mountaineering Guide* (due late 2009) has full coverage of 25 peaks including most of the trekking peaks described here plus more technical climbs and even Everest.

IMJATSE / ISLAND PEAK (6173m/20,252ft)

The name was coined by Shipton, who thought this peak looked like 'an island in a sea of ice'. Finding a route to the top could be a challenge in itself were it not for the fact that as many as 25 people a day reach the summit during the busy season, October

---

Glaciers for the uninitiated

When falling snow doesn't melt quickly enough, it accumulates, consolidates and is compressed to ice. Its weight forces it slowly downhill, literally bull-dozing its way down to a warmer area where it melts.

The névé is the glacier's accumulation area (the Western Cwm below Everest, for example) where snow falls in avalanches from the steep walls to the basin below and is squashed to ice.

Next, as it moves down, it bends and catches on the valley walls, the uneven pressures forming cracks or crevasses. In the Himalaya these may be hundreds of metres deep, and in Greenland and Antarctica more than a kilometre. When snow falls, rather than fill the bottom of the crevasse it often sticks to the top of the sides forming cornices. Instead it can also, dangerously, cover the crack, sometimes with a snow bridge little stronger than a playing card.

Sometimes the ice drops down a steep slope and completely breaks up into a mess of building-sized blocks of ice, known as seracs. The icefall above Everest Base Camp is a good example. Here the danger is not so much the huge cracks but of being squashed flat by them as they fall. The Drolambao Icefall on the Tashi Labtsa route is particularly risky.

The big glaciers shovel rocks up on themselves, especially where they meet another glacier. These rocks appear to be held in gravity-defying poses – that is until you put your weight on one. Rocks tend to protect and extend the life of a glacier.

◆ IMJATSE PEAK SUGGESTED ITINERARY

Before attempting this peak it's essential to include an acclimatization trip (eg to Lobuche and Kala Pattar or any of the other Chukhung Valley peaks). The table shows the absolute minimum number of days required to allow for relatively safe acclimatization for most climbers. Night stops are shown. Note that it is better to spend more time in the region than this, if possible.

Day	Altitude guideline	Overnight stop	Actual altitude
01	2-3000m	Phakding/Monjo	2650m/2850m
02	2-3000m	Namche	3450m
03	3000m	Namche	3450m
04	3000m	Tengboche/Khumjung	3860m/3790m
05	3300m	Tengboche/Pangboche	3860m/4000m
06	3900m	Dingboche/Pheriche	4350m/4280m
07	3900m	Dingboche/Pheriche	4350m/4280m
08	4200m	Thuklha	4600m
09	4500m	Lobuche	4940m
10	4800m	Lobuche (Climb Kala Pattar)	4940m
11	4800m	Dingboche/Chukhung	4350m/4750m
12	5100m	Base Camp	5150m
13	5400m	Climb Imjatse	5150m
14		Extra day for safety	
15		Pangboche	
16		Namche	
17		Lukla	

to November. This does not, however, detract from the fact that it's a hard climb that many people fail to complete, either because of a badly-planned acclimatization itinerary, or because they set off too late in the morning or the winds become too strong. Occasionally deep snow makes even reaching the Base Camp difficult.

Chukhung to Base Camp (5150m/16,896ft)

This walk, on the well-defined track, accurately marked on the 1988 National Geographic map, takes a short afternoon. The long thin Base Camp area is a real cesspit despite being cleaned up occasionally. Other problems here include the frequent howling winds and a lack of water, sometimes only a trickle available a ten-minute walk above the camp near a couple of cairns on the rock fan south and above the Base Camp. As well as this it's not safe

to leave a tent unattended, not so much because things will be stolen (though this is starting to happen) but because of the birds. They seem to enjoy ripping through even the toughest of tents so leave them packed up and, with all your other gear, well covered with rocks or, much better, leave someone to mind the camp. The high camp suffers from this problem as well, and so does the 8000m South Col on Everest.

The route up

As early a start as possible is best: before dawn or at dawn at the latest. It can be a long day and the wind sometimes arrives just before lunch. From the high camps, leaving just as the sun hits may be sufficient.

A trail heads clearly up the hill and then branches into direct and zigzag yak routes up to the high camp which is a series of tent platforms in several groups. From the high camp beside the steep stream, ascend the dry gully immediately to the left of the stream. After about a 50m ascent (measured vertically), cross the gully with the (frozen) stream in it and traverse on one of several cairned trails continuing around to the right. It's important here to find one of the correct routes.

Do not continue ascending the gully or you'll come to a tricky white rock wall that is difficult to solo. Beware, also, of many misplaced cairns, some in the oddest of places. You should traverse around and continue ascending on black and brown rock to reach a further gully that steepens, bringing you onto the spur which shortly leads to the glacier.

There is a convenient spot to put on crampons but take care where you sit – it's amazing where some people have the audacity to shit. (If you really need to go here, do so on a rock and toss it off the north-east side, ie away from your water supply.) Well-acclimatized groups have occasionally set up a camp just on the snow. From here there should be a track threading through the maze of gaping holes and crossing snow bridges to the flat, but still lightly crevassed, glacier above.

If there's no clear track, route-finding can be difficult and possibly fatal without a rope. Head up the smooth, sometimes crevassed glacier and look for a line of weakness where the snow extends to the summit ridge. Beware of the bergschrund; often it is only barely visible and messy, ie easy and dangerous to fall into. The two general routes are either straight up (120-200m of fixed rope) or a diagonal traverse away from the summit. The wind can be savage on the ridge.

The summit ridge presents the last surprise. Once it was straightforward, but in the last few years it has broken up. It is essential to rope up for this section because what is underfoot can be loose and rotten. In total around 250m of fixed rope is required for this section.

The north ridge

Lots talk about it but few ever do it. Firm snow would make it a nice proposition with a rope and a few screws, stakes and a piton. Getting on/off the ablation valley by the Lhotse Shar Glacier can be tricky.

MERA PEAK (6476m/21,246ft)
[Map D]

Mera is one of the most popular of the trekking peaks and, despite being considered little more than a walk to the summit, it is also one of the most dangerous. It's often attempted by people who have flown in to Lukla and not given themselves adequate time to acclimatize. Several people each year pay for their lack of altitude awareness (or their foolhardiness) with their lives. See box pp276-7.

 Which Mera?

Since the turn of the millennium there has been some debate and confusion as to which peak exactly is the real Mera Peak. A discrepancy was noticed by a Finnish climber in the details given by the NMA; the latitude and longitude plus the altitude (which was noticed by many) didn't match the commonly climbed peak. Rather they pointed to another peak, labelled 'Mera' on Nepali maps, 8km to the north with a height of 6650m or 6648m. The alternative name for this peak is Peak 41.

After further research it turns out that the people who suggested and researched the peaks that became the NMA's 'trekking peaks' always meant Mera to be the 6476m peak: however, when more details were added to the list, the wrong details taken from the Nepali district maps were transferred. And that is how the error crept in.

In January 2002, Peak 41 appeared on the list of newly opened expedition peaks and it has now been climbed.

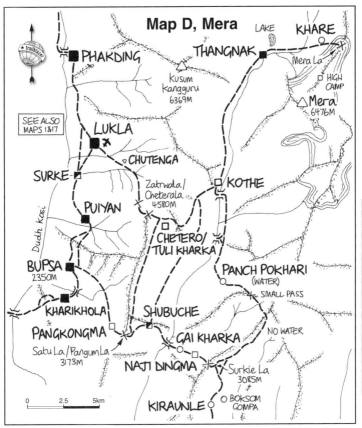

Map D, Mera

SEE ALSO MAPS 1&17

Once this area was wilderness, and was a full camping expedition. Now there are basic lodges all the way to, and including, Khare. Camping is still required on the mountain.

Some place names on the *Shorong/Hinku* Schneider map are incorrectly placed according to locals: Gondishung is often referred to as Orshela, Dupishung is Gondishung, Lungsamba is Dupishung and Lungsamba is the name for the whole region, not a single place name. Got it?

Over the Zatrwala La / Chetera La (4580m/15,026ft)

Note that the alternative Chilli La / Zatr Teng (4943m/16,217ft) is infrequently used, being steeper and higher and impractical for loaded porters. A number of groups have got into trouble trying to use this trail in, although it is occasionally used to exit the region.

The first camping place is often **Chutenga**. Although only three hours out of Lukla it's a sensible choice for the purposes of acclimatization.

MERA PEAK SUGGESTED ITINERARY

As with all climbs to 6000m or more careful acclimatization planning is critical but the hard reality is many companies, foreign and Nepali, use an itinerary that is bound to cause altitude problems. The added danger in the Mera area is that descent and a rapid exit are not always possible.

The ignorance of the trekking companies that sell expeditions based on the table opposite is hard to believe but many groups approximately follow this itinerary. Typically, out of a group of ten members two to four might make the summit, perhaps eight or nine will feel sick and two or three might not even make the Mera La. In most large groups at least one person will get ataxia and without immediate descent, death is only a day or so away.

If you do consider an expedition using this itinerary ensure that a PAC/Gamow bag, ie a portable altitude chamber, is carried and the guide is trained in its use. The Hinku and Hongu/Hunku areas are particularly isolated so groups planning to go faster than the recommended acclimatization rate MUST carry a Gamow bag and should have trained Western medical personnel with them who have altitude experience. In addition, all exits mean crossing a high pass.

There are many itinerary alternatives that provide better acclimatization preparation. If time is at a premium consider visiting Namche first or flying in to Phaplu and taking the alternative Pangkongma routes. While superior to the shortest itineraries these still bring you to altitude at a rate that is slightly too quick for some people; a course of Diamox may help. With more time why not walk in from Jiri (the bulk of the crew need only join you at Lukla) or for more adventure try the Salpa-Arun route via the Surkie La and Panch Pokhari. For better preparation, first trek to Kala Pattar then over the Amphu Labtsa. There are many more variations, the only limits are time and your imagination.

Once you have summited the peak it depends on where you get to that day as to how many days it will take to get back to Lukla.

Recommended itinerary

Day	Altitude Guideline	Overnight stop		Actual altitude
01	2-3000m	Phakding 2650m	Fly Lukla	2850m
02	2-3000m	Namche 3450m	Chutenga	3050m
03	3000m	Namche 3450m	Chutenga	3050m
04	3300m	Lukla 2850m	Mid/High camp	4100m/4200m

The **second camp** (or the first if the group is acclimatized) is at 4200m/13,780ft where there's the last reliable water source until well down the double pass. This area can be entirely snow-covered in March-April.

The trail traverses steep terrain but is straightforward if snow-free. In snow, however, it gets icy and several hundred metres

of handline for porters in a couple of spots is advisable.

Chetero/Tuli Kharka camp (4300m/ 14,107ft) is marked by a huge boulder that offers fine weather shelter for porters, and there is a simple porters' lodge as well. Beyond the views open up spectacularly. Half an hour on is another camping place, part of the same kharka and also with a

Recommended itinerary *(cont'd)*

Day	Altitude Guideline	Overnight stop		Actual altitude
05	3600m	Chutenga/High camp 3050m/4200m	Tuli Kharka	4300m
06	3900m	Tuli Kharka 4300m	Kothe	3500m
07	3900m	Kothe 3500m	Tuli Kharka	4300m
08	4200m	Thangnak (Tagnag) 4350m	Thangnak (Tagnag)	4350m
09	4500m	Thangnak (Tagnag) 4350m	Thangnak (Tagnag)	4350m
10	4800m	Khare 5000m	Dig Kharka	4750m
11	4800m	Khare 5000m	Khare	5000m
12	5100m	High Camp/Mera La 5800m/5400m	Khare	5000m
13	5400m	Summit, Mera La/Khare 5400m/5000m	High Camp/Mera La	5800m/5400m
14		Thangnak (Tagnag)	Mera La/Khare	5400m/5000m
15		Kothe		
16		Tuli Kharka		
17		Lukla		
18		Fly Kathmandu		

Dangerous itinerary
The following is a dangerous acclimatization planner as followed by many groups.
Do **not** book on such a trek.

Day	Altitude guideline	Overnight stop	Actual altitude
01	2-3000m	Fly Lukla, stay Chutenga	3050m
02	2-3000m	High camp	4200m
03	3000m	Tuli Kharka	4300m
04	3300m	Kothe	3500m
05	3600m	Thangnak (Tagnag)	4350m
06	3900m	Thangnak (Tagnag)	4350m
07	3900m	Khare	5000m
08	4200m	Mera La	5400m
09	4500m	High Camp	5800m
10	4800m	Khare	5000m
11	4800m	head out 3-4 days	

ROUTE GUIDE AND MAPS

huge boulder. The exposed trail is usually cairned although it descends several streams.

The next camp and a usual stopping place is **Kothe** (Kothé). The trail (in October, the expressway) alongside the Hinku Khola is small and confusing in a few places; follow porters who will know the most direct route. At first, views here on either side are not very inspiring – rough,

barren country – but ahead is the awesome Peak 43 (6769m/22,208ft) a real eye-catching pyramid and also a sacred mountain (and now open for mountaineering). Then the west face of Mera comes into view, sheer and horrible, but climbed once via a buttress by a Japanese expedition.

Thangnak/Tagnag (4350m/14,271ft)
(see p219) is a summer grazing area with the simplest **lodges** and shops beginning to

develop. It has been mis-named by myself
and others as Tagnag for years. An acclimatization day is essential here and a visit to
the Sabal Tsho or the cairn (5271m) on the
flanks of Kusum Kangguru can be rewarding, if the views are not reward enough
already.

It's a slog to **Khare 5025m/16,486ft**, a
regular camping spot, where another
acclimatization day or short trekking day is
necessary. For the energetic there are plenty of exploring possibilities. Alternative
camping spots are Dig Kharka or near the
snout of the Hinku Nup Glacier. There are
two trails on the western side of this glacier,
a higher one (for the lake) and a lower trail
that both lead around to near the Kangtaiga
Glacier.

Conditions on the climb to the Mera
La (5415m/17,766ft) are variable. When
the glacier is dry and the crevasses open, it
presents few problems but in new snow a
rope (at the very least for the leaders) is
essential. A camp may be made either on
top of the savagely windy pass, or slightly
the other side, but even with a slow ascent
it's likely that you'll suffer the effects of the
altitude. Porters without crampons should
be watched and assisted; indeed, it is better
they are not up there at all.

Climbing Mera Peak
It is particularly important for the climbing
leader to assess the crevasse dangers for the
climb to the Mera La, to the high camp and
to the summit. The majority of Nepali
guides are far too gung-ho. If the glacier ice
is hard and with a packed trail over it, the
risk of falling in a crevasse is low, but not
quite zero. If it has snowed recently or there
is soft snow without a trail you **must** rope

up; quite a number of people have fallen
into crevasses here.

The standard route up is through a
potentially dangerous crevassed area to the
top of the rock band, marked by a large
cairn. Here it's possible to establish a high
camp either in the snow or on the rock at
5800m. From here the views are outstanding, with Everest, Makalu, Cho Oyu and
more piercing the skyline.

In recent years especially as the season
progresses into November and December,
the snow has almost completely melted off
the glacier leaving hard bare ice. Even with
crampons caution is required as they don't
always grip, especially if the points are
blunt.

Mera has two summits: the easier one
attempted by most groups is accessed by
taking a higher line to the eastern 6461m/
21,197ft peak, with its steep last 20m or so;
the true 6476m/21,246ft summit can either
be reached by a drop and traverse – beyond
many people by this stage – or by initially
taking a more westerly lower line out of the
high camp for a steep haul to the true summit. Note that both these routes are
crevassed.

Approaching Mera from the Surkie La
There are two routes to the Surkie La: from
Hille/Tumlingtar via the Arun Kosi, or via
Bupsa from Jiri or Phaplu.

The trail junction, a little east of the
Surkie La, is by a crumbling mani wall and
soon leads on to the high and pleasant
ridge, passing through pastures. A couple of
these are suitable for camping if water is
available.

The holy lakes of **Panch Pokhari** (see
box below), where there is a Hindu shrine,

Bring your mother-in-law
Panch Pokhari (meaning five lakes) is a holy area where pilgrims gather on
the holy days of Baisakh Purne and Rishi Tarpani. There are five holy lakes in
the area, believed to be father, mother, two sons and a daughter-in-law. The mother
pond is believed to seek sacrifices from those persons who come near it.

also offer good camping but from the Surkie La they would be a rapid ascent to do in one day. Finding your way out of the lakes area is a little tricky. The trail now contours in and out of numerous gullies where, if the monsoon run-off has dried up, there is no water until the Mojang Khola/Drangka and quite a descent to the Hinku Khola.

You can cross the bridge to Tashing Ongma or go up the valley to Mosom Kharka, where there's another bridge and a camping area. The trail then crosses the Hinku on temporary bridges, joining the regular route from Lukla near Kothe.

Approaching Mera from the Satu La / Pangum La

This is an alternative to the standard route over the Zatrwala if coming from Jiri or Phaplu or even from Lukla. Although the route from Lukla is longer, it does give useful acclimatization time.

The route to the Pangum La is covered on p259; from here, just east of the pass is a trail that follows the ridge. This route is used occasionally but it is not always obvious. It joins the Lukla–Chetero La/Zatrwala approach around Chetero/Tuli Kharka.

The trail from Shubuche

Between 1998 and 2000 a new trail was constructed from Shubuche to Kothe (Kothé) making it easier to supply Thangnak (Tagnag) from the south, and easier to enter or exit.

From Shubuche ask the way to the beginning of the new trail. In sections the trail is narrow and steep, difficult in rain. Nungsar, a kharka surrounded by rhododendrons and magnolia trees, is a good camping spot with water. It is a couple of hours away on a trail that winds around big spurs. It is best to stay here and plan with that in mind because the next reliable camping place, Chautra Khola, is perhaps seven hours' walk away.

The trail climbs switchbacks on a rocky and sometimes narrow path to a height of around 3250m before undulating through the rhododendron forest. After approximately one and a half hours there is a steep, sometimes treacherous descent to a waterfall and landslide area, a good spot for lunch. The trail now winds around to a steep climb up stone steps. At the top of the ridge is a sign stating three hours to Chautra Khola; there is a small campsite here with enough room for perhaps three tents. Three hours of slogging and climbing does indeed bring you to a small waterfall and bridge.

Approximately three minutes after crossing is a small turnoff that leads to the campsite, which has enough room for a single group. Alternatively by the waterfall there are a few small spots and some caves. From here it is approximately four hours at a group pace to the main trail from Lukla and a further three hours to Kothe.

After Mera

Some groups backtrack or head to Lukla for a quick exit. The more daring head east down the Mera La then north to reach the Khumbu via the Mingbo La (5866m/19,245ft; see p224), or into the Chukhung Valley via the Amphu Labtsa (5787m/18,986ft).

Note that the logistics of getting fully laden porters over the Amphu Labtsa early on in the expedition are difficult. It's easier later in the trip when the majority of the supplies have been consumed and packs are lighter.

LOBUCHE PEAK (6105m/20,029ft) [Map 6, p199]

This is the hardest of the trekking peaks that ordinary commercial groups attempt and while many clients attain the ridge top, virtually none attain the false summit, and never the real summit.

There are two routes to **Base Camp**. If you're coming down from Lobuche, where the track to Thukla crosses the creek, stay instead on the west bank. From the first flat area, that valley ascends to the Base Camp area via a short rope pitch. To reach Base Camp without using a rope continue around the huge spur between Tsola Tso (Tshola

Tsho) and Thukla and at the large, roughly flat area a cairned track heads up the valley. The Base Camp is pleasant with lots of snow for water.

Good conditions and a dawn or pre-dawn start are essential for **the climb**. The average angle for the entire climb is not steep but there are some areas of messy ser-acs that require two axes, front pointing and belaying. The ridge route is sometimes eas-ier. Many people stop at the top of the ridge thinking this is the false summit. It isn't; continue on the knife-edged ridge (groups fix a rope) to the false summit, if you are game.

PARCHARMO (6273m/20,580ft)
[Map A, p265]

There is some confusion over the height of Parcharmo. The height given on the Schneider maps is 6273m, the Nepal Mountaineering Association state the height to be 6187m/20,298ft and surveyors on the first expeditions calculated it to be 6318m/20,700ft. However, it's over the magic numbers 6000m and 20,000ft.

There's a reasonable view of the least difficult route up as you approach Parcharmo and from the Tashi Labtsa, but a cursory glance here may lead you to under-estimate the difficulties. Although at mod-est angle, the access to the ridge is crevassed and, further up, seracs tower. Basic equipment should include a rope (or two) with a few stakes and screws, and two tools (at least for the leader).

POKALDE/DOLMA RI (5794m/ 19,009ft)

When snow-free and with clear weather, the top of Pokalde is a great place to have lunch. Although below 6000m or 20,000ft, the view is reward enough for a few hours' scrambling.

There are **two routes**: there's a splen-did base camp by the lakes below the Kongma La. From this large lake pick up a small trail that leads to the small lake to the east, which isn't visible until you have climbed a bit. Then scramble over glacier-smoothed rock to a trail up the **east ridge**.

Approaching the top of the peak the going gets more difficult and less experienced climbers may want a hand line or other help. Rather than climbing directly up it is easier to swing around the top pinnacle and approach from another side.

The **north ridge** route runs directly up from the Kongma La and is a little more hazardous. There are some exposed moves, requiring steady feet and nerves, that pru-dent climbers would not attempt solo. Safer would be to take 10m of cord (or a real rope), a sling harness, a couple of slings and a tool or two.

If there's no snow lying around then both routes are solid rock, but beside a sec-tion of the north ridge is an ice/snow slope that is convenient to climb with crampons and axe. If there is snow, the conditions are infinitely more variable, requiring a real rope.

Kyazo Ri / Kyajo Ri / Gyajok Ri (6189m/20,300ft)

The least difficult climbing route is accessed up the magical Kyajo valley, although it has also been attempted from the Bhote and Gokyo valleys too. It has proved to be a tough peak to climb, but the challenges are mainly logistical. Acclimatize elsewhere then plan a week or more up the valley. See p227 for the trek-in to the valley.

After the successive rock steps is a glaciated area, camp somewhere here, if possible, with the climbing route mostly visible. Consider whether you want to camp near the base of the peak for the ear-liest, best start. Once climbing on the snow slopes, the trickiest section is some smooth rock bulges, a third of the way up. It is moderately steep, that sort of angle that makes it awkward in crampons; rock shoes would be useful for the leader, but consider the cold. Fixing around 100m of rope here might be sensible. Good luck!

OTHER TREKKING PEAKS IN THE REGION

● **Kongma Tse (5817m/19,084ft)** (see Map 11, p223) Originally called Mehra, this can be climbed from either the east side or from the south. The south route from the superb camping spot below the Kongma La goes up beside the glacier, at times on slippery rocks, then continues on steep rock to the summit ridge. A rope (plus limited gear) is widely considered necessary.

● **Ramdung-Go (5930m/19,455ft)** (see Map A, p265) Usually climbed from the north and combined with a crossing of the Tashi Labtsa. The southern approach is long, difficult to follow and crevassed but otherwise isn't technical.

● **Kongde (6187m/20,298ft)** Seldom attempted. It's a serious climb, not a scrambling peak and requires a stocked rock rack and bivvy gear.

● **Kusum Kangguru (6369m/20,895ft)** This is rarely climbed; its razor ridges provide a challenge for the serious and well-prepared.

Unclassified peaks

These peaks are not on the expedition list yet are interesting mountains to attempt. The prudent might get a permit for one of the nearby trekking peaks, such as one of the Lobuche peaks.

● **Kangchung Shar / Pyramid (6103m/ 20,023ft) and Kangchung Nup (6089m/ 19,975ft)**
The twin peaks of Kangchung (see map p209) are eye-catching from all the high points around the Gokyo region, sticking up like islands from the surroundings. The Sherpa name means 'small mountain'. Maps mark a pass between the peaks and approaching from the south is fairly straightforward up an icefall. The north side, however, is impossible, not a pass at all.

The eastern Kangchung (Shar) is, if viewed from Dza Bua (Knobby View; see p264), a steep pyramid. Camping on the col will give the best chance of success. The angle of the snow on the face changes season to season, perhaps depending on wind loading. However, expect the steepest pitch to be around 60°, and an average of 40° or so.

The west (Nup) peak is best attempted from a rock saddle south-west of Surprise Lake. This rock ridge meets the snow summit ridge and in good conditions is a fairly straightforward climb to this point: the fun begins from there. The whole area is a delight to explore. These peaks are not yet on the trekking or expedition peak lists.

● **Changri Lho (6189m/20,304ft) and pass (5690m/18667ft)** Slightly north of the Tsho La/Cho La/Chugyima La is another pass, one that was used for crossing with yaks until the snow level dropped. It is considerably higher, but except for variable conditions for the last 10m, is quite straightforward. The approaches are gentle although crevassed.

From the Gokyo side access the glacier by skirting under the Kangchung Shar peak. On the Dzonglha side the route is lightly cairned to the glacier. From the pass itself it is possible to ascend Changri Nup (unnamed on most maps). The ridge is a series of seracs and under most conditions requires some ice-climbing gear.

ROUTE GUIDE AND MAPS

APPENDIX A: ITINERARIES

The trail guide was deliberately not written on a 'Day 1, Day 2' basis to encourage trekkers to travel at their own pace and not stop all in the same places. Some guidelines are, however, necessary for overall planning. Overnight stops are given in the tables below.

ACCLIMATIZATION PLANNER

Awareness of the time taken for your body to acclimatize is the key to planning itineraries in this region. Although the process of acclimatization begins even at altitudes as low as Kathmandu (1400m), planning only becomes important if heading above 3000m. The usually ignored medical recommendation is that a minimum of two to three days (and better four to five days) should be taken to reach 3000m or 10,000ft, followed by a daily altitude gain of 300m or 1000ft with a rest day every 900m or 3000ft, as shown on the table below.

Some people acclimatize slower than others but you should find that your body will tolerate deviations of plus or minus approximately 300m from these figures. Larger deviations may bring on symptoms. For example, if after Night 8 at 4200m/13,779ft you spend Night 9 at 5000m, this may cause some symptoms, although sometimes a night later. Spending Night 8 at 4800m/15,748ft, however, is much less likely to bring on mild AMS especially if you stay a further night there to synchronize with the table again.

Night		Night		Night	
00	below 2000m/6562ft	05	3600m/11,811ft	10	4800m/15,748ft
01	2-3000m/6562-9842ft	06	3900m/12,795ft	11	4800m/15,748ft
02	2-3000m/6562-9842ft	07	3900m/12,795ft	12	5100m/16,732ft
03	3000m/9842ft	08	4200m/13,779ft	13	5400m/17,716ft
04	3300m/10,827ft	09	4500m/14,764ft		

LUKLA TO NAMCHE

The table below shows the safe rate of ascent if you have flown from Kathmandu (1400m) to Lukla (2850m). The recommended maximum altitude for each day (as laid down by AMS specialists) is indicated. Ascending above Namche in four days, which is the schedule followed by most trekking companies, has been shown to cause troublesome mild AMS in about 50% of trekkers. Diamox will help – as mentioned rather too many times.

	Altitude guideline*	Itinerary 1	Itinerary 2	Unwise option
01	2-3000m	Phakding/Monjo 2650m	Lukla 2850m	Phakding/Monjo
02	2-3000m	Namche 3450m	Phakding/Monjo	Namche
03	3000m	Namche	Namche	Namche
04	3300m	Namche	Namche	(higher)
05	3600m	(higher)	(higher)	

ALTERNATIVE ROUTES TO NAMCHE

	Jiri (sedate*)	Jiri (rapid)	Phaplu (medium)	Tumlingtar (sedate/medium)
01	Kathmandu–Jiri (bus)	Kathmandu–Jiri (bus)	Kathmandu–Phaplu§ (plane)	Kathmandu–Tumlingtar (plane)
02	Shivalaya	Bhandar	Jubing	Balawa
03	Bhandar	Sete (short day)	Surke	Phedi
04	Sete	Junbesi	Monjo	Sanam (long day)

ALTERNATIVE ROUTES TO NAMCHE *(cont'd)*

	Jiri (sedate*)	Jiri (rapid)	Phaplu (medium)	Tumlingtar (sedate/medium)
05	Junbesi	Kharikhola	Namche	Bung
06	Junbesi (rest)	Chourikharka	Najing	Naji Dingma
07	Nuntala	Namche		Pangkongma
08	Kharikhola			Surke
09	Puiyan			Monjo
10	Phakding			Namche
11	Namche			

* or group pace   § overnight at Ringmo

Note that it's possible to get from Jiri to Namche in four days but only if you are extremely fit. To walk from Kathmandu to Tumlingtar takes three to four days. For Tumlingtar to Namche, whether you are fast or slow, allow 10 days.

NAMCHE TO LOBUCHE / GOKYO

For acclimatization, you should spend two nights at Namche (or three if you flew to Lukla), two nights at Tengboche or similar altitude and two nights at Dingboche or Pheriche, before reaching Lobuche and attempting Kala Pattar. Note that an alternative to spending three nights at Namche is to spend just two nights there and an extra night at somewhere near Lukla.

	Altitude guideline*	Itinerary 1	Itinerary 2	Itinerary 3
00	(additional night at Namche for people who flew to Lukla)			
01	3000m	Namche 3450m	Namche	Namche
02	3300m	Namche	Namche	Namche
03	3600m	Tengboche 3860m/ Khumjung 3790m	Tengboche/ Khumjung	Namche/Khumjung or Thame
04	3900m	Tengboche/Pangboche	Pheriche 4280m	Phortse/Phortse Tenga
05	3900m	Dingboche/Pheriche	Pheriche	Dole 4040m
06	4200m	Dingboche/Pheriche	Duglha 4600m	Machermo§ 4410m
07	4500m	Lobuche 4940m	Lobuche	Gokyo 4750m
08	(day)	up Kala Pattar	up Kala Pattar	up Gokyo Ri
08	4800m	Lobuche	Lobuche	Gokyo
09	(down)	Tengboche	Pangboche	Phortse Tenga/ Namche
10	(down)	Namche	Namche	Lukla
11	(down)	Lukla	Lukla	

This acclimatization plan seems to work quite well for most people but obviously the more time spent acclimatizing, the better you will feel. Conversely if you cut out just one of the nights listed above the risk of minor altitude sickness greatly increases.

* The altitude guideline shows the fastest recommended rate of ascent.

§ or Pangka

GRAND TOUR – NAMCHE TO CHUKHUNG, LOBUCHE & GOKYO

	Itinerary 1 (long)	Itinerary 2 (short)	Itinerary 3 (reverse)
00	(additional night at Namche for people who flew to Lukla)		
01	Namche	Namche	Namche
02	Namche	Namche	Namche
03	Tengboche/Khumjung	Tengboche/Khumjung	Namche/Khumjung/Thame
04	Pangboche/Tengboche	Pangboche/Tengboche	Phortse/Phortse Tenga
05	Dingboche	Dingboche	Dole
06	Dingboche/ Chukhung Ri	Dingboche	Machermo/Pangka
07	Chukhung	Lobuche/ Kala Pattar	Gokyo/ Gokyo Ri
08	Dingboche/Duglha	Lobuche	Gokyo
09	Lobuche/ Kala Pattar	Pangboche/Phortse	Gokyo/ Gokyo area
10	Lobuche	Machermo/Gokyo	Gokyo
11	Pangboche/Tsho La	Gokyo	Phortse/Tsho La
12	Machermo/Gokyo	Gokyo	Pheriche/Dingboche
13	Gokyo Around Gokyo	Phortse/Dole	Lobuche/ Kala Pattar
14	Gokyo	Namche/Monjo/Phakding	Lobuche
15	Phortse/Dole	Lukla	Tengboche
16	Namche		Namche/Monjo/Phakding
17	Namche		Lukla
18	Lukla		

RETURN – NAMCHE TO JIRI OR TO THE ARUN

	Itinerary 1 (medium)	Itinerary 2 (rapid)	Itinerary 3 (sedate)	Itinerary 4 (rapid)
00	Namche	Namche	Namche	Namche
01	Surke	Puiyan	Surke	Puiyan
02	Nuntala	Trakshindo	Pangum	Shubuche
03	Junbesi	Tragdobuk	Najing Dingma	Bung
04	Kenja	Bhandar	Bung	Salpa/Thulofokte
05	Shivalaya	Jiri	Sanam	Balawa Besi
06	Jiri		Phedi	past Tumlingtar
07			Balawa Besi	Leguwa Ghat
08			Tumlingtar	
09			Leguwa Ghat	

APPENDIX B: HEALTH

Special thanks to Dr Helena Swinkels at CIWEC Clinic, Kathmandu for thoroughly reviewing this section, but there is of course no liability implied.

STAYING HEALTHY WHILE TREKKING

In developed countries we take for granted treated drinking water, hygienically packaged food and comprehensive sewage systems, none of which exist in the villages of Nepal. New arrivals to Asia will be lucky to escape a visit to Nepal without some form of upset stomach, although in some cases this is relatively mild and can clear up of its own accord. Trekking for a long period and in extreme conditions involves new challenges, particularly with the high altitude nature of the trek. This comprehensive section has been thoroughly researched to help you cope with these environments.

Given the high likelihood of getting sick you should be prepared with your own small personal drugs kit. Most of the drugs are prescription medicines and some are expensive; it is much less hassle to put together a kit in Kathmandu where you can buy most of them directly from a pharmacy.

DIET

The food you will eat in the mountains is generally nutritious and healthy. The diet is carbohydrate-weighted and, intriguingly, a high carbo diet seems to slightly reduce AMS. Protein comes mainly from eggs, nuts, beans and dal and on a long trek getting enough protein becomes important.

The diet is short on fibre, which comes mostly from fruits, vegetables and legumes, and many people get constipated while they are trekking. Bringing dried fruits as snacks and focusing on vegetables when ordering can help avoid this. Some people who have a tendency to constipation should bring some metamucil with them. Walking every day, breathing harder and the cold at higher altitudes all mean that you'll burn far more calories than normal. Don't be afraid to eat as much as you like! A vitamin tablet every day or two will do no harm and women may want to take an iron supplement too.

Snack frequently to avoid hypoglycaemia (getting low on energy); always carry some spare energy bars with you. Be sure to drink plenty too. Alcohol should be drunk in moderation, if at all at altitude, and while a good cup of tea or hot lemon is refreshing, drinking a good volume of fluids means drinking plain water; a glass of hot water can also be surprisingly pleasant, as can swigging icy cold mountain water.

DIARRHOEA

This is a common problem in developing countries, especially Nepal, and few trekkers escape without contracting some stomach disorder. Ideally, you should visit a good doctor for a stool test if it doesn't clear up in a few days. While trekking, however, this is impossible so some self-diagnosis may be necessary.

The causes are many, only some of which are in your control, so even people who are particularly careful still sometimes get sick. While on the trail it seems to make little difference whether you trek with an expedition-style group package or stay in lodges. Most group cooks working for the bigger agencies have completed a basic hygiene course. Their assistants, however, usually have not and the conditions under which food is prepared are far from perfect. Most lodge owners have attended basic hygiene courses: their working conditions are better, they attempt less-adventurous dishes and their hygiene has improved significantly in the last decade. The last often overlooked factor is your own personal hygiene and contact with paper money and other items that harbour bacteria.

During the winter months there is much less sickness: April, May and June are probably the worst months because of the more numerous flies; even if you eat only in the best restaurants that are serious about cleanliness at this time, you may still get sick.

In Kathmandu it pays to be particularly cautious with water. The normal town supply water comes through pipes that are uncomfortably close to sewage pipes, and sometimes both are broken. Some hotels use water pumped from the ground, which is becoming increasingly contaminated too.

Many people over-react and start taking medication at the first loose stool. Diarrhoea will not normally kill you so urgent treatment is neither necessary nor always recommended. If not too troublesome it's better to wait a few days and see if it goes away on its own. Do drink lots of water and listen to your body: if you feel hungry, eat, and if you don't, take soup and light foods. If the diarrhoea is particularly severe or still troublesome after a few days and you are fairly sure what type it is you may want to treat it. Unless the diarrhoea is particularly severe there is no need to stop trekking.

The bugs that cause diarrhoea can be divided into a few categories: parasites (amoebas and giardia which travel as cysts), bacteria and viruses. Giardia and amoebic dysentery are caused by a protozoan that survives outside the gut in a tough protective shell, and are vulnerable to similar drugs. Similarly the many different bacteria that cause bacterial diarrhoea are all killed by a separate class of drugs. Surprisingly the exact cause of over 20% of cases of diarrhoea is as yet unknown. So first decide if the diarrhoea fits one of the descriptions then consider whether you want to treat it. Even when treating with drugs you can expect only about an 80% chance of being cured rapidly. If the drugs don't work the diarrhoea will normally clear by itself with time.

Precautions
There are two basic schools of thought: one is that you may be able to avoid an upset stomach if you are extremely careful. This involves only drinking purified/boiled/bottled water (including for brushing your teeth), avoiding salads and other uncooked food and only eating fruit that you have peeled. Only eat meat that has been well cooked. Eat only with cutlery (not your hands), and off plates and glasses that were served dry. Wash your hands carefully or, better still, use the water-free hand cleaning gels. You should only eat in the best restaurants in Kathmandu. This can be an appropriate strategy for a shorter visit, but even taking all of these precautions you still might get sick.

For a stay of more than a few days in Kathmandu, though, this becomes impractical but it would still be a good idea to eat salads sparingly, use only purified/boiled/bottled water, and eat at the cleaner-looking restaurants.

If trekking with an expedition-style kitchen crew, the sirdar or leader should give a good pre-trek hygiene briefing to the crew and regularly check that the kitchen is clean. Many less educated Nepalis don't realise that there are germs that you can't see. Towels should be cleaned regularly or everything air-dried. The best solution is the new gel hand cleaners that don't require any water but don't expect the trekking company to provide these.

Once you are hit
Take it easy and drink oral rehydration solutions or less fizzy soft drinks. Some people subscribe to the idea that you should 'starve' diarrhoea. From a scientific point of view this is wrong, though if you do feel like eating, do so in moderation; if you don't feel like eating, don't – but do drink enough. Certainly plain food seems easier on the stomach, but that doesn't mean you should limit yourself to bananas, toast or plain rice; just avoid food that is spicy or oily.

Occasionally if you're afflicted with a stomach bug, eating or drinking will induce an immediate run to the bathroom. Don't worry about this, it is a normal reaction and if you eat after this, normally your body will accept food.

Stoppers

All the drugs that fix the root cause of diarrhoea are prescription medicines so doctors commonly hand out Imodium or Loperamide (Lomitil), drugs that simply stop you up, but don't fix the root cause. These drugs can be useful if you need to take a long bus journey but in a lot of cases by following the instructions, you might be stopped up for a week. So either avoid them or use them carefully. Don't use them in case of dysentery (diarrhoea with blood and mucus in it).

Travellers' / bacterial diarrhoea

If you are new to Asia you will have to be lucky to escape a bout of 'Travellers' diarrhoea'. The onset is often preceded or accompanied by a fever and/or chills, nausea and cramps followed by fairly sudden, frequent, watery diarrhoea. It is this reasonably sudden onset that distinguishes a bacterial diarrhoea from others. Sometimes people feel off-colour for a day, usually with a light fever or chills; then only a day or so later, the diarrhoea strikes.

The cause is usually eating food or drinking water that is contaminated with strains of bacteria different to those that your body is used to, or simply plain nasty bacteria, and is responsible for roughly 80% of diarrhoea cases in Nepal. It could be from flies, dirty money, your own habits, the cooks' habits, dirty water, a less than spotless kitchen – there are a multitude of possibilities.

Treatment The sooner you take drugs, the quicker you will be better – assuming that you do actually have a bacterial diarrhoea. And this is the reason to consider taking drugs to cure it. The alternative is to wait for your body to fight it off: the diarrhoea should lessen in a few days, and after another few be gone. Occasionally if you are weakened or at high altitudes bacterial diarrhoea can take a long time, 7-10 days, to go away by itself. The most effective treatment is to begin a short course of Norfloxacin or Ciprofloxacin.

Dosages For Norfloxacin, 400mg, every 12 hours, for 3 days. For Ciprofloxacin, 500mg every 12 hours for 3 days. In most cases you will begin to feel better in around 12 hours, and should be back to normal after perhaps 24-36 hours. If you are not better after 36 hours you don't have bacterial diarrhoea (or the bacteria was drug-resistant).

It is possible to use these drugs prophylactically but while this strategy can work against bacterial diarrhoeas, as with all drugs longer term use often has real side effects so is not recommended except in special cases.

Food poisoning

Symptoms 'I don't feel so good' or turning white and then 'uh-oh, I need the bathroom **now**'. This comes on suddenly and severely about two to eight hours after eating contaminated food. It is more usual to vomit repeatedly first then sometimes spout both ends but occasionally it can be explosive diarrhoea only. Often it strikes at night; you'll be thankful if you have an attached bathroom. Luckily, the misery usually lasts 4-12 hours and recovery is quick, though you will probably feel weakened.

The classic cause is pre-cooked food that has been infected when allowed to sit. It is also sometimes thought to be from contamination in the fluffy egg-white-based cake icings. Sometimes it can strike all the eaters of a meal, but sometimes only one person is affected, ie there is only one small area of contamination on the food.

Food poisoning is not an infection of the body so there are no drugs that can help – the body just has to eject all the contaminated food and rid itself of the toxin. Resting and drinking plenty of fluids helps. Oral rehydration solutions and soft drinks (shaken after opening to reduce the fizz) are helpful.

Irritated bowels

The payback for eating chilli the night before is to wake up early the next morning for a long dump; once the offending chillies are flushed out, however, relief quickly follows.

Rich curry gravies, too, are made with plenty of ghee or oil that sometimes lubricates the bowels rather too well, especially with a few too many lagers.

There are many other causes for mildly irritated bowels that can cause some uncomfortableness or diarrhoea. Many drugs, even the ones to fix diarrhoea, can cause loose stools. A change in diet, time zones and stress all can affect your body unpredictably.

After a bout of diarrhoea has ended, whether by drugs or by time, your system can still be sensitive, gassy and not particularly regular for quite a period afterwards. In other words if you are back to defecating roughly once a day but your movement isn't quite normal, don't, in general, worry. Sometimes staying off coffee helps.

Giardia

This generally takes 7-10 days to develop and does not come on suddenly. The classic often-quoted symptoms are sulphurous (rotten egg) smelling farts and burps but this does not necessarily mean giardia: these are just as common in bacterial infections and are therefore not useful whatsoever in coming to a diagnosis.

Distinguishing symptoms are a churning, upset stomach, bloating, cramps, and on-off diarrhoea. Nausea (without vomiting) and fatigue are normal. There is usually no fever, chills or vomiting. Frequently the sickness follows a pattern: an uncomfortable stomach or mild diarrhoea after food, often in the morning, for a few days, followed by a day or two of feeling relatively better. This pattern alternates, sometimes with a bit of constipation in between, but gradually the trend is to worsening symptoms.

Giardia can also be virtually symptomless: just a slightly rumbling stomach with occasional soft stools or even constipation. Some forms may go away on their own after several weeks but treatment is usually required. If you have been in Nepal (or India) for less than a week, it is extremely unlikely you have giardia.

Giardia is caught from infected water, especially from washing salads in Kathmandu and from high mountain streams near areas where yaks graze.

Treatment There's a choice of two drugs: Tinidazole (Tiniba), of which the dose is 2 grams, ie 4 x 500mg, taken all at once. It's better taken in the evening because the usual side effects (nausea and a strong metallic taste in the mouth) may be slept off. Do not mix with alcohol: other medications in this class of drug are used to get alcoholics off alcohol by provoking a sometimes violent reaction. Take the same dose again 24 hours later.

Alternatively Flagyl / Metronidazole may be used but is harder on the body. The dose is 250mg, three times a day for 5 to 7 days. This should also not be mixed with alcohol.

Amoebic diarrhoea

An amoebic infection usually has similar symptoms to giardia, with a low-grade diarrhoea alternating with days of being normal or even constipated – symptoms that can almost, but not quite be ignored. Fatigue and weight loss are common over time. Most infections with amoeba are actually without symptoms, but the illness can vary greatly in severity – though the sudden onset of bloody diarrhoea, like some bad bacterial diarrhoeas, is rare. It can also be dormant for a time and recur months later. Only about 1% of all diarrhoea cases are caused by amoeba. Amoebas are easily confused with other things that are commonly found in diarrhoea and so is highly overdiagnosed at most clinics in Nepal (except CIWEC! see p118). You will often be recommended to take treatment for amoebic infection (Tinidazole 2g daily on each of three days) by drug-store owners and doctors, even though it is unlikely you have it. Proven infection needs to be followed by a second medication called Dilamide to completely clear it from the system.

(Opposite) Top: The popular Buddhist prayer chant *Om Mani Padme Hum* is carved onto countless flat stones and slates (mani stones, see p140) and painted onto chortens.
Bottom: Weaving a doko, the basket used by porters, from split bamboo.

Viral diarrhoea

At least 10% of diarrhoea is caused by viruses. Similar to the common cold, drugs can't fix the root problem, instead your body just has to fight it, and after a couple of days you should begin to feel better and after perhaps five days it should have cleared up.

Cyclospora

Any diarrhoea between April and September that doesn't clear up with the above drugs could be cyclospora (see below). You should consult a doctor in Nepal. The cure is Cotrimoxazole.

WATER PURIFICATION

Part of avoiding diarrhoea is drinking clean water. All water from taps, streams and rivers in Nepal (even at high altitudes) could be contaminated to some degree and should not be considered safe to drink without purification. Only spring water and water made from clean snow is safe without being treated. There are several methods of purifying water but first it helps to know who your enemies are. The most difficult to kill of the various pathogens are the cysts that cause cyclospora, giardia and amoebic dysentery; even just one or two cysts can cause disease. These can survive in very cold water for several months and can even survive when the water freezes. High concentrations of chemicals are required to penetrate their protective shell. They are, however, killed immediately by bringing water to the boil. Bacteria and viruses are less resilient. Larger numbers are needed before infection occurs and they are destroyed by very low concentrations of chemicals.

Boiling

Water that has been brought to the boil, even at 5000m/16,404ft, is safe to drink. It need only be pasteurized (heating to 75°C/162F, or 68°C for 10 minutes), not sterilized (boiling for 10 minutes). At 5800m/19,000ft water boils at around 81°C/177°F so hot drinks, like tea, coffee and hot lemon etc, are all safe.

Iodine-based methods

● **Iodine tablets** The active ingredient is tetraglycine hydroperiodide. If the water is very cold allow 30 minutes rather than the usual 10; if it is cloudy double the dose (ie 2 tablets per litre). These tablets are convenient and easy to use but only sometimes available in Kathmandu. The recommendation for water that is possibly giardia-contaminated is two tablets per litre, but I have never met anyone who has got giardia while using only one tablet. The two main brand names are Potable Aqua and Coghlan's Drinking Water Tablets.

● **Polar Pure** This method relies on dissolving a small amount of iodine directly in water. It is effective and cheap. The iodine crystals come in a glass bottle with a system to prevent the crystals from falling out of the bottle and there's a temperature-sensitive strip on the side to determine the dose needed.

● **Betadine / Povidone** This method uses a non-iodine based molecule to bind free iodine. For a 10% solution use 8 drops per litre of water. If the water is 20°C wait 15 minutes before drinking; if very cold, one hour.

● **Lugol's Iodine Solution** Unless purchased in the West, the solutions come in different concentrations that are often not indicated on the bottle: the solution could be 2%, 4% or 8%. In addition, the free iodine (the active ingredient) is dissolved in potassium iodide so the total amount of iodine consumed is much higher than necessary. However, if you have no choice, it's definitely better than nothing. For 2% solution use 5 drops per litre of water and leave for 15 minutes before drinking. If the water is very cold, or cloudy, it should be left 30 minutes or 10 drops should be used.

(Opposite) **Top**: Yak (shown here in the foreground) and dzopkio (several in the background), a yak/ox crossbreed. **Middle**: Tibetan snowcocks (left) near Dole; pika (right). **Bottom**: Musk deer (left) and Himalayan tahr (right) often seen above Namche. See p304.

Note that **Iodine solutions are messy**, so put the bottle in several plastic bags, and the iodine (except Betadine) should be kept only in a glass bottle.

Chlorine-based methods

● **Sierra Water Purifier** This uses super-chlorination, a high dose of chlorine that is later neutralized by adding hydrogen peroxide. It is effective.

● **Chlorine-based tablets** (Steritabs, Puritabs) If used alone, they aren't effective against giardia. However, if used with a fine filter (to remove the giardia), half a tablet is adequate. Note that standard **Micropur** tablets are not effective for trekking conditions. Having said that, I have met trekkers who used only Steritabs or Micropur and none got sick. There's also a system called **Pristine** which is chlorine dioxide based: it needs to be mixed and left to sit for five minutes before being added to the water and is therefore a bit finicky. After adding to the water, it needs to be left for 30 minutes. It leaves no aftertaste and claims to be effective against protozoa including giardia and cryptosporidium (but no word on cyclospora).

Water filters

There is quite a variety on the market. Follow the manufacturer's instructions carefully, especially with regard to cleaning and maintenance. Filtering water requires more effort than many methods but if you can develop the habit it's a good method for longer trips. The drawbacks with filters are that they can freeze plus their size, weight and cost. Also, most filters are not considered adequate for removing viruses from the water and therefore should be used only in conjunction with chemical methods.

UV light

● **SteriPEN** Using UV light to kill pathogens, this battery-operated device is perhaps the most convenient for regular use. They are available in Kathmandu.

Using bottled water

This can be obtained along the trail almost everywhere. Because it must be carried in, its price rises dramatically. The leftover bottles are also unsightly and difficult to dispose of so using purifying methods or buying boiled water is a far better solution.

ALTITUDE AND ACUTE MOUNTAIN SICKNESS (AMS)

Going to high and extreme altitudes is exceptionally hard on the body: it is a testament to the complex adaptability of body chemistry that humans can usually survive the experience. Commonly called altitude sickness, AMS can affect all trekkers in Lukla and above. It's caused by going up too fast to and can be fatal if the warning signals are ignored. Your body needs

---

❏ Barometric pressure table

Altitude	mmHG	Pressure	O₂ sat	Altitude	mmHG	Pressure	O₂ sat
Sea level	760	100%	99%	5000m/16,404ft	404	53%	80%
1000m/3281ft	670	88%		5500m/18,044ft	380	50% *	
2500m/8202ft	554	73%		6000m/19,685ft	356	47%	75%
3000m/9843ft	520	68%	93%	7000m/22,966ft	314	41%	
3500m/11,483ft	489	64%		8000m/26,247ft	277	36%	
4000m/13,123ft	460	60%	88%	8848m/29,028ft	249	33% **	
4500m/14,764ft	431	57%					

* (Kala Pattar) ** (Everest)

Pressure is the air pressure relative to sea level

O₂ sat is the average level of oxygen saturation in the blood at rest. Readings +/- 5% are still within the normal range.

time to adjust to the smaller quantity of oxygen present in the air at altitude: this involves dramatic changes in your body chemistry. At 5500m/18,044ft the air pressure is approximately half that at sea level, so there is half the amount of oxygen (and nitrogen) in it (see table left). For treks below an altitude of about 2500m/8000ft, AMS is not normally a problem.

Altitude sickness is preventable. Go up slowly, giving your body enough time to adjust. The 'safe' rates of ascent for 95% of trekkers involve spending 2-3 nights between 2000m/c6500ft and 3000m/c10,000ft before going higher. From 3000m you should sleep at an average of 300m/c1000ft higher each night with a rest day approximately every 900m/c3000ft. These rates are marked on the sample itineraries on pp28-9 and pp282-4. Be aware of the symptoms of AMS and only ascend if you are symptom-free.

The process of adapting to higher altitudes is called **acclimatization**. Firstly, you want to go up at a pace slow enough that you acclimatize and not get altitude sickness. Secondly, the longer you stay at altitude, the more you acclimatize and the stronger you become.

Note that the altitudes attained while trekking in the Khumbu are more extreme than virtually anywhere else, requiring a more cautious approach than, for example, skiing at 3000m/c10,000ft in Colorado, USA.

NORMAL SYMPTOMS

Don't expect to feel perfect at altitudes of more than 3000m. These are the normal altitude symptoms you should expect but **not** worry about. Every trekker will experience some or all of these, no matter how slowly they ascend:

● Periods of sleeplessness
● The need for more sleep than normal, often 10 hours or more
● Occasional loss of appetite
● Vivid, wild dreams especially at around 2500-3800m in altitude
● Unexpected momentary shortness of breath, day and night
● Periodic breathing
● The need to rest/catch your breath frequently while trekking, especially above 4000m
● Runny nose
● Beer and soft drinks don't taste so good until you have been at altitude for a long time
● Increased urination while moving to/at higher altitudes – a good sign.

Many people have trouble sleeping in a new environment, especially if it changes every day. Altitude adds to the problems by inducing periodic breathing (see further on) and the decrease of oxygen means that some trekkers experience wild dreams. This often happens at Namche, on the way up. You need to sleep well most nights so ensure you are warm enough – a hot water bottle is luxurious – and if you have persistent problems certainly consider taking some drugs. When you are ascending day after day there comes a point where suddenly you pee an unexpectedly large volume and many times and every night you have to pee a few times. After this you find water moves through you quickly. This is your body making changes and is an excellent sign that you are adapting to altitude. At Gokyo, Sean from Canada's record was 18 times in one day. A really large pee will be almost a litre! If you are ascending and are not peeing more than normal you need to drink more. After you have stayed at the same altitude for a day or longer or begin descending this extra urination stops.

MILD AMS SYMPTOMS – NEVER GO HIGHER!

Many trekkers in the high valleys of the Khumbu get mild AMS: admit or acknowledge that you are having symptoms. You need have only one of the following to be getting altitude sickness.

● **Headaches** are very common among trekkers. A headache is usually frontal, all over or simply all-round pressure, and often comes on during the evening, remaining into the night until you fall asleep. Raising your head and shoulders while trying to sleep sometimes offers partial relief. Ensure you have drunk enough fluids and then consider taking something for it. At the point of getting mild AMS a slight headache may come and go, sensitive to the difference between exercising and rest, or even simply breathing less or more.

● **Nausea** can occur without other symptoms but usually develops with a bad headache. If you are better in the morning, take a rest day; if you still feel bad after breakfast descend.

● **Lightheadedness or mild dizziness** If this occurs while walking, stop out of the sun and have a rest and a drink. Stay at the closest teahouse.

● **Appetite-loss** or generally feeling bad is common at altitude after too rapid an ascent.

● **Sleeplessness** or generally feeling lazy.

● **Dry raspy cough** This may sometimes be painful, use throat lozenges.

In other words, anything other than diarrhoea or a sore throat could be altitude sickness and you should assume it is. If, for example, your headache is due to dehydration ascending further is not dangerous but if it's due to AMS the consequences could be serious. You cannot tell the difference so caution is the safest course. Don't try to deceive yourself. Accept that your body needs more time to adapt. The basic AMS rule is: **never go higher with mild symptoms**.

What to do about mild AMS symptoms
There are two basic choices: the natural way and the drug way.

● **The natural way** If you find mild symptoms developing while walking, stop and relax (with your head out of the sun) and drink some fluids. Drink frequently.

● **The drug way** If mild symptoms develop while walking, stop have a rest, drink some fluids and take 125-250mg Diamox. Diamox generally takes one to four hours to begin alleviating symptoms. Drink more water and consider staying close by.

If symptoms develop in the evening take 125-250mg Diamox and drink plenty of fluids. If you have a headache/nausea perhaps take some Ibuprofen or Paracetamol (but not aspirin). Be prepared to make many toilet journeys or obtain a pee bottle. If symptoms partially go away but are still annoying it is safe to take another 250mg Diamox 6-8 hours later. If similar symptoms return consider taking 125-250mg of Diamox every 12 hours until you begin descending in sleeping altitude.

In both cases If the symptoms (including a headache) do not go away completely, stay at the same altitude. If symptoms get worse, go down. Even a small loss of elevation (100m/328ft or so) can make a big difference to how you feel and how you sleep. You should descend to the last place where you felt fine.

If symptoms develop at night, unless they rapidly get worse, wait them out and see how you feel in the morning. If the symptoms have not gone after breakfast have a rest day

---

❏ What happens if you ascend too quickly?
Many people say that the 300m a day guideline is too cautious; some people consider 500m a day more realistic. Certainly a few people can handle 500m a day, but many people cannot – a very few cannot even handle 300m a day. Consider this French group. They followed this itinerary on the advice of a less than professional Kathmandu trekking company.

Night stops at: Kathmandu (1400m), Namche (3450m), Tengboche (3860m), Dingboche (4350m), Lobuche (4940m), the HRA Pheriche clinic. On reaching Lobuche the group immediately turned back: 3 out of 12 had cerebral edema (HACE) that would have killed them if it wasn't for the HRA doctors, and two still had to be helicopter evacuated. The rest came down with moderate AMS (not mild) but felt better at the Pheriche clinic after taking Diamox. Nobody made it up Kala Pattar.

or descend. If they have gone, you should still consider having a rest day or at least only an easy day's walking. Continued ascent is likely to bring back the symptoms.

Note that there can be a time lag between arriving at altitude and the onset of symptoms. In fact, statistically it is just as common to suffer mild symptoms on the second night of staying at the same altitude.

Altitude sickness must be reacted to when symptoms are mild: going higher will definitely make it worse. You trek to enjoy, not to feel sick.

SERIOUS AMS SYMPTOMS – IMMEDIATE DESCENT

- **Persistent, severe headache**
- **Persistent vomiting**
- **Ataxia** – loss of co-ordination, an inability to walk in a straight line, making the sufferer look drunk
- **Mental confusion and/or hallucinations**
- **Losing consciousness** – inability to stay awake or understand instructions
- **Mild symptoms rapidly getting worse**
- **Difficulty breathing**
- **Severe lethargy/fatigue**
- **Marked blueness of face and lips**
- **Very persistent, sometimes watery, cough**
- **Rapid breathing or feeling breathless at rest**
- **Liquid sounds in the lungs**
- **Coughing clear fluid, pink phlegm or blood (a very bad sign)**
- **High resting heartbeat** over 130 beats per minute.

Ataxia is the single most important sign for recognizing the progression of cerebral AMS from mild to serious. This is easily tested by trying to walk in a straight line, heel to toe and should be compared with somebody who has no symptoms. Twelve hours after the onset of ataxia a coma is possible, followed by death, unless you descend. Take note of the second basic AMS rule: **immediate and fast descent with serious symptoms**.

That is the basic rule but here are more details. Firstly, remain calm. If there is a doctor consult them first. If bottled oxygen is available use it before descending or, if they are unconscious, while descending. If there is a PAC bag (see box p294), use this for at least an hour before descending.

If far away from both expert care and these tools consider carefully which type of AMS – HACE or HAPE (see below) – give the appropriate drug treatment and begin descending. The patient must be taken as far down as possible, even if it is the middle of the night. Ensure the descent party is well equipped and there are enough people to carry the patient if they collapse since his or her condition may get worse before getting better. Exercise makes HAPE worse: carry the person. Later the patient must rest and see a doctor, even if well recovered. People with serious symptoms may not be able to think for themselves and may say they feel OK. They are not. If you are at or above Lobuche head to the Pyramid. If at Chukhung or higher, or Thukla or Dingboche or Dzonglha head to the Pheriche HRA post, if open, otherwise head further down. Ask at the Gompa Lodge in Upper Pangboche (ask for Namka) or the Rhododendron lodge in Deboche.

Note that the HRA and Khunde doctors are frequently called out to sick people. Normally their first action is to get them back to the clinic where there is light and all the tools. So, if you are considering calling a doctor out, it may be wiser to begin descending towards the clinic first. If at Gokyo, head down to the hospital at Machermo, and the PAC bag there. In all cases you have to pay for services.

Medical conditions at altitude

- **High Altitude Cerebral Edema (HACE)** This is a build-up of fluid around the brain. It causes the first five symptoms on the mild list (see pp291-2) and the first five in the left column of the severe list (see above). Coma from HACE can occur in as little as 12 hours from the onset of symptoms, but normally takes 1-3 days to develop. At the first sign of ataxia begin treatment with medication, oxygen and descent. Usually 4 to 8mg of dexamethasone is given as a first dose, then 4mg every 6 hours, Diamox every 12 hours and 2-4l/min oxygen.

❏ **Using a portable altitude chamber**

Increasingly, trekking companies/groups rent a PAC/Gamow/CERTEC bag and occasionally there is nobody trained in their use. Each of these is basically a large plastic tube that you can put someone in then pump up the pressure thereby simulating a lower altitude. Used properly they are very effective. For moderately severe HAPE/HACE one or two one-hour sessions may be enough; for more severe cases, longer periods or more sessions will be required.

If there are instructions, follow them; the PAC bag has instructions printed on the side. Briefly:

● Pumping up and releasing the pressure should be done slowly, patients may need time to equalize their ear drums: when pumping up they can hold their nose and blow, when deflating the bag, swallow with the mouth wide open.

● With severe HAPE use a sloping surface, the head being 30-40cms higher.

● Put a sleeping bag in with the patient, or if in the sun, shield the bag.

● Maintain eye contact and communication.

● Pump regularly otherwise CO_2 can build up to dangerous levels in the bag.

● Never sit on the bag.

Descent is necessary, but a PAC Bag will often be used first if available. This can make an unsteady, uncooperative, difficult to manage patient into one that is more able to assist in his/her own evacuation. An O_2 sat reading is an unreliable indicator of HACE.

● **High Altitude Pulmonary Edema (HAPE)** This is an accumulation of fluid in the lungs and is very serious. It is responsible for all the other mild and serious symptoms and it is often accompanied by a mild fever. By far the best treatment is oxygen at 4 litres a minute but PAC bag treatment is a good substitute. If there is neither oxygen nor a PAC bag descent will be life saving. Drugs are of limited necessity in HAPE because oxygen and descent are such effective treatments. However, if oxygen is unavailable and descent is delayed, it is reasonable to give 10mg of regular (fast-acting) Nifedipine (swallow the gel capsule intact) or, if unavailable, Nifedipine 30mg slow-release tablets; in both cases, descend as soon as possible. Asthma medications (Salbutamol, Ventolin, Asthalin) help in mild cases although this has not been studied in detail. It is common to suffer some HACE as well so Diamox should be given. It is far more common for serious HAPE to strike while sleeping so with mild HAPE during the day descent or treatment is essential. HAPE patients have low O_2 sat readings. Administering medication and waiting for a helicopter is **not** adequate treatment.

Before much was known about AMS, HAPE was often misdiagnosed as pneumonia and since the treatment was antibiotics rather than descent, most people died.

While the symptoms of AMS are usually clear, occasionally the symptoms don't follow the usual pattern or other problems show up in conjunction. This could be because of complications or in rare cases, it is not altitude sickness at all. The patient may have suffered a heart attack, a stroke, a blood clot in the lungs or kidney failure and there are many other possibilities.

● **Periodic breathing (Cheyne-Stokes respiration)** Less oxygen in the blood affects the body's breathing mechanism. While at rest or sleeping your body seems to feel the need to breathe less and less, to the point where suddenly you require some deep breaths to recover. This cycle can be a few breaths long, in which after a couple of breaths you miss a breath completely. Alternatively it may be a gradual cycle over a minute, appearing as if your breathing rate simply goes up and down regularly. It is experienced by most trekkers at Namche, although many people are unaware of it while asleep. At 5000m/16,404ft virtually all trekkers experience periodic breathing, though it is troublesome for only a few. Studies have so far found no direct link to AMS.

If periodic breathing wakes you sometimes during the night seriously consider Diamox an hour before bed; this usually works very effectively.

● **Swelling of the hands, feet, face and lower abdomen** An HRA study showed that about 18% of trekkers experience some swelling, usually minor, and women are more susceptible. It is a sign that you are not acclimatizing as well as you could, but is not a cause for concern unless the swelling is severe. Continued cautious ascent is OK. Rings should be removed. People who have experienced swelling should not push themselves hard on the trail.

● **Altitude immune suppression** At base-camp altitudes, cuts and infections heal very slowly. Your body is unaffected in its ability to fight viral infections but is much more susceptible to bacterial infections. For serious infections, especially bronchitis, descent to Namche level is recommended.

● **High Altitude Retinal Haemorrhage (HARH)** A study conducted in the Khumbu found that 30-35% of trekkers at 5000m suffered retinal haemorrhages. Small bleeds in the retina can result in specks in your vision, often noticed when lying down looking at a uniform ceiling. There is no pain and they clear after time. If severe, ie blurred vision or readily noticeable during the day, descend and see a doctor.

● **High Altitude Flatulence Expulsion (HAFE)** This is commonly known as HAF (High Altitude Farts). The cure – let it rip! You're not a balloon that needs blowing up.

Re-ascent after severe AMS

This entails risk, but is not impossible; you should discuss it carefully with an AMS-experienced doctor.

Useful drugs at altitude

● **Diamox (Acetazolamide)** This is a mild diuretic (it leads to increased urination) that acidifies the blood to stimulate breathing. It also reduces cerebrospinal fluid formation. Often it is not recommended to take it as a prophylactic (ie to prevent AMS, before you have symptoms) unless you ascend rapidly, unavoidably (eg flying to a high altitude – Lhasa, for example – or on a rescue mission), or unless you have experienced undue altitude problems previously. However there is no harm in taking it as a prophylactic. Once you have some troublesome symptoms it is a good drug to take.

It is a sulfa drug derivative, and people allergic to this class of drugs should not take Diamox (sulfa allergy is uncommon). You could test your reaction to this at home prior to being in the mountains. The normal side effects are increased urination (you should drink more when this happens), and tingling sensations in the lips, fingers or toes but these symptoms are not an indication to stop the drug. In rare cases it causes a rash or other allergic symptoms and it can soften the eyeball to the point that vision is affected. In that case don't take Diamox again. It can ruin the taste of beer and soft drinks. It should not be used at the same time as full-strength aspirin (this also acidifies the blood slightly).

The recommendations are to carry Diamox and consider using it if you experience mild but annoying symptoms, especially periodic breathing if it continually wakes you up. The dosage for prevention and treatment of mild symptoms is 125-250mg every 12 hours until you descend in sleeping altitude or after 2 days at the same altitude. For aiding sleep try 125mg about an hour before going to bed. It is not necessary to take it in the morning as well, although Diamox does appear to assist more effectively if taken for several days. In case of real altitude sickness and HACE the exact effective dosages have not been established so the guideline is as follows: the sicker you are, the bigger the dose you should consider taking. This could be up to 500mg three times a day.

Diamox actually goes to the root of the problem, it does not simply hide the problem. So if you feel better, you are better. However, this does not mean that you can ascend at a faster rate than normal, or ignore altitude sickness symptoms since it is quite possible to still develop AMS while taking Diamox. If you are experiencing altitude sickness problems the further away you are from medical care, the sooner you should consider beginning Diamox. Note that if you are going high rapidly Diamox can be used to best effect by beginning a course 24 hours before. If you are already at altitude and are going to take a large jump in sleeping altitude, ie greater than 600m, Diamox begun one day before should help significantly.

● **Gingko biloba** Two controlled trials revealed that Gingko at 80-120mg a day begun before going to altitude and continued at altitude reduced the incidence of AMS. It also assisted circulation to the extremities. The mechanism of how it works is not understood and while it does help some people, subjectively Diamox seems to be slightly better but with more side effects. More work is needed on this. Many people believe that homeopathic/ayurvedic/herbal medicines are somehow different from the other drugs listed here. Remedies are still drugs; remember that Aspirin comes from willow bark.

● **Dexamethasone (Decadron/Dexasone)** This is a potent steroid but taken for periods of only a day or two has few side effects. It should be used in treatment and should **not** be used prophylactically, ie to prevent AMS before it happens. It does not aid in acclimatization and therefore there is a potential rebound effect, ie once the drug wears off, you may feel worse than before, particularly if you haven't descended in the meantime.

● **Aspirin (Dispirin/Bufferin/Ascriptin/Ecotrin)** Some altitude experts say that Aspirin increases the risk of retinal haemorrhages and should not be taken at altitude (perhaps above Namche), and definitely not on high-altitude expeditions. At lower altitudes the usual dose is one to two 325mg to 500mg tablets every six hours (to a maximum of eight per day). In some countries 650mg tablets are also available and only one is taken at a time. Even small amounts (50-75mg) reduce the ability of the blood to clot. It can also reduce fevers, although doesn't fix the underlying problem. Plain aspirin is hard on the stomach lining but most preparations add a buffer to minimize this. It is, however, still better taken with food. It should not be taken at the same time as Diamox.

● **Ibuprofen (Advil, Nurofen, Motrin, Nuprin, Midol)** Tablets come in 200mg, 400mg or (a rather strong) 600mg. The maximum daily allowance is 2400mg, usually divided into four or five doses. This is probably the best drug for tendonitis and inflammation of joints. It is also considered the best drug for high-altitude headaches, and should be used to avoid further increasing your risk of HARH. It also decreases fever, but can be hard on the stomach (even buffered versions).

● **Naproxen (Aleve, Naprosyn)** The usual dose is 220mg. It is similar to Ibuprofen but its effects are longer lasting so you need only one tablet for 12 hours or more of relief. No studies have been conducted about how well it works for altitude headaches but it is probably less effective than Aspirin or Ibuprofen.

● **Acetaminophen (Tylenol Paracetamol, Panadol)** The usual dose is one to two 325-500mg tablets up to four times a day and it can be combined with Ibuprofen or Aspirin. It is a good painkiller (but doesn't reduce inflammation) and has fewer side effects than anti-inflammatories like Aspirin. It reduces fevers, although it does not fix the cause of the fever. It should not be used by people who regularly consume more than about three alcoholic drinks a day.

● **Nifedipine** comes in two forms: quick-acting gel capsules and the more normal slow release small tablets (Nifed, Adulat, Retard). For HAPE the capsules are preferable and the

---

❏ **Aspirin, Ibuprofen and Naproxen – caution**
At altitude many people end up taking far more drugs than normal. Aspirin, Ibuprofen and Naproxen are all related drugs (and therefore should not be mixed) and because of the way they work they are hard on the stomach so are better taken with a snack, meal or at least a drink. They should not be taken continuously for extended periods, ie more than a week without consulting a doctor to help determine what is causing the problem and to discuss potential side effects. If a lower strength tablet works, take a lower dose.

dose is 10mg, swallowed whole. If the person is still sick another 10mg can be taken an hour later and then every 4-6 hours. If only the slow-acting form is available the dose is 20-30mg, and this is effective for approximately 12 hours. Nifedipine should only be taken if no other treatment is available for HAPE. Smaller doses can be useful for warming up fingers or toes in an extreme situation, providing your core is warm and you are exercising.

● **Sleeping tablets** The majority of sleeping tablets depress the breathing instinct and the effect on trekkers at altitude has not been studied in depth so generally they are not recommended (Ambien doesn't). Also tablets can leave you drowsy the next day. Identifying the cause of the sleep problem, such as periodic breathing or aches and pains from trekking, may mean taking Diamox or Ibuprofen is a sensible and effective option.

The acclimatization process
When you move to a higher altitude your body quickly realises less oxygen is available and its first reaction is to get you to hyperventilate (breathe more). More oxygen (O_2) is inhaled but more carbon dioxide (CO_2) is breathed out and with the O_2-CO_2 balance upset the pH of the blood is altered. Your body determines how deeply to breathe by the pH level (mainly the dissolved CO_2 in your blood). If you exercise hard at sea level, your muscles produce large amounts of CO_2 so you breathe hard and fast. While resting, your body is using little energy so little CO_2 is produced. When this balance is upset your body may believe that it needs to breathe less than it really does. Over several days it tries to correct this imbalance by disposing of bicarbonate (carbon dioxide in water) in the urine. (Since it's not very soluble you need to drink plenty.) Diamox assists by allowing the kidneys to do this more efficiently thereby enhancing many people's ability to acclimatize. In addition, after a day or two, the body moves some fluid out of the blood thus increasing the haemoglobin concentration. After several days more new red blood cells are released than normal. A changed blood pH also affects how oxygen sticks on the red blood and other chemical changes take place to compensate for this.

Intentional hyperventilation, ie consciously breathing harder for several minutes is potentially harmful. Less oxygen is the main reason the body needs to adapt, but less air pressure alone also has effects on the body.

Rates of acclimatization
Individual rates of acclimatization are dependent on how fast your body reacts to compensate for the altered pH level of the blood. For slow starters Diamox provides a good kickstart but for people already adapting well its effect is minimal.

Interestingly it is this reaction of breathing more when there is less oxygen (Hypoxic Ventilatory Response: HVR) that is most important initially; being fit or having a higher lung capacity has nothing to do with it. A quicker reaction (ie higher HVR) means that while ascending you will feel better – acclimatize more quickly – and feel stronger than someone whose reaction is slower. However, once you are acclimatized, ie have stayed at a similar altitude for 3-7 days, overall fitness matters and the fitter will be stronger. So people who do not acclimatize easily may still perform well at altitude if given time.

Your HVR is mainly genetic but importantly the mega-fit, ie marathon runners and people who train regularly for long periods at a similar work rate, have a depressed/blunted HVR, often very significantly, and can have a tough time acclimatizing initially. In some cases pushing yourself harder and using a stop-start pattern can assist in developing a lower HVR. In other cases pushing hard can be detrimental, in the worst cases bring on HAPE.

Sherpas have genetic adaptation to altitude but they can still get sick. Sherpas who live in Kathmandu occasionally get AMS upon returning to the Khumbu. Studies have shown that people who live at moderate altitudes (1000m-2000m/3281ft-6562ft) are acclimatized to those altitudes. They are much less susceptible to AMS when ascending to around 3000m/9842ft (ie going to Namche). However the benefits decrease once higher and they should follow the same acclimatization programme as others.

❏ **Climb high – sleep low?**
This often quoted dictum is partly correct in some situations, plain wrong in others. If you are already well acclimatized climbing higher and returning to a similar altitude may help further with acclimatization.

If you are still in the early stages of acclimatizing process, ie still ascending to a higher altitude each night, be careful. If you feel any symptoms of AMS at all you are probably better taking light/moderate exercise only with little or no increase in altitude. If you feel really good you could consider climbing a bit higher (200-400m), but climbing significantly higher, ie 1000m or more higher will almost always result in a headache on the way down or upon returning to the lodge. You may have had a good day but it is not so sure that you have actually helped your acclimatization.

Trekkers who fly from sea level to Kathmandu and then almost immediately fly to Lukla are more likely to suffer AMS than people who have spent a few days in Kathmandu (1400m/4593ft) on the way. Unfortunately it is usually these people who are in a hurry to go higher. This is why group trekkers are initially more susceptible to troublesome AMS than individual trekkers, who often walk from Jiri or spend time in Kathmandu first.

Effects of long-term exposure to altitude
If you stay at altitude for several weeks there are more changes: your muscles' mitochondria (the energy converters in the muscle) multiply, a denser network of capillaries develop and your maximum work rate increases slowly with these changes. Expeditions have run medical programmes with some interesting results. Climbers who experience periodic breathing (the majority) at base camp never shake it off and have great difficulty maintaining their normal body weight. Muscles will strengthen and stamina is increased but not the muscle bulk. Sherpas who have always lived at altitude never experience periodic breathing and can actually put on weight with enough food.

How long does acclimatization last?
It varies, but if you were at altitude for a month or more your improved work rates could continue for weeks so you'd still feel fit upon returning to altitude. You should not, however, ascend faster than normal if you return to sea level for a few days since you can still be susceptible to HAPE. If you have been up to 5000m/c16,500ft and then go down to 3500m/c11,500ft for a few days, returning rapidly to 5000m/c16,500ft should cause no problems. Thus, having been to Lobuche and Kala Pattar, then rested for two days in Namche, you should be able to ascend to Gokyo or a trekking peak fairly quickly.

Appetite
Altitude causes some people to lose an interest in food but you should try to eat as much as you can since your energy consumption, even at rest, is significantly higher than normal. Your body needs to generate heat to combat the constant cold, especially while sleeping. Very energetic trekkers, no matter how much they eat, will barely be able to replace the huge quantities of energy used.

The pill and fertility
The risk of a blood clot at high altitude while on the combined oral contraceptive pill is theoretically slightly higher, but no studies have been undertaken to see if there is significant risk. However, no problems have been reported while trekking or at the medium-altitude ski resorts in the States. It is important to keep hydrated. For an 8000m expedition more caution is suggested. There is no increased risk of thrombosis with the mini-pill.

A common trick while trekking to avoid the mess of a period is to take two cycles of the combined oral contraceptive pill back to back. There are no special altitude-related reasons not to do this. Prolonged exposure to altitude does reduce men's fertility, although this quickly returns to normal.

Oxygen saturation meters (O_2 sat)

With the arrival of some relatively cheap battery-powered models some trekking companies now carry them. Oxygen saturation levels vary with altitude (see the table on p290) and vary from individual to individual; values plus or minus approximately 5% are still within the normal range. O_2 sat values also vary enormously between resting and exercising and eating. Normally only resting rates are meaningful. A low O_2 sat is an indication that HAPE may be developing (or that you have a low HVR), or has developed. However, it gives no indication of HACE: somebody can be dying of HACE and still have an O_2 sat that is perfectly normal for that altitude.

OTHER HEALTH PROBLEMS

The Khumbu Cough

Few trekkers manage to escape this one. The extra amounts of cold dry air that you need to breathe in at altitude irritate your bronchi (windpipes). Your body reacts to this as it would to an infection like flu, producing large quantities of phlegm, a mild cough, mild sore throat and a runny nose. Since there is, in fact, no infection it's pointless taking antibiotics but throat lozenges might help so take plenty along. Before you appear to get it use non-medicated ones; once you get the cough try using anti-bacterial ones occasionally because you are more susceptible to a bacterial infection.

Other solutions are to wear a thin scarf over your mouth to keep your breath moister, inhaling steam and keeping well hydrated. An inhaled nasal decongestant can help you breathe through your nose so that the air reaching your throat and lungs is more moist and therefore less irritating.

Bronchial infection

Bronchitis is an inflammation of the bronchi: sometimes it is caused by dryness (as in the Khumbu cough), asthma or allergy, but sometimes it can be caused by a virus or bacteria. An infection may be accompanied by a fever, shortness of breath, chest pain and a cough producing more and greener phlegm. It can be a viral infection, in which case antibiotics will do nothing, or at altitude it would more likely be a bacterial infection. It's best to see if the above measures for the Khumbu cough work; otherwise get some rest or return to a lower altitude, eg Namche, and see a doctor.

Dehydration

Trekkers lose large quantities of water, not just through sweating but by breathing harder at altitude. Water vapour is exhaled with each breath and the thinner air means more breaths are required. If the fluids lost are not replaced, dehydration will result making you feel lethargic and sometimes resulting in a headache. The symptoms are similar to AMS so the easiest way to avoid confusion is to always keep hydrated.

A happy mountaineer always pees clear! If your urine is a deep yellow or orange colour you are not drinking enough. Even if you are not feeling thirsty you should still try to drink more. This can include any liquids (soups and tea but not alcohol) and as much water as possible. Many people find that with supper they often drink more than a litre of water, catching up on what they should have drunk during the day.

Hypoglycaemia

Especially after prolonged bouts of exercise, the body can quickly run out of energy (hitting the wall). The solution is to snack frequently and stop often.

Snow blindness

This is sunburn of the cornea, a painful affliction that feels like hot sand in your eyes. It is entirely preventable by wearing sunglasses that block UV light. This precaution is most important not just in snowy areas but also at altitude since the concentration of UV light increases with altitude. Porters often get snowblindness because they don't realize the importance of wearing sunglasses in snow.

Exposure

Also known as hypothermia, this is caused by a combination of not wearing enough warm clothes against the cold, exhaustion, high altitude, dehydration and lack of food. Note that it does not need to be very cold for exposure to occur. Make sure everyone (porters included) is properly equipped. Symptoms of exposure include a low body temperature (below 34.5°C or 94°F), poor co-ordination, exhaustion and shivering. As the condition deteriorates the shivering ceases, co-ordination gets worse making walking difficult and the patient may start hallucinating. The pulse then slows and unconsciousness and death follow shortly. Treatment involves thoroughly warming the patient quickly. Find shelter as soon as possible. Put the patient into a sleeping-bag with hot water bottles (use your drinking water bottles). Another person should get into the sleeping-bag with the patient to warm him or her up.

Frostbite

When flesh freezes the results are very serious. Amputation may be necessary. Frostbite occurs usually in fingers or toes and takes time to develop unless bare flesh is exposed to winds at low temperatures or is holding cold metal.

Treatment When cold, fingers or toes feel numb, clumsy and lose power. If it's still possible to move them they aren't likely to be freezing although at this point the skin surface can partially freeze unnoticed. If you are worried, stop and rewarm. For fingers swing your arms around to promote circulation and stick them in your armpits. Pain on rewarming means either you frost-nipped them or came close.

With partial thickness frostbite, the flesh turns cold, blue and numb, but the underlying tissue remains normal – soft and pliable. With deeper injury, fingers or toes become wooden, incapable of movement. If you suspect deep frostbite, make plans for evacuation immediately. Don't begin rewarming until in a situation where refreezing cannot occur since this is infinitely more damaging than the affected part staying frozen a bit longer. If evacuation is guaranteed, if only the hands are affected or if damage to the toes is minimal and pain will not impede walking, rewarming should be done as soon as is practical. Warm slowly and evenly: blood temperature or a bit warmer (up to 42°C) is optimum. If possible, a bath which allows the affected part to be warmed without it hitting the sides of the container is ideal. Rewarming can be excruciatingly painful so consider giving narcotics if available. Ibuprofen 400mg should be administered before rewarming and continued every 6 hours afterwards to prevent formation of natural chemicals which can actually harm the tissues further. Blisters will probably form – clear ones are indicative of partial thickness injury whereas bloody ones mean more extensive damage. Gently dry the affected limb and place clean gauze between the fingers or toes to protect them. The most important part of the treatment of frostbite is preventing further injury and infection. A bulky dressing and not allowing the affected part to be used **at all** is the best way to achieve this. See a doctor as soon as possible for an assessment of the damage and continued care. Nifedepine (Adulat) can also be used to help prevent frostbite (5-10mg of the fast-acting type of tablets only) if your core temperature is good but the side effects are an increased heart rate that can occasionally have unpredictable results at altitude.

Unwelcome bed companions

If you're using your own sleeping bag it's very unlikely you'll have problems. Renting sleeping bags always carries a very small risk of scabies but not fleas or bedbugs, and this can be further reduced by airing the bag for a day or two in the sun. If you ever use local blankets the risks increase considerably.

● **Bedbugs** Bedbug bites are normally small, itchy and in neat lines. Bedbugs do not normally live in sleeping bags because when they are aired there is nowhere to hide.

● **Fleas** All local dogs are carriers and fleas also hide in quilts, blankets and old carpets. Occasionally trekkers pick them up. The small, red, itchy bites are usually congregated around areas such as the tops of your socks, waist, armpits or sleeves. You should try not to scratch, but do wash yourself and your clothes thoroughly. If you can find some flea powder, use this as well.

● **Scabies** Caused by a microscopic parasite this is luckily rare amongst trekkers. It can be caught from sheets or rented sleeping bags (but only if they have not been aired properly) or contact with an infected person, sometimes another trekker. To avoid scabies you should use a sheet sleeping bag within your sleeping bag. The itchy red spots look like pimples without the pus and may, at first, be confused with flea bites. As the parasites multiply, the marks spread widely but not usually on the face or head. Go to Khunde Hospital or Pheriche Clinic, if possible, or visit a health post. Treatment is a head-to-toe dousing with Scabex. All clothing should be washed and thoroughly aired and your sleeping bag should be left in the sun for a several days. It takes a few days to a week or more for the symptoms, including itching to disappear, even if the treatment has been successful. Occasionally a second treatment may be necessary.

Leeches
These monsoon terrorizers are able to put a sizeable hole in you completely painlessly. Found in profusion in damp forest and damp, deep grass, leeches are adept at penetrating socks and even boot eyelets. Do not try to pull a leech off but apply salt, iodine or a lighted match and it'll quickly drop off. Leeches don't transmit disease but the wound can get infected: clean with antiseptic.

Blisters
Since you spend most of the time on your feet, looking after them properly to avoid blisters is of paramount importance.

Prevention Start with boots that have been worn in. This means not just for a short walk on level ground but with a pack in hilly country. If a blister starts to develop while you're trekking you can usually feel it. There'll be some rubbing, localized pain or a hot spot. Stop and investigate, even if it occurs during the first five minutes of walking or just in sight of the top of the hill. The trick is to stop and tape before the blister develops. Carefully apply moleskin or Second Skin, or a strong adhesive tape. Check that the hot spot is not being caused by the seam of a sock or a seam in your boot. Once you've applied a dressing, recheck it periodically to ensure that the problem is not getting worse.

Treatment If you develop a blister there are several approaches. If it's not painful surround it (don't cover it) with some light padding, eg moleskin, and see how it feels. If it is painful you may want to drain it. Clean the skin carefully, sterilize a needle by holding it slightly above a flame for few seconds and pierce the blister. Do not cut away the blister skin until it has dried out and is no longer useful for protecting the delicate skin underneath. Put protective tape over it with some cotton wool as padding. Some people, however, put strong, carefully applied tape straight over the blister, with no dressing.

Cuts and scrapes
Most important is getting and keeping them clean and dry so they can heal on their own. Wash with lots of (clean) water to get out bacteria and dirt. A bit of dilute betadine or other antiseptic is fine, but does not substitute for washing with lots of water. Do not clean wounds daily with antiseptics – this will slow the healing. Covering wounds with a dressing, perhaps

with some antibiotic ointment underneath, promotes healing. If wound edges are gaping, using steri-strips to pull them together is a good idea, then find a doctor to fix it properly.

Vaginal infections
If you have experienced these before it is worth bringing a course of the medication you were last prescribed in case the infection recurs.

Dogs and other animal bites
These are fortunately rare, but potentially very anxiety inducing. If you get bitten, or even receive a scratch that draws blood, the first thing that needs to be done is thorough washing of the wound (unless serious bleeding is occurring in which case stopping it is the priority!). First use copious quantities of soap and water and then clean again with an antiseptic such as betadine. Animal injuries that break the skin carry the potential for rabies in Nepal. The treatment depends on whether you had the pre-exposure rabies vaccine series (most trekkers don't get it – the likelihood of needing it is so small). Whether you had the pre-exposure series or not, a break in the skin from an animal needs to be assessed by a physician (preferably not a local one – rabies treatment in Nepal is inadequate). If a potential exposure has occurred, the vaccines, which are 100% effective if given in a proper and timely manner, should be started within about 4-5 days. Wounds should not be stitched/sutured until rabies treatment has been given.

FIRST-AID KIT

This is a basic list to cover the more common ailments that afflict trekkers. Climbing groups, expeditions and trekkers going to isolated areas will need a more comprehensive kit. Quantities stated are for one person.

Drugs easily purchased in Kathmandu:
● **Acetezolamide Diamox for altitude sickness** This comes in two forms, 250mg tablets (in Nepal) and 500mg time-release capsules. One strip of 10 tablets is enough.
● **Norfloxacin or Ciprofloxacin** for bacterial diarrhoea. Norfloxacin is cheaper. They are both broad spectrum antibiotics and can be used to treat many other infections. One strip of tablets.
● **Tinidazole (Tiniba) for giardia**. One strip of ten tablets.
● **Oral rehydration salts** Some people can drink this stuff, others hate the taste. It is worth remembering that they all are good for you, replacing essential salts. In Kathmandu the nicest-tasting one is 'Electrobion' but there are more brands, the best known is Jeevan Jal. Take 1-3 packets for the replacement of salts and fluids lost by vomiting and diarrhoea.
● **Throat lozenges** Basic Strepsils, Halls and Vicks brands are usually available.

Better purchased in the West:
● **Tape for blisters** Moleskin/Second Skin/zinc oxide based tape (Leukoplast) – for blisters. Cheap low quality tape is available in Nepal.
● **Painkillers** Useful as mild painkillers for headaches, for reducing fever and reducing tenderness or swelling. For longer treks take plenty. Some brands are available in Nepal.
● **Cold medicines/Decongestants** and/or nasal spray are handy for short-term use.
● **Plasters/Band-Aids** Assorted plasters and perhaps a stretch bandage would be useful. If you have had knee or ankle trouble previously a good **support bandage** is well worth bringing.
● **Betadine/Savlon/Dettol Antiseptic** for cuts.
● **Anti-bacterial throat lozenges** Bring several packets for the Khumbu Cough.
● **Gel hand cleaner** A small bottle is particularly handy for trekking and means that you are not washing your hands with possibly contaminated water.

RESCUE PROCEDURES
Assessing the situation
You don't need helicopter rescue for moderate AMS. For severe AMS, oxygen, PAC bag treatment or immediate descent is vital, so get the patient down rather than waiting for a helicopter that may take hours or even days to arrive.

For other emergency situations think carefully: are you better off going to the Pheriche HRA post or Khunde hospital, or calling their doctors to you – or calling a helicopter? In addition, there are always a surprising number of doctors on treks themselves. For non-life-threatening situations it may be that after seeing a doctor you can descend yourself or be carried down saving the expense of a helicopter rescue, not to mention being able to continue the trek when things have improved, rather than being stuck in Kathmandu.

If somebody has had a serious accident, don't panic. If there is bleeding, apply pressure over the wound, keep them warm and take stock of the situation. Look at all your options logically and carefully.

Summoning a helicopter
The process of summoning a helicopter can take 24 hours or longer once the message reaches Kathmandu because there must be a guarantee of payment (by a trekking company, insurance company or your embassy). How quickly the helicopter comes also depends on the weather. While a helicopter can magically appear in several hours it isn't unusual for it to take several days to reach an injured patient – there are no golden hour rescues.

There are telephones everywhere. When sending a message include as much clear detail as possible: your names and nationalities, the exact location, the reason for the rescue request and an assessment of the seriousness. Helicopters require a flat area to land on, below approximately 4500m/14,764ft.

APPENDIX C: FLORA AND FAUNA

The best all-round guide to the flora and fauna in this region is *The Story of Mt Everest National Park* by Margaret Jefferies but it can now only be found in libraries.

FLORA
From October to the spring the Khumbu is dry and brown, almost desert-like. In contrast, during the monsoon the greenery is surprisingly intense and flowers dapple hillsides. The wide range of flora includes the rhododendron, gentian, primrose, edelweiss and the beautiful mountain poppy. The forests of the deep Khumbu valleys comprise blue pine, fir, and juniper with birch and rhododendron forests at lower altitudes. Above the tree line is dwarf rhododendron and juniper scrub. The latter is prized by the Sherpas for its fragrant and instantly recognizable smell when burnt, a scent that soon becomes familiar. The highest plant of all is the tiny snow rhododendron.

WILDLIFE
In the Khumbu few wild mammals live above the treeline: even fewer are regularly seen.
● **Himalayan tahr** A large and handsome goat adept at rock climbing. The males are around a metre high and sport a luxuriant coppery-brown coat, with a paler mane. They are often seen during the first day or so of the walk above Namche, eyeing trekkers with disdain.

- **Snow leopard** Hauntingly beautiful solo cats, hardly ever seen by trekkers.
- **Wolf** Rarely seen, wolves live at the top of the tree line. Their coat is thick and sandy or grey and they use their bushy tail to keep their nose warm while sleeping.
- **Weasel** Quick eyes may see a blur of tan fur around grass and rocks near villages above Namche, even to as high as 5500m/18,044ft.
- **Himalayan mouse hare** A small tail-less mammal that is surprisingly tame.
- **Musk deer** Well under a metre high, this delicate deer is occasionally seen near Dole or around Tengboche in the dark forest. It is illegally hunted for its musk, produced by a gland in the male and used for making perfume. The male has large distinctive fang-like teeth (see photo opposite p289).
- **Common mouse** At night in the lodges there's the telltale pitter-patter across the roof and the occasional scream (not of mouse origin!).

DOMESTIC ANIMALS

In the warmer lower hills a variety of animals are kept. Chickens are kept mainly as egg-producers. There are dogs; and goats are numerous, being sacrificed and eaten during important Hindu festivals and ceremonies. They are very destructive, stripping the ground and shrubs bare of leaves and are responsible for much of the deforestation close to villages. Buffaloes provide milk and meat, and pull ploughs. At high altitudes they are replaced by yaks, naks and various crossbreeds.

BIRDS

Nepal is on some major migration routes and is famed for its varied bird life. Since the local people don't hunt birds, and they are all protected in the park, with keen eyes you should seen the majority of the birds mentioned below. Serious birdwatchers should consult: *Birds of Nepal* by RL Fleming or *Birds of the Central Himalayas* by Dorothy Mierow, both usually available in the Kathmandu bookshops.
- **Lammergeier/bearded vulture** This large and beautiful soaring bird is a scavenger and it is often seen gliding along the mountain sides above Namche.
- **Griffon** Similar to the lammergeier, but slightly heavier with a shorter, wider tail.
- **Golden eagle** This raptor hunts pheasants, snow cocks and smaller mammals rather than being a scavenger. It is smaller and more agile than the other soaring birds.
- **Danphe/Impeyan pheasant/Monal** The national bird of Nepal, often seen in pairs. The male sports nine iridescent colours and is plump, almost heavy. The female is a plainer brown and white. Good places to spot them are along the trail to Thame and Tengboche, and around Phortse.
- **Blood pheasant** The male has a red throat, red and white tail and bright red legs. They are seen around Tengboche and Dole.
- **Tibetan snow cock** Both male and female are striped: black, white, grey and brown with orange legs. Easy to approach, they congregate in noisy groups at altitudes above Namche right up to the snow line, especially on freshly dug fields.
- **Snow pigeon** They fly in compact flocks and as they wheel around in the sky their colour alternates between light and dark.
- **Yellow-billed and red-billed chough** Black with red legs, choughs are curious and playful but have the annoying habit of attacking tents, ripping the material with their beaks. Together with crows, they are known as 'gorak' by the Sherpas.
- **Jungle crow** Black and slightly scrawny, crows are great camp scavengers.
- **Tibetan raven** ('Caw caw') Completely black, these ravens attain nightmarish proportions in the Khumbu.

APPENDIX D: NEPALI WORDS AND PHRASES

Many Nepalis, especially those used to dealing with foreigners, can speak some English. It is, however, really worth making the effort to learn even a few Nepali phrases since this will positively affect the attitude of the local people towards you and you'll be made all the more welcome.

Derived from Sanskrit, Nepali shares many words with Hindi and is also written in the Devanagari script. For many of the people you speak to (Sherpa, Rai etc) Nepali will, in fact, be their second language. Whilst Nepali is not a particularly difficult language to learn up to a basic level, Sherpa is much harder.

Nepali includes several sounds not used in English. The transliterations given below are therefore only approximate. However, since pronunciation varies across the country your less-than-perfect attempts will probably be understood as just another regional variation.

Namasté
Probably the first word learnt by the newly arrived foreigner in Nepal is this greeting, which is spoken with the hands together as if praying. Its meaning encompasses 'hello' and 'good-bye' as well as 'good morning', 'good afternoon' or 'good evening'. *Namaskar* is the more polite form.

General words

How are you?	*Bhaat khanu-boyo?* (lit: Have you eaten your dal bhaat?)
Fine thanks	*Khai-é* (lit: I have eaten)
Please give me	*..... di-nus*
Do you speak English?	*Angrayzi bolnoo-hoon-cha?*
Yes/no	(see Questions and answers below)
Thank you	*Dhan-yabad* (not often used)
Excuse me (sorry)	*Maf-garnus*
good/bad	*ramro/naramro*
cheap/expensive	*susto/mahongo*
Just a minute!	*Ek-chin!*
brother/sister	*eai/didi* (used to address anyone of your own age)
Good night	*Sooba-ratry*
Sweet dreams	*Meeto supona*

Questions and answers
To ask a question, end the phrase with a rising tone. An affirmative answer is given by restating the question without the rising tone. 'No' is translated as *chaina* (there isn't/aren't any) or *hoi-na* (it isn't/they aren't).

What's your name?	*Topaiko* (to adult)/*timro* (child) *nam ke ho?*		
My name is	*Mero nam ..... ho.*		
Where are you from?	*Topaiko/timro dess kay ho?*		
Britain/USA	*Belaiyot/Amerika*		
Australia/New Zealand	*Australia/New Zealand*		
Where are you going?	*Kaha janné?*	I'm going to ...	... *janné*
Are you married?	*Bebah bo sokyo?*		
Have you any children?	*Chora chori chon?*	boy/girl	*chora/chori*
How old are you?	*Koti borsa ko boyo?*		
What is this?	*Yo kay ho?*		

306 Appendix D: Nepali words and phrases

Directions

Ask directions frequently and avoid questions that require only 'yes' or 'no' as a reply.

Which path goes to ....?	.......janay bahto kun ho?
Where is ...?	.....kaha cho
lodge/hotel	bhatti
shop	possol
latrine	charpi
What is this village called?	Yo gaon ko nam kay ho?
left/right	baiya/daiya
straight ahead	seeda jannus
steep uphill/downhill	bhiralo matti/talla
far away	tadah
near	nadjik

Numerals / time

1 *ek*; 2 *du-i*; 3 *tin*; 4 *charr*; 5 *panch*; 6 *chho*; 7 *saat*; 8 *aatt*; 9 *nau*; 10 *dos*; 11 *eghaara*; 12 *baahra*; 13 *tehra*; 14 *chaudha*; 15 *pondhra*; 16 *sora*; 17 *sotra*; 18 *ottahra*; 19 *unnice*; 20 *beece*; 25 *pochis*; 30 *teece*; 40 *chaalis*; 50 *pachaas*; 60 *saati*; 70 *sottorri*; 80 *ossi*; 90 *nobbi*; 100 *say*; 200 *du-i say*; 300 *tin-say*; 400 *charr say*; 500 *panch say* ; 600 *chho say*; 700 *saat say*; 800 *aatt say*; 900 *nau say*; 1000 *hozhar*

How much/many?	*Kati?*	today	*ajaa*
What time is it?	*Kati byjhay?*	yesterday	*hidjo*
It's three o'clock	*Tin byjhay*	tomorrow	*bholi*
hours/minutes	*ghanta/minoot*	day after tomorrow	*parsi*

Food and drink

restaurant/inn	bhatti	bread	roti
Please give me...	......di-nus	cheese	cheese
mineral water	khanni-paani	boiled egg	phul
tea	chiya	omelette	unda
coffee	coffee	salt	noon
milk	dood no	spicy hot	piro
chillis	korsani china	sugar	chinni
boiled milk	oomaleko-dood	beer	beer
honey	maha	rice spirit	ruxi
Cheers!	Khannus!	rice	bhaat
chicken	kookhura-ko massu	lentils	dal
buffalo	rango-ko massu	potatoes	aloo
pork	sungur-ko massu	vegetables (cooked)	takaari
It tastes good	Ekdum meeto		

APPENDIX E: GLOSSARY

ama	mother
bergschrund	gap where a glacier parts from a rock wall
bhanjyang	pass
bhatti	simple hotel
bivvy (bivouac)	small shelter for camping
Brahmin/Bahun	Hindu high priest caste
cairn	pile of stones marking a route ('stone men')
chang	home-brew made from barley or rice; also 'north' direction
chhu	river
chhusa	crop-growing area above main village
chimneying	climbing a vertical crack just greater than body width
chomo/jomo	mountain goddess
chorten	Tibetan stupa (see below)
chotar	prayer flag pole beside house
crampons	spikes that strap on boots to aid walking on ice
crevasse	dangerous cracks in a glacier
cwm	valley shaped like an amphitheatre (Welsh)
dal bhaat	staple meal of lentils and boiled rice
deorali	pass
dhai	curds
dingma	clearing
doko	woven, load-carrying basket
drangka	stream
ghat	river bank or bridge
goan/gau	village
gompa	Buddhist temple (literally: 'meditation')
goth 'goat-h'	shelter or temporary house
gunsa	'winter place', where early crops are grown
himal	snowy mountains
jumars	device used for climbing up a fixed rope
kang	mountain
kani	entrance arch
kharka	grazing ground
khola	stream
kosi	river
kund	lake
la	pass
lha	fenced herding area, also spirits
lho	south
mani wall	wall of stones carved with Buddhist mantras
mantra	prayer formula
neve	smooth high snow-field, accumulation area of a glacier
nup	west
phu	high-altitude grazing area at the end of a valley
piton	spike hammered into a rock crack for climbing security
pokhri	lake
prussiks	loops of cord used to climb a vertical rope
rakshi	local distilled spirit
ri	ridge or soft peak

satu	flour
serac	large block of ice typically found in an icefall
shar	east
Sherpa	of the Sherpa people
sherpa	trekking group assistant
solja/suchia	salt-butter tea
stupa	hemispherical Buddhist religious monument
suntala	mandarin orange
tal	lake
tarn	small lake without entry or exit stream
trisul	trident carried by worshippers of Shiva
tsampa	roasted barley flour
tse	peak
tsho/cho	lake
yersa	crop-growing area above main village

APPENDIX F: BIBLIOGRAPHY

TRAVEL GUIDES

Armington, Stan *Trekking in the Nepal Himalaya*, Lonely Planet Publications, Australia,

MAPS

Khumbu Himal, Freytag-Berndt und Artaria, Vienna, 1978 and 1985
Lapchi Kang, Freytag-Berndt und Artaria, Vienna, 1974 and 1985
Mt Everest, National Geographic Magazine, 1988
Planimetric Map of Satellite Images for National Remote Sensing Centre (Nepal)
    Institute for Applied Geosciences, Germany 1986
Rolwaling Himal (Gaurisankar), Freytag-Berndt und Artaria, Vienna, 1981
Shorong/Hinku, Freytag-Berndt und Artaria, Vienna, 1974, 1979 and 1987

TRAVELOGUES / HISTORY

Bernstein, Jeremy *Wildest Dreams of Kew*, George Allen & Unwin UK 1970
Boardman, Peter *Sacred Summits*, Hodder & Stoughton, London 1982
Bonington, Chris and Clarke, Charles *Everest the Unclimbed Ridge*, Hodder & Stoughton, London 1983
Bonington, Chris *Everest South West Face*, Hodder & Stoughton, London 1973
Bonington, Chris *The Everest Years*, Hodder & Stoughton, London 1986
Eggler, Albert *The Everest Lhotse Adventure*, Geo Allen & Unwin, UK 1957
Franco, Jean *Makalu*, Jonathan Cape, London 1957
Gillman, Peter *Everest – The best writing and pictures from 70 years of human endeavour*, Little, Brown & Co, London 1993
Hillary, Edmund *Nothing Venture, Nothing Win*, Hodder & Stoughton, London 1975
Hillary, Louise *High Time*, Hodder & Stoughton, London 1973
Holzel, Tom and Salkeld, Audrey *The Mystery of Mallory and Irvine*, Jonathan Cape, 1986
Hornbein, Thomas *Everest the West Ridge*, Vikas, New Delhi 1982
Howard-Bury CK *Mount Everest: The Reconnaissance 1921*

Hunt, John *The Ascent of Everest*, Hodder & Stoughton 1953
Kolhi, Capt MS *The Himalayas – Playground of the Gods*, Viking India 1983
Kolhi, Commander M S *Nine Atop Everest*, Orient Longman, New Delhi 1969
Mulgrew, Peter *No Place for Men*, AH & AW Reed, Wellington, 1964
Norton EF *The Fight for Everest: 1924*, Edward Arnold, 1925
Salkeld, Audrey *People in High Places*, Jonathan Cape, London 1991
Shipton, Eric *That Untravelled World*, Charles Scribner's Sons, NY 1969
Shipton, Eric *The Six Mountain-Travel Books*, The Mountaineers, Seattle 1985
Taylor-Ide, Daniel *Something Hidden Behind the Ranges – a Himalayan Quest*
    Mercury House, San Francisco 1995
Tichy, Herbert *Cho Oyu By Favour of the Gods*, Methuen & Co, London 1957
Tichy, Herbert *Himalaya*, Anton Schroll, Vienna 1970
Tilman, HW *The Seven Mountain-Travel Books*, The Mountaineers, Seattle 1983
Unsworth, Walt *Everest*, Oxford Illustrated Press, UK 1989
Von Furer-Haimendorf, Christoph *Exploratory Travels in Highland Nepal*, Sterling
    Publishers, New Delhi 1989
Weir, Tom *East of Kathmandu,* The Travel Book Club
Wignall, Sydney *Spy on the Roof of the World*, Canongate, Edinburgh, UK 1996

RESEARCH

Bista, Dor Bahadur *Fatalism and Development Nepal's struggle for Modernisation,*
    Orient Longman, Calcutta 1991
Jefferies, Margaret *The Story of Mt Everest National Park,* Cobb/Horwood, Auckland, 1985
Fisher, James F *Sherpas – Reflections on Change in Himalayan Nepal,* University of
    California Press, Berkeley, 1990
Mierow, Dorothy *Birds of the Central Himalayas,* 1988
Ortner, Sherry *Sherpas through their Rituals,* Cambridge UP 1978
Sharma, Pitamber *Assessment of Critical Issues and Options in Mountain Tourism in Nepal,*
Stevens, Stanley *Sherpa Settlement and Subsistence – Cultural Ecology and History in
    Highland Nepal* for University of California
Subba, Chaitanya *The Culture and Religion of Limbus*, Subba KB, Kathmandu, 1995

Route map key

☐☐ Simple lodge/ large simple lodge	◢◤ A few lodges/ a few large lodges	◣■ Many lodges/ many large lodges
▽ Tea shack	○ Other	✈ Airstrip
Trail	Pass	Bridge
Difficult Pass	▲ Peak	△ Trekking Peak
Ridge	Stream / River	Glacier

INDEX

Page references in bold type refer to maps

BOXED TEXT INDEX

TRAILBLAZER'S BRITISH WALKING GUIDE SERIES

We've applied to destinations which are closer to home Trailblazer's proven formula for publishing definitive route guides for adventurous travellers. Britain's network of long-distance trails enables the walker to explore some of the finest landscapes in the country's best walking areas and they are an obvious starting point for this series. These are guides that are user-friendly, practical, informative and environmentally sensitive.

● **Unique mapping features**
In many walking guidebooks the reader has to read a route description then try to relate it to the map. Our guides are much easier to use because walking directions, tricky junctions, places to stay and eat, points of interest and walking times are all written onto the maps themselves in the places to which they apply. With their uncluttered clarity, these are not general-purpose maps but fully edited maps **drawn by walkers for walkers**.

● **Largest-scale walking maps**
At a scale of just under 1:20,000 (8cm or 3¹/₈ inches to one mile) the maps in these guides are bigger than even the most detailed British walking maps currently available in the shops.

● **Not just a trail guide**
Includes where to stay, where to eat and public transport Our guidebooks are a complete guide, not just a trail guide. They include: what to see, where to stay (pubs, hotels, B&Bs, campsites, bunkhouses, hostels), where to eat. There is detailed public transport information for all access points to each trail so there are itineraries for all walkers, both for hiking the route in its entirety and for day walks.

Coast to Coast *Henry Stedman* ISBN 978-1-905864-09-6, £9.99
3rd edition, 240pp, 109 maps & town plans, 40 colour photos

Cornwall Coast Path *Edith Schofield* ISBN 978-1-873756-93-5, £9.99
2nd edition, 224pp, 112 maps & town plans, 40 colour photos

Cotswold Way *Tricia & Bob Hayne* ISBN 978-1-905864-16-4, £9.99
1st edition, 192pp, 55 maps & town plans, 40 colour photos

Hadrian's Wall Path *Henry Stedman* ISBN 978-1-905864-14-0, £9.99
2nd edition, 192pp, 60 maps & town plans, 40 colour photos

North Downs Way *John Curtin* ISBN 978-1-873756-96-6, £9.99
1st edition, 192pp, 60 maps & town plans, 40 colour photos

Offa's Dyke Path *Keith Carter* ISBN 978-1-905864-06-5, £9.99
2nd edition, 208pp, 88 maps & town plans, 40 colour photos

Pembrokeshire Coast Path *Jim Manthorpe* ISBN 978-1-905864-03-4, £9.99
2nd edition, 208pp, 96 maps & town plans, 40 colour photos

Pennine Way *Keith Carter & Chris Scott* ISBN 978-1-905864-02-7, £11.99
2nd edition, 272pp, 135 maps & town plans, 40 colour photos

The Ridgeway *Nick Hill* ISBN 978-1-905864-17-1, £9.99
2nd edition, 192pp, 53 maps & town plans, 40 colour photos

South Downs Way *Jim Manthorpe* ISBN 978-1-873756-95-9, £9.99
2nd edition, 192pp, 60 maps & town plans, 40 colour photos

West Highland Way *Charlie Loram* ISBN 978-1-905864-13-3, £9.99
3rd edition, 192pp, 53 maps, 10 town plans, 40 colour photos

*'The same attention to detail that distinguishes its other guides
has been brought to bear here'*. **The Sunday Times**

TREKKING GUIDES
Europe
Corsica Trekking – GR20
Dolomites Trekking – AV1 & AV2
Scottish Highlands – The Hillwalking Guide
Tour du Mont Blanc
Trekking in the Pyrenees
Walker's Haute Route: Mt Blanc to Matterhorn

South America
Inca Trail, Cusco & Machu Picchu

Africa
Kilimanjaro
Trekking in the Moroccan Atlas

Australasia
New Zealand – The Great Walks

Asia
Trekking in the Annapurna Region
Trekking in the Everest Region
Trekking in Ladakh

The Walker's Haute Route – Mt Blanc to the Matterhorn
Alexander Stewart 1st edn, 256pp, 60 maps, 30 colour photos
ISBN 978-1-905864-08-9, £12.99
From Mont Blanc to the Matterhorn, Chamonix to Zermatt, the 180km walkers' Haute Route traverses one of the finest stretches of the Pennine Alps – the range between Valais in Switzerland and Piedmont and Aosta Valley in Italy. Includes Chamonix and Zermatt guides.

Tour du Mont Blanc   *Jim Manthorpe*
1st edition, 208pp, 60 maps, 30 colour photos
ISBN 978-1-905864-12-6, £11.99
At 4810m (15,781ft), Mont Blanc is the highest mountain in western Europe, and one of the most famous mountains in the world. The snow-dome summit is the top of a spectacular massif stretching 60 miles by 20 miles, arguably the most magnificent mountain scenery in Europe. The trail (105 miles, 168km) that circumnavigates the massif, passing through France, Italy and Switzerland, is the most popular long distance walk in Europe. Includes Chamonix and Courmayeur guides.

Corsica Trekking – GR20   *David Abram*
1st edition, 208pp, 32 maps, 30 colour photos
ISBN 978-1-873756-98-0, £11.99
Slicing diagonally across Corsica's jagged spine, the legendary red-and-white waymarks of the GR20 guide trekkers across a succession of snow-streaked passes, Alpine meadows, massive boulder fields and pristine forests of pine and oak – often within sight of the sea. Physically demanding from start to finish, it's a superlative 170km, two-week trek. Includes guides to gateway towns: Ajaccio, Bastia, Calvi, Corte and Porte-Vecchio. '*Indispensible*'. **The Independent** '*Excellent guide*'. **The Sunday Times**

New Zealand – The Great Walks   *Alexander Stewart*
2nd edition, 272pp, 60 maps, 40 colour photos
ISBN 978-1-905864-11-9, £12.99
New Zealand is a wilderness paradise of incredibly beautiful landscapes. There is no better way to experience it than on one of the nine designated Great Walks, the country's premier walking tracks which provide outstanding hiking opportunities for people at all levels of fitness. Also includes detailed guides to Auckland, Wellington, National Park Village, Taumaranui, Nelson, Queenstown, Te Anau and Oban.

Himalaya by Bike – a route & planning guide
Laura Stone 336pp, 28 colour & 50 B&W photos, 60 maps
ISBN 978 1 905864 04 1, *1st edn,* £16.99
An all-in-one guide for Himalayan cycle-touring. Covers the Himalayan regions of Pakistan, Tibet, India, Nepal and Sikkim with detailed km-by-km guides to main routes including the Karakoram Highway and the Friendship Highway. Plus town and city guides.

Trekking in the Annapurna Region *Bryn Thomas*
4th edition, 288pp, 55 maps, 28 colour photos
ISBN 978-1-873756-68-3, £11.99
Fully revised guide to the most popular walking region in the Himalaya. Includes route guides, Kathmandu and Pokhara city guides and getting to Nepal. '*Good guides read like a novel and have you packing in no time. Two from Trailblazer Publications which fall into this category are* 'Trekking in the Annapurna Region' *and* 'Silk Route by Rail' '. *Today*

Trekking in Ladakh *Charlie Loram*
3rd edition, 288pp, 75 maps, 24 colour photos
ISBN 978-1-873756-75-1, £12.99
Fully revised and extended 3rd edition of Charlie Loram's practical guide. Includes 75 detailed walking maps, guides to Leh, Manali and Delhi plus information on getting to Ladakh. *'Extensive...and well researched'.* **Climber Magazine** *'Were it not for this book we might still be blundering about...'* **The Independent on Sunday**

Scottish Highlands – The Hillwalking Guide
1st edition, Jim Manthorpe 312pp, 86 maps, 40 photos
ISBN 978-1-873756-84-3, £11.99
This guide covers 60 day-hikes in the following areas: ● Loch Lomond, the Trossachs and Southern Highlands ● Glen Coe and Ben Nevis ● Central Highlands ● Cairngorms and Eastern Highlands ● Western Highlands ● North-West Highlands ● The Far North ● The Islands. Plus: 3- to 4-day hikes linking some regions.

Dolomites Trekking Alta Via 1 & Alta Via 2 *Henry Stedman*
2nd edn, 192pp, 52 trail maps, 7 town plans, 38 colour photos
ISBN 978-1-873756-83-6, £11.99
AV1 (9-13 days) & AV2 (10-16 days) are the most popular long-distance hikes in the Dolomites. Numerous shorter walks also included. Places to stay, walking times and points of interest, plus detailed guides to Cortina and six other towns.

Kilimanjaro: the trekking guide to Africa's highest mountain
Henry Stedman, 2nd edition, 320pp, 40 maps, 30 photos
ISBN 978-1-873756-97-1, £11.99
At 19,340ft the world's tallest freestanding mountain, Kilimanjaro is one of the most popular destinations for hikers visiting Africa. It's possible to walk up to the summit: no technical skills are necessary. Includes town guides to Nairobi and Dar-Es-Salaam, excursions in the region and a detailed colour guide to flora and fauna. **Includes Mount Meru**. *'Stedman's wonderfully down-to-earth, practical guide to the mountain'.* **Longitude Books**

TRAILBLAZER GUIDES — TITLE LIST

For more information about Trailblazer and our expanding range of guides, for guidebook updates or for credit card mail order sales visit our website:

www.trailblazer-guides.com

ROUTE GUIDES FOR THE ADVENTUROUS TRAVELLER

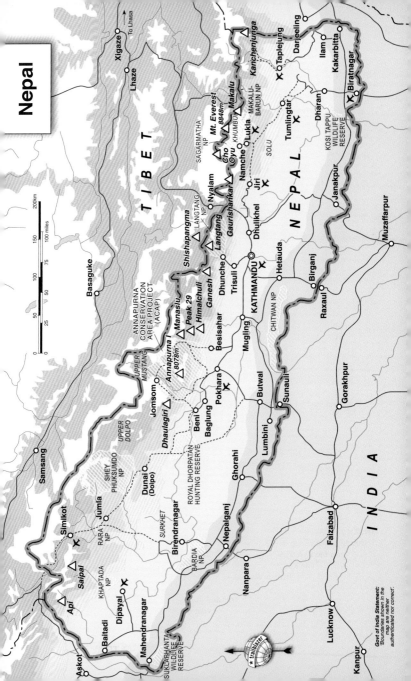

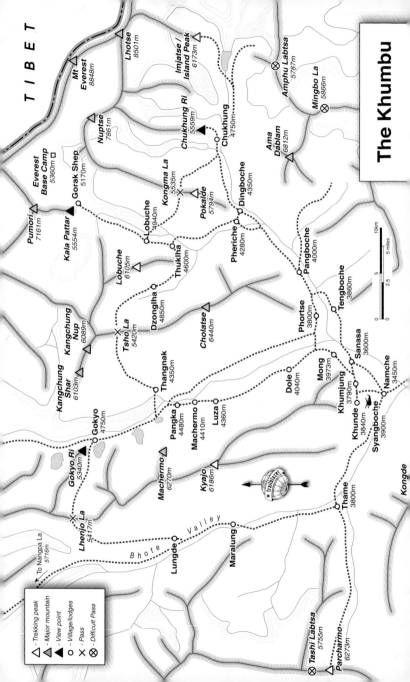

The Khumbu

T I B E T

Mt Everest 8848m

Lhotse 8501m

Imjatse / Island Peak 6173m

Amphu Labtsa 5787m

Mingbo La 5866m

Nuptse 7861m

Chukhung Ri 5559m

Chukhung 4750m

Ama Dablam 6812m

Everest Base Camp 5360m

Gorak Shep 5170m

Kongma La 5535m

Pokalde 5794m

Dingboche 4350m

Pumori 7161m

Kala Pattar 5554m

Lobuche 4940m

Pheriche 4280m

Pangboche 4000m

Lobuche 6105m

Thukhla 4600m

Tengboche 3860m

Kangchung Nup 6089m

Dzonglha 4850m

Cholatse 6440m

Phortse 3800m

Sanasa 3600m

Kangchung Shar 6103m

Tsho La 5420m

Thangnak 4350m

Dole 4040m

Mong 3973m

Khumjung 3790m

Namche 3450m

Gokyo Ri 5340m

Gokyo 4750m

Pangka 4480m

Machermo 4410m

Luza 4360m

Khunde 3840m

Syangboche 3900m

Machermo 6270m

Kyajo 6186m

Thame 3800m

Kongde

Lhenjo La 5417m

To Nangpa La 5716m

B h o t e   *V a l l e y*

Lungde

Maralung

Tashi Labtsa 5755m

Parcharmo 6273m

Trailblazer

△ - Trekking peak
▲ - Major mountain
◢ - View point
○ - Village/lodges
✕ - Pass
⊗ - Difficult Pass

10km

5 miles

5

2.5

0   0